601 WAYS TO BE A GOOD PARENT

601 WAYS TO BE A GOOD PARENT

A Practical Handbook for Raising
Children Ages Four to Twelve

Michele Elliott

A Citadel Press Book

Published by Carol Publishing Group

To John Hadjipateras, who told me that my next book should be a "how to" and so the idea for *601 Ways* took hold. John has also helped the Kidscape charitable organization, which works to prevent child abuse and bullying. Without his support I don't think any of the work on protecting children would have been done. He is a great friend and the father of five wonderful children.

First Carol Publishing Group Edition, 1999

601 Ways to Be a Good Parent is an expanded and enlarged edition of *501 Ways to Be a Good Parent,* which was originally published in Great Britain by Hodder & Stoughton in 1996.

A Citadel Press Book
Published by Carol Publishing Group
Citadel Press is a registered trademark of Carol Communications, Inc.

Editorial, sales and distribution, rights and permissions inquiries should be addressed to Carol Publishing Group, 120 Enterprise Avenue, Secaucus, N.J. 07094.

In Canada: Canadian Manda Group, One Atlantic Avenue, Suite 105, Toronto, Ontario M6K 3E7

Carol Publishing Group books may be purchased in bulk at special discounts for sales promotion, fund-raising, or educational purposes. Special editions can be created to specifications. For details, contact Special Sales Department, Carol Publishing Group, 120 Enterprise Avenue, Secaucus, N.J. 07094.

Manufactured in the United States of America
10 9 8 7 6 5 4 3 2 1

Library of Congress Cataloging-in-Publication Data

Elliott, Michele.
   601 ways to be a good parent: a practical handbook for raising children ages four to twelve / Michele Elliott.
     p. cm.
   "A Citadel Press book."
   Includes index.
   ISBN 0–8065–2072–8 (pbk.)
   1. Child rearing—Handbooks, manuals, etc. 2. Parenting—Handbooks, manuals, etc.   I. Title. II. Title: Six hundred one ways to be a good parent.
HQ769.E5644 1999
649'.1—dc21   98–51436
                                              CIP

Contents

Acknowledgments

It has been a pleasure to write for *Family Circle* magazine. The people there have supported the publication of this book from the start. Some of the chapters started life as *Family Circle* articles. Special thanks to Deborah Murdock, Gilly Batterbee, and Gill Adams for their great patience, excellent editing, and cajoling.

The Kidscape staff put up with my writing and long periods away from the office, which I think they quite enjoyed. A big thanks to Gaby Shenton, Lisa Flowers, Angela Glaser, and Daphne Joiner. Daphne is also a proper nanny who has raised about thirty children over the years and is a fount of wisdom.

My husband, Edward, has been my strongest supporter and a loving and kind father to our sons, Charles and James. We think they are the world's best kids, but you will have to ask them in a few years how they think we did.

Finally, many thanks to my editors at Carol Publishing, Andrew Richter, and at Hodder, Rowena Webb, and Dawn Bates. They are a writer's best friend—humorous, accessible, and full of good ideas.

Introduction

Amy was bouncing around the garden having a great time. Her mother, Nicola, and I were talking. Nicola was worried about her daughter.

"I don't want her to become too forward," she said.

"But she's a lovely kid," I protested. Amy was one of the most secure, happy children I knew. I always looked forward to my children playing with her. "Are there some problems with Amy?" I asked.

"Oh, no, she's a wonderful kid—everyone loves her," replied Nicola.

"Then why change what you're doing?"

"Because someone told me that too much praise might spoil her."

Isn't it amazing that we parents are so quick to listen to what others tell us about our children, even if our own instincts tell us that everything is OK?

Nicola was starting to doubt her own good common sense. Amy is a delightful child, full of self-confidence. Nicola was not praising bad behavior, she was reinforcing good behavior. She was doing the right thing, and all she needed was for someone to tell her she was doing a great job and to keep up the good work. I only wish there were more children like Amy.

The real problem for Nicola was that she didn't have anyone to share her worries with—like a favorite aunt who had raised four children, perhaps. When we were concerned about raising children in times past, we would go next door and talk to a neighbor or phone family members. Now we don't have the time to talk. I remember my grandmother having endless conversations over the back fence or on the telephone with her grown-up children about their growing-up children. These days it seems we are all bringing our kids up alone and we're feeling unsure of ourselves. We also believe that the problems we run into are only happening to us. Not so. The same problems face every parent, but we just don't know it because we are so busy and live so far apart from each other and from our extended families.

This book is for busy parents. (Are there any other kind?) You can dip into it for ideas when you're stuck, or read a chapter when you have a few minutes peace from the demands of parenthood, work, chores, and so on. As a mother who works both inside and outside the home, I know only too well how difficult it is to juggle everything and remain relatively sane. (Many who know me would say I haven't succeeded!) I hope you find some comfort knowing that none of us gets it right all the time. I've owned up to most of my mistakes (my kids will say so if I haven't), and have taken credit for things that have gone well. I have injected some humor because it is one of the only ways, in my opinion, to survive parenthood.

If there is one underlying theme of this book it is that children need their parents to be parents first and friends second. There is no harm in being friends with our children, but our primary role is as parents. Children will push and shove and test the boundaries, but we have to hold firm. Giving in for the sake of an easy life when children are young just creates problems for them, and for us, when they get older.

I hope you enjoy the book and wish you well, from those frantic younger years to those preteen and teenage years, when your lovely, fun-loving, and charming children begin turning into grunting, noncommunicative, hormonally driven creatures who blame you for everything. Don't despair, they eventually come out of it and discover that you weren't so bad, after all. Keep in mind the famous comment from Mark Twain: "When I was a boy of fourteen, my father was so ignorant I could hardly stand to have the old man around. But when I got to be twenty-one, I was astonished at how much he had learned."

There is no point in holding you up in a long introduction. Good luck being a parent. We all need it! And I'd love to hear from you if you have any ideas you think would be good for the next edition. (Perhaps it could be entitled *1001 Ways to Be a Good Parent*.) Contact me through the publisher at the Kidscape Charity address:

Michele Elliott
Kidscape
2 Grosvenor Gardens
London SW1W 012H

PART I

Getting Through the Day

1

23 Ways to Stop Your Children From Fighting With Each Other

If it often seems that your children do nothing but fight, take heart. We all had a vision of happy, laughing children—and then we became parents.

You hear the scream from two rooms away, and you know it's serious: "I HATE YOU!" You know from experience that your children are standing nose to nose, toe to toe, fists clenched.

"I hate you a thousand times more than you hate me," says the other one.

Blows are struck and both run in to you. The older one shouts, "She hit me first." "But he hit me back first," yells the little one.

Your own anger starts to match theirs as you attempt to untangle fingers from hair, right from wrong.

Why?

Why, you ask yourself, are they always fighting? From observations of my own two, I'd say children fight for the same reasons adults do:

- It's exciting.
- It gets attention from grown-ups.
- They like it.
- Because one of them feels less loved than the other.
- Because they haven't yet learned, or have forgotten, how to share.

- Because one of them is angry at the general unfairness of life.
- To prove that they are in charge—if only for a moment, if only with a brother or sister—in a world where children, and people, often feel they have little power.
- Because they see others fighting—in the family, at school, and on television.

The problem for parents is deciding when, and whether, to live with the fighting or fight back.

Is Fighting Normal?

There is a great debate among "experts" about whether fighting is normal and healthy, or whether it occurs so regularly it just *seems* normal. One book says that fighting is not good and can be avoided, another says that a fight a day keeps the psychiatrist away. Some time I would like to put all the experts together with tired, fractious children on a daily basis and see what they actually do about it. I would also say never trust a friend who says her children don't fight. She's lying.

Kate, nine, and Paul, five, were sitting next to each other. Kate was doing her homework while Paul was building a boat out of Lego. Mom was out of the room. Paul moved over next to Kate. She tried to ignore him and moved over herself. Paul pushed his boat on to her paper. "Get off," said Kate, annoyed but still doing her homework. Paul poked Kate in the face and giggled. She shoved him away. He stuck his finger into her lip, at which Kate grabbed his hand and bit it....Paul screamed. Mom rushed in. Seeing Paul's hand, she yelled at Kate and comforted Paul, saying to Kate: "You know you shouldn't pick on him, he's much younger than you."

Speaking as a working mother who often doesn't get it right, I think that a certain amount of fighting is normal, and even healthy. Everyone has to learn to settle differences—and what you learn sorting out the everyday perils of growing up may help you stay on your feet on the front line of work and in relationships as an adult.

Paul engineered the fight, but Kate got the blame. She shouldn't have bitten him, but Paul clearly needs to know what's likely to happen if he continues bugging someone. Sometimes the rough justice of children works better than anything we can do. The mother might have done better to comfort Paul (after all, he had suffered in order to learn), and had a quiet word with Kate later—but none of us is perfect. This "let them sort it out for themselves" philosophy is fine as long as the odds are fair and it works. When they aren't fair and it doesn't work, however, we need to know that although fighting is normal, it is never simple; there are always undercurrents, only some of which we can fathom.

Strategies

Parents need strategies to prevent things from getting out of hand—when nerves are shot, for example, or when damage is about to be inflicted on children or home. In cases when you can't just let the fight run its course, try:

1. Being Specific

Give very specific instructions such as: "Do *not* touch his car"; "Do *not* hit"; "Leave the room." Children do not respond to "Be nice." Nice is for wimps.

2. Marking Territory

Find a place for each child's toys and games that is his own. Ideally, give each a lockable box to keep special things in. This makes it clear that certain things belong to certain children and helps if you have to sort out a dispute.

3. Giving Them Ideas

Give children their own strategies. Ten-year-old Sam went berserk every time his sister said "Sam is a sissy." She loved taunting him. Sam's mom helped him work out things to say that made him feel less tense so his sister couldn't get to him. He came up with "Buzz off, elephant breath." His mom got him to try: "I love you, too," and "Yes, all great men are sissies," or "Twinkle, twinkle little star, what you say is what you are."

4. Staying out of It

Keep out of the everyday fights as much as possible. If you only seem to give them attention when they fight, try giving them attention only when they *don't* fight.

5. Cooling Things Down

Make it less awful. When one of them says, "I hate her," say, "Yes, you hate her right now. You don't have to like everyone all the time." If you tell them, "You don't mean that really; you love your sister," you'll just create more anger.

6. Preventing Real Harm

Pry them apart. When things look nasty, try "time out" in different rooms or threaten withdrawal of allowance for both unless they cool down.

7. Discovering the Problem

Take the children aside separately and find out if there is a basic reason for their continual fighting—something that just keeps eating away at them.

Karen and Anna's constant niggling and fighting was driving their mom nuts. She had tried everything, and finally sat down for a long talk with each. Karen thought that Anna got more attention and she was angry. Anna thought that Karen got away with too much and she felt cheated. Their mom asked them to come straight to her with their grievances next time and to ask straight out for some extra attention or privileges. Once the girls knew that what they wanted was available, they needed it less.

8. Finding Out When They Fight

See if there's a fighting time: It may be bedtime, bathtime, or when visitors come.

James, eight, was always picking fights at bedtime because he didn't like his older sister staying up later than him. His parents told him that age had its privileges, but they decided to give James an especially nice bedtime away from his sister and with his father reading him a story.

Similarly, I noticed that my boys fight more after watching TV for more than an hour. The funny thing is that it doesn't really seem to matter what the program is about. They just get nasty and their best solution seems to be to bother each other. I think they need to move around to work off boredom instead of sitting there, so I ration their television viewing and make them go outside. It works. (See chapter 10 on video and television watching.)

9. Avoiding Self-fulfilling Prophecies

Don't tell your children they always fight or say it in front of others when the children are listening. It becomes a self-fulfilling prophecy. "That's what we do best—fight!" they begin to believe. And so they do.

10. Allowing Anger

Allow children to be angry, but safely. I invite them to draw awful pictures of each other; then they know you understand that they are angry. And they learn that drawing is a better way to vent their anger than hitting.

11. Using Humor

I think humor is a great weapon that parents should use as often as possible. A flippant remark often can work better than a long analysis. "I'll trade you in for a teapot"; "I'll give you a million dollars to stop fighting"; or some such gem might defuse the situation. The challenge is trying to be humorous when you want to kill them!

12. Noticing Good Behavior

If you can, catch your children being peaceful. Some days it may not seem possible, but there will always be times when they are little angels.

Julie noticed one evening that Tom and Katherine were actually discussing something without killing each other. Instead of saying anything, she wrote them each a little note: "I like the way you talked to each other at dinner tonight. Love Mom."

It might sound sappy, but it can work wonders. Julie's other kids kept trying to do things so they could win a note, as well.

13. Undoing Bad Deals

Life is all about give and take, and a good-enough deal. Kids learn this from an early age and practice it relentlessly. Needless to say, as they're so important, deals cause horrendous fights.

Tony, six, is hysterical. "I want it back," he sobs repeatedly. "It isn't fair."

Lucy, his eight-year-old sister, walks in, steps over his sobbing form, and asks, "What's for dinner?"

"Give it back," yells Tony.

"No," says Lucy, very calmly and decisively. "We made a deal."

"What deal?" you ask, deeply suspicious of the transaction.

"He swapped his car with me and now he wants it back. I gave him three stickers that glow in the dark. It was a deal and we shook hands on it. Now he wants his car back and that's not fair." Lucy is confident her case is airtight.

"The stickers definitely aren't as good as my car." Tony is furious.

"But we shook on it and you can't go back on a deal."

They look at you expectantly. The car is worth five dollars; the stickers fifty cents. Lucy knows this; Tony doesn't but still feels wronged. While you don't want to undermine the initiative of a future businesswoman, you don't want her unfairly throwing her weight around, either.

The better child-rearing books say you should talk with the children individually and get all the facts. Then, democratically, you should ask them to help you sort it out. I find that this approach can often cause a burnt dinner and an exhausted mother.

"Sorry Lucy, it isn't fair," you pronounce, rushing back to the stove to rescue the potatoes. "The deal's off." This is usually followed by howls of both rage and delight, and it provides the basis for a comeback fight at a later date. Perhaps this can be dealt with after dinner.

Power struggles are the basis of so many fights, for kids and adults. At some stage, when the potatoes aren't boiling over and tempers are cooler, we need to teach children to exercise power and fairness at the same time. I believe we need to talk with our children about the subject of power. It's a subject they take very personally. Ask them to understand that everyone has power—even a little baby (if only to burst your eardrums). We have power over children; an employer has power over you; and children have power over brothers, sisters, other children, pets.

Play "what if" games relating to power, such as:

- What would you do if you knew someone in the playground was picking on a much younger child?

- What would you do if I made a deal with you that wasn't fair?
- What would you do if someone paid $100 for a toy of yours and then wanted it back? Would it matter how much the toy was worth? It could be worth $4, $100, or $200.
- What would you do if you made a deal with your best friend and she changed her mind? Would it make a difference how long it took before she changed her mind? Two minutes after the deal? Ten minutes after the deal? A week later?

From this, agree on ground rules for future "deals," which include a cooling-off time during which either party can back out.

What we want children to learn is that there is a way to use power so that people aren't taken advantage of or left feeling angry. Misusing power causes unhappiness.

What to Do if They Won't Stop Fighting

Try putting them on a desert island and letting them exhaust themselves. Better still, put yourself on the island and leave them at home. If you don't have a desert island handy try some last resorts, such as:

14. Making Them Laugh

Again, use humor to divert them—make a funny face, stick out your tongue, juggle, dance, stand on your head (carefully!), and just generally make a fool of yourself. Invite them to join in. It's hard to keep fighting when you're laughing.

15. Confiscating the Goods

Take away whatever it is they are fighting over. If it is a television program, turn off the television.

16. Restraining

Physically restrain them, if necessary, but don't hit them. Hitting only proves to them that it's valid to use force to end arguments.

17. Chilling Out

Put them into different rooms to cool off, make yourself a cup of coffee or tea, and think pleasant thoughts, such as where you're going to go on your summer vacation *alone*.

18. Diplomacy

Find out both sides of the story, then make a final judgment, telling them that is *it*—finished and over. No more discussion.

19. Giving a Time Limit

Set a timer and tell them to sort it out before the timer rings or you will. This works especially well if you point out that they probably won't like your solution much.

20. Offering Alternative Pursuits

Give them more constructive ways to get rid of their anger, such as punching bags, making clay models, or a three mile run.

21. Helping Them Find Their Own Solution

At a quiet time, involve them in finding a long-term solution to recurrent arguments. For example, if the fighting is always about who got the bigger share, do what my aunt who had six children did: Make the children divide the portions themselves. Whoever divides gets last pick. Take turns dividing and picking. I watched my cousins take incredible care to fill the glasses exactly or cut the cake with medical precision. My sister and I were made to do the same; it kept us interested and quiet while we measured to the very last drop.

22. Loss of Privileges

Take away a privilege if the fighting continues. Try to agree which privileges might have to go in advance, so they can decide whether the fighting is worth it!

23. Toning Down the Language

Teach children that they can use words to sort out disagreements. Starting sentences with "I don't agree with you" is better than "You're so dumb," or worse. If you find your children are repeating your words when you fight with your spouse or partner, you might have to tone down or change your own way of arguing—and that's not easy! If possible, take them along to listen to a debate so they can see how issues can be argued out without fisticuffs or name calling.

Above all, don't despair. Most relationships do improve with age. When my sister and I were teenagers, I drew a line down the center of our bedroom. She wasn't allowed into my side, and I wasn't allowed into hers. We argued about everything. I thought *she* was wrong all of the time, and she thought *I* was wrong all of the time. Today, she is my best friend in the whole world (even though she is *still* wrong about lots of things!).

2

10 Tips for Modern Manners

After the dust has settled from your ten-year-old's birthday, you ask him to write to his granny to tell her he liked the book she sent.

He is looking sullenly at a blank piece of paper. "I didn't like it."

"Well, thank her anyway. It will make her feel good." There's a slight edge to your voice.

"I can't think of anything to say."

"I just told you!" Exasperation sets in.

"Why can't I just call? I hate writing sappy notes."

"Because it's polite to write and..." You stop. Why can't he just call and not go through all this hassle? The answer is probably that, like most of us, you're not sure why not. This immediately threatens to undermine your insistence that the blank page gets filled.

Good manners are becoming harder to define. In our not-too-distant past we knew what manners were was expected of us: If you got a present, you wrote a thank-you note, however much it hurt.

I remember, when I was about seven, agonizing over how to thank my Aunt Pat for the excruciatingly awful sweater she'd sent me for my birthday. It was three sizes too big and a horrible mixture of brightly colored wools. Nevertheless, I was obliged to put pen to paper and be thankful in writing. But my parents had also taught me not to lie, so I was totally honest about what I was going to do with the present.

Dear Aunt Pat,
Thank you very much for the sweater. It is very big. There are many cold children in the world who do not get presents, so I will donate it to Good Will.

Love,
Michele

My parents' philosophy of manners didn't extend to being quite that honest, so the note was altered before being mailed.

Dear Aunt Pat,
Thank you for the sweater. It is really nice of you to knit it for me. It must have taken a very long time. Thank you.

Love,
Michele

But where do we stand on an old-fashioned concept like thank-you letters when we live in a world of e-mail, fax machines, cordless phones, and highways that take us to Granny's and back in a day? In any era there should be good, solid reasons for asking our children to do things. And, for me, that's the hard part—working out the reasons and explaining them.

Some traditions make sense to me, such as saying "please" and "thank you," because it makes other people feel good, or giving up your seat on the bus to someone who is less able because it's kind. Others don't make sense—such as children not speaking until they're spoken to. It seems to me that we need to work things out as we go along.

So, what about those thank-you notes? In fact, I do usually make my boys write them when presents come by mail. Receiving a thank-you letter makes the recipient feel special, and because grandparents, especially, like to reread notes and show them to friends.

There's another reason, too, which is hard to define. I think it's that sitting down to write focuses your thoughts and the result is a little part of yourself that's unique (provided you didn't copy it from your sister).

Remembering my own struggles, I do try to make it easier on my children, so here are a few tips.

1. Postcards and Pictures
It's hard to think kind thoughts when faced with a big sheet of blank paper, so picture postcards make good thank-you notes. You can let

the child choose one from some you've bought, and even address and stamp it for him or her. Older children should write a few lines; younger ones can just write "Thank you" and sign their names. Little ones who can't write yet can draw a picture of themselves playing with the gifts, or perhaps donate one of those crackly paintings, which you may now be using to decorate your refrigerator door.

2. Telephone

We don't live in a perfect world, and sometimes I do let the children phone their thanks, keeping my fingers crossed that they will include words in the "thrilled" and "wonderful" category.

3. E-mail and Faxes

If you are lucky enough to have access to such facilities, well, why not? In our house we don't, so it isn't an issue. I still confess to a nostalgic love of receiving a handwritten note, but my kids quite rightly point out that I was "practically born before the invention of the airplane."

4. Be Realistic

Whatever method you use, common sense should prevail. When my youngest son was seven, he took a gift to a party attended by twenty children. Two days later, he received a thank-you note from the birthday boy. The child's mother had made her son write twenty thank-you notes the day after the party, to people who'd been there to receive thanks in person. In our house we're lucky to find all the gifts at the end of a party, let alone know who gave what. You must be realistic about your expectations.

But it's realistic to expect basic table manners, isn't it?

Are Table Manners Important?

This is a subject of great debate. When I was a kid you stayed at the table for the entire meal, even if you were bored witless. Should we continue to be ruled by the expectations of the previous generation? In our house, the answer is yes and no. It is, of course, up to you to decide, but here are my guidelines.

5. Yes

Children should keep their mouths shut when they chew, should say "please" and "thank you," should wash their hands before sitting down, and should not touch every piece of bread before choosing the best one.

6. No

Children should not be made to wait at the table while adults discuss the state of the world. Family meals with conversations that include the children are a joy, and sometimes the only time in a day for exchanging news. When the children have finished eating and talking, why can't they say "Thank you" and "Please may I leave the table?" Seems fair to me.

But You Can't Win 'Em All

You're in the middle of a meal when your thirteen-year-old slouches through the door. He says nothing, pulls up a chair, does a boardinghouse reach for the bread and grunts when you ask questions. Your eight-year-old smiles and asks you to please pass the potatoes, so you think at least you've got it right with one of them. Believe me, in five years time your baby may be just as bad. When children reach adolescence and start working out their own codes of living, they often start by rejecting most of the things they've been taught. So manners lose out—temporarily. My only advice is to keep up your own standards; you have rights, too!

It's worth remembering that normally well-mannered adults have their lapses, as well, if only at certain times of the day. Hysteria in our house reaches a high point around evening dinnertime. A few nights ago I heard myself inviting the boys to "Sit down, shut up, and eat."

By contrast, friends Anne and Tom took their two children to a restaurant for the first time. The waitress handed them their menus and then said to five-year-old Andrew, "What would you like to eat, young sir?" He couldn't believe his ears. "Did you hear that, Dad? She treated me like a real person." Manners take time to learn, and children learn best when they're praised rather than criticized. If we try to teach them with a barrage of instructions and criticism, children soon stop feeling good about themselves. Respect and praise makes them feel "real."

Should They Be Made to Clean Their Plates?

Once, I stayed with an aunt who served me a huge helping of cooked carrots. They were overcooked, yellow, and thoroughly disgusting. I tasted them and said "no thank you." In that house, though, manners dictated that you ate what was on your plate, even if you hadn't served yourself. There were, after all, starving children in the world.

Believe it or not, I had to sit at the table until bedtime. The next morning, the carrots reappeared on my breakfast plate. I was a stubborn little creature and never did eat them, nor did I stay with that aunt again. And I will not eat cooked carrots to this day. Children shouldn't be abused in the name of manners.

7. Helping Themselves

Since we want meal times to be a pleasure, I think the best way, if possible, is to put the food in serving dishes and let children help themselves. Have "rules" about manners that you all agree to but, above all, make meal times fun. If you're too strict, too critical, meals become tense.

8. Trying a Little

If you are thinking "How on earth do we get them to at least try different vegetables or other foods," suggest that they have one spoonful and make it a little one. Bribe them with an extra helping of something they like! Or, if you are clever like my friend Linda, make the vegetables into interesting shapes and try to serve them raw. Vegetables really do taste better raw and retain their nutrients, too. Get the children to help you prepare things, because they enjoy it and quite often nibble along the way. They are also more inclined to eat something they've helped to get ready because they are proud of their efforts.

Greetings—Beware the "Hairy-chinned Aunt"!

Sometimes being polite is just too hard, especially during school holidays or when the house is jam-packed with visitors.

Four-year-old Joseph hadn't quite mastered good manners when his grandparents turned up for Easter. "Where's my Easter egg?" he demanded. "What's the magic word?" asked his mother, trying to make the best of a bad job. "Abracadabra," he yelled.

9. Rules Vary

Joseph could have at least said "Hello" first, although he could have botched that, too. The way you greet people depends on your manners policy, although you may not have been aware you had one. Greeting rules vary between families, nationalities, and cultures. In some, everyone, including men, hug each other; in very "correct" households, contact is avoided. Hugging is great, but I think it is wrong to insist a child kiss or hug someone if she doesn't want to.

Jennifer, forty-three, had a great aunt who engulfed every young visitor in a big bosomy hug. "*My aunt always wore a big brooch. I dreaded seeing her because she'd seize me and crush my cheek for what seemed an eternity to this terribly sharp, lumpy brooch. I loved her, she was a dear woman, but this dread of her hugs is a vivid memory.*"

10. They May Have to Be Rude

Beware of teaching children that good manners must mean unquestioning obedience or you could be asking for trouble. One day, they may need to be rude to adults in order to protect themselves, so it's important to teach children that their bodies belong to them. I will expand on this in Chapter 5, "46 Things They Need to Keep Safe."

Talk About Manners

The good thing about social conventions is that that's all they are— conventions. As such, they're subject to change, and thank goodness, some of them have changed. But, all in all, we still need good manners; it shows we care about other people and that there are parameters for the way we can behave toward others. In any event, children are basically the same. They want to be spoken to nicely, they don't want to eat with slobs, and they like to be thanked if they send Granny a present. If you can talk about why you insist on certain things (admitting if you're not always sure of your motives) and work out adaptations to rules together for the good of everyone, then manners and kindness will become part of your children's way of life.

3

11 Ideas for a Peaceful Bedtime

Five-year-old Marie comes out of her bedroom at least a dozen times a night asking for food, drink, a story, or assistance in getting the monster out from under her bed. Her exhausted parents cannot remember having a full night's sleep since she was born.

Eleven-month-old Peter constantly cries when he is put to bed, so his mother has slept in his bedroom with him every night for the past three months. Whenever she tries to sneak out, he wakes and screams his head off.

Conversely, ten-year-old Bethan and her four-year-old sister have never had a problem sleeping, except for the nightly request for an extra story or the occasional nightmare.

Are some children purposely trying to drive us to distraction at bedtime? Is there an "I'm not going to bed quietly" gene we can blame? Most importantly, what are Bethan's parents doing right?

Here are some tried and true tips that do help with getting children to bed. You may have others that work just as well.

1. Give Sufficient Warning

- *One hour before you want them in their bedrooms:* As the clock rolls round or digitally clicks towards bedtime, give your children an hour's notice that it's coming. I know they should be able to figure this out for themselves, but they do seem to run on a different time line and certainly have better things to do than go to bed, anyway.

Look at it from their viewpoint: They are having a good time and don't want to stop. It's your idea that they need sleep; they are convinced that they don't. Besides, they might *miss* something if they have to go to bed. Nevertheless, we know they need sleep, so the battle lines are drawn. Kids pull out lots of weapons, such as hunger, thirst, need to use the toilet, monsters, "not tired," and "haven't finished my homework." The sixty-minute warning helps them to start winding down and getting into the right frame of mind for bed, and gives them no excuses once "lights out" comes.

- *Forty-five minutes:* Tell them they have fifteen minutes until they have to start washing, brushing teeth, and getting ready for bed.
- *Thirty minutes:* That's it—time to get ready. Don't wait until the last minute. The faster they get ready, the more time they'll have to themselves before going into their bedrooms.
- *Five minutes:* Countdown. Time to get ready for the story, reading, listening to music, or all three.
- *Lights out:* No excuses. Time to go to their rooms, get into bed, and settle down for stories, hugs, and kisses. I now give my children half an hour to read and listen to music before lights out, but they are not to get out of bed.

So the entire ritual takes about an hour, plus whatever time (if any) you give them before finally turning off the lights. It isn't as complicated as it seems; it just means you have to keep an eye on the time or set a timer or alarm clock to remind you.

I once babysat for a friend's little girl, three-year-old Alison, who hated going to bed. Alison liked coming to look at the clock to see how much longer she had. When the timer went off, she scampered into her bedroom, had a story, and asked to keep the timer to see when I was going to come back to turn off the light. This method worked wonders and continued to work for her parents, who were thrilled.

2. Allow Staggered Bedtimes

As children grow older they expect to have later bedtimes than their younger brothers and sisters. This makes your life more complicated, but it is fair. When my older son asked for a later bedtime, we allowed him to go to bed half an hour after his little brother. It meant two sets of timekeeping, but it was worth it. Also, it gave me more individual time to spend with each child before bed.

You'll have problems sorting it all out, especially if your children share a room, as mine did. In order not to disturb the younger child, both children got ready at the same time—teeth brushed and into pajamas. The older one then spent time either in the living room or kitchen; the going-to-bed activities had to be adapted. After a short while, we went into the room to tuck him in and, his younger brother stayed sleeping.

The other main problem is convincing the younger child that it is fair. We set up a bedtime schedule according to age and told both children that when they reached a certain age, they would have a certain, predetermined bedtime. You have to ignore protestations from your child that he is the "only one in the entire school/world/ universe" who goes to bed that early. Reply, "If you don't go to bed you will be the only child in the school without a head," or some other suitable comment. Say it with a demonic smile.

3. Have Bedtime Rituals

Children find it comforting to have the same thing happen before going to sleep every night. In our house, the boys still ask for nightly hugs and some sort of fruit, such as an apple, even though they are both teenagers. When they were little, they always had a story and a song. Now they read themselves to sleep listening to their own music, which is quite awful in my humble opinion.

If your children have a special blanket, toy, or bit of rag that they need to help them sleep, be sure to have that handy. Don't worry, they won't sleep with a stuffed animal when they're forty. Anyway, if it's a comfort to them, it's a comfort for you, too.

If you are a "split" (divorced or separated) family, as so many are today, and your children go back and forth between two households, try to ensure that both parents are being consistent. It doesn't matter if the rituals are slightly different so long as they are fairly consistent in each parent's household. What does matter is if the children are unsettled, or if you allow behavior that is not in their best interests.

4. Try Using Night-Lights

If children don't like to sleep in the dark, why not have a night-light? The soft light can be quite comforting, though for some children the shadows thrown up by the light are more frightening than the dark. Other children prefer flashlights. I used to hide under the covers and read with mine, never thinking that my parents could see the glow through the bedspread.

Another possibility is to give the children those high intensity lights that only direct a small beam on a book. If your children share a room, give those that don't like the light a nightshade to cover their eyes.

5. Tackle the Monster Problem

"But Mommy, there *is* a monster under my bed. I see him!" Sigh! There are some wonderful books—*There's a Monster in My Wardrobe, Alexander and the Dragon,* and others—that deal with children's fears of strange beings in their rooms. Try reading them one of these stories or asking them to make up their own. If they are still concerned, look under the bed and in the wardrobe, but be sure to say that you *don't* believe in monsters and there aren't any here. One mother wrote to me to say that when she was little, her parents made a big deal of "looking for the monster," which convinced her even more that there was one!

There is a deeper, more frightening reason for the fear of monsters which fortunately doesn't affect most children. Several years ago I met a group of teenagers who had all been sexually abused and were now under care in a children's home. Of the nine young people, seven still had a fear of monsters and looked under the bed and in the closet every night, even though they were fifteen and sixteen years old. For them, the abuse that happened in their bedrooms continued to produce monsters that many are still being counseled for.

6. Use Humor and Laughter

Laughter relaxes children and grown-ups alike. Remember jokes you hear or take out a book from the library—something like *Three Hundred Corny Jokes.* The humor might be very low-level: "What's green and bounces?" "I don't know, what's green and bounces?" "Spring Cabbage." But it can add tremendously to the fun of going to bed if there is some sort of laughter every night. Ask your children to find a joke, too. Not a sick one, please.

7. Avoid Wild Activities and Distractions

Years ago, I think it was easier to get children to bed quietly. Yes, there were the noisy fathers (at least in my house) and the chasing-around-the-house games, but there weren't all the possible distractions our children have to deal with today. For better or worse, parents didn't try to make children mini-geniuses by making sure their beds were festooned with mobiles, mirrors, horns, drums, and all sorts of colorful paraphernalia. Don't get me wrong, my children had all those things and more, but I sometimes wonder if the theory that beds are meant only for sleeping has some merit. Funny I managed to do all right in school without all that kind of stimulation as a baby, but I didn't want to take a chance that my kids would miss out, so I bought it all.

Anyway, put aside the stimulating toys that talk and teach, and things like the television, loud stereos, dishwashers, and dryers—necessities of modern life—and try to avoid games and activities that wind the children up to a frenzied pitch. I remember the parents of three who came to see me because their children never seemed to settle down. The father was a character and a practical joker. It turned out that he loved to put the kids to bed with wild horseback rides, and games that involved running around with lots of competition to see who would win, and he also liked to surprise the children by jumping out from behind doors. I became hyper just listening to his antics. Imagine how excited the children were—hearts racing, minds excited, sleep out of the question.

Bedtime isn't the time to horse around and get keyed up. Better to do that in the morning if you want to hurry them along. Try cozy, low-key, gentle activities such as singing, relaxing exercises, rubbing backs, listening to story tapes, or thinking of what Teddy might wear tomorrow. All of this should be done in a soothing voice bordering on monotony. Softly, softly, off they'll go to sleep. Using that voice continues to work right up through the teenage years.

8. Use Praise

So often we comment on how badly the children behave at bedtime. Try catching them doing something good and praise them for it.

"You're such a good girl for brushing your teeth and being in bed on time. God job!"

"I'm so pleased you managed to get all your homework done and go to bed without a fuss."

"You're ready ten minutes early, so you have ten minutes to do something you like before going to your room. That shows you are growing up. You're wonderful!"

Reward them with an extra story or five minutes longer staying up—it's worth it and much more relaxing than having to scold them or hurry them.

9. Give Them Extra Attention

There will be times when your children do need a little extra attention. In that case, go to them rather than letting them get up, and rub their backs or pat them. But be careful not to let this extra time become part of the nightly ritual.

If they begin to use hunger or thirst as an attention grabber, then leave a thermos of water or an extra apple by the bed so they can't use those old excuses.

For Marie's parents, this cut down their trips to her room by half. They combined that with looking for the monster *before* they left the room, and a firm nightly ritual that included one trip back to Marie's room and no more. Marie did throw a fit at first, but I advised them to go into another room, shut the door, and turn up the music. After about two weeks of hell, Marie now goes to bed like a lamb.

Peter's parents, too, have broken his habit of having to have mom or dad sleep in his room. Peter didn't like it, but they held out and he soon learned that they weren't going to come. "Listening to him cry himself to sleep was horrible," said his mother, "but we are all happier now and he really likes his bedtime stories and cuddles. I do, too. Before, I used to dread bedtime and I was in a bad mood most of the day because of lack of sleep. Now, after the story and cuddles, I put on a tape and out I go. He knows that when the tape starts that is my good night." Peter's parents won't have to go through the traumas that Marie's parents had for all those years.

10. Recognize True Distress

Of course, at times our children's needs will supercede the bedtime routine. They may be truly distressed about something that's happened, or sick, or having nightmares. The answer is common sense—go to them. You may have to take them into your own bed for a while, sometimes simply for your own convenience.

When our sons were babies and were still needed nursing, that long walk down the cold hallway in winter (I had both children in the autumn—silly me) got to be a bit much. One night, when my first child was about three weeks old, I told my husband to leave him with us in bed because if I had to get up next time (we took turns), then my milk and I would surely freeze and we didn't have any baby bottles.

Experts often say it isn't a good idea for children to get used to staying in their parents' bed, or they might still be there five years

later. I agree that allowing kids to be permanently ensconced in their
parents' beds is not a good idea. In our case, this didn't happen
because we made sure the boys' room was a more fun place to be. But
I can't see anything wrong with occasionally allowing a distressed or
sick child into your bed. Of course we don't want them moving in
and taking over, but some times when extra warmth and human
contact is a much needed tonic.

Take, for example, the night after my younger son's hamster died.
He was inconsolable and felt guilty that he hadn't taken better care
of the nasty, biting, little rodent. After I put him to bed, I could hear
him gulping down big sobs, and I felt he needed to be hugged and
comforted. My husband carried him in, which wasn't easy considering he was a strapping eight-year-old, and we both talked to him and
cuddled him to sleep. The next night everything was back to normal.

I remember a father who came to see me soon after his wife had
unexpectedly died. He expressed some concern that his twelve-year-
old son wanted to sleep in bed with him. "I really want him to, but
what would people say?" Personally, I think that it is more important
for the child to have comfort and love than for the father to worry
about others' opinions. The man was simply a caring father who
most likely needed the comfort of his son, as well, at a very difficult
time.

Later, the son told me that just being in the same bed his mother
used to sleep in and having Dad put his arm around him helped
enormously when coming to terms with his mother's death. The son
was more than a little afraid his dad might die, too, so it was easier to
sleep knowing his dad was there to look after him.

As with all these issues, parents have to use their own common
sense, which is usually ten times better than so-called "expert"
advice.

11. Prepare for Guests

"I was mortified," Ellen told me. Here we were in the middle of an
important dinner party we had planned and worked hard to prepare,
and suddenly my eight-year-old was putting on a tap-dance show.
The guests clapped politely; I smiled, covering murderous thoughts.
My daughter had never done that before, but we rarely have guests so
I hadn't thought about how to deal with her bedtime. After that
exhibition, I don't think we'll have many more guests anyway!" Ellen
was in despair.

If you have guests and your child suddenly decides that he is a budding actor, musician, magician, or dancer, it may be because you aren't able to read the ritual story or give the obligatory snack. Or it may be that your stagestruck child has finally found a captive audience.

If your guests are good friends or relatives, you might arrange in advance for a short show, which they may love, especially when they know it is going to end. I was once stuck at a dinner party that was constantly interrupted by the host's children, and after a while I began to smile through gritted teeth as I thought about what little show-offs and creeps they were. The third time you hear "I'm a Little Teapot" sung out of tune with "cute" antics is enough to make you want to run screaming from the house. I just managed to stay seated and was dying for the parents to pick up the precocious brats and sling them into their bedrooms. Instead they looked on with parental pride and indulgence. As Charlie Brown would say in *Peanuts,* "Arghhhhhhh!!!"

One way around the problem is to farm your children out to friends or to bring in a babysitter. If your children are old enough and it is a weekend, why not allow them to have guests of their own? Get their food ready in advance, arrange to play a video or have games set up, and let them be the host or hostess. This worked quite well with my children when we ordered take-out pizza and let them choose the videos they wanted. At one point it was so quiet I thought they had disappeared.

As a last resort, you can tell your guests you are trying to stop the children's bad behavior, and ask them to help by paying no attention to whatever your children try to do. (Don't do this on the night you are entertaining the boss, however!)

One way to handle the guest-bedtime dilemma is to warn your children the night before that you won't be able to spend time with them the next night and promise to make up for it the night after that. Alternatively, you might be able to make time earlier in the evening, or record a special story on a tape that the children can listen to once the guests have arrived. If you do this, make it a big deal so that the children look forward to it. If they ask you to do it other nights when you would normally read to them, don't! (Anyway, the ungrateful little monsters shouldn't prefer a tape to the real thing, but then kids will be kids.)

If you have guests and cannot yell out the fifteen-minute warning, use a timer or alarm clock so that they know when to start. Of course, that doesn't mean they will, but if you tell them you are counting on them and that you know they are grown-up enough to do this, their reaction might surprise you. Be sure to praise them like mad and tell them how proud you are of the fact that they can behave this way.

After years of parenting and helping other parents, one thing I know for certain about bedtime is that the rosy picture of the Von Trapp children singing their way to bed while the guests smile and applaud portrayed in *The Sound of Music,* just ain't how it is in real life. But then I'm sure you already know that.

4

10 Ways to Help Your Child
Make Friends

"But, Dad, I don't want to go to school. No one likes me. I don't have any friends."

Carol's father was nearly in tears when he came to see me. "She is so miserable that I don't know what to do. I can't manufacture friends for her, and I don't want to do the wrong thing and make matters worse."

Your heart goes out to Carol and her father. It is such a lonely feeling when you have no one to sit with at lunch, play with on the playground, or go to visit after school. Yet other children never seem to lack friends. They appear to have a natural ability to attract people and are full of confidence. Are there some things we can teach children about finding friends and being a friend to others? You bet there are, and some are very simple. The earlier we start, the better. But there is one caution: Some children will be very happy having one or two friends or a small group, while others like being friends with everyone.

Even in the same family, children will differ in how they perceive friendship. Harry, age eight, loves being in the midst of a shouting, rowdy, tumbling group of children. As far as he is concerned, the more the merrier, and he isn't happy unless there is action most of the time. His brother Thomas, age ten, has always had a few close friends and likes to play games, go to the movies, or take walks in the woods with them. Their parents can't understand how they could be so different, but they are both content, so there is no need to try to change things. If it isn't broken, don't fix it.

If you do need to fix it, here are some pointers about making friends that you can try with your children:

1. Identify the Problem

Did Carol have friends at one time or has she always been a loner? Has a group of her friends left her out in the cold? It turned out that Carol was a bright eight-year-old who usually had one or two friends, but who had always related better to adults. One of her friends had moved away during the summer and the other, Susan, seemed to be moving on to form new friendships—something Carol felt unable or unwilling to do. Carol was a slightly introverted child, and her previous friendships had come largely through the efforts the other children made to get to know her. She didn't approach them, but she was delighted to be approached and included in things. She had no family, behavior, or academic problems; she was just unhappy about her lack of friends.

A discussion with Carol brought out some of her anxieties. Because she had never thought about or felt the need to make friends, the very idea of approaching a new person or group terrified her. She simply did not know how to begin, or even who she might like to be friends with. She also felt rejected by Susan, who was spending less and less time with her because of the new friends she was making.

Some children will have other types of problems. Another child may be bullying her or deliberately excluding her (see chapter 27 on bullying). Or she may irritate other children by doing something like wiping her nose on their sleeve or burping all the time. Or she may live a long way from the rest of the class and miss out on socializing with the others after school and on weekends. Or she may, of course, be picking on other children herself. It always pays to find out as much information as possible about the problem before you begin to try to solve it.

2. Form a Plan

I asked Carol if I could help her make a list of children she might like to know. The list included Susan and three other girls. We figured out a plan that Carol felt she could achieve. One of the girls on her list, Jasmine, seemed quite nice but also a bit shy. This was an ideal person for Carol to try to approach, because Jasmine would probably welcome someone attempting to get to know her. The plan was:

- Carol and her dad sat down together and figured out what Carol liked in a friend and what friends might like from her.
- Her dad spoke with the teacher to ensure that everything possible was being done to include Carol with the other children, and to find out if there were any problems he didn't know about.
- Carol role-played with me to give her the confidence she needed to seek out friends. (I will explain how to do this later in the chapter.)
- Invite Jasmine over.

Depending upon the circumstances, your plan might not include all these steps. If your child is new to a school, doesn't know anyone yet, and feels uncomfortable about making new friends, you might just help by letting your children practice on you what to say, or by getting advice from the teacher. Inviting children to your house might be all that is required.

3. Enlist the Teacher's Help

Most friendships are formed in school, so it is vital to get the teacher's help. Perhaps the seating arrangements could be changed to encourage more friendships. In Carol's class, the teacher had allowed the children to choose who they sat next to every day. After being alerted by Carol's father, she decided to assign seats and change the seating plan every three weeks. This gave children a chance to get to know more people, and it helped develop new friendships. It certainly helped Carol, as the teacher made sure she sat at a table with Jasmine, giving the girls an opportunity to get to know each other.

You can also ask the teacher to discreetly monitor your child in the lunchroom and on the playground so that conflicts or hurtful incidents can be stopped before they get out of hand. It is best if this is all done with the knowledge of your child, but if this is not possible, you should contact the teacher in confidence for the good of your child. Most teachers are only too pleased to help.

If you get no cooperation, or feel that the teacher might make it worse, which unfortunately does sometimes happen, see if there is someone else at the school with whom you could have a quiet word to enlist help. Often the playground supervisors or lunchroom staff are people from your neighborhood, and they might be able to let you know how they feel your child is getting on with the other children. Also, they might be able to intervene in less obvious ways, because they know all the kids and their parents.

4. Figure Out What Makes a Good Friend

Recently, I conducted a survey of 200 children ages seven to eleven and asked them what they looked for in a friend. I also asked teachers to make observations about why they thought some children were more "popular" than others.

When children are seeking friendship they are drawn to someone who:

- smiles and is happy most of the time
- likes to join in and play with them
- isn't bossy
- helps them with their school work
- shares things
- makes them laugh and is fun to be with
- listens when they want to talk
- is kind
- sticks up for them
- doesn't change—they aren't nice one day and mean the next

Teachers observed that children who were "popular" with both students and teachers:

- were self-confident
- were good at organizing games and activities
- could shrug off disappointments and setbacks
- were good listeners
- had a good sense of humor
- had parents who were supportive
- had good communication skills, including being able to find something to talk about with other children and adults
- were healthy and often good at sports
- were able to sort out conflicts between children
- complimented others and were not critical

It might be a good idea either to duplicate this list and discuss it with your children, or make up a list of your own with them. Better yet, let them make one up themselves and then discuss it with them. It is an excellent exercise that gets children thinking not only about what they want in a friend, but how they are acting with other children. You might suggest to your child's teacher that, if time can be found, they try a similar exercise with the class. When I was teaching, I found it very useful to get the children talking about friendship because it prevented problems from forming.

Carol and her father came up with a list. What Carol wanted in a friend was someone who would:

- like her
- enjoy drawing, talking, reading, playing
- be with her at lunch and playtime
- come to her apartment and sleep over sometimes
- be nice

Carol thought a friend might like her in order to:

- be liked
- share activities
- eat and play together
- talk about things
- think of things to do

When we met, Carol thought she could be kind (in fact, she was a very kind child, just a bit too sensitive) and that she could start thinking of things she and friends could do, like roller-skating or going to the park. Her father, a single parent, was more than willing to provide opportunities for Carol and her friends to do some fun things.

Carol also thought she had to work on a way to start a conversation with Jasmine. She tended to get tongue-tied, so we decided to practice—just the two of us, so she wouldn't be em barrassed.

5. Ice Breakers

Initiating a conversation with someone or going up to a group to talk can be daunting. Many adults find it difficult, saying that every intelligent thought they've ever had vanishes and they become blithering idiots. If that's how they feel it's no wonder they hold back. Children need a practice phrase or two that slips out easily and gets them over that first hurdle. Carol and I came up with the following ideas for opening sentences:

"Did you see the program last night about...? What did you think of it?"

"What did you think about the story we had in reading this morning (or yesterday or whenever)?"

"I liked your drawing in class. What kind of things do you like to draw?"

"What did you do over the weekend?"

"Would you like to go over there and play that game? Or would you rather do something else?"

"Would you mind if I sat here next to you?"

We practiced with Carol as herself and me as the various children, such as Susan and Jasmine. Carol felt silly at first, but her confidence increased tremendously and she was soon able to try it out with the children. She was thrilled to tell me at our next meeting that it worked, and children actually talked to her and sat with her at lunch.

If children are old enough to understand, explain the difference between a "closed" question and an "open" question. A closed question is more likely to elicit a plain yes or no response: "Do you like milk?" "Yes." These kinds of questions usually start with words like *do, did, is, are,* and *was.* Open questions are more likely to elicit a longer response with more opportunities for conversation: "What sort of things did you do when you were on vacation?" "Oh, we went swimming and out in a boat. We played tennis a little bit, but I'm not very good at it."

There is no guarantee that the person your child talks to will give a better answer to an open question, but at least the odds are better.

6. Invite Children Over

In order to cement friendships and foster new ones, it often helps to have your children play at your home with others. This not only gives them the chance to get to know each other away from school, but gives you a chance to observe how your children interact with others and what their friends are like.

Try to make sure the children have a good time. Help your child to think of fun things to do, such as a trip to the movies or an expedition to the park with a picnic. Maybe there is a swimming pool or an ice rink near you. It is also fun to do things the other children might not do at home. I remember teaching a group of my son's friends how to play Monopoly and some card games. They had never done that before, which amazed me. (I guess computer games took over the world when I wasn't looking!)

Carol invited Jasmine over and they made homemade pizza, watched a video, played with Carol's cat, had a water-pistol fight, and generally enjoyed themselves. Carol now plans to include Susan and the other girls in a party she and her father are planning for her birthday.

7. Observe Your Child

If you can unobtrusively observe your children when they are with friends or trying to make friends, you can find out lots. Obviously you can't be in the room the whole time, but you can be "reading" next door, rearranging pictures in the hallway nearby, or weeding the garden while they are outside. Leave a door ajar so you can overhear what's happening, or set up a game or a snack in the kitchen and busy yourself in the background. See if your child is being friendly, judgmental, bossy, shy, too sensitive, tactful, humorous, aggressive, or complaining. Then, try to encourage the traits from the survey to enhance friendships, and gently suggest ways to change the negative traits, one at a time.

If your child is too sensitive, you might suggest that sometimes people misunderstand what others are saying because they take things too seriously. Explain that crying or going into a shell doesn't help because it makes others withdraw. Help your child see that the other person did not mean to hurt her feelings and that she should not take things to heart so much.

Carol's father reported that she was very friendly and solicitous of her friends. She shared things and was good at taking turns and complimenting others, but was inclined to be hurt too easily.

"She seemed to take everything to heart, even silly little comments. Luckily, the other girls didn't seem to notice too much, except once when Carol felt hurt because she thought Susan was talking too much to Jasmine and Soon-Yi. Susan just turned to her and told her not to be so stupid. I could see Carol trying to control her emotions, which she did very well, but I thought she was too thin-skinned. I'm sure it's because she still feels rejected after her mother left, but we'll work on it. She knows she has to try to laugh things off more—actually we both do, so I guess it's partly my fault as well."

Good for Carol's father for admitting that he too might be overly sensitive. It gives children hope to know that we have to struggle with the same problems as they do.

If I could tell parents of newborn babies one thing to do with their children (beyond loving them), it would be to laugh a lot and help them develop a sense of humor.

8. Change Undesirable Behavior

In Carol's case there was no undesirable behavior to change, unless you count her sensitivity. I wouldn't call that bad behavior—more a sense of perspective. However, some children don't have friends because they put people off.

If children are aggressive, have a quick temper, are bossy, or refuse to share, other children will not want to play with them. If they have nasty habits like farting, burping, picking their noses, or spitting, they will find everyone taking a wide berth. If they have poor personal hygiene, such as body odor or greasy hair, then it is not surprising if they lack friends.

It is possible to change children's behavior or personal hygiene if they, and their parents, are willing to try. I remember one boy who was so smelly that no one could bear to be around him. When I gently and, I thought, tactfully tried to talk with his mother about it, I was told it was none of my business and the family, which seemed normal in other respects, didn't believe in washing much because it was harmful to the body. Oh dear. The boy knew he smelled and hated it.

I circumvented the mother on this one, something I rarely do. We arranged for him to shower at school and put on fresh clothes we kept for him. So, every day he would arrive in the clothes from home, wash, change, and spend the day in his "school clothes," then change back into his "home clothes" to go home. His mother never did find out, and the boy went on to become a very clean carpenter.

If your child is acting in a way that clearly needs to be changed for her own good and for the good of others, don't hesitate to wade in. Practice alternative ways to behave until they become second nature to her. Arrange a time-out place for her to go when she is feeling aggressive so she won't bother someone else. Let him now when he is bossy and explain how to approach people in a nice way. Role-play with him asking kids to do things instead of telling them what to do. Don't look the other way if a child is picking or her nose. Confront yucky habits, tell the child this is unacceptable in polite society, and reward her when she doesn't do it.

9. Some Friendships Just Don't Work Out

Friendships don't always go according to plan. A child may try to be friends with someone, but it just may not work out for reasons beyond your or her control. It could be that they simply can't find anything in common. It might be that they used to be friends but now enjoy doing completely different things. Or it may be that a friend may have personal problems and just wants to be left alone for a while. Friends may also decide to do something your child cannot or will not do, such as stealing. At least weall hope our children would draw the line at that kind of destructive friendship.

The message to get across to your children is that friendships do come and go. Some will last a lifetime, others only a day. If they have tried their best, perhaps it just wasn't meant to be. Talk with them about friendships that fail, if they want to talk, and assure them that there are lots of people out there to become friends with, and not to despair. It does help if you can talk about a time when you lost a friend and what it meant to you. After all, your children can see that you've survived it, and that is a good model for them.

10. Enhance Your Child's Talents, Interests, or Activities

Help your children increase the number of people they can be friends with by encouraging them to develop their skills and interests. If a child is good at sports, find out about Saturday sports clubs or after-school lessons. Look into swimming, dance, tennis, and gymnastics classes. Check out the local Scout troops, Brownie packs, or acting or martial arts classes. See if you can arrange group music lessons. Not only will these things increase your children's self-confidence, they will have whole new groups of people from which to find friends.

And, whatever you do, please encourage your children not to discard old friends as they make new ones. I don't know the rest of it, but I remember this song from my childhood.

> Make new friends
> But keep the old;
> One is silver
> And the other's gold.

5

46 Things They Need to Know to Keep Safe

A child playing outside can be snatched off a bike, bundled into a car, and dragged out of sight in seconds. News of child abusers seems to surface weekly in the papers. Parents today face a difficult dilemma: how to give children the freedom to develop their independence, yet stay safe.

Things were so different when I was a kid. Remember leaving early in the morning with a bag of peanut butter and jelly sandwiches and a drink? Mom would give a wave, absently tell us to be careful and not to get into trouble. "Be back before dark" was the only definite rule. We got back on time, but even then we played out with our friends after dark, hiding behind neighborhood trees and in dark alleys without a thought that we might be in danger. In the summer we were often out until past ten P.M.

Of course, we were warned not to go off with strangers, but we also said "hello" politely if any grown-up talked to us. We were not aware of child abuse, or that danger might come from someone you knew.

I look back with rose-tinted glasses to those days of my childhood with a yearning for what appeared to be a safer and kinder time. But sometimes I worry about how on earth we can bring children up now so that they are safe in today's very different world, but still allow them to have some of that lovely innocence and sense of wonder we had.

It's no good asking our own parents for advice. When they were bringing us up, they didn't seem to be hit by shocking news of yet another child murder. Nowadays, it's not just a little scary to let our children go out to the park on their own for an hour or two; we wonder if it's safe to ask them to run a quick errand to the corner store. As parents of this generation, we have to keep things in perspective and we have to work out new rules—and it's hard being a pioneer. The vast majority of children go through life without any serious harm, but we still must warn all children that the danger is there. How can we go about this?

1. Accept That Children Will Lose Some Innocence

There is a danger that our children will lose their innocence as they are no longer shielded from many adult worries and responsibilities. No one can blame us for wanting to keep our children safe, but there is a cost. Children are, of necessity, more vigilant and aware of dangers. For example, in the past no one warned kids about people they knew who might try to abuse them. So when children were abused, they didn't tell or weren't believed. Now they are told to tell if anyone tries to secretly touch or kiss them, but the price is they learn earlier about things we would rather they didn't ever have to deal with. But I think we have no choice, unless we never let our kids out of our sight, that is.

2. Judge When to Let Them Out Alone

I remember vividly the day I finally relented to my eldest son's burning desire to go, on his own, to the corner store. He was eight, I was thirtysomething. We lived on the sixth floor of an apartment building. Charles waved goodbye and got into the elevator. I waited until the doors closed on his little freckled face, then rushed down the stairs. He went out the front door, looked left and right about ten times, and crossed the road before heading to the corner store. Peering out from behind the door, I took deep breaths until I saw him return. I then charged up six flights of stairs to arrive back in the apartment just ahead of him. When he came in bursting with pride and announced, "I did it, Mom," I could only gasp, with assumed nonchalance, "Good boy."

Allowing your kids out is exhausting! And, it would seem to us, dangerous. There's no denying that children are vulnerable. Every parent's nightmare is that a psychopath will take them away, horrifically abuse them, and murder them. But the reality is that the vast majority of children are quite safe; moreover, most who are in danger are harmed by someone they know.

Sometimes, however, children are missing and stay missing. Some are found dead. It's no use then telling us that psychopaths are few and the chances are one in a million that a child will be in the wrong place at the wrong time. That won't stop us being terrified of letting our kids out.

Seeing those lovely young faces staring at us from newspapers, or even milk cartons, hearing their parents' anguished pleas on the news, and knowing that "there but for the grace of God goes my child" brings a chill of dread to any mom or dad. You know it will never be possible to protect all children from all harm and horrid people, but you must try your best. That they are far more likely to be harmed by someone they know than by a stranger doesn't quell that dread.

3. Beware Being Overprotective

One mom I talked to, Jackie, thought she had solved the problem by shelving it. "Whenever my children ask me if they can go out on their own, I tell them 'next year.' The difficulty is that when next year comes, it's always too soon." Her son will probably still be asking if he can go to the store when he's forty!

We all know parents who never let their children out of their sight. Sometimes it's understandable—for a short while. As one mom, Susan, told me, "After a man attempted to snatch a girl from the playground at my daughter's school, I followed her everywhere. But soon I realized the shadow behind the tree wasn't a wicked stranger—it was me, worrying all the time."

We cannot teach our children to mistrust everyone, even if we feel that way. Most people like (or at least tolerate) children and would never hurt them. We have to curb our natural tendencies to protect children, or they will never learn to stand on their own feet.

4. Prepare Them for the Outside World

But what do you do when your children want more freedom than you think they can handle? Every parent's heart will sink when they hear these accusations:

- "You always treat me like a baby."
- "My friends stay out until midnight."
- "No other parents want to know where their children are."

It's natural for children to try to gain that extra bit of independence, but we can't give in when we know they shouldn't be roaming the streets at an unearthly hour. We should stoutly resist (even if we're pleased that they've the guts to try it with us).

We must, however, let them spread their wings. We owe it to kids to teach them to cope in the world. We must show them how to develop strategies to use—in case they come into contact with someone who tries to harm them.

And talking about it isn't enough. You don't just tell a child to look both ways before crossing the road—you take them by the hand and practice crossing the road with them. The same applies when teaching children about yelling, kicking, and running away from dangerous situations—don't just say it, get them to do it until you are satisfied they could summon up a really convincing yell at anyone who tries to molest them.

The following are some typical situations when children may be vulnerable, and some tips on preparing them how to act.

Using Public Transportion

Andrew, age twelve, was on his way back from a soccer match. He caught the train home and somehow ended up in a car on his own. A gang of youths got on at the next stop and started taunting him. Though Andrew ignored them, they shoved and pushed him around. Finally, they beat him and kicked him in the groin. They left the train and Andrew staggered home without reporting the attack.

His mother, horrified, sought medical help and telephoned the police. When the officer pointed out he could have pulled the emergency cord, Andrew said he'd considered it, but thought he would have to pay a fine as the sign said "only use in an emergency." The poor boy hadn't realized this was an emergency!

We need to ensure that children, particularly ones brought up to have good manners, understand they have a right to protect themselves at all costs. Talk about basic rules for travel on public transportion with your children. Tell them to:

5. Always travel in cars where there are other people.
6. Ride in the conductor's car.
7. Find the emergency lever or cord, read the instructions, and use it if necessary.
8. Stay on the bus, subway, or train if they think they are being

followed, tell the conductor or driver, and ask to call home from the manager's office.
9. Use only licensed taxis.
10. Turn around and go back to where there are other people if someone follows them from the stop or station.

Using Public Restrooms

Frances told me that when her son, Martin, was nine, they were at a fast-food restaurant and he went to the restroom. He came out looking pale and agitated. A man, attracted by the number of children known to go there, had hidden just inside the door. When Martin came in, the man pounced, fondled him, and left. Martin had been too frightened to run, let alone cry for help. There were many people around who would have heard him and helped, but he didn't know how to react—fast and at once.

11. Are You OK?

Many's the time when I have stood outside the men's restroom shouting to my boys, "Everything OK?" The men's room is one of the first places moms get excluded from, but it is also one of the most likely places where a pervert might try to grope a child. Fathers out alone with daughters can't go into the Ladies' room but thankfully this kind of offense is rare in female restrooms. Do remember that girls have been assaulted in isolated restrooms, so they should be warned as well.

Talk to your children about what they should do if they find themselves alone in a public restroom and in trouble. Suggest that they should:

12. Leave immediately if someone tries to touch them or to start a conversation with them.
13. Tell an attendant if there is one.
14. Never go into a stall with anyone, no matter what he says.
15. Never be afraid to make a fuss if there's a chance someone will hear.
16. Never go into isolated public restrooms by themselves.

Using Elevators and Staircases

Paula, age ten, had lived in the same building all her life. Her mother says she is fairly streetwise, but recently a terrible thing happened.

Paula's mom found her daughter crying at their front door. Between sobs, she blurted out her story. Her mom said it was all she could do to keep from screaming as she listened.

Paula had gotten into the elevator and noticed a man she instantly felt uncomfortable about. But it didn't occur to her to get out again, and in a moment the doors had closed. Suddenly, the man reached over, stopped the elevator between floors and turned off the light. He told Paula he'd kill her if she yelled or made a fuss. He then stripped her and indecently assaulted her. The child did as she was told because there was no chance of escaping. She told her mom she'd wanted to get out when she saw the man, but hadn't wanted to appear rude.

Little Paula did the right thing by not fighting back when the man said he'd kill her. But if only she'd been prepared to follow her instincts and get out of the elevator in the first place, it might have prevented the traumatic assault. Discuss the dangers with your children. Tell them to:

17. Be prepared to leave an elevator immediately if they feel uncomfortable for any reason about another person.
18. Wait until the next elevator—an empty one or one with lots of people in it. Anytime your child feels unsafe, she can get out.
19. Use the stairs if they are safer.
20. Be wary of dark staircases and wait to walk up with other people.
21. Get away as quickly as possible if someone threatens them on a staircase—They should run in the opposite direction or run up to the door of a house or apartment and knock loudly. (If you live in an apartment building you could talk with neighbors and arrange with other parents where kids can go to in case of emergency.)
22. Yell if there's a chance of being heard.

Going Out and About

Twelve-year-old Melissa was waiting for a bus when a man joined the line. He moved close to Melissa and whispered something to her. She froze when she heard the stream of filth. Although there were at least ten people in the line, Melissa was too frightened to move away. The obscenities went on for what seemed like forever before the man calmly walked off.

Melissa told no one until three months later when she approached me after I'd given a talk to her class. She repeated what the man had said and then broke down. She'd been having nightmares and, each time she waited for a bus, was scared that the man would reappear. It had never occurred to her to leave the line and walk into a nearby store or to ask for adult help.

Explain to your children that if someone talks obscenely or exposes himself, they should:

23. Ignore him—put their fingers in their ears, or turn or look away.
24. Always walk toward shops or houses or, if on public transportion, move purposefully elsewhere.
25. Tell their parents, their teacher, or the police.

Coming Into Contact With an Abuser

Children may be at risk from someone they know who might try to abuse them. Children need to know strategies they can use to either get away or tell someone should something happen. Here are some suggestions for talking with children about this difficult subject.

26. Not Everyone Can Touch

Explain to children that their bodies belong to them. No one should touch them in a way that makes them uncomfortable or confused. Touching, kisses, and hugs should *never* be kept secret.

27. Tell All

Tell children to tell you if anyone asks them to keep touches, kisses, or hugs secret, even if it feels good. Sometimes abuse is not physically painful; it can even feel good. This confuses the child even more.

28. Some People Have Problems

Explain that most people love children and would never harm them, but that some people have problems that might lead them to touch children where they should not. It is OK for children to touch their own bodies, of course.

29. Don't Say Too Much to the Abuser

Tell your children that they should never threaten an abuser by saying that they will tell. They may have to go along with what is asked and then tell you. If they threaten an abuser, he or she could turn nasty and hurt the child. Better that the child should get away and tell you.

30. Role-Play

To reinforce the idea of safety, play "What if?" games with your children. Ask things like, "What would you do if someone you knew asked you to keep a kiss a secret?"

Be low-key when talking about all of these things. You will find that children take it in their stride. Be sure to work out with them who they would tell if something did happen. Help them make a list of people they know and trust.

When Do You Allow Them Out?

When I was setting up Kidscape, which teaches children how to keep safe, I asked more than 4,000 parents what they did about giving their children freedom in safety.

The only thing they all agreed on was that the maturity of the child and where you lived were important in determining when to allow children out to play. How do you judge maturity? Each parent has to decide, but the general consensus was that they allowed:

31. children, age nine, to go to local shops and cross small roads.
32. children, age eleven to use public transportation in daylight.
33. children, age twelve, to go shopping or to the movies with a friend in daylight.
34. young people, age fifteen or sixteen, to go out at night with a curfew of eleven P.M. (or later for special events).

There are hundreds of safety tips I have worked out at Kidscape, and the great reward for me is when a child tells me, "It works!"

Tom, age ten, told me he'd been on his way to school when a man drove his car up on to the sidewalk right in Tom's path. The man leaned out of the car and tried to grab him. Tom backed away, yelled a deep, loud yell, and ran all the way to school, where he collapsed like a heap of Jell-O. He'd been taught in one of my classes just the previous week the lesson of yelling, running, and getting away. He had practiced it and it may have saved his life.

The positive way to look at this problem is to realize we can instill confidence in children by teaching them practical things they can do if they come under attack. It's something we can work on a little bit at a time, as soon as they are old enough to understand about learning to fight for themselves.

It isn't a cozy, safe world. Bringing up kids just seems more difficult these days. Even riding a bike has become a major safety issue. When my eldest son's bike was stolen, we replaced it, along with a new cycling helmet, knee pads, and gloves, at our local bike store. Recalling my carefree, bike-riding youth with none of these accouterments, I remarked to the old gentleman who runs the store that it was amazing that any of us ever grew up, lacking as we were in safety measures. "Times were different then," he said, shaking his head. I think he's right.

"Can I go out to play?" "Yes, my love, but remember to run away quickly if anyone tries to grab you, don't talk to anyone you don't know and scream your head off if you feel in danger. Have a good time and be home by dark."

Practicing Safety

Here are two exercises every parent should do with their children when they are old enough to go out on their own.

35. The Yell

Yell "No" from deep in the stomach. Do this plenty of times, then repeat it in front of a mirror until the child is not shy about doing it. Polite children are most at risk of being unable to yell at an attacker.

36. The Yell and Run

Practice yelling while running away at the same time.

General Tips to Make Children More Streetwise

Teach your children:

37. Never take short cuts.
38. Don't wear personal stereos on the street—it makes you an easy target.
39. Keep enough money to make a phone call.

40. Don't carry large sums of money.
41. Stay in a group if possible.
42. Always to tell your parents where you are going and with whom.
43. How to make an emergency telephone call.
44. If someone they don't know talks to them, pretend not to hear. The other person may be looking for a fight. Look confident and walk quickly away.
45. They don't always have to be polite. They can scream, kick, or ignore an adult if their safety is at risk.
46. Their safety is more important than anything and they can break any rule to keep safe.

6

50 Ways to Boost Your Child's Learning Power

Alarm bells are ringing. No, not fire alarms, the "Monday morning and it's time to get the family ready for school" alarm clock. Your children, still exhausted from their strenuous weekend playing with friends, are ignoring the alarm. Somehow, Mondays are always like this. In you go.

"Good morning. Time to get up." No response.

Five minutes later. "Time for school." Groan.

Another five minutes and your friendly, "I'm a positive parent" line is wearing thin. "Come on, get going. You only have a half-hour."

Three minutes later. You turn the lights on, and with a glass of cold water in hand, shout, "If you don't get out of that bed immediately, I am going to throw this entire glass of water over you."

Finally you get then out the door and on the bus. Now it's completely up to the teachers. Or is it?

Twenty minutes later, as you are going out of the door to your second job—you know, the one that pays the rent—you reflect on your first job, being the parent of school-age children. When you get home tonight there will be homework to supervise: helping Sam with his math, Natalie with her spelling. Not for the first time you wonder how we can help kids to do well, to like school, to love reading and writing. (Perhaps to become rich and famous novelists who will keep you in your old age so you can give up your job? Dream on...)

Teaching children is too important to leave it all up to the schools. Without your help, it won't work as well as it should. Parents can do some basic things with children that will encourage their learning power.

Teach Them to Love Reading

We can instill a love of reading in our children, which will help them in anything they do in school and in life. It is probably the most important skill they need to learn. You might try some of the following strategies.

1. Keep Books Around

The most obvious way to start is by having lots of books, magazines, and newspapers around your home that appeal to you and to your children, and to spend time reading them—without the television blasting away. It is hardly surprising that children who grow up in homes like this learn early that reading is a valued activity. Magazines such as *National Geographic* and *Reader's Digest* are great to have around. I remember not being able to read all the words in *National Geographic,* but pouncing on it for the wonderful and exotic pictures. Even with the advent of television, I think the fascination of absorbing the photographs and stories at your own pace still holds true for both adults and children. *Reader's Digest,* with its bite-size stories, points to ponder, and humor is ideal to draw children into the joy of reading and to hold their interest. Also look for other publications and books specifically for children. If you can't afford to buy them new, look at yard sales or go to the library.

2. Use the Library

You don't have to be a millionaire to have books around—remember your local libraries. Take your children and help them select books they are interested in. By all means suggest books, but don't impose your own tastes on them. Give them time to browse and discover things for themselves.

3. Read to Your Children

From the time they are small right up until they turn into teenagers, most children love to have a story read to them. In fact, at a conference about children's books at which I was speaking, one of the other speakers, late in the day, announced that she was going to read us a story. You should have seen the reaction in that audience of 200 adults when she began to read. People who were starting to leave stood transfixed at the doors, those sitting down relaxed back into their seats, and everyone had a smile on his or her face. We sat listening for twenty minutes to this wonderful storyteller, and when she finished a collective sigh could be heard before thunderous applause. There is, I firmly believe, something magical about being read to, especially for a young child sitting on a parent's or grand-parent's lap.

Besides the benefit of learning to associate reading with warm and loving feelings, children who are read to develop a solid vocabulary base and an ear for pronunciation that will help them when they begin school. If you read books about things that interest them and leave other books about these same subjects lying around, they will pick up the books and start reading on their own.

4. Get a Good Dictionary

Reading dictionaries can be fun, especially the illustrated children's dictionaries. If grandparents are trying to decide on a gift, why not suggest a dictionary instead of a toy. I know, I know—kids love toys, but the dictionary will last for several years and I suspect the toy might not make it through the holidays. As your children get older, ensure that you have dictionaries that will be useful to their age group.

5. Buy Them a Flashlight and Put the Lights Out

Liz, approached me because her son Andrew found reading boring. He also had a hard time falling asleep and, because of this, had trouble in the mornings being alert at school. She had done everything she could think of to no avail. He was having problems at school, and she and her husband were worried that their bright child was not succeeding.

We established that Andrew was allowed to watch television after dinner and homework, right up until bedtime, as a way of relaxing. It was fairly easy to come up with a solution to Andrew's difficulties and it had nothing to do with my years of experience as a child psychologist and everything to do with my grandmother.

When I was a child, the lights went out at a certain time and that was that. The problem was that my sister and I were usually in the middle of reading something and complained bitterly about how unfair it all was. My grandmother bought us each a flashlight and said we weren't to use it for reading at night. She was a sly old fox. We spent many a happy night under the covers finishing that crucial chapter.

So, for Andrew, it was decided that he would go to bed at the normal time and the lights would go out fifteen minutes later, but only if he was reading something of his own choosing. Otherwise the lights went out when he got into bed. Well, give a kid that kind of choice and guess what he opts for?

Andrew was also given a flashlight (one that goes out automatically when laid down, to prevent any danger of burning) with the same admonishment that my grandmother gave. I also suggested curbing his television viewing gradually so that he wouldn't see it as punishment. He was turning into a couch potato and this had to be addressed. His parents also enrolled him in after-school sports activities to get him more exercise.

Within a month Andrew graduated from reading comics to reading short stories, started sleeping better, and improved at school. The only thing his parents had to do was to make sure the flashlight was out of his bed before they went to bed. Who needs experts when you have such a wise grandmother?

6. Giving Gift Certificates

It is fun going to the bookstore to choose your own book. Put a gift certificate in your child's Christmas stocking or give it as a present for whatever holidays you celebrate.

7. Listening to Your Child Read Aloud

Reading aloud is a skill that helps children learn to pronounce words properly and to develop confidence in speaking. It also helps you assess your child's understanding of what is being read. Try having your child read for just a few minutes at first, and do it often. Vary the length depending upon age and concentration level. The object is to enjoy it, not turn it into an onerous task.

Let's say you are doing this with your seven-year-old daughter. If she is struggling, help her out by reading it with her. Give masses of praise and emphasize what she does right, not what she does wrong. Ask specific questions to see if she understood what she read. Take, for example, the Grimm Brothers fairy tale Hansel and Gretel.

"Why do you think that Hansel and Gretel were taken into the forest?"

"What plan did Hansel think of to help them find their way back?"

"How do you think that Hansel and Gretel felt when they were lost in the forest?"

"Why do you think the witch was so mean?"

"How did the children defeat the witch?"

"Do you think the children were angry at their father for being left in the forest?"

You can, of course, ask general questions about how she liked the story and if she has any ideas for ending it differently. This is good for fostering ideas and creativity. You may even give her an opportunity to write her own story.

Teach Your Child to Enjoy Writing

Fourteen-year-old Nick has just completed his first novel. It isn't going to set the world on fire or even be published, but Nick loved writing it. He began writing stories at the kitchen table when he was about four. His parents praised his stories and always displayed them on the front of the refrigerator. They stapled them into a little cover, on which Nick drew a picture. They proudly showed them, in front of Nick, to their friends and relatives, who also gave Nick lots of encouragement. Someday Nick may be published, but he likes writing so much that he doesn't care.

How can we get our children to be as enthusiastic about writing even if they aren't destined to be the Dickens of their generation? Most of us would even settle for a child willing to write a brief thank-you note! Try the following ideas.

8. Show an Interest Yourself

It is no accident that parents who are writers produce children who write. If Mom or Dad have a place where they regularly write, whether it's letters, books, or articles, children usually end up sharing that interest in writing. It is reinforced by the parents.

It is the same for reading, music, science, and other subjects. It is very motivating for a child when he sees parents engaged in an activity they clearly enjoy. Let your child see you writing, talk about it at mealtimes, read aloud some of your own words, and encourage your child to do the same.

9. Create a Place for Writing

It's easier to sit down to write if there is a place that doesn't have to be cleared. Arrange a spot for each child to write, even if it is just a corner of a desk you managed to pick up at a used furniture market. In fact, a desk or table and a quiet place to work help most children with whatever they are learning. I know that this isn't always possible, and that some kids can shut out the world and work, but most cannot.

10. Keep a Journal

Give your child a journal or diary and encourage her to write in it daily. It gets her into a lifelong habit of expressing herself in writing for her own pleasure and use.

11. Get Your Child a Pen Pal

Pen pals are fun and children love to get mail. If your child's school does not have a pen pal program, find out from your local news paper, library information center, or even a foreign embassy if they have a list. Another way to find one is to write to a local newspaper in a country or area your child is interested in and ask for correspondence. Make sure that the person your child is writing to is another child and not someone who preys on children. It might help if you made contact with the child's parents.

12. Use Computers

In the world our children are growing up in, computers are essential for communication. Although I certainly want my children to be able to write legibly, it would be unrealistic to expect that they would laboriously write out everything by hand. I had a different opinion on this from another author, who believes that his books are superior to those written on word processors because they are handwritten and that "Writing should be painful." My reply was, "Rubbish. Writing is expressing yourself; the method you use is not as important as the words and messages you write." The debate will go on, but I happily confess that this and all my other books are word-processed.

13. Don't Always Correct Their Work

If your children start writing for pleasure and show you their work, focus on the good things. Praise their choice of words, the way they

describe the characters, the humor, and the drama. Don't immediately correct grammar or sentence structure. It might turn them
off. There will be plenty of time for helping them with the nitty-
gritty of writing after they've caught the writing bug.

14. Writing at School

Check with your child's school to make sure they are giving children
time and encouragement to write. I was horrified one year to find
one of my sons had a teacher who only used workbooks where the
children filled in the answers. In my humble opinion, these
workbooks should be burned, because filling in blanks leads to
blank minds and lack of creativity.

One way to handle a situation like this is first to have a word with
the teacher, who may have a perfectly rational explanation for the
workbook method. Say that you understand the use of workbooks,
but that you feel children also need to practice writing letters,
journals, essays, and so on. to hone their skills and develop their
creativity. It is possible that the teacher will take your point and
change. If not, have a word with the principal to find out the
philosophy of the school and how they teach writing. If you are still
not happy, you can continue to make a fuss or start giving your child
extra work at home, perhaps by introducing him to the joys of
keeping a diary or journal. Better yet, encourage your children to
write their own books and "publish" them, complete with covers and
pictures. Children love to see their books "in print." (All you need is
a stapler, glue, and steady hands to "bind" the book.)

The final step would be to look for another school, but that might
be a bit drastic if everything else is going well. You could offer to help
the teacher by setting up a "write and publish your own book" club
with the children. It takes time, but it really is fun.

Teach Your Children to Spell

Winnie the Pooh said it best: "My spelling is wobbly. It's good
spelling but it wobbles and the letters get in the wrong place." The
spelling of the English language, with all of its irregularities and
quirks, has got to be one of the most difficult things children have to
learn. Just think about the different sounds that go with the same
letters and how confusing it must be for children. We teach children
that g is for *girl,* and then along comes g for *giant!*

When I was in school, we had spelling bees and tons of helpful little quotes to get us through, but it was never easy.

15. Use Helpful Hints

If your child is having difficulty with a particular word or category of words, try teaching them some memory aids such as:

- *I* before *e* except after *c,* unless it sounds like a, as in *neighbor* or *weigh*.
- Knock off the *e* when adding *ing*.
- To spell *occasion*—remember: two *c*uffs on one *s*hirt
- Egypt—say Egg Ypt (pronounced "egg wiped") to remember where the *y* goes.

16. Teach Them a Word a Day

Try teaching one or two words a day. Put them on the fridge. Put the words up in the bathroom or in their rooms. At the end of the day, ask them to try to spell the word or words from the previous day, so by Friday they may be able to spell all the accumulated words in that week.

17. Listen to Their Spelling

Set some time aside for your children to spell words aloud before they are tested at school. Be patient and don't criticize. Yoy can acknowledge that it is a bore learning how to spell, but it is important.

18. Reward Good Spelling Grades

When your child brings home a good spelling test, make a big deal of it. Post it where everyone can see. Make a special treat or a star chart. Give them lots of praise and tell the rest of the family how well they've done. There is nothing intrinsically rewarding about memorizing spelling, so you have to make it as painless as possible.

19. Using the Dictionary

Make sure your children know how to use the dictionary and how to search for a word if they aren't sure how it is spelled. If you have a word processor with a spell-checker then by all means use that too. These are a godsend for children with learning difficulties such as dyslexia (see below).

Teach Your Child Math

Now this is something I can only ask other people about. It's not that I am a math illiterate, but I do come close. Oh, I have no problem adding, subtracting, dividing, and multiplying, but algebra and trigonometry utterly defeated me. (However, I can beat my sons" calculators in adding columns of figures.) I am assured by math experts that there is no such thing as a math illiterate and that everyone can learn math. Perhaps my motivation wasn't strong enough. Certainly one of my sons seems to have overcome any genetic defect he may have inherited from me and is doing well in math. So what can we do to foster good math skills with our children?

20. Shopping

An obvious way in our family was to take the children shopping and let them figure out which products were the least and the most expensive. Now, many supermarkets do this for you on the little tags under the products, but your children can still try it for themselves. They can also figure out approximately how much the shopping will cost by adding the products together and rounding up or down to get a ballpark total.

21. Allowance

Give your children their allowance and help them work out a budget. They can use a piece of paper or a little book to record what they spend or save (save?!). Help them decide how to be more efficient with their money before they ask you for a raise.

22. Sort Things Into Categories

Ask your children to sort their toys into categories and count how many they have in each category. For example, your daughter may have four categories, such as soft furry toys, drawing materials, books, games. Ask her to count how many she has in each category. You can also point out how food stores put things on the shelf in sections, such as vegetables, fruits, dairy products, bread, and so forth. See if your children can come up with their own categories.

23. Counting

When your children are learning to count, think about all the things you can use to help them. Count the segments in oranges, the

M&Ms in a bag, the houses on the street as you walk by, the segments in a chocolate bar, the stairs you climb—anything. The only problem is that this can become an obsession. A woman who works with me, age forty-nine, still counts everything in threes because of a game she played as a child. She drives us bonkers!

24. Measure Things

My youngest son loved the tape measure left in his Christmas stocking one year. He measured everything in the house and we carefully recorded his measurements in a book he carried around in his pocket.

25. Use Flash Cards

For some things like learning tables, there seems to be no way around memorizing. Many a long night we spent in the kitchen with both children reciting their tables and us using flash cards. We couldn't afford the printed ones, so we made our own.

Teach Your Child Science Skills

Many of the questions children ask are in some way related to science. Why is the sky blue? Where does rain come from? What is snow? How does the clock work? Where did I come from? A child's natural curiosity can be used to help her develop skills needed in science.

26. Answer Questions

This isn't as easy as it sounds. One of my children asked me how nuclear power plants worked. Though I know a little about them, the question was beyond me. But the library had some wonderful books with illustrations, so we both now know how they work. My son won first place at the school science fair with his project—he built a model nuclear power plant from cardboard tubes, pipe cleaners, and sugar cubes. (Thank goodness for drawers full of those bits and pieces I could not bear to throw away in case "they came in handy one day"!) The moral: If you can answer, do; if you can't, find help.

27. Encourage Observation

Encourage your children to touch, smell, and look carefully at things. By pointing out size, shape, texture, color, and other characteristics, you can start children on the road to analyzing materials and objects they come into contact with in everyday life. As they get older, they can use certain tools to measure, weigh, and generally to compare and observe their world. Scientists are keen observers, and this is probably one of the most important skills we can help children develop. Don't forget that game many of us played as children: looking at ten or more objects on a tray for twenty seconds, then covering the tray, trying to remember what the objects were, and describing what they looked like.

28. Noticing How Things Work

If a child is interested in how clocks run, find an old clock, take it apart and explain it. If you don't know, ask someone who does. Many mechanical building toys are on the market that make good presents, but these are sometimes too expensive. Old toys can be just as good. Why not take apart a windup toy and tinker with it?

Hands-on science museums are marvelous places to take children, because they can push the buttons, turn the levers, and pump the handles to see what happens. Some factories and plants have public tours, too, so you can go along and find out how cars are put together, how water is filtered, how steel is made, or how ceramics are fired.

29. Make Things, Do Experiments

If your children are interested in building something or setting up an experiment, get the tools together and help them. Draw a plan, forage for old pieces of wood or whatever, and give it a try. If it doesn't work out, learn from it. Edison, when asked by his staff if they should give up on an experiment that had failed 900 times, was reported to have said, "Give up? We now know 900 ways it doesn't work—carry on." (They eventually succeeded, and we now have Corning Ware.) Some very good books give step-by-step instructions for doing simple home experiments. Check with your library or with the school.

30. Enjoy Nature with Your Child

Go for walks, notice how the animals live, talk about why the leaves change color and fall in the autumn, discuss how plants are necessary for life on earth, look at the stars and talk about navigation skills....The list is endless, and exciting. The opportunities to enhance your child's interest in science are there for the taking.

Teach Your Child Test-Taking Skills

I remember studying like mad for tests and dreading them. I wish someone had given me a few test-taking hints. Explain to children that there are some guidelines about taking tests.

31. Don't Cram

Studies have shown that cramming for tests the night before is not a good way to learn. No surprise there, but kids still try to cram everything in at the eleventh hour.

32. Organization

Make sure your children have the necessary papers organized so that the information they need can be found without hassle. If they use notebooks, get dividers and help them label them so they can easily find their work. As they get older and have more subjects to study, buy, beg, or borrow a used two-drawer filing cabinet. Using files, they can instantly lay their hands on the materials they need.

33. Repeat Aloud

One very effective way to remember information is to repeat it aloud several times. Give your child time to practice saying the information aloud, and then have him repeat it to you. It is also effective for him to write down the information and then to say it aloud.

34. Practice

Whenever possible, give your child a mock test based on the information that is likely to be covered. It can increase confidence, but you must make sure your child understands that the test she is taking might be different. Check with the teacher if you are unsure of the format or materials to be covered.

35. A Full Stomach

Make sure your children have a good breakfast and plenty of time to get ready during the morning of the test. A relaxed, well-nourished child has a better chance of doing well than a harried, hungry one.

36. Last-Minute Review

On the morning of the test, go over anything your child is unsure of. Not too many things, but one or two crucial ones. This is not the time to cram.

Difficulties

Some children will have problems with some subjects because they aren't interested or talented in them, or they don't like the teacher. That can be overcome. But some children find it difficult to read or write or spell or do math because they have some form of dyslexia, which scrambles things or makes them incomprehensible.

Dyslexia is an information-processing difficulty. It is estimated that about 10 percent of children are affected by it. A friend of mine who is dyslexic said that I might understand what it is like if I tried reading the newspaper upside down and backwards, and then tried writing the same way. "You could do it eventually," she explained, "but think of all the extra time and effort it takes me to get the same information you get so easily."

The irony is that, most often, children with dyslexia are just as bright, if not brighter, than other children in their class. So, not being able to learn in the same way as their peers can be very frustrating and discouraging.

If your child seems to be bright but is having trouble keeping up with classmates, you may want to seek help. Ask the school to refer you to an organization that specializes in teaching or helping children who are dyslexic. If the answer is "yes" to most of the following questions and your child is age 7 to 11, you would be wise to seek advice. Is your child:

- bright in some ways, but has a "block" in others?
- having particular difficulty with reading and spelling?
- writing figures or letters backward, such as 15 for 51, or b for d?
- reading a word and then failing to recognize it farther down the page?
- spelling a word several different ways without recognizing the correct version?
- exhibiting poor concentration when reading or writing?
- having difficulty understanding time and tense?
- confusing right and left?
- answering questions orally, but having difficulty writing them down?
- unusually clumsy?

There may be other explanations for any of these problems, but if your child seems to have several of them, it is worth checking to see if dyslexia is the cause. One other important clue is that this does run in families, so if great uncle George was the same way, it might mean your child needs help.

Don't despair. Lots of extremely creative, intelligent, and successful people are dyslexic. One even became one of the best-known authors of children's stories: Hans Christian Andersen. It does mean that your child will need special teaching and advice to make learning easier or, in some cases, simply possible.

Study Habits

No matter what subjects your children are learning, a few vital points about study habits will help them:

37. Set aside a quiet, well-lit place to work.
38. Have a set time for homework with no telephone calls or distractions allowed.
39. Establish a routine for studying: when, where, and how.
40. Allow children to take short breaks. Studies have shown that we learn best in twenty to thirty minute segments with five or ten minute breaks in between.
41. Organize schoolwork. Children should use a small notebook to write down assignments and a monthly or yearly planner to plot out long-term work such as term papers and revisions.
42. Encourage them to ask for help if they don't understand something.
43. Insist on practice. Languages, music, art, physical education, and other subjects all require practice in order to master specific skills.
44. Teach them to take good notes in class.
45. Keep up with assignments. A little work every day prevents last-minute panics.

Parents should set aside some time to look at homework. If your child claims "There is no homework" and you don't buy it, check with the teacher. Whatever the philosophy of the school, children benefit when parents are interested in the work they are doing. Ask about what your child is studying and offer to help with any difficulties.

The Five Most Important Things to Do

My husband, a history teacher, is going to be very annoyed that there isn't a separate section on history! (By the time he realizes it, the book will be in print.) The point is that there are too many areas to go into detail about here without turning this into an academic exercise. Many of the skills and suggestions in the sections above will be useful in history, music, art, and languages.

If there were only five important things to remember about helping children to learn, I believe they would be:

46. for parents to set an example of loving to learn.
47. to be an "approachable" parent—one who encourages a child to find out the answers and helps if they can't.
48. to keep in contact and cooperate with your children's teachers, so you can work together to create the right environment for kids to enjoy learning.
49. not to dwell on failures. Nothing so undermines a person as having failures brought up again and again. If a kid doesn't do well with something when he should have, then discuss it and drop it. No one's perfect.
50. to say something positive to your children about their achievements or their attempts to achieve. It's that word again: praise.

7

10 Ways to Stop Kids From Swearing

Penny, age eight, and her brother Ben, age six, were playing with their friends in the park. Their father, Brian, was talking with some of the other parents while keeping an eye on them. He noticed a few older children playing with the younger ones, but thought nothing of it until Ben came running up to ask if he could get an ice cream.

"Sorry, I don't have any money with me," explained Brian.

"Oh, sh—!" said Ben in disgust, and started to walk off.

"What did you say?" exclaimed Brian, who was incredibly embarrassed and shocked as he made it a point never to swear around his children.

Ben stopped short and turned scarlet. "I said 'Oh, sh—.'"

Brian thought all the other parents were looking at him and judging him to be a rotten, foul-mouthed father. In fact, they were sympathizing—they'd all heard their children repeating words they themselves didn't use.

The reality is that children swear, adults swear, and who knows what the dog is really saying when he barks his head off at the doorbell. That doesn't mean, however, that we have to condone or put up with it.

Poor Ben. He had just been playing with older kids who were busy proving how much more grown-up they were than the little kids by swearing a blue streak. Now he was in trouble and not getting any ice cream either. What could Brian do, and how can we make sure kids don't turn into trash mouths?

1. Explain

If your children use swear words they don't understand, explain to them what the words mean. Children may use the f— word, for example, without knowing that it is slang for sexual intercourse. So, if your children are old enough and you have explained to them about sex, tell them what it stands for. Likewise explain the many offensive words used thatr refer to sexual organs or to bodily functions.

Also explain that some words are considered offensive for religious or cultural reasons. When I first moved to England from the United States, I was amazed when someone took offense at the word "bloody." In England it is a swear word, supposedly a contraction of "by our Lady," and is blasphemous. When I was growing up in Minnesota, it just meant someone was being difficult!

2. Give Them Substitute Words

Many swear words are short and emphatic and are easy to get into the habit of using, especially when we are angry. Help your child come up with a list of acceptable words that serve the same purpose. I had an acquaintance who used to say things like "Oh, poopy doo" when she was angry. To tell the truth, it almost caused me to swear at her. Don't make the words so bizarre or silly that your child won't use them. Try words like *shoot* or *darn* or *drat* or *heck*—one syllable and easy to shout out when he is annoyed.

3. Set a Good Example

Obviously, if we swear our children will copy us, so we have to set a good example. I remember swearing once in front of my then three-year-old son, who proceeded to repeat the word from his car seat until I thought I would scream. When I told him to stop, he just said, "But Mommy, you said it." Out of the mouths of babes....Believe me, there is nothing like a parroting three-year-old to make you clean up your language quickly.

4. Friends Swear

Even if you don't swear, your children will have friends who swear, or will go to homes where swearing is a normal part of the conversation. If your child comes home and says, "But Jay Smith's brother swears and he doesn't get into trouble," tell him that you know other people swear, but that isn't what is done in your family.

Or tell him that your last name isn't Smith (or invite him to go live with the Smiths if it becomes too much—just kidding). Stick to your guns and don't let him swear around you. Of course, it is more difficult to ensure that kids don't swear when they are away from home, unless you have an army of spies.

5. Don't Go for Shock Value

Children swear to shock and to get attention. Say, "I don't like or appreciate that language," and then get on with what you were doing. Don't react by getting angry or shouting, as that will only make the child realize that she can use swearing to upset you. If you think it helps, tell your child that she can swear to herself in her own room, but you don't want to hear that language. Personally, I don't want the language anywhere in my house, including the bedroom!

6. Ignore Them

Some parents just ignore bad language entirely and pretend they don't hear it. They will carry on with what they were doing as if the child has said nothing unusual at all. Parents I know who use this method say that the child then uses the words louder and more frequently for a time, but eventually gets bored trying to get their attention this way. Debbie told me that her child kept saying, "Did you hear what I said?" in an attempt to see if she was shocked. Debbie didn't overreact, explain, correct, or punish, and her child did stop swearing. There was no point in carrying on because no one paid the slightest bit of attention.

7. Play Dumb

When eight-year-old Khalid came home and used profanity, his father looked up from his work and quietly asked him, "I'm afraid I don't understand, Khalid, what does that mean?" Needless to say, Khalid's sojourn into profanity was quite short. Can you imagine how embarrassing it is to actually have to explain to your parents what a swear word means?

Asking a child to explain the words she knows are nasty embarrasses the child, but you can use that embarrassment to your advantage by explaining that is how other people feel hearing swear words. Go on to explain that it is not right to use words that embarrass people.

8. Monitor Television and Films

I remember getting into terrible trouble as a girl because I saw a film that used the words *damn* and *hell* and then told my grandmother about it. It seems that I should have got up and left when the first *damn* was uttered, but the film suddenly became much more interesting just because those words were in it. The same applies today, except the words are several degrees stronger. Words that I would have been killed for using are now standard fare, making the parent's job more difficult. If your children are exposed to bad language on television or in a film, explain that the language is still not acceptable and that, sometimes, the people who write films like to shock and use swear words. Reiterate that it is still unacceptable, just as murder might be portrayed in films but that, too, is unacceptable.

9. Consequences

When I was growing up, if a child swore, the bar of soap came out and the little mouth was left foaming. Ugh! I guess it worked, but it does seem a cruel and unusual punishment. I would never use it with my children. If children do continue to swear in spite of your best efforts, warn them that there will be consequences and tell them what they are. Try:

- taking away a privilege such as watching television.
- giving extra privileges if they don't swear.
- asking them to leave the room and not come back until they can talk in a more civilized manner.
- telling them to repeat the word 100 times (boring!).
- fining them a certain amount every time they swear. This works best if you are giving them an allowance and can either deduct the fine source or ask them to put the money into a jar kept for that purpose. If you use this method, grown-ups have to pay up as well!

10. Praise Clever Use of Words

Some people swear because they have a limited vocabulary and, in my opinion, limited intelligence. Encourage children to use descriptive words instead of swear words. If they hate that "@*!" homework, help them look up and use more clever words, such as "onerous" homework, and tell them how clever they are when they do use them.

I once endured a two-hour train ride with a group of young men going to a soccer match. They were well-dressed and seemed quite nice until they started talking. I have never heard the f—word used as much in my life, and I have heard it used. A typical sentence went something like: "Did you f— see how that f— player f— kicked the f— ball into the f— net?' Although I moved farther up the car, their voices were loud and there was no escape. I guess I should have said something, but they probably would have been amazed that anyone would care how they talked, and I wasn't feeling all that brave. Anyway, it was kind of sad because they weren't trying to shock, they just had no other adjective to use.

Ben knew the word he used would shock his father, even though he was only six. Even much younger children know this, though most are just copying words and don't understand their meaning. Ben was annoyed that Brian wouldn't buy him an ice cream and was angry. He had heard the older boys swearing and filed it as a possible new skill that he, too, could use. Ben's father took him aside and told him that it was wrong to use that word, and that polite people did not talk like that. When Brian turned back to apologize to the other parents, he found that it wasn't necessary; they were full of stories of their own about their children's language.

Probably all children will experiment with swearing, and I think we have to accept that. What we don't have to accept is swearing around us or in our homes. They may insist that they have a right to talk as they wish, but, *darn* it, we have a right not to listen.

8

8 Ways to Help Kids Deal With Money

"How on earth are we going to manage this month? Back-to-school clothes, new sneakers, music lessons, food, mortgage, car insurance…what can I sell?"

"The children?" said my spouse hopefully.

"Well, I'm not sure how much they would bring." The idea was tempting. "But why would anyone buy kids who can devour half the refrigerator in a nighttime raid and think that life's necessities include computers, televisions, mobile phones, roller blades, *and* a weekly allowance? By the way, they've asked for an increase in their allowance."

"*What?* When I was their age, I…"

I interrupted him. When he was their age you could go to the movies for a quarter. "Yes, I know, dear."

"Can't we teach them to manage money better?"

"Yes, I think perhaps we can."

Children, just like us, need to learn how to budget, save, and spend money. Unfortunately they are not born with a money sense—unless it's the feeling that parents have an endless supply of it!

One of the more difficult things we have to teach children is how to manage their (and our) money. Granted, it is more difficult today because children see and want so many things that cost money, and lots of it. An average child will be subjected to hundreds of thousands of advertisements before he reaches the age of sixteen. It seems to me that most of those adverts are inviting my children to spend my money on things they don't really need or won't use for longer than two weeks.

We can rail against this modern madness, but what we really have to do is to develop a money sense in our kids.

1. Explain Family Finance

My children attended a school where most of the other children's families had lots more money than we did. My husband was a teacher there, so we didn't have to pay for tuition, which was great. What wasn't great was that the kind of money many of their classmates had to spend was, in my opinion, crazy.

Once, when my elder child was six and going with a group to a birthday bowling party, he casually asked me for $20 to spend. His allowance at that time was $1 a week, so he was asking for twenty weeks' money at once. I couldn't believe it.

It turned out that some of the children were given that kind of money when they went out, and that they blew it on candy, arcade games, fizzy drinks, and the like. Even more disturbing was that some of the children had an unlimited allowance—and still were given nearly everything they asked for, such as remote-control cars that reached twenty-five miles an hour and cost as much as $300. In contrast, my son had saved his allowance, done little jobs around the house for pay, and asked for birthday money to buy a $30 remote-control car that chugged away just about as fast as you could walk. Poor deprived kid? I think not.

I sat down with him and explained in simple terms the kind of money his father and I earned, what we had to pay for food, mortgage, clothes, and expenses, as well as what we were putting aside in case of emergency and for college. I think I used a package of candies to show him the proportions. Then I explained that the parents of the other children might earn more or have perks from their companies so that they had more money to spend.

After I explained all this briefly and told my son that he had chosen the wrong parents and better luck next time, he very sweetly offered to take a cut in his weekly allowance. I guess I overdid it!

Seriously, it is important that children know what you can and can't afford, and why. Obviously, you need to tell them that this is private business (or you will get them "bragging" about how poor you are) and that it is just between members of your immediate family. Also, you don't want them to worry that you cannot provide the next meal, so don't go into great detail or paint a gloomy picture that will keep them awake at night. Some parents just say they can't afford certain things and leave it at that, but I would opt to include the children as much as possible because it gives them a sense of responsibility in the family (and it may spur them on to become millionaires—who knows).

2. Be Fair and Consistent With an Allowance

When children are given an allowance on a weekly or monthly basis, they quickly learn that no money means no treats and that money spent is money gone. The worst thing you can do is to agree on an allowance and then bail your children out when they spend it all in the first ten minutes. It won't kill them to wait until next week for more candy or comics, even though they will claim it is a fate worse than death. Stand firm and you will teach them the value of budgeting and saving in the kindest possible way.

One decision you have to make is what the allowance should cover. Some parents arrange it to include transportation, school lunches, and treats. Others reserve the allowance only for treats. Some don't give an allowance at all, and just respond to requests for money, which I personally think is a big mistake (unless they cannot afford to give an allowance on a regular basis). The problem with this last approach is that you are bombarded with "I want" and "I need" for every little thing.

Start giving a regular allowance from about the age of five, when children start school. Try to give about the same amount that other children are given (within reason, of course). Check with other parents and talk with your children about what they think is fair.

If you have children of different ages, I think it is fair to give them different amounts of money. My children are three years apart in age, so the older one gets more money than the younger because he goes out more with his friends. As my younger child becomes more independent, his allowance will go up, too. Of course, the younger one never thinks it's fair and the older one never thinks he has enough, but I always tell them they can trade us in for new parents as soon as they save enough money. So far, we're safe!

Sit down with your children and help them work out a budget. Explain that if they spend it all every week, then they won't have anything saved in case they want to buy something special or go somewhere with friends.

3. Discuss Advertising

Because we are all subjected to advertising, it helps to talk about how the advertisers try to tempt you to part with your money. There is no point in attacking the advertisers; they are doing their job. What you need to do is instill a bit of realism and cynicism so that your children are not so easily taken in by every new product that hits the market.

One way to do this is to sit with your children and watch advertisements on the television. Point out that those toys zooming through space are being "zoomed" by children's hands that can't be seen on the screen. Children often think they look like more fun than they turn out to be. Discuss how much these things cost, what percentage of their allowance it would take to buy them and whether they really want them or are being manipulated into wanting them because of the superb advertising spiel.

4. Teach Them Comparative Shopping

When children go shopping with you, regardless of if it's for groceries or something they need or want, always try to do some comparison between prices and products. Then, when children are spending their own money on something, they will get into the habit of making sure they are getting the best deal. Take them to sales and show them why it is often best to wait to buy something until the price drops. That way, they save money, which enables them to buy something else too.

Look at the ads in the newspapers and magazines and point out the differences in prices for the same or similar objects. If you are shopping for a big family purchase like a car or refrigerator, include your children in your deliberations. Ask what they would do if it was their money.

If you are having some decorating done and receive two or three different quotes for the same job, use this as an opportunity to explain why you finally decide to go with one firm instead of another, or whether you decide to do the job yourself. At times you will not choose the cheapest option because you don't think the quality is good, and children need to understand that as well.

Another way to educate them is to go to flea markets, where it is usually possible to bargain. Initially, this tends to embarrass children. I remember taking my sons to a flea market and having them tug me away when I offered less money than the trader asked. "Mom, give him the money," hissed my youngest. "Whose side are you on?" I hissed back. I guess I should have prepared them better before we went, but now they are old hands at bargaining and I think it's great.

5. Let Them Have Their Own Savings Account

As soon as your child has saved a little money, or perhaps gets some birthday or vacation money from relatives, consider opening up a savings account. Check with your bank to see when children can sign up for their own accounts. This is a big thrill for children, especially if the bank gives a small gift for new accounts. Also find out at what age children are allowed to open up an account with an ATM card, which really teaches them self-discipline.

It might be a good idea initially to set aside a small amount of their allowance, which you agree they will save, just to get them into the habit. When they are older, you may want to put their allowance into their account and let them try to manage their own finances for a month. It is a safe way to learn before they are turned loose in the big wide world. It may save them from getting into debt—a trap many young people fall into when they leave school or try to manage on a budget when going to college or learning a trade. Don't penalize them for doing well, however. One sixteen-year-old boy managed to save more than he ever had when he was given full control of his money. His parents then decided that he could live on less and cut his monthly allowance. The lesson they were teaching him was spend, spend, spend—or you'll be sorry! If kids do manage to save some extra, for heaven's sake don't take it away. Give them a bonus!

6. Encourage Part-time Jobs

A part-time job is an excellent way to enable kids to become more self-confident and to learn firsthand about discipline, business, and finance in the real world. You do a job, you get paid, and you feel good about yourself. You can also spend and save more, and eventually buy things you need or want.

My sister and I opened up a lemonade stand on the corner outside our house in Minneapolis one hot summer when we were about six and seven years old. We squeezed the lemons, added sugar and water, and sold the concoction for a nickel. We made a fortune and immediately spent it on comics. The next day we were ready to do it again, when my grandmother informed us that if this was to be a regular business then we needed to buy our own lemons and sugar. What a rude awakening—until then we hadn't realized that businesses incurred expenses.

My first job was as a waitress when I was sixteen. I remember going for the interview and the thrill of being hired. Getting there on time, being neatly dressed, getting my first meager paycheck—it was wonderful. Even spilling a whole glass of water on my first customer, which reduced me to tears, had its rewards—he left me a tip because he felt so sorry for me! I have always been grateful that my father encouraged me to work part-time, because it gave me a solid sense about money and also convinced me that continuing my education was the best option for me.

Kids have many opportunities to get part-time jobs babysitting, delivering papers, washing cars, or mowing lawns. There are two notes of caution. The first is to make sure it doesn't interfere with their schoolwork and cut off future education options. The second is to thoroughly check out the situation. Don't, for example, allow your child to go for an interview with a private individual you don't know, or to a strange place. One thirteen-year-old girl saw a card in a supermarket advertising for a babysitter. There was no number to call—the instructions were for her to leave her number on the board and the person would call her. The "father" called, arranged to meet her at what turned out to be a deserted house, and sexually assaulted her. If an individual wants your child to do any kind of work, they should never object to meeting with you. You should insist on it.

Finally, if your child does get a job, give as much advice as is needed and then let her handle it. If she doesn't show up on time or fails to do what is asked, then she may lose the job. If that happens, it will teach her about the responsibility of keeping a job and what it takes to get along in the world of work. Help her learn from the experience and try again. This, I know, from unfortunate first-hand experience. That wonderful first job I had as a waitress ended abruptly. Six weeks after I was hired, I left some money on the till, intending to ring it up after I cleared the table. When the supervisor saw it, I was summoned and dismissed for not following the rules. I was crushed. I eventually landed another waitressing job, which I kept for two years, so I guess I learned my lesson.

7. Explain Credit

Explain to children what it means to buy something on credit. If you have a mortgage, explain about the monthly payments and how long it takes for the house or apartment to belong to you. (Forever is the right answer, I think.) You might show them a statement from a credit card, and explain that if the balance is not paid off on time then interest charges are incurred.

One of our sons wanted to buy a particular CD player and had saved quite a bit toward it. One afternoon he saw the CD on sale at a considerable discount, but he still did not have enough. We agreed to lend him the money if he paid it back to us, interest free, on a monthly basis. The first two months were fine, but on the third, he begged off, saying he had "heavy expenses." We postponed the payment, but the next month the excuse was the same. This time we said absolutely not and made him come up with the money. I felt like an ogre, but he needed to realize that he had committed himself and we had trusted him. We told him the banks and credit card companies would never be so kind. He paid it off, grumbling but wiser.

8. Be Realistic

All these lessons not withstanding, there may be times when you either have to come to your child's rescue and give a little extra money, or negotiate a new deal. One Saturday, all of my elder son's friends decided to go to the movies for one boy's birthday. Although he had the money to get into the movies, he didn't have enough for popcorn and a drink. I really didn't think it was an unreasonable request, so I gave him money for popcorn.

Your children may find something while on a school journey or on vacation that is not budgeted for, and they ask you to buy it. Or they find they cannot manage on the money they are being given or are earning, and they are really struggling. After going through their budgets with them, you may agree and help them out. If it happens every week, you'd better look into what's going wrong. But, on an occasional basis, I think it's absolutely fine to save them—after all, we are parents first (and loan sharks second!).

9

10 Ways to Chores Without Tears

If there is one thing that seems certain to cause families to fight, it is getting children to do work around the house. Not only do children resist, body and soul, to avoid moving one dish from the table to the sink, parents fight with each other because they disagree on what, how many, how often, and when chores should be done. I remember vividly a fight with my sister about washing the dishes and setting the table. My father always said we could have done the work and walked to China and back in the time we were arguing. "It *is* your turn, I did it yesterday." "No, you didn't." "Yes, I did." "Didn't!!" "Did!!!!" As the noise and indignation rose, one or the other parent would fly into the kitchen and demand that we got on with it "or else." Usually that did it. We were never quite sure what "or else" meant, but neither of us was prepared to be the first to find out.

It is even harder today for parents as most of the time, both parents (or a single parent) work outside the home. Help from the children is vital if the household is to run with any semblance of order.

So what are the tricks to get children to share in the work at home without having to resort to threats and murder? Try some of the following and see what happens.

1. Let Them Do It

Children will always allow you to do their work for them. Wouldn't we all if we could get away with it? There is very little that is intrinsically rewarding about taking out the garbage or washing dishes, so it isn't surprising that they quickly figure out how to get out of things. Look on the bright side: It means they are clever.

A favorite ploy of children is to do a chore so slowly or badly that we become frustrated and step in. I once bit my tongue and dug my fingernails into my hand to stop myself leaping in and making my son's bed. It had taken him forty-five minutes to put on the sheets and the blanket. Must be a world record.

Sometimes, your child really is trying to get it right and needs lots of encouragement from you. Say how pleased you are he stuck with the task and got it done. Offer suggestions or minimal help if he's just learning. Tell him he is doing a good job and that it sometimes takes a while to learn to do something new.

If you jump in and do the chore for the child, he will quickly learn the skill of "getting mom or dad to do it." Yes, it is easier to do it yourself, but in the long run your children will learn how to be responsible only if you let them do it, no matter how long it takes. Be sure not to ask them to do something that is impossible for their age and maturity. I was horrified when a friend complained that her nine-year-old was so irresponsible because the child had run a bath for his sister and the water was too hot. That kind of responsibility belongs with the parent, not with the child.

2. Don't Expect Them to Enjoy It!

Children will not be thrilled that they have to do chores. Don't expect them to whistle while they work and be cheerful because they are being allowed to help. When my sons were about two or three, they loved helping Mommy. Now that they are teenagers, help is four-letter word. So, ignore them if they are glum and insist that they do it anyway.

You might try saying, "What do you think I'm going to say?" instead of "This is the tenth time I've asked you to clean your room?" or "What should you be doing now?" Keep your voice calm and just keep repeating your request or question.

Having agreed earlier that he is not to do anything else until he finishes the chore, turn off the television if he has diverted to it. Or give her notice that she has one minute to hang up the telephone if that's what's preventing her from finishing the chore. If after the warning she doesn't hang up, hang it up for her. Ignore her howls of protest. It will give her something to talk with her friends about— being a misunderstood teenager.

When they finally do a chore, give them lots of praise and point out that next time they could do it in half the time, if time is important to them. Be sure to notice and comment whenever they do act responsibly. Praise works wonders for all of us.

3. Organize the Chores Beforehand

It helps if there is a list of chores that need to be done and children are allowed to choose, in turn, which they prefer. You can alternate who goes first every week. It also helps if you can estimate the time, so that children get equal measure as far as possible. It may seem a pain to do at first, but it does work. The following is a list we worked out.

To Do	Time	Who Will Do When
Set table	5 mins	_____
Clear table	5 mins	_____
Sweep floor	5 mins	_____
Clean toilet	5 mins	_____
Vacuum living room	10 mins	_____
Vacuum hall	10 mins	_____
Clean balcony	10 mins	_____
Dust living room	10 mins	_____
Mop bathroom floor	10 mins	_____
Shake out rugs	10 mins	_____
Water plants	10 mins	_____
Rake leaves	15 mins	_____
Sweep path/sidewalk	15 mins	_____
Wash dishes	20 mins	_____
Dry/put dishes away	20 mins	_____
Make cake	20 mins	_____
Pack lunches	20 mins	_____
Prepare dinner	30 mins	_____
Do one load laundry	30 mins	_____

Notice that ironing and cleaning up bedrooms are not included on our list because these are personal chores, not chores for the entire household. Obviously, the list of chores has to be adapted for your own family, and for the ages of your children and the "breakability" of your dishes. With the list above, your child will do between an hour and two hours housework a week. You will need to take into account the amount of homework demanded of your children and that they do need time to relax and enjoy being children. The idea is not to turn your house from a battlefield into a labor camp, but simply to eliminate the "It's not fair" or "I did it last time" argument.

If you have a pet that the children begged you for and promised to help with (promises, promises), then devise a separate list. In our house, one boy is responsible for walking the dog each day after school, and it is recorded. They swap, as long as someone walks him. The real hassle is getting them to clean up the mess, but we have gloves and bags specially designed for the purpose.

4. Show Them How to Do the Task

Children are not born knowing how to do chores. We have to show them how to get things done in the easiest and most efficient way. If they then go on to do it in their own way, fine, as long as it gets done to a certain standard. When I was showing my six-year-old how to wash dishes, I:

- made sure my good dishes were not in use. There was no sense setting up an impossible situation where I would explode as my dishes did the same on the floor. (Actually, my son was an excellent dishwasher, but he seems to have completely lost the skill now that he is a teenager. Strange.)
- helped him to get out the detergent and put a small amount into the sinkful of warm water. I also explained that we use dishwashing detergent, not the soap powder designed for clothes. My poor father once came home and found that my sister and I had very helpfully waxed his car. No one had pointed out to us that floor wax was only for floors. As far as we were concerned, wax was wax. Not so, I'm afraid. The car had to be refinished and we learned the hard way that different substances were for different jobs. Luckily, my father had a sense of humor and we survived to tell the tale.
- gave him the washcloth and a stool to stand on. I showed him how to wash the first plate and then let him do it. As he progressed, I explained that we wash the glasses and cups first, then the plates, and so on. Each family does it their own way, but that's what

happens in our household. He also learned to rinse all the dishes. All in all it was a great success, and he was quite proud of his achievement.

Most chores will need to be demonstrated and explained. Remember: Patience is a virtue.

5. Motivate Them to Work

Now comes the crunch. They've chosen their chores and learned how to do them. You have the expectation level about right and you are willing to let them do it. And you wait...and wait...

Help them get into the mood by asking, "Which task do you want to get out of the way first?" It usually helps if you can be doing something in the same room. Children sometimes like the company, and chatting together makes the time go faster. "You can get started on the dishes while I clean the front of the cupboard" or "Let's listen to the radio or a tape while we're working," might work.

You can also link the chore to something they want to do. "We'll go swimming as soon as you finish clearing the table," or "I'll get out the storybook so I can read it to you as soon as you sweep the floor." You can also say, as I do now with my sons, "You can go out with your friends as soon as you wash the dishes." Getting away is a big motivator at times! "No television until you water the plants," or "You can watch for an extra half hour if you water the plants now," are ways to motivate the procrastinating kid. Bribery also works (see chapter 23). The problem here is that you might run out of bribes, or patience, or both after a while.

Another idea is to set up a chart and offer points to those who finish their chores. Points can lead to a special treat, like staying up later or being allowed to go for icecream. If your children are young enough, one way to motivates them is to play "Beat the Clock." Set the timer and see who can get her chore done first, but the job has to be done properly.

6. Don't Spring Chores on the Children

Most people appreciate knowing what they are going to have to do at work during the day. We might be aware that certain chores need doing, and expect a child to remember that if it is Tuesday she should be cleaning the toilet. OK, you've set up the chart, but it helps if at breakfast you remind children of the chores they are doing that day, so that when they are mentally prepared to do them.

There will be times, though, when everyone just has to pitch in and help, regardless of the chart and your best intentions. So, prepare your children for that eventuality with reminders that unexpected visitors arrive or an emergency occurs, it's "All hands on deck." Plans will go out the window and you will count on them to help.

Whatever happens, remember to continue to give praise even though you expect their help. Children, like all living creatures, love to be recognized for the good they do.

7. Allow Them to Exchange Chores

If your children sign up for or agree to do a task, but arrange a swap, that's great. If the exchange works to everyone's satisfaction, don't get involved. But sometimes an older child takes advantage of a younger one. Intervene if there is a dispute that is obviously unfair. You can undo deals (see chapter 1, about fighting), and that, too, is a learning experience.

You can also exchange chores with your child. Peggy, mother of six, hates to vacuum. Her son doesn't mind because he does it while listening to his personal stereo. He hates cleaning up his room, so they have an agreement to swap.

Please note one special time when no one should have to do chores: birthdays! This includes parents!

8. Agree in Advance on Consequences for Not Doing Chores

You may never need this step, but if your children are not doing the chores in spite of your best efforts, gather the clan together and decide on consequences. Then, no one will be surprised when he ends up having to pay for his lack of action.

Tony and Jill and their children have worked out the following consequences to choose from if someone doesn't complete chores.

- Someone else does the chore. The culprit must pay back the time spent by doing an equivalent task, which the person who has done the chore can choose. That person can also choose when and where the task is done; the culprit has no choice in the matter. It can't be something horrible and nasty. It has to be another chore, not an invented slave-labor job.
- The culprit loses privileges, such as going out or watching a program, for the equivalent amount of time, plus penalty time (say an extra 30 minutes).
- The culprit gets up an hour early to do the chore. My sons have

had to do this to complete homework they "forgot" until bedtime. It's a great ploy for a child to say that she can't go to bed, after having read, played games and watched television, because she suddenly remembered her math wasn't finished. Nice try!

You will come up with consequences of your own. It does help if everyone knows the penalties, and that they will be enforced.

9. Label Your Children as Good Workers

Brag about how helpful your children are and make sure they hear you. Too often we say things like, "Justine is the messiest kid I know. Her room is a pigsty." It may be true, but Justine is getting the message that she is messy and may even start saying, "I'm just messy." It all becomes a self-fulfilling prophecy; Justine becomes "the messy one."

On the other hand, if Justine hears her parents complimenting her neatness and her helpfulness, that is a much better label. "I'm helpful and neat" is a good message, not a negative one. If Justine's parents also say that her work was good or that she really tried hard, that will reinforce the idea that she is a good worker. It wouldn't hurt to ask Justine to tell you how she thinks her work is. She'll start to develop her own sense of pride.

The only note of caution here is not to turn your child into a perfectionist by demanding military-style standards. Not only is it unrealistic, but some studies have shown a link between eating disorders and extreme perfectionism. This doesn't apply to most of our children, even if they like to keep their things very neat, but beware of overdoing the "perfect worker" bit. Stick with "You really stuck to that job," "Good," "Well done," "Great effort," and "Nice try," and so forth.

10. Withdraw Your Labor!

If you have tried everything and the children still don't follow through, try withdrawing your labor. If one of your responsibilities is to drive the children to soccer or some other activity they enjoy, but they haven't completed their chores, go on strike. If you are supposed to make dinner and no one sets the table, make yourself a cheese sandwich and retire to read or watch television. When people complain they are hungry or that "You have to drive me to soccer right now," say "Sorry, but why should I be the only one fulfilling responsibilities when I haven't had any cooperation?" Better yet, ask your children if they have any idea about why you are doing this. Then ask them if they have a solution. It is amazing how the shock of it all can bring about a new attitude toward chores.

If it gives you any hope, I have been told by many friends with grown children how neat and clean their children became when they got their own places. But you can't set up your ten-year-old in an apartment, so you just have to keep encouraging them to be good workers. When I was growing up, my sister was incredibly messy, while I was very neat, and we shared a room. She drove me nuts when clothes, both clean and dirty, tumbled out every time I opened anything. Her half of the room was horrible. As I mentioned earlier, one day while she was out, I drew a white chalk mark down the center of the room and thereafter refused to let her into my half. I was a real creep about it, and she became messier and messier. But there is justice—my sister, now a lawyer in California, turned out to be quite house-proud, but her children drive her crazy. She telephoned me long distance to complain that, "They are so messy I can't even get into their rooms." Who says there isn't a God?

10

17 Suggestions About What They're Watching on Videos and Television

It's the year 2084 and Douglas Quaid (Arnold Schwarzenegger) is escaping from the henchmen of a treacherous tyrant. As Quaid runs up an escalator, shoving and pushing bystanders out of the way, the enemy opens fire, killing an innocent man. Quaid grabs the man's body and uses it as a shield. The man's body is shot several times more, in close-up gory detail, then is discarded as the fight goes on, people diving for cover as automatic weapons rip in every direction.

No one gives a thought to the human shield. He was disposable and unimportant to the plot of *Total Recall*. Definitely not my kind of film. So why did I watch it? In fact, my twelve-year-old son borrowed it from a friend, also age twelve. The friend got it from his local video store with the help of his older brother.

Until then, I'd thought I had the video and television business licked. The rule in our house is supervised television viewing after nine o'clock, and no violent videos. Any other videos are judged on their merits. But I'd forgotten about what happens when children get together. I'd managed to catch *Total Recall* and felt I could at least influence my son's reaction to it. I knew, though, that he'd be exposed to others at overnight stays and for birthday party "treats." I spoke to my son and he just said: "Don't flip out, Mom. It's no big deal. Anyway, it's just like watching television."

Wrong! At least with television viewing I felt fairly safe if the kids were watching early in the evening because programs then are supposed to be "child friendly," and usually, but not always, are. But with a video there is no "safe" time. They can get a copy of a film you consider totally inappropriate and watch it over and over.

Are Violence and Sex Scenes Harmful?

Should we accept that our kids will see violent videos and ones with degrading sex scenes sooner or later? Should we save our "freak-outs" for something we can really hope to affect?

As usual, the experts are divided. One recent study said that children were not affected by violence on film or TV, especially if it was in fantasy or cartoon style. (Personally, I think there's a world of difference between a flattened cartoon tomcat, which is easy to accept as fantasy, and the realistic portrayal of people being violently murdered.)

Another study showed that children *are* affected by what they watch, and their behavior *does* become more violent. This is countered by another study that suggests that it's not the content that matters, but the amount of movement and action. The conclusion is that children become just as aggressive watching a fast-moving soccer match as they do when seeing a violent, blood-and-guts film.

I dislike, and shield my children from, unnecessary and graphic violence. I don't mind my children seeing loving and appropriate sex scenes (now that they're older), but I will not allow anything that portrays sex in a degrading fashion.

The Evidence

Are children affected by television and videos? Well, in a local school I have worked in, the real experts—the children themselves—conducted their own survey. Pupils looked at the power of TV and videos. They asked a group of eleven- and twelve-year-olds which media influenced them the most. The results would not surprise parents, though it might surprise the young researchers.

- What influences you most?

Videos	63%
TV	37%
Magazines and books	0%

- Would you switch off a program because of:

  Boredom   93%
  Violence   0%
  Don't know   7%

- Do you watch videos that are supposed to be for older people?

  Yes   90%
  No   10%

The pupils went on to question some eight- and nine-year-olds and found that the majority said they had seen videos such as *A Nightmare On Elm Street*. A small minority had seen sexually explicit videos.

It's clear from this that many children do have access to videos that most parents would prefer they did not see. It's also clear that young children are seeing quite violent and sexually explicit videos, if not at home, then at the homes of their friends—and they're not switching off unless they find them boring.

The most telling statement of all is that children themselves say that videos influence them more than TV, books, or any other media. My common sense tells me that they will be influenced by good or bad videos, because children learn from what they see and hear. (Anyone who has ever sworn in front of a young child, and then had the embarrassment of hearing him repeat it in the middle of a crowded supermarket, will agree that children *do* pick up on adult behavior!)

It seems clear to me that, whatever the experts say, we live in the video age and need to make decisions *now* about what our kids might be watching tonight.

The message of many readily available films is that violence, physical and sexual, is all right. The way to solve problems is to torture someone and then "blow him away." If the job is done in as bloody and violent a way as possible, so much the better. These messages can be especially influential in homes where such issues are rarely talked about.

Careful parents can have trouble, too. Eight-year-old Colette began having persistent nightmares, waking up sobbing in terror. Her mother couldn't figure out what was wrong at first. Gentle questioning revealed that Colette and a friend had watched *A Nightmare on Elm Street*, rented for the friend's older brother's birthday party. Colette's mother was shocked and upset. She had been so careful about what her children watched and had even restricted TV to an hour a day. She had heard horror stories about children seeing harmful videos but, like me, she never expected it to happen to *her* kids.

What Should We Do?

Most homes in the U.S. now have video recorders, so it is becoming almost impossible to ensure that your children will never see inappropriate films.

One young mother was shocked when she arrived early to collect her three-year-old from the babysitter's and walked in to find the children watching a particularly nasty video. Horrified, she watched for a few minutes and counted twenty-four violent and bloody deaths, including a mother and two young children being blown up in a car. The babysitter said they were "too young to be bothered by it." Needless to say, she found a new sitter.

If You Want to Protect Your Children

1. Tell People

Ensure that whoever is minding your children does not show them videos you do not approve of. Say something like, "Jenny has terrible nightmares and I don't want her to see these videos."

2. Use Reputable Shops

Deal only with reputable video shops that cater to a family audience. Some national chains, such as Blockbuster, have family-oriented policies. Make sure that your video store knows the ages of your children and will not give them videos for an older age group. Ask your local video store to place videos that are sexually violent of degrading on the top shelves or in another room, or for the cover pictures to be removed so that only the titles show.

3. Check What They Are Watching Elsewhere

Check what your older children are watching at their friends' houses. Make sure an older child is not treating your younger children to inappropriate videos.

4. Talk to Other Parents

If you can, agree with other parents not to rent certain videos. This eliminates the "Everyone does it" argument.

5. Make a Decision and Stick to It

Ensure that you and your partner agree that the children shouldn't see certain types of videos and stick to your agreement, even if the kids argue like mad. Your decision is what counts; never mind about another parents" opinions. If you feel the video is harmful, protect your child from it.

6. Explain Your Reasoning to Your Child

Talk to your children about why you dislike certain videos. Explain that sex should not be degrading or violent and that you object to the images and the way people are depicted as being particularly nasty to each other. Explain why you dislike violence and bad language and how you think it affects people.

7. Tell Them It's Fiction

If they have seen a bad video or late-night fictional television program that you object to, explain that it isn't real life that the people in it were only acting—that it is not how people should behave toward each other.

8. Help Them Avoid Peer Pressure

Help your child decide what to do and say if he is at a friend's house where a shocking video is shown. If he feels very brave, he can walk out of the room and say why. If he can't do that, he can pretend to be ill, go to the bathroom, or say he's bored or sleepy.

9. Have a Code

Work out a code so that your child can call you if she wishes to get out of a situation. One child I know calls and asks, "Has Aunt Jill arrived yet?" This is her parents' cue to call back in a few minutes to say a relative has arrived and they need to collect her.

10. Watch the Video Beforehand

Try to watch videos, especially before younger children see them. Some parents think "PG" means "OK for children to watch with their parents." Sometimes it does, but sometimes it doesn't!

11. Don't Be Afraid to Turn It Off

If the door is closed and there is a lot of giggling or too much silence, drop in on the kids and offer them popcorn—anything actually, as it's only an excuse. Never underestimate the power of surprise as a parent. If the video is unsuitable, stop the show and explain why. They know why, but it doesn't hurt to tell them again.

12. Use Caution

Ensure that you don't leave any videos around that you don't want them to see. Children like nothing better than to sample forbidden fruit.

Decisions, Decisions

Of course, sometimes you don't mind your child seeing certain television programs or videos. At home, in spite of our no violent videos rule, I wanted my children to see *Mississippi Burning* because it was based on a true-life incident and dealt with racial prejudice. We watched it together, discussed what happened, and learned how harmful and stupid prejudice is.

Another time, however, I made the mistake of letting my young son, then five, see *Jaws* on TV. He was terrified and I spent ensuing days explaining about special effects and how they built the shark, and anything else I could think of to assuage his fear (and my guilt). Although that was years ago, he still tells me it's my fault he doesn't like horror films because I let him see *Jaws*. One of my many mistakes as a parent, I'm afraid.

The Positive Effects of Television and Videos

In spite of the dire warnings and the bad effect that television and videos can have, I think we have to remember that they can be a brilliant way to open up new possibilities for children. Think of all the wonderful and creative things that children learn from programs such as *Sesame Street* and *Reading Rainbow*. My children know so much about the world from watching documentaries and the news they ask me searching questions about important issues such as ecology, poverty, wars, and so on—questions that have come directly from their exposure to television. It wouldn't be fair to leave out the good points, so here are some ways we can help television and videos benefit our children.

13. Pick Out the Best

There are so many interesting and, dare I say it, educational programs on television that it is worth going through the week's offerings and marking the best. It is also worth renting a good video if it portrays something you feel is important for your children to see. My feeling is that we should use the tele vision as a friend and mentor, or we should get rid of it entirely. I think it is unrealistic to expect our children to live in a television-free environment, so I've opted to make the best of it.

14. Allow Some Junk

Have I gone mad? No. There are some programs that I think are a waste of time but are not particularly harmful. They are just rather mindless. All the other children watch them and not letting my children see them could deprive them of a social tool.

Also, everyone needs to vegetate occasionally, and it won't kill them to watch one or two mindless things a week. The other reason is that if you make everything off limits, the forbidden-fruit syndrome sets in, and the program becomes an icon. Is this a cop out? Maybe, but we all have our foibles.

15. Use Television to Inspire

When I was a child I was taken to see *Peter and the Wolf,* which inspired me to learn to play musical instruments. I only saw it once. My children have been lucky enough to see *Peter and the Wolf* in the theater, on television, and on video. They both play instruments—yes, because of my example, but also through the inspiration of the television.

Television can also inspire good deeds. The plight of starving children, earthquake victims, or refugees shown on TV has inspired some quite selfless acts and made my children more sensitive to the needs of others. I only heard about children in need when I was a child; they *see* the children. The picture, in this case, really is worth a thousand words.

16. Tie the Programs to Books and Activities

Little House on the Prairie was one of my favorite books as a child, as was *20,000 Leagues Under the Sea* and *The Time Machine.* Since kids are going to watch programs, give them the books first and reinforce the books with videos or television.

Follow up a program on space, electricity, or the human body with a visit to a local science museum. Or use a program about history to spark a visit to an exhibition of artifacts from that period. A program about finding the tomb of Tutankhamun, combined with a visit to see an Egyptian mummy, can fire a child's imagination for life.

17. Create a Fun Atmosphere

If you are going to use television and videos for family time, make it an occasion. Choose an especially good video or program, order a pizza or pop some popcorn, turn off the lights, and have an evening together. It really is great fun.

The Value of Books

Whatever we do, we won't always get it right. Parents never do. But at least we can keep learning, and I've learned something extremely important from the high school students' survey I mentioned earlier. When the eight-year-olds were questioned, it was found that not a single one had a parent who read to him.

Yes, it's true most of them can read quite well on their own by that age. But sitting close to someone and reading with her or to her from the same book beats everything else for a cozy time—even the family television evening. It can also lead straight into important discussions about life, death, love, brutality, tenderness, the universe—everything. It would be tragic if the video age robbed us of this way of conveying our values to our kids.

11

23 Ways to Deal With Those Blasted Computer Games

It's a glorious sunny day outside, but your child is glued to his computer game indoors. Does this sound familiar? "Mother to son: Over." Silence. "Come in Son: Over." Silence. That's more or less the extent of conversations in our house these days. For there are aliens in my home—small, spaced-out creatures sitting with hunched shoulders, hands fused to small square boxes of controls, eyes glued to a fast-moving, homicidal maniac on a screen.

That's the bad news. The good news is that these aliens make few demands and almost no mess. They've learned enough English to say "I'm hungry," they can shout "Nooooo!" or "Yesssss!" according to the antics of their maniac, and are able to cry "Pleeease don't turn it off!" when the object of their obsession is threatened with disconnection. Yes, I allow my children to play computer games. You may as well know this from the start. I swore it would never come to this, but I have succumbed to the inevitable. I may as well confess the rest, too. Both of my children have also had a go at Virtual Reality. If you saw *Lawnmower Man* or *Terminator 2,* you will know what Virtual Reality (VR) is at least in principle. It gives the illusion of being inside and part of a life-size computer game (see Virtual Reality explained later in this chapter, p. 95).

But to experience VR properly, you have to go to an arcade that features this new technology. It's fairly expensive, and if you are lucky, there won't be one near you. That said, I am sure there must have been a similar reaction to the introduction of electricity, telephones, radio, and television, and would you want to be without any of those? And I'm conscious of family history repeating itself. I remember my grandmother lamenting the fact that I refused to go out to play when *The Lone Ranger* came on TV. "Your brain will turn to mush," she prophesied (correctly, some will say).

I guess though that, like me, many parents feel uneasy about computer games and VR. Aren't they removing kids too far from the real world? Well, watching television and talking on the telephone to distant countries, or worse to an answering machine, has already removed all of us from the everyday reality known in previous centuries. So, before we condemn computer games out of hand, let's try to acknowledge their good points.

- Children don't make a mess when they are playing with them. It's better than dropping paint or modeling clay on the carpet.
- They are relatively quiet, eliciting only a few grunts and shouts, and occasional unprintable phrases, interspersed with sighs of despair.
- Studies claim computer games improve hand-to-eye coordination and stimulate a child's imagination and creativity. They also may develop their powers of logic, memory, problem solving, and intuitive skills, as well as get a child used to being challenged.

It's a pretty impressive list, isn't it? But, personally, I suspect that those studies were paid for by computer-game manufacturers. I do have to add another bonus point to the list, however: Playing these games helps research skills. My children carefully researched several studies to convince me of the games' benefits!

Here are the good points to acknowledge about Virtual Reality.

- VR, say its supporters, makes us all active participants in technology, unlike television, which is passive.
- The technology is being used to advance knowledge. For instance, it may soon be possible to dissect a frog without harming it (see Virtual Reality explained, p. 95). My biology teacher was a sadist who would come around the class to check on our progress on a dissection while munching on a tuna sandwich and joke. "Great frog-leg sandwich." A man of sophisticated humor.
- A VR game is also being developed that will allow you to ski while curled up on a sofa in your living room. No broken bones, no frozen fingers, no kamikaze snowboarders. I could get into this.

Last year I tried to learn how to ski down some real beginner slopes: no poles, bending my arms and body, repeating "I am a bird." As I slid, screaming, down the hill on my back and dressed in yellow, I did resemble a bird—a canary in its death throes.

To be honest, part of the reason I worry is because I don't understand the games. They are part of the new world of technology that children pick up with enormous speed and that, even when I try my hardest, I can only manage slowly.

When we had children I thought they would grow up like my husband and me and we could teach them the ways of the world. Hah! The other day I couldn't get the VCR to work, so in despair I called for my younger son. He fixed it in seconds—something he and his brother have been able to do almost from the time they could walk! In the old days you'd call for the man from the repair store. Let's face it, they're teaching us the ways of the world. Maybe our children really are aliens—super intelligent aliens sent to help us!

But I have serious concerns about computer and video games. How do these games influence children? Are children relating more to games than to other children? One television documentary concluded that children who were addicted to playing the games showed more anti-social and aggressive behavior. This wasn't a scientific study, but it seems to make sense that, if children have a steady diet of winning points for aggression in the games, they will learn that being aggressive is good.

Additionally, don't forget that children might also suffer physical harm from the games. As parents, we need to be aware of a slight risk of epileptic seizures, even in children with no family history of the problem (see the precautionary measures below). The number of cases is tiny compared with the overall number who play the games, but some manufacturers have now added health warnings to labels. Japan has launched an investigation into reported cases of deaths induced by computer games.

One objection I have to the games is that they make it harder to get kids to read. When a child's mind is reeling from the fierce battle that has just taken place on the screen, it's hard to switch to the gentle activity of reading a book. But I want my kids to read and here's why.

- Reading improves their vocabulary, spelling, and grammar.
- It expands their imagination.
- It increases their knowledge of the world and allows them to experience things beyond their own lives.

- It helps them to learn about other cultures and customs.
- It increases their attention spans, which in turn help them to concentrate better on school work.
- It gives them a chance to mentally try out different situations to work out what they might do in various circumstances.
- It gives them ideas to talk—and think—about. Good old-fashioned moral dilemmas, such as whether the hero should do a bad thing for a good reason.
- Reading is not accompanied by annoying little beeping sounds.
- It's a lot cheaper. I calculated that you could buy five or six books for the price of each game.

A further problem for me is the way that computer game fights have no moral themes—no justice, nothing to give us insight into ourselves. You just zap as many people as you can. The ethos is simply "Kill 'em all and get to the next level." My fear is it's possible that, in later life, some of these little aliens might become completely divorced from reality and zap other people just as they learned to zap their on-screen enemies.

The bottom line is that these games deliver self- absorption, but not self-enlightenment. If our children insist on playing them, it's up to us as parents to provide some sort of balance, by plugging away at them to read, to discuss, to think. And if we are worried about the continual zapping and killing, then we'd better sit down and talk about that with them.

Parents shouldn't pretend the games aren't there. We need to find out more about them.

1. Ask what happens in the games.
2. Sit down with your children and watch them (the games, not the children) in action.
3. Discuss any violence and ask the children what they feel about it. Ask if they think it might make children who play the games be violent toward real people.
4. Praise anything worth praising so you are not seen as totally anti-games.
5. Should you disapprove of a game, don't be afraid to show it and turn it off.
6. Watch out that you don't get addicted yourself!

I talked with my kids about the violence, but they seemed to be quite clear that this was a silly, if fun, game and that of course they knew it wasn't real life. "It's like the *Tom and Jerry* cartoons you said you liked as a kid," exclaimed my youngest with a certain amount of pity and embarrassment that his mother could have liked *Tom and Jerry.*

But I do worry a lot about kids who play constantly without parental input or discussion. It seems to me that getting points for shooting, decapitating, or knocking down opponents cannot be good for impressionable, growing minds.

I'm not forgetting how we all watched *Tom and Jerry* and *Road Runner* cartoons as children. Talk about violence for the sake of it! None of my friends has grown into Hannibal Lecter, so I try to keep my worries in perspective. And I'm not quite as concerned about video games that have graphics like *Tom and Jerry* does as I am about Virtual Reality, in which you appear to become the person doing the killing. My kids think I'm overreacting, but I disagree.

The problem is that Virtual Reality seems to be *the* birthday party thing to do, and kids love it. That means either banning them from parties, which I won't do, or lots of discussion to get things into perspective, which I can and will do.

Precautionary Measures

Because of the danger of computer-related epileptic seizures, you should seek medical advice if your child is already subject to fits. Do this before allowing him or her to play these games. In any case, encourage your child to:

7. Take lots of breaks. Never let them play for more than an hour at a time.
8. Sit as far away from the screen as possible. If you think your child may be at risk of a seizure, make sure he or she sits at least eight feet away and covers one eye with a patch—for a seizure to occur, the flickering on the screen needs to register in both eyes simultaneously.
9. Keep hand-held games at arm's length.
10. Turn the room lights are on. The less contrast between room and screen, the better. And be careful about children using hand-held games in a dark car.
11. Never play when sick or tired.

You may not always manage to impose all these tips, but do make sure you:

12. Negotiate

We had a real tussle when it came to negotiating how long and when my children could play. We finally agreed on weekends and nonschool days—with a time limit.

13. Plot

Software is available that allows the screen to be used for a limited period. You can program it for each child. (Admittedly it won't help if your children know how to hack in and reprogram the device!)

14. Confiscate

If necessary, take away some vital part of the game—such as the controller—and simply ignore their squeals of protest.

15. Advertise the Rules

If your children are left in someone else's care, ensure that the guidelines are known. You cannot monitor them when they are out of sight, but you can at least try to influence the adult in charge. Don't make it so unpleasant, however, that no one ever invites your child over to play.

16. Encourage Other Interests

Take your children skating or bike riding, or sign them up for a pottery class or music lessons. Sometimes children play computer games simply for lack of anything else to do. (See chapter 6, "50 Ways to Boost Your Child's Learning Power.")

17. Good Health

In addition to the danger of computer-related seizures, parents need to be aware of the other health risks, whether using a TV, monitor, or hand-held game. These include:

- eye strain.
- lack of exercise during endless hours of play, which can affect body development, particularly of leg and shoulder muscles.
- headaches and neckaches.
- teeth-grinding, which can often be caused by tension.
- constipation, or even hemorrhoids, from sitting for too long.

To be fair, a lot of these problems affect children who don't play video games, so keep things in perspective. I know an overweight, antisocial pain in the neck whose mother never allows her to do anything that is pure fun.

Let's face it, some kids will be affected and others will play the games with no ill effects. (Then again, maybe this is just my way of justifying my lack of character in submitting to my sons" pleadings for their computer games in the first place.)

18. Warning Signs

There are a few things to look out for if you suspect your children are turning into couch-potato television or video-game addicts. Get tough and turn it off if your child seems to be:

- unwilling to walk anywhere and wants to be driven even the shortest distances.
- overweight or nonenergetic, yet still consuming large amounts of candy and chips.
- bored all the time.
- uninterested in going outside, cycling, skating, or playing any kind of sports with friends.
- completely out of shape and unable to walk up stairs without pausing for breath or being winded.
- only interested in watching television or playing video games.

Parent Power

For most of us beleaguered parents, there has to be a middle ground. We must ensure that we and our children carry a sense of morality into the future. You see, it was worth my Gran uttering those solemn warnings about watching TV—look how I've remembered them to this day.

This is a computer age and there's nothing we can do to change that. But we can be aware of the dangers and make sure the kids don't turn out to have mushed brains or soggy muscles. (I wish we could blame computer games for our lack of exercise and blurry eyes!)

One last thought: Video games may improve hand-to-eye coordination, but give me a book any day. Think of all that hand-to-eye page-turning coordination you get.

Virtual Reality Explained

It started as a military system for simulating combat. Now it's one of the buzzwords of the decade. In the long run Virtual Reality could revolutionize work, education, and play.

VR, computer-generated pictures with sounds and sensations, is so authentic that it seems real. With VR game machines, each player wears a helmet fitted with two tiny TV screens that give 3D vision. In more advanced games, they also wear gloves, which give the illusion of tactile sensation—you see an object and can pick it up and move it as though it were real.

As computing power advances, it will be possible to give biology students, for example, classes in dissection without real specimens. And, with new fiberoptic cables, it may be possible to create an illusion of being in the same room as people on the other side of the globe.

Something Nasty on the Computer

Parents should be up-to-date with the Internet. Jay walked into his twelve-year-old son's room and found him engrossed in a "very nasty pornographic image on his computer." Jay pulled the plug. His son was actually relieved because he had gotten in over his head and didn't quite know how to extract himself.

Children have easy access to pornographic pictures in full color: sadomasochism; women bound, gagged, and tortured; group sex; bondage; children having sex with animals.... And much of it can be pulled up by our children, if they have access to the computer Internet.

"Surfing the Net" (looking at the various things that are available) has become a favorite occupation of children and young people. Of course you can click on to lots of wonderful information through the Internet—current news, the latest sports scores, new book publications, and even bird-watching and beekeeping guides. But some parents are not aware that our children can also gain access to horrendous and degrading pornography, as well as put themselves at risk from pedophiles who surf the Net to contact potential victims.

This isn't pie in the sky. In a recent case, two children were lured away from home by people they'd been corresponding with on the Internet, and police are prosecuting individuals who have downloaded pornographic images of children. Children have also joined "Chat Rooms," party lines that can have all kinds of participants, from other children to pedophiles posing as innocent "penpals" to get children's names, addresses, telephone numbers, and photographs.

The good news is that you generally need to know certain codes or have a clued-in friend to access the pornography. The bad news is that many teenagers do know the codes and, having pulled up the material, can load it on to disks that can be used by younger children on their own computers, even if they are not connected to the Internet.

We can't forbid our children to use computers—they are an essential tool. Children have to be computer literate or they will not be able to cope in the world, but we have to protect them at the same time. Here are a few suggestions.

19. Explain to your children that there are some things to beware of when using the Internet:

    • Remember that anyone can use the Net and pretend to be someone else. The person they think is another child or teenager may be a "dirty old man" (or woman).
    • Never give their name, address, telephone number, or other personal details on-line.
    • Never arrange to meet anyone without checking with you first.
    • Never send anyone a photo without checking with you first.

20. Find out about how to restrict access to these "services." There are some software packages, such as Net Nanny, that can block access to pornographic sites. Check with computer stores and internet service providers about how to do this.
21. Put the computer in a room that everyone has access to.
22. Drop into the room if your children are using the computer and take an interest in what they are doing. Get them to explain to you how to use the Internet.
23. Monitor the amount of time your children are spending online. If they are using lots of online time, especially late at night, they may be in danger.

We may not be able to shield children completely from the harmful parts of the Internet and its millions of channels. Children will experiment and forbidden fruit has a strong lure, but we need to be aware, to monitor, and to talk with children so they can make good safe choices while surfing the Net.

12

22 Hints for Getting Together for Family Meals

The family meal is losing out to TV, take-out, and teenage schedules. Why should we reinstate the tradition?

My husband called at four P.M. "Looks like I won't get away for ages. Go ahead with dinner without me." When I got home from the office, my elder son, Charles, was rushing out, a sandwich in one hand and a drink in the other. "Rehearsal night, Mom, see you later." Exit, stage left.

"Well, it's you and me for dinner, dynamite," I said hopefully to James. The look on his face informed me what was coming: a request to watch TV. So much for a family dinner.

Why did it worry me so much? What were we missing? I thought of my earliest meals, when our family was living at grandmother's. I could smell the aroma of her homemade stews or casseroles that simmered on the stove all day.

We children would eagerly hang around the kitchen, hoping for a taste. At six o'clock sharp we sat around the table to eat, often with friends or visiting relatives. Dinnertime was noisy, interesting, delicious, and could go on for hours.

This meal was the focus of our day and we all vied with each other, children and adults alike, to tell the most interesting thing that had happened to us that day. At the center of it all was Gran, dishing out the food, telling us not to talk with our mouths full, and ensuring that this nightly ritual was more than a simple refueling of stomachs. Dinner, and what happened around it, gave us a sense of belonging and it confirmed us as a family.

Why Family Meals Are Important

A few years ago, I began to look at my own family. Yes, we did do quite a bit together—weekend outings, vacations, that sort of thing—but we did not have the same sense of togetherness I remember from those daily family meals when I was a child. I was left feeling that there are many moms who, like me, are breaking with a tradition they would prefer to keep. Did we have the same opportunity to develop family unity? Did it matter if I wasn't that old-style pillar of the family, or if we had thrown-together meals so often, or take-out pizza eaten from the box? What else were we missing?

Family meals are good for communication. We find out all sorts of things when we can sit down to family supper. While reviewing the events of the day just past, it's also a good time to pick up on the beginning of problems.

Is Sara being bullied? Is Paul in over his head with that new girlfriend? Do the kids understand the various issues being talked about, such as AIDS and drugs?

It's also a good time for parents to air their views. I remember when my sister, age eight, had been picked on by some local children and we were discussing it at dinner. "She deserved it," I said from my superior, year-older position.

"Did you help her?" asked my father.

"No, why should I?"

"Because you stand by your family," said my mother. "You can disagree all you like at home, but outside you stick together." This conversation took place over a chicken stew. I can recall it as if it were yesterday.

It's also a good time to show you care. One generation back, the mother was the pillar of the family. I do know that part of me still likes and hankers after "being a pillar"—organizing, cooking, cementing my family together.

I also know that I don't want things to go back to my mother's time. I have no desire to perform her role. I like my life; I enjoy lots about the fast, busy modern world, yet I also want to give my children that warm, cocoonlike environment that fostered all those old-fashioned values that my parents passed on to me. I want my children to experience the parental caring that the home-prepared, shared meal communicated.

And what a difference it makes when parental care isn't there. One of my son's friends, Andrew, loves coming for meals at our house because his parents are often out to dinner. When they are in they like to eat separately later. Andrew prefers even our hastily produced spaghetti and bread sticks, which we eat all together at the kitchen table, to the food he and the babysitter get at home. He once said when going home to dinner, even though he knew there was steak waiting, "I'd rather stay here—it's so empty at home." He's right; although I loved the home cooking of my childhood, it isn't the quality of the food that matters most, it's the quality of the company.

Helpful Hints

1. Share the Chores

Many things are better these days. I'm glad that one of the bad messages from my childhood no longer prevails: the idea that girls do housework and cooking while the boys can be free to play. In our house we all pitch in with the work—I refuse to raise boys who cannot take care of their personal needs themselves. Then, they can decide for themselves about upholding the tradition of family meals.

2. Make the Decision

We got together for a family chat. Did this tradition of eating together matter to us all? We decided that we:

- liked the idea of sitting down together. Much to my delight the kids said they actually missed family meals.
- would try to get up a little earlier in the morning so that we could have breakfast together. Controlled chaos is the best way to describe mornings in our house, with the children wanting an extra five minutes to sleep, the dog whimpering to go out, my husband ironing a clean shirt, and me groping around for my contact lenses. Nonetheless, we decided to try!
- would arrange a dinner time each morning and all be home for it, if at all possible.
- would all help prepare breakfast and dinner and clear up afterwards.

- would not watch TV while eating, so our attention could be focused on each other, making real communication possible.
- would make every supper a family meal. Even for a last-minute-rush take-out pizza, we'd get out the check cloth for the table and stick a couple of household candles in empty wine bottles to make it a candlelit supper.

3. Accommodate Everyone's Tastes

One of the dilemmas we face is that healthy eating and food allergies mean that not all family members can always eat the same things. When my mother put food on the table, the whole family ate whatever was offered and no one even dared think about having his own special meal. Now you might have to make a vegetarian or vegan meal for your animal-loving thirteen-year-old, pudding with no additives for your E-allergic eight-year-old, and free-range roast chicken for the rest of them. You probably didn't want to be a short-order cook but that's how things are. So, sitting down together doesn't necessarily mean harmoniously nibbling on the same dish, but that doesn't matter (except, of course, to the cooks) as much as the talking, debating, and sharing that should go on in mealtimes.

If folks need or like different foods, then accommodate as much as possible and enlist everyone's help to make it as pleasant and easy as you can.

4. Encourage Your Child to Talk

Children are most inclined to interrupt and talk when adults are deep in a good conversation. Sometimes, unwelcome bits of half-chewed dinner accompany the interruption. Children aren't deliberately being rude—they are stimulated by what they hear and want to contribute.

Though manners are necessary and no one wants children who are unappetizing to be around, don't quash enthusiasm. We don't want children who are so worried about being polite that they're nervously silent. To me, it's better to excuse a bit of food accidentally spilling out of a mouth because a child is so excited to tell you something than to reprimand her for poor manners. This might be the only time everyone gets to talk together in a busy day.

Making Family Meals Happen

5. Plan a time at least three times a week when you will all be together and can sit around the table. It can be breakfast, lunch, or dinner.

6. Don't worry if your child doesn't want to eat at the meal; just being there is enough. Our sons sometimes stop for "healthy" french fries or candy on the way home—and then say they aren't hungry. Fine, we want their company anyway, even if it's only for fifteen minutes.

7. Encourage your children to invite their friends over and always be welcoming. "What's one more at the table?" my Gran said whenever someone was hanging around at dinner time.

8. Whenever possible, go to a restaurant with your family. Without the normal distractions, it is amazing how much more talkative everyone is and (knock on wood) children are usually polite and charming when you're out. Yes, I know there are horror stories about Johnny screaming the walls down because they didn't serve his favorite kind of ice cream, but they are mostly well behaved!

9. Turn off the television. That favorite television program can be taped, or dinnertime negotiated around it. Better still, unplug the damn thing.

10. Take the phone off the hook. Train everyone to answer the phone by saying: "We're just sitting down to eat, I'll get him to call you back after dinner," or "I'd love to talk but the pie is just coming out of the oven."

    Ask your children to tell their friends not to call during supper. And when you call anyone around dinnertime, start with, "Are you eating? If so I'll call back." Chances are that the kids will pick up on your style.

11. Use any occasion for a special meal. Good reports, sports awards, Fridays, the shortest or longest day of the year, 'unbirthdays', pets' birthdays—anything for a change and a bit of unexpected fun.

12. Make it happy. If you've got a bone to pick with anyone, don't do it at the table. Making the dinner table into a battleground destroys the reason for having it in the first place.

13. Give everyone a ten-minute warning before the meal is ready to eat. It drives cooks nuts when the meal is getting cold during last minute visits to the bathroom and "the program's just finishing— I'll be right there" comments. To avoid tension, plan dinner to coincide with the end of the favorite program or activity.

14. Don't do it all yourself. Many hands do make light work. Mealtimes shouldn't make anyone the martyr of the family: the "Look what I did for you" attitude is enough to put us all off eating together for life.

Eating Out

At least when you eat at home you are (somewhat) the master of your own fate. Going to restaurants with young children, however, can be a disaster. Here are a few things you can do to make eating out more enjoyable, learned the hard way by Yours Truly.

15. Choose the Right Restaurant

It would be crazy to take young children to a very expensive, fancy restaurant. The other diners are most likely trying to get away from noisy, playful, chatty children and you wouldn't be very popular. Anyway, it would be impossible to relax and have a good time yourself. Choose a child-friendly place, especially for your first outings. As much as I dislike fast-food places, we practically lived in them when our children were small. No one minds your kids being there and it's a great way to introduce children to the joys and rules of eating out.

16. Telephone Ahead

If you are going to a restaurant you are not familiar with, telephone ahead to see if they are prepared for children. Better that than arriving to find that you aren't welcome or they aren't prepared.

17. Go "Off-peak"

If possible, take the kids to the restaurant early, before it gets crowded.

18. Take Toys and Entertainment

Keep your children occupied with games, toys, crayons, and paper. Bring along any special equipment they need, such as cups with spouts and bibs.

19. Ask for Small Portions

If the restaurant doesn't have a children's menu, ask for a smaller portion, or two get plates and split the dinner between your children (if you can get them to agree on what they want to eat).

20. Avoid the Exotic

Most children are not terribly adventurous when it comes to food. Try to order food they know and like. If you want to let them try something unusual, order it yourself and let them taste a bit. Whatever you order, try to make sure it doesn't take hours to prepare—the quicker the better for young children.

21. Sit by a Window

My children always loved sitting near a window, and so did I. We could play "I Spy with My Little Eye" or just watch all the people and cars going by. It just made the whole experience more pleasant.

22. If All Else Fails, Leave!

If the children freak out, cut your losses and go. You can always ask for a doggy bag. It isn't fair to spoil the meal for the other diners.

Our two boys are really quite a pleasure to go out with now. The only trouble is, they have a taste for those expensive restaurants I mentioned earlier. I can't wait until they are working and can afford to take *us* out! (I always have been an optimist.)

Enjoy Them Now and Plan for the Future

Family meals are not a feature of our lives for long. Children grow up and quickly prefer to do their own thing. I will miss the hustle and bustle and hassle of it all, but I hope the tradition of our family suppers will carry on to my grandchildren. I like planning ahead. Even though my children are only teenagers and definitely not ready to be parents yet (is anyone ready to be a parent?), I'm sure my grandchildren will love my chicken dinners!

13

The 5 Basic Rules of Scolding

All parents need to scold their children—it's a part of our job description! But it can be done well and helpfully, so badly it's useless, or so scathingly that it's wounding worse than useless. Should we review ourselves as critics?

- "That's the last time I let you go on your own to get your hair cut—you look terrible!"
- "You spilled your milk all over the carpet, you stupid boy!"
- "How could you get such low grades? I am so disappointed with you."

Do these sound familiar? How well do you think they rate as constructive? Can we learn to do better? Is there a best way to criticize?

Maureen, a friend of my grandmother, used to criticize her children in the most inventive way. She gave them points out of ten, like the judges for ice-skaters. So, if Barry came home with poor grades, she would take out her cards and silently give him one out of ten. Maureen only added a remark when Barry did something good. Then the cards would come out with eight or nine out of ten and a comment like: "Well, Barry, that was really clever of you," which was her highest praise.

Despite low grades when he first went to school, Barry ended up going to university and now works as an engineer. He laughs about his mom's strange method, but admits that it worked—and that he uses the same cards with his own kids.

I'm not suggesting we all rush out and get a set of cards. In fact, children need definite rules and the totally silent system, the complete avoidance of criticism that Maureen used over the school grades, definitely wouldn't be right for all occasions.

Let's see which way you react and how you criticize—and then use the marks to rate how well you are doing. Granted, we all react differently depending on how energetic or how exhausted we are feeling. So give yourself the benefit of the doubt. When you are choosing your answers, pretend that you are in your *best* parenting mode!

QUIZ: How Do You Rate as a Scolder?

1. My child is so careless

Robert, age ten, is carelessness personified. He knocks things over and spills things, and generally drives you nuts. Today, he is working on a school project and you walk into the living room just in time to see him tip over a glass of juice on to the carpet. Do you:

a. Put him up for adoption at once.
b. Lose your temper and call him a stupid fool.
c. Scream "Watch out!," rush over and try to stem the flow of juice and say, "I told you not to bring drinks in here. Now get a cloth and help."
d. Smack him and make him clean it up.
e. Calmly leave the room, asking him to deal with it himself.

Points

a. *Score one (for humor).*
b. *Take two points (for honesty).*
c. *Score five. This is a natural way to react. If Robert shouldn't have been drinking juice in the room then he should help to clean it up. You haven't called him names or belittled him.*
d. *No marks. Hitting a ten-year-old over a spilled drink only teaches him that making mistakes will lead to violence.*
e. *Minus five (for lying—it's impossible for anyone to be that saintly!).*

2. My child plays his music too loud

Charles loves music, especially if it is loud, has a driving beat, and no discernible tune. His younger brother has the room next to Charles and cannot concentrate. Charles claims he cannot do his homework without his music. You are constantly battling with him to "turn that thing down." It has come to a head. Do you:

a. Throw his sound system out when he's at school and deny all knowledge when he returns.
b. Sell his sound system while he is away, then claim there was a burglary and say that only his sound system was taken. Offer him your sincerest sympathy, but explain that the insurance money doesn't cover his loss.
c. Tell him firmly and calmly what volume you (and his brother) can stand. If he won't cooperate, impose a "silence time," when no music can be played, so everyone can get work done.
d. Go in every night and turn it down. Keep going in every time he turns it up. Don't back down.
e. Offer to help him find another family to live with until he starts showing an appreciation for Bach and Mozart.
f. Buy him a set of earphones for his birthday.

Points

a. *One point for trying, but no more because of lack of inventiveness.*
b. *Two points for imagination, but watch out when your child asks to see the police report.*
c. *Five points if you manage to stay calm; three if you don't. This is one of those times you just have to be the firm parent for the sake of your other children and your neighbors, let alone yourself.*
d. *Three points for being tenacious. You may eventually win just because your child gets tired of you continually coming into the room.*
e. *No points. Well, but two points if you can get your child to see the sense in recent studies that have shown that you learn more effectively and remember more when you listen to calming classical music such as Bach and Mozart than when you listen to the Top 40.*
f. *Four points, but only if you ensure that he doesn't go deaf from playing the music in the earphones too loud. Researchers are finding that kids who listen to loud music suffer long-term damage to their hearing.*

3. My child is so messy

Theresa has left her room in a complete mess. She told you it had been cleaned up when you gave her permission to go out. When she returns, do you:

a. Tell her she didn't live up to her part of the bargain and keep her in for an agreed length of time. Then make her clean up her room immediately.
b. Yell at her.
c. Make her move out.
d. Tell her that you now know she is a liar and that you'll never trust her again.
e. Icily call her a sloppy pig and refuse to talk to her for a few hours.

Points

a. *Of course, this reaction gets five. We can all figure out that this is the most logical and constructive thing to do. (Unfortunately, we don't always do it, though.)*
b. *Well...two points. Maybe you think she deserves it, but it doesn't really solve anything.*
c. *Fifty points. (Just joking.)*
d. *No points. Never call a child a liar or a thief—she may live up to these labels.*
e. *Score one. Shame can work, but not nearly as well as reason. She may well be a sloppy pig, but this method won't make her change her ways.*

4. My child was rude

Kathryn calls a neighbor a "silly old woman." The neighbor complains to you. When you call Kathryn, do you:

a. Smack her, march her to the neighbor, and force a tearful apology.
b. Ask her what happened. If she has been rude, make her apologize in person and explain that even if your neighbor provoked her, calling people names will not be tolerated in your family.
c. Tell your neighbor she *is* a silly old woman and challenge her to a fistfight.
d. Call your daughter a nasty little creep and give her a harsh punishment.

Points

a. *No points. Your daughter will learn nothing about manners, but a great deal about fear.*
b. *Award yourself five. You have given your daughter a chance to explain her side of the story. If she has been rude, then you have also allowed her to learn from her mistake, to take the logical*

consequences of her actions (apologizing), and to understand that you value being kind and polite.

c. *Minus one. She may be silly, but watch out for her left hook.*

d. *No points. All you are teaching her is that calling people names is acceptable.*

5. My child isn't doing school work properly

Tim's teacher reports that he is not trying and is getting poor grades. Do you and your partner:

a. Express your disappointment, tell Tim you can't understand what the problem is, and inform him he can't watch TV or go out until he improves.

b. Get really angry and tell him he is a stupid good-for-nothing who will never amount to anything in the future.

c. Trade him in for a gerbil—they don't have to study.

d. Ask him what he thinks the teacher said. Find out if there is any reason for his poor performance (other than sheer laziness) and see if you can think of some way to help. Figure out how he can catch up or change his study habits, and tell him he can do better—and that you'll help.

e. Sigh and look hurt and exasperated. Ask him how he could do this to you after all you've done for him.

Points

a. *Three points. This is such a normal reaction, and at least you admit to it. However, Tim doesn't get a word in, which may be part of his problem.*

b. *No points. If he's a good-for-nothing, why should he bother to try at all?*

c. *One point. Gerbils are good company.*

d. *Score five. Lucky Tim—someone really cares how he feels and is willing to help. He knows you are not happy with his perform ance, but there is hope.*

e. *Minus five. Loading a feeling of guilt on to a child without helping with the problem is clearly going to make things twice as hard for him.*

6. My child is so quarrelsome

Stephanie is constantly bullying her younger brother. You've just heard a thud and a piercing scream. Here comes your son, crying, "She hit me." Do you:

a. Grab your daughter by the arm and say, "I'm fed up to here with you! Go to your room immediately."
b. Say, "Get out of my sight, both of you. I am sick and tired of this constant bickering."
c. Take a deep breath, comfort your son, and find out what has been happening. Has your son been bugging your daughter or is she picking on him because she is angry, annoyed, or frustrated about something else? Give appropriate punishment or counsel.
d. Wonder why the devil you ever had children. Life used to be so peaceful.
e. Call the travel agent and book a trip anywhere, as long as the plane leaves within the next ten minutes.

Points

a. *Score two. But only if you didn't grab her so hard that it hurt. Sometimes getting the child out of the way saves her from being murdered.*
b. *Three points for this one. It's fine to give yourself an occasional break from children until you can decide what to do. Don't feel you always have to come up with the right solution instantly. Sometimes a little "time out" will cool things off until everyone feels more ready to talk about it reasonably.*
c. *Take five points. Finding out what the problems are might just save you a lot of future aggravation. Children's squabbles are not always what they seem. This action will probably only be possible when you feel that you can cope.*
d. *Two for this. Join the crowd, and don't trust anyone who says they have never thought of it. By the way, you only get the points if you didn't say it aloud in front of the children. If you did, score minus one.*
e. *One point for creativity. It would have been four, but I booked before you!*

How Did You Score as a Critic?

- 25 to 30 points: You're brilliant!
- 20 to 24 points: You're normal, but could improve.
- 15 to 19 points: You're tired and need a break.
- 10 to 14 points: You've gone beyond the expiration date. Get help.
- Less than ten points: You've got a good sense of humor, but you should have stuck to raising goldfish.

Kids can drive you up the wall, and no parent gets ten out of ten every time. But knowing how to criticize in a positive, helpful way is one of the most important skills we can learn. There are a very few basic rules I think we can all follow.

1. Take a "Time-Out"

Sometimes we need to give ourselves time to calm down before we come down like a ton of bricks and do something we'll regret.

2. Remember That We All Make Mistakes

Children need our guidance to help them learn not to repeat mistakes, but they will make lots of them anyway. That's what growing up is about. If we expect our children to always get it right, we're in for a lot of aggravation.

3. Remain in Control

We need to scold and discipline children at times; children need to learn that there are consequences to bad behavior. But if we can scold in a fairly calm and reasoned manner, they will hear what we're saying instead of cowering in the corner because we're yelling like a banshee. (Who, me? Yell? Never!)

4. Admit Mistakes

If we get it wrong, we have to make amends and apologize. It's only fair.

5. Maintain a Sense of Humor

That doesn't mean we laugh while we are talking to the kids. It just means we have to keep all of these transgressions in perspective and maybe have a little moment of humor between the adults after it's all over. Of course, this doesn't apply to the more serious problems (see chapter 23). I don't know how people without a sense of humor survive parenthood. I certainly feel sorry for their children!

14

16 Ways to Avoid Spanking Your Child

I know that most parents hate the idea of spanking; no good parent could enjoy inflicting pain on his own children. But parents also want to make sure their children do not grow into horrible, obnoxious creatures, and sometimes a quick smack seems to be one of the answers.

Regardless of your philosophy of raising children, the problem is that spanking is easy and, sometimes, parents act impulsively or just don't have the time to think of other more constructive ways to deal with things. If you want to keep some alternatives to spanking in mind for those occasions when you feel like throttling your child, then here are some suggestions.

1. Hold the Child Firmly

Some parents say that the only way to teach young children about dangers such as fire or cars, or to stop a temper tantrum, is to administer a quick smack. The theory is that the child then associates the danger with the pain of the smack. If your young child persists in getting into a dangerous situation or a throwing tantrums that places her in danger, grab the child and hold her firmly to you and say "Stop" in a strong voice. Continue to hold the child until she calms down, then explain the danger and your displeasure that the child didn't listen.

2. Ignore Tantrums Whenever Possible

Children have tantrums, but rarely do they have them without an audience. Supermarkets seem to be a popular place. It can be incredibly embarrassing to have your child writhing around on the floor screaming his head off while self-righteous people stare at you and whisper, "That child needs a good spank." You may have to pick the child up and carry him out of the store, but the best way to stop tantrums is to walk away, completely ignore the tantrum, and watch from a distance (where the child cannot see you) to ensure that he or she is safe.

3. Reward Them When They're Good

Children want to please their parents, but they also want attention of any kind. If we only pay attention to them when they are being naughty and we smack them, they will act up until they are smacked, because any kind of attention is better than none.

Do your best to tell them how pleased you are when they are being good. Tell them how much you like the way they are playing together nicely, or how glad you are that they acted so grown up while you were shopping. They will tug your sleeve and say, "Aren't I being good?" to get your attention, instead of doing something awful. (See chapter 22 for reward ideas.)

4. Tell Them What Bothers You

Explain to children that certain things drive you to distraction (if they don't already know!) and that you will be less likely to punish them if they avoid doing those things.

5. Tell Them the Consequences in Advance

Tell children what will happen if they continue bad behavior, and follow through. Knowing in advance that they will not be allowed to see their favorite program if they insist on fighting often stops the fight dead in its tracks. If it doesn't, don't let them see the program.

Possible consequences can include:

- missing television.
- sitting facing a blank wall for five minutes (an hour is far too long).
- not being allowed to go on an outing.
- taking away a toy for a period of time.

• not allowing a treat, such as a sweet.

None of these things actually helps the child learn good behavior, and it is better to use rewards. However, there will be times when you feel you need some sanctions because nothing else will seem to be working and you'll be at your wits' end. Ideas like this may help you avoid spanking, but do work on positive rewards too.

6. Set Limits

All children need limits, and to know what those limits are. Tell your children the kind of behavior you expect and what will happen if they transgress. (Also tell them what will happen if they behave.) They will test the limits—all kids do. I told one of my sons that he was not allowed to go out on a school night and that I always wanted to know if he was going to be late home from school. One night he didn't call, and came waltzing in two hours late. I was hysterical, imagining all sorts of terrible things happening to him. First I hugged him, they I yelled, "Where have you been? You know the rules of this house," etc. It turned out that a group of kids had gone for a pizza after school and invited him. He didn't want to seem "like a baby" who had to call home for permission.

Although I sympathized with his desire to be independent, as far as I was concerned he knew the limits and had chosen to break them, so he lost some privileges as a result. We then set up new limits as, clearly, he was starting to need a bit more leeway after school. But I still insisted that he call me, even if he did it in secret.

7. Don't Expect Too Much from a Young Child

Be sure that you are not expecting the child to do something that is impossible for her age and level of maturity. You would not expect a two-year-old to fully understand the dangers of moving cars, so supervision and constant explanations are in order. You would expect a nine-year-old to understand the dangers of playing with matches, so punishment would be in order if he or she persists in playing with them.

Penelope Leach, the world-renowned childcare expert, feels strongly that we should never hit children. She aims to change attitudes toward children, and to help people recognize that it is as wrong to hit a child as it is to hit an adult. It is an uphill struggle, but she has written some very clear guidelines for parents, some of which she has kindly given me permission to quote from her pamphlet, EPPOC (End Physical Punishment of Children) here.

8. Tell Often

With young children, it can take hundreds of tellings over months to get them to do something like put their toys away. Patience and lots of little tricks such as: "I bet you can't put your toys away before the timer goes off," work wonderfully. They will forget, but they aren't being naughty, just very busy getting on with all the things they have to do in their young lives.

9. Ration Don'ts

Your child will simply stop hearing them. "Don't" works best for rules you want him to keep whatever the circumstances, like "Don't climb trees, it's dangerous." Try not to make rules that vary according to circumstance and which might have to be broken. "Don't interrupt me," for example, is a silly rule, because you may need to be interrupted in an emergency or if a child needs to go to the bathroom.

10. Driven to Distraction

If your child will not listen to you and you've started to deliver a smack, divert the blow to the table or to your knee (ouch!). The sound will interrupt the behavior and the child will hear what you say far better than if she or he was crying.

11. Cool Down

If you feel your temper going, make sure your child is safe and leave the room until you've cooled down. The child or baby may cry at being left, but that's better than crying for being hit.

12. Grab

Little hands that get into danger are better grabbed than smacked. Grabbing them is quicker and attracts just as much attention.

13. Superior Size

Use your superior size to lift a child who won't come or carry a child who won't walk.

14. Substitute

If you've started to say, "Stop that this minute or I'll..." you may have time to substitute "scream" for "smack." Do it, as loudly as you can. Your child will be surprised and impressed and your tension will vanish (or at least diminish).

15. Punishment Fits the "Crime"

If you feel you must use punishment, make sure that it follows directly from the "crime" so she or he has the chance to learn the lesson you mean to teach. If a child rides a bike on to a road you've forbidden, take the bike away for the afternoon or longer. As for spanking: nothing will make your child believe that you do it for his or her sake: "I hurt you because I don't want you hurt" is too devious a message for any child or adult.

16. Talk to Other Parents of Professionals

If you are troubled by your own reactions to your children, please seek help from a professional counselor or a support group. Parents Anonymous has chapters nationwide; consult your yellow pages or local social service agency. Remember that you are not alone. Getting yourself help when you need it is a big part of being a good parent.

PART II

Getting Through Life

15

20 Questions: How Well Do You Know Your Child?

Do you know what your children want to be when they grow up? What they like and dislike about themselves? Or what they would wish for if you gave them one wish?

Give a copy of this quiz to your child and fill one out yourself, then compare the results and see how you score. I reckon we don't know our kids as well as we think we do!

1. What is your child's favorite food?
2. What food does your child dislike the most?
3. What does your child most like about himself?
4. What does your child dislike most about herself?
5. What do you do that most embarrasses your child?
6. What would your child like to change about himself?
7. What does your child like best about you?
8. What would your child like to change about you?
9. What would your child change about her siblings?
10. What does your child want to be when he grows up?
11. What would your child do with a $100 gift?
12. What does your child most worry about?
13. What is the thing your child is most frightened of?
14. Who is your child's best friend (or boyfriend or girlfriend?)
15. Who is your child's least favorite person and why?
16. What subject does your child like best at school?

17. What subject does your child like least at school?
18. What is your child's favorite activity away from school?
19. Who would your child like to talk to if she had a problem?
20. If your child was granted one wish, what would it be?

Score

Give yourself one point for every time you match your child's answer. Before you score your answers it might help to know that none of the parents I tried this out on scored higher than 15, and the parents who scored the highest had the youngest children. I think that means the older they get, the less we know our kids—or the more they don't tell us. But then that won't surprise parents of older children, and perhaps we don't really want to know everything about them (or what their favorite activity is!).

- 15 to 20 points: Amazing. You deserve a gold star and a vacation.
- 10 to 15 points: Well done. You must be a good communicator and your child must like to talk to you.
- 5 to 10 points: Not bad. Try to find out more about what your child is thinking and be more observant.
- 0 to 5 points: Not good. Sit down and talk with your child, then take the quiz again.

Of course this quiz is just a bit of fun, but it is a good way to start finding out more about your kids. Ask your children to make up their own quiz to give to you. I promise you it will be much more difficult than this one!

16

10 Tips for Getting Kids to Talk to You

"What did you do in school today?"
"Nothing."
"Did you have a good time at the party?"
"Yea."
"How was the field trip?"
"OK."

In our house, getting kids to talk is sometimes like pulling teeth. In fact, I would like to pull their teeth when they answer in monosyllables. I want to know every detail of what happened. (Other times, like when I am ready to go out or am rushing around like mad trying to juggle telephone calls, dinner, writing, and sanity, they saunter in and start chatting away like jay birds!) So how on earth do we get our children to talk to us?

1. Ask Specific Questions

Children may talk more if the questions are phrased in a way that requires a longer reply. Frankly, I'd be happy with full sentences at times. Try opening up the conversation with questions like:

- "What book are you reading at school?"
- "What was the funniest (weirdest, worst, and so on) thing that happened in school today?"

- "What kinds problems are you doing in math?"
- "What did they give you for lunch at school? What did you like best?"
- "What kinds of experiments are you doing in science?"
- "What songs are you singing in music? Do you like them or think they aren't very good?"
- "Who do you think had the best time at the party?"
- "What kinds of food did they give you to eat at the party? What did you think of it?"
- "How would you rate school today on a scale of one to ten? Why?"
- "You seem sort of thoughtful tonight, I wonder what you're thinking about? I'd like to know if you feel like talking about it."

Don't fling all these questions at them at once or they will think you've gone mad, which will probably confirm what they've suspected all along!

Notice that these questions ask for more than a yes or no answer. There is no guarantee that children will be more forthcoming if you ask them specific questions, but low-key, information-seeking questions are more likely to elicit a response. If your children don't carry on the conversation, let it drop and go on to talk with someone else. At least you've given them a chance.

2. Swallow the Editorial Comment—Don't Judge

Julie: My teacher is stupid!
Mother: Don't talk about your teacher that way. It's rude.
Julie: But she is.
Mother: I said don't talk like that.

End of conversation. As parents we all have feelings and judgments about how children should behave and talk. Julie was trying to get her mother to talk about a problem with her teacher, but she didn't succeed because her mother wasn't prepared to listen and take Julie's feelings into account. We've all done it. I remember my younger son telling me once he was hungry and my saying "No, you're not, you've just finished eating." After all, he couldn't be hungry unless he had a hollow leg. But I was wrong—he has a hollow leg!

How could Julie's mother have encouraged Julie to talk?

Julie: My teacher is stupid!
Mother: Oh?

Julie: You won't believe what she did today.
Mother: What?

Notice that Mother isn't agreeing that the teacher is stupid, but she is trying to get Julie to tell her more about what happened. Julie's mother is keeping her judgments to herself, even though she may think Julie's teacher is the best thing since sliced bread. As parents we often seem to deny our children's feelings, to jump to conclusions that somehow they are at fault, to give advice without finding out enough about the facts, or to defend the other party if our children are complaining about someone. One little boy called his mother at the office in tears because some children had picked on him. Before he could finish his first sentence, she interrupted with "What have you done to them?"

Face it, we all make mistakes when our children try to com municate with us, but the bottom line is that if we listen and give children a chance, they'll be more inclined to tell us things. Granted, it will still be on their terms, but at least they'll have the opportunity.

3. Allow Your Children Their Opinions

Children usually end up with many of the same values and opinions as their parents—when they are parents themselves. Until then, we can help communication by discussing issues, but not acting threatened if our children disagree with us. Even very young children have strong opinions about what they like to eat and wear, which may not suit us.

Lynn, a friend of mine, forces her children always to be color co-ordinated. I'm not kidding! Whenever they go out together as a family, everyone wears red or blue or beige, or whatever. Her eldest son, aged eight, is beginning to rebel. In his opinion, this is a silly idea. He wants to wear what he chooses to wear, regardless of what the rest of the family does. Lynn, an otherwise normal person in my opinion, has to adjust her own views about this, or her son has stated he won't go out with them. At least he is talking to his mother about it, and if she doesn't allow him to form his own opinions about this relatively trivial matter, I predict problems in the future over larger other issues.

Encourage your children from a young age to tell you what they think, and praise them for telling you, even if you don't agree. You don't have to change your opinions, however, and you may want to have calm discussions about your differences. For example, if your ten-year-old comes home and declares that eating animals is disgusting and she is now going to be a vegetarian, and you don't agree, tell her you are glad she is thinking about these issues. Let it ride for a while, and then let her know in a non-judgmental way what you think. But, at the same time, do not force her to eat meat.

One of the most exciting aspects of raising children is watching them grow and develop into their own people. As the oft-quoted prophet Kahlil Gibran once said about children: "You may strive to be like them, but not seek to make them like you." I would humbly add that most of us secretly hope they will adopt our more enlightened opinions and values and somehow shrug off our own worst faults.

4. Compliment Them

When your kids talk, try to find a way to say something complimentary about what they've said or how they've said it. When one of my sons decided to talk with some bizarre accent, I thought he sounded like a moose with marbles in his mouth. But I told him that I was impressed with his talent to mimic. Very few people tire of hearing praise about themselves or about something they have done. In our parental role, it seems as though we spend a great deal of time talking to our children about what they've done wrong, and how to correct their faults. No wonder they are often wary of talking to us. They have learned that the less they say, the fewer things we can find to criticize. I'd be quiet, too, if the majority of my conversations ended up with someone saying, "What's wrong with Michele and how can we fix it?"

Here are a few ways to compliment children when they are talking to us.

- "I admire the way you said that."
- "You've really thought this through, haven't you?"
- "You're clever."
- "I like talking with you."
- "I can see that you feel strongly about this. Strong opinions can help to change things."

Beware of complimenting without conviction or cause. Kids can see right through false compliments. Better not to say anything than to fake it.

Use compliments frequently, even if you are not having a discussion. Find a reason to tell your child that:

- you are glad he is persevering and learning his math even if it isn't his favorite subject.
- you are delighted she has cleaned up her room.
- you are pleased he was responsible and came home on time.
- you are proud she stood up for a friend.
- you know he was disappointed he didn't get the part he hoped for in the school play, but you think he has been very mature in handling the situation.

All these little communications will encourage your children to talk more, because they will feel good about being with you and good about themselves.

5. Be Light-hearted

If we can maintain a sense of humor and stay fairly laid-back, kids will be more likely to talk. A father I know, Tony, treats everything as a crisis. The minute a subject is raised he is yelling, tearing his hair out (what little is left), and going on and on about how terrible it all is. When one of his children gets in trouble at school for a minor infringement, you would think the world is going to end. I wonder what will happen if he has to deal with a real crisis. It is no surprise that the children in his family never bring anything up for discussion, and mealtimes are eerie. No one wants to venture an idea or bring up a problem for fear he will be hung, drawn, and quartered.

Another father who is a friend of mine, Gary, says that his family has shouting matches. His children feel confident enough to state their views strongly and they all enjoy these discussions. Listening to these free-for-alls as an outsider, his children might seem rude and difficult. But if you listen carefully, you will hear mutual laughter and respect for one another as points are argued. Gary is very laid-back and funny and has clearly given his children permission to talk. And talk they do. He says, "Sarcasm is out. Facts are always corrected. Feelings are allowed. Humor is essential." A good formula if ever I heard one.

6. Allow Them to Shine

We went to dinner with an elderly aunt recently. She is probably the most self-centered and talkative person I have ever met. She had not seen our children for several years. The gist of the conver sation was:

Boys: How do you do?
Aunt: Not very well. My arthritis is acting up. My children never come to see me. When I was your age I...

We surfaced two hours later, shell-shocked, and dying to get away as quickly as possible. She never asked a single question about the boys or us, or the outside world, for that matter. The only thing we knew for certain was that, whatever else might be bother ing her, her lungs and tongue were fine.

I asked the boys what they thought of the evening. "She wasn't very interested in anyone else, was she?" commented one. "I can see why her children never come to visit," said the other. "I bet she never asks them anything about their lives."

Kids, and the rest of us, like to have the spotlight at least once in a while. If all conversations are about the adults and adult concerns, children will soon learn not to talk. Try asking children about areas you know they are good in or can talk about with some authority. With young children, it might be the drawings they have done or the song they have learned to sing. Let them sing it, and give lots of praise. Older children might have expertise in sports, music, academic subjects or hobbies. Asking anyone about something they like or do well will usually bring a good response, especially if you pay rapt attention when he is talking. Obviously we don't want little show-offs who pout if someone is not paying constant attention to them, but we need to remember to give kids that chance to shine, even if we have to engineer it.

7. Avoid Lecturing

If you ask kids what irritates them most about parents, the top answer always is: "They're always lecturing." Our job is to incorporate teaching, and lecturing is part of teaching. If children think that talking with parents will result in some kind of lecture about either the good old days or the bad habits of children, they will clam up. They need to brush their teeth, clean up their rooms, do their homework, be kind to others, and turn off the television, and, sometimes that means a lecture, but it doesn't have to always be like that. Try:

- Using fewer words. For example, if Marina keeps forgetting to brush her teeth, say, "Toothbrush," instead of "You've forgotten to brush your teeth again." If Alex has neglected to take the dog out, say, "Dog," instead of "You're being irresponsible about the poor dog again—he has to go out now."
- Describing the situation factually instead of directing your anger at your child. For instance, if Charles should have emptied the

dishwasher, say, "I see the dishes are still waiting to be put away," instead of "You lazy boy, you haven't put the dishes away." If, as at our house, the children are constantly using the telephone, say, "Please, I need the telephone now," instead of "Get off that telephone this minute."

- Writing notes. Darcy, mother of two, uses this method often and swears by it. For example, children know they should not turn on the television until after a certain time, so she puts a note on the television saying, "Only turn me on at six P.M., please. Thank you." If Bethan has forgotten to clean her room, she puts a note on the door saying, "Room—Clean Please."

I know some of this won't be possible in a bustling family with working parents. We might be tempted to put a note on George's door saying: "Room for Rent, Kid Leaving," because he didn't get off the telephone immediately. However, it does work, especially if you give your children the choice between lectures and a few words. And it is such a relief to your vocal cords and frayed nerves!

8. Respect Their Silence

Sometimes kids just don't feel like talking. For that matter, neither do we. Give your children the space to think and reflect when they need it. One of the mistakes new counselors and psychologists make is to try to keep people talking. When I listen to the tapes I made with my first clients in 1968, I shudder. Every time they were quiet for longer than about thirty seconds, you could hear me coming in with some inane remark. My supervisor kindly pointed out that silence was useful, and people need time to collect their thoughts and to decide what, if anything, to say next. Talking is important, but silence can be a tonic as well.

9. Share Your Feelings

When talking to your children, be sure to explain that you, too, sometimes find things difficult. We often think that, as parents, we have to be perfect. It helps kids tremendously to know that we made mistakes growing up and to find out if we talked with our parents or grandparents. My sons have heard all about the time when I was eleven I decided to lead a school rebellion against our hated uniforms. I organized all the girls to come to school in strange outfits, or so I thought. On the day, only six of us turned up inappropriately dressed. Our parents were called and we were sent home in disgrace, though I suspect the teachers did see the funny side of it. My father had a chat with me that evening and I still recall that he asked me why I did it, told me that he understood, and said that peaceful protest was the democratic way of changing things we didn't like. He said he wasn't going to punish me, but asked how I was going to handle the situation. I wrote a note to the principal and ended up wearing the uniform every day.

I learned that a better way might have been to ask for a meeting with the principal before going all out on strike. My other crimes, such as pelting cars with eggs, taking apples from a neighbor's tree, going to a friend's house without telling anyone—thus sparking off a police search, and other things too numerous to mention, help when my boys do silly things they should have done differently. At least they know they have a misguided mother who also did silly things and somehow survived to become a (more or less) responsible adult.

10. Find the Best Time and Place to Talk

Whatever skills we use when talking with children, nothing will work when they are doing homework, watching their favorite television program, or getting ready to meet a friend. Attempts to converse will almost always end in failure. It is frustrating for both parent and child. When someone calls me at the office and I'm in the middle of finishing something im portant, I'm afraid I don't listen well, nor am I much of a conversationalist. Kids are no different. They are moving at their own pace and have their own agendas, so we have to adjust if we want to get through.

Try, instead, talking to your children while they are in the bath (if they haven't reached the privacy stage) or at bedtime, when they welcome the extra time because they don't have to go to sleep immediately. Some of the best and more rewarding conversations I have had with my sons have been at night with the lights out. In fact, even my eldest teenager still likes talking then. Now that they are older I might rub their backs and ask them how things have gone or if they are having any problems I can help with. When they were little, I read to them and cuddled them and we talked. If they were worried about something, like starting school or the dark, I tried to find a book about those issues so we could talk some more.

All this has paid dividends, but don't get me wrong, my kids still say "Nothing" if I happen to say "What did you do in school today?"

17

19 Ways to Deal With Those Important and Sometimes Embarrassing Questions

"What's the *Kama Sutra?*" my niece Laurie piped up in a voice that brought the conversation at adjoining tables to an immediate halt. Laurie was five and we were in a restaurant crowded with thousands of stern, disapproving types. Or so it seemed to my sister and I as we exchanged pained glances and told Laurie to "Speak a little more softly, dear." (The "dear" was said through clenched teeth. Why do they always find the most public time and place to ask the most embarrassing questions? I guess it's a gift children are born with.)

I patiently and carefully stepped through an answer. "Well, you know that men and women have sex...." Laurie interrupted. "To have babies," she said brightly. "That's right. There's a book that is kind of like a reading book with pictures, that gives men and women ideas about different ways to have sex." Laurie listened carefully, along with all the people at every table within 100 yards. "Oh," said Laurie, "but why did King John have to sign it?"

Magna Carta, Kama Sutra—they do sound a bit alike. Poor Laurie, she couldn't understand why we were weak with laughter, tears streaming down our cheeks. Looking back (Laurie is now twenty-six), my first response should have been a casual, "Where did you hear about that?" It would have saved Laurie a lot of confusion and us some embarrassment, but it has made a great family story over the years.

How can we avoid the pitfalls but still answer the important questions children ask us? I asked all my friends who are parents to come up with the most awkward, unusual, or difficult questions their children had asked, and I've added suggested replies. In most cases, the children had asked the question in a loud voice in a supermarket line, in the middle of a solemn religious service, or on a very quiet crowded bus. I'm sure you have many examples of your own that could top these!

1. What's Sex?

If possible, start when your children are very small and, when the opportunity presents itself—a pregnancy in the family is ideal—explain sex to them in simple. If you do this, you are less likely to receive this question out of the blue. If your child does ask, find out where he heard the term *sex*, to make sure someone has not been using it to explain or attempt abuse. One child sex offender I talked with said he told children that he was teaching them "sex" so they would know what to do when they grew up. Most likely your child will have come across the word on television or heard it discussed on the playground.

Explain that when grown-ups love each other they sometimes show it by having sex. This means that the man puts his penis into the woman's vagina, and they hold each other very close, and they like it. For a young child, this is usually more than enough explanation before they look at you in complete disbelief and go "Yuck!", followed by "Why?" When you explain that that's the way babies are made, but that having sex doesn't always produce babies, they'll say something like, "You and Daddy don't do that!" For older children a more complete description is in order, usually with books and drawings. I found several books with wonderful illustrations that were very helpful with my sons when they were each about four. As they grew older, we answered more and more questions until they got to the age when they'd rather giggle with friends than ask us.

I remember one evening sitting with my five-year-old on my lap watching a program about a seal cow being mated by a huge bull seal. I thought we'd done a good job of explaining the facts of life, especially when he said confidently, "I know what they're doing. They're having sex." "That's right," I replied. "With animals they call it mating." He watched for a few more minutes, then looked up at me and said in disgust, "Is *that* what you and Daddy do?" Back to the drawing board....

When fielding questions about sex answer them as completely as necessary for the child and be straightforward. I think it is a good idea to teach children the correct names for the parts of the body and to try not to be embarrassed by the mention of sex. This is the best way to ensure that our children have a healthy and natural outlook about sex. Most adults I know got their sex education from books left lying around by their parents in the hope that their children would read them and not ask anything. Usually, parents put the books out about five years too late.

2. What's AIDS?

My elder son, then eight, came home from school one day and declared that he wasn't sleeping with his little brother anymore because you could die from sleeping with someone. He had got the wrong message from a campaign to prevent the HIV virus spreading. As far as he was concerned, sleeping meant just that, and he wasn't taking any chances.

Older children will often have a better understanding of AIDS (Acquired Immune Deficiency Syndrome) than we adults because of informative teaching in schools. Younger children need to know that AIDS is a disease that affects mainly grown-ups, and that it is difficult to "catch" the "germ" that causes AIDS. To go further and explain that AIDS is only one consequence of infection by the Human Immunodeficiency Virus is more than children need to know. It may be the most correct explanation, but it is too confusing. Children need to know that you and they are not going to die from AIDS—that is often their overriding concern.

If a child or adult they know has AIDS, then seek professional help from an AIDS support organization or from your doctor.

3. What's Safe Sex? What's a Condom?

Because of the publicity about some diseases that can be sexually transmitted, like herpes and the HIV virus, children now ask questions about things many of us didn't even know about until we were adults. If children ask this before they know what sex is, you will need to start at the beginning with an explanation about sex. Then explain that, sometimes, a germ or virus can be given to a person through sex, but that there are ways to make sure this doesn't happen. One very good way is for the person with the virus not to have sex with anyone. Another way is for the people having sex to use something to keep the germs from spreading, such as a condom. Then draw a picture or show the child what a condom is and how it works. As your children become teenagers, it is imperative that you bring the subject up with them for their own protection. With the younger ones, I would wait until they ask.

You may, on the other hand, find yourself in the situation of the teacher who overheard two children on the playground. One child, age six said to the other, "I found a condom on the patio." Her friend replied, "What's a patio?"

4. What's Oral/Anal Sex?

For older children and young teenagers, explain that some people like to have sex in different ways. One way to have sex is called oral sex—people kiss and suck on the genitals. Another way is called anal sex—this involves putting a penis into someone's bottom. For younger children, you could say it is when people "have sex with each other's bottoms." I don't think you need to go into lots of detail with young children. It is better to give information in small bits until they are satisfied with the answer. Too much detail can be counterproductive.

5. How Do Babies Get Into the Tummy? How Do They Get Out?

Explain that sperm rush up to the egg in the mother's body and that the sperm and egg as tiny, as the head of a pin. Then the sperm and egg get together and form the very first cells of a new baby. As this new little baby grows, the mother's stomach grows to make room for it. When the baby gets big enough to live outside, the mother's body has a tubelike place wide enough to let the baby out. Of course, you can go into as much detail, with drawings, videos, and books, as you wish. Many children think that the baby comes out with the "pee pee," so I made sure my children knew it was a different tube! I didn't tell them that having a baby was like passing a watermelon.

6. What Will Happen to Me When We Get a New Baby?

A wise midwife friend, Audrey, told me never to tell my older son that when the new baby came, my older son would become my "big boy."

Children don't want to become the big boy or girl when it means they won't get all that wonderful attention they had before. Audrey told me to say, "You'll both be my babies. You'll always be my baby, even when you're grown-up!" She was right—it worked brilliantly.

7. What Is the Matter With That Person?

Children are often quite direct when they see someone who has a deformity, is in a wheelchair, is blind, or has an obvious birthmark or burns. Children don't mean to be hurtful; they are just curious. Try to prepare them in advance so they won't embarrass someone. Explain that we don't stare at people just because they are different from us. If they make the comment in public, take them aside and explain that some people are born that way and some people have accidents or diseases that cause them to look a certain way. It isn't funny or weird, it is just how they are, just as some people have blue eyes and some have brown. Ask them to remember that no one likes to be stared at or made fun of, so we should treat them just like everyone else.

8. What Does It Mean to Be Gay/Lesbian/Homosexual?

Explain that most men fall in love with women and most women fall in love with men, but some men fall in love with other men and some women fall in love with other women. If you are a man who loves a man, people call that gay or homosexual. If you are a woman who loves a woman, some people call that lesbian or homosexual. With older children, explain the liguistics that heterosexual means different sexes and homosexual means same sex.

9. Why Do People Hurt Children?

A is kidnapped, abused, or murdered child makes headlines, and children ask questions. I used to say that people who do this are sick, until a friend got sick and my children wanted to know if the friend would turn into a child abuser. Now I say that most people love children and would never harm them, but that some people have bad problems and they might hurt a child.

10. Should I Worry About All the Bad People Who Might Hurt Me?

Reassure your children that there are very few bad people who want to hurt children. Then explain that you cannot tell just by looking at someone if he might be bad, so it is best not to talk to people they don't know, especially if they are on their own. Draw up a list of "safe" people, such as police officers, with your child. It is easier to have a "I can talk to these people if I'm on my own" list than for a child to try to determine who is safe. Or make a blanket rule that your child should not talk to or go off with anyone unless she checks with you.

11. What's Rape/Incest/Sexual Abuse?

Find out where your child heard the term and then give enough information to satisfy him. With a young child, rape can be described as someone touching his genitals or "private parts" in a way that he doesn't like or want. Incest or sexual abuse can be described as a relative or another adult or teenager touching genitals and asking the child to keep it a secret. For an older child, you will have to describe the term more fully. With the many programs and news articles referring to rape, incest, sexual abuse, AIDS, and so on, children will be asking questions whether we're ready or not.

12. Why Don't They Have a Baby?

When friends or relatives don't have children, your kids may think it strange and ask awkward questions. Daphne, an experienced nanny, but with no children of her own (probably because of her many years of experience!), was approached by one of her young charges, Sarah. "Nanny, I know why you don't have a baby. You've got to sleep with a man. I don't know what you do when you sleep but that's the only way you'll get a baby." Daphne laughed, but some people are sensitive about the issue, so we need to tell children that not everyone wants to have children and that some people cannot have children. Also explain that it is a private matter, and we don't ask people about it because it might make them feel bad.

13. What Happens When We Die?

How you answer this depends upon your beliefs. Some parents tell their children that you go to heaven or hell, or you become part of the universe, or you come back in another life. Others say that there is no afterlife and that when you die there is nothing. I think children find it more comforting to believe that a loved one who has died has gone somewhere like heaven, rather than just "gone."

Another aspect of this question is what happens to our bodies. Tell them that our bodies go into the earth to become part of nature and that it doesn't hurt. (See chapter 29 for more ideas).

14. What's That?

Your child comes into the bathroom pointing to your penis, or vagina, or breast, and asks what it is. Without embarrassment, tell them what it's called and what it's for and carry on. Some fathers get worried that the child might go to school and say, "I saw my Daddy's penis," setting into motion a social work investigation of child abuse! As long as you don't tell children to "keep this a secret," it is highly unlikely this would happen. If you are still worried, be sure to lock the bathroom door.

There are hundreds of questions children ask, and we will never get it right all of the time. But there are some pitfalls we can try to avoid when talking with our children.

Pitfalls to Avoid

If a child, particularly a young child, asks a question that startles you because it doesn't seem appropriate to his or her age:

15. Swallow Your Surprise or Embarrassment

Parents have to be fairly good actors or our kids will never ask us anything remotely embarrassing. They'll remain in the dark or ask another child, who will either misinform them or tell them too much.

16. Find Out the Real Question

If we had asked my niece Laurie where she'd heard of the *Kama Sutra,* we would have answered her real question about the Magna Carta. Laurie's class was having a storybook read to them, and she somehow confused it with a line overheard from adult conversation. However, it was remotely possible that there could have been a more sinister reason for Laurie's question—that someone was abusing her and had shown her pornography—but this wasn't the case. Most questions turn out to have innocent explanations, but it always pays to find out.

17. Don't Avoid the Questions

Probably the worst thing we can do when children ask us questions is to say, "I'll tell you when you're older," or "You don't need to know," or "Don't worry about that." Children ask when they need to know or are worried about something. If we avoid answering or indefinitely postpone our replies, then they have learned an important lesson—not to ask us. If we answer them now, later they may come to us with questions that could literally save their lives—questions about drugs, safe sex, or drinking. They may also feel more comfortable about telling us if something untoward happens, such as abuse, if we have established that we are willing to listen and try our best to answer their questions and concerns.

18. Honesty Is the Best Policy

Although we have to keep our amusement or horror to ourselves when children ask certain questions, it is a good idea to admit that we don't always know the answers. But we should always say that we'll find out, and let them know as soon as we can. This also gives you time to think about how to respond to questions that throw you, or to check out your ideas with someone else.

19. Give Age-Appropriate Answers

If Laurie *had* been asking about the *Kama Sutra,* then the answer we gave was enough information for her. The rule of thumb is to give children the facts gradually until they are satisfied with the answer. Let them keep asking questions, rather than bombard them with tons of information they don't need or want.

Keep these last few points in mind and you'll never be in the position of the father I heard about from a speaker at a conference. He told of a four-year-old boy who came into a room full of people and asked in a loud voice, "Dad, where did I come from?" His father excused himself, took his son into another room, sat him down, and patiently explained about lovemaking, how the sperm and egg got together, and how the baby grows inside his mother's womb and then comes into the world. The son listened intently and then said, "But where did I come *from?* Fred says he's from Boston."

18

9 Ways Through the Moral Maze

Horrifying newspaper reports of children robbing, or even raping and murdering, make us ask what is going wrong with parenting. Do today's parents find it too difficult to teach right from wrong?

When Your Child Disappoints You

Jenny was driving her nine-year-old son's friends home after a play date. The boys were giggling in the back seat of the car. "Did you see it trying to fly away?" whispered Paul. She heard flapping noises and more giggles. Not wanting to be left out, Jenny asked "What's so funny?" Suddenly there was embarrassed silence and her son Alex said, "Oh, nothing." Jenny was curious, but didn't pursue it until she had dropped off the other boys. On the way home, she noticed that Alex was quiet. "What was all that about?" asked Jenny again.

Alex squirmed. Jenny could see he didn't want to talk about it, but this only added to her growing sense of unease. "Come on, tell me about it," Jenny urged. "Well, we found this bird when we were playing and it had a broken wing. It was flapping around. Paul said we should put it out of its misery, so we started throwing stones and things at it." Alex bit his lower lip and stopped. "Go on," said Jenny. She listened, but dreaded what she was going to hear. Alex took a deep breath, "We chased it and killed it."

Jenny was thunderstruck. Her sweet, gentle Alex, who she thought she had raised to be kind and compassionate to all living things, was confessing to heartlessly killing a poor, wounded creature. So much for the values and morals she thought she had instilled in him.

Values? Morals? Are we allowed to mention the words—is it politically correct to do so? If we teach our children to be kind and generous to others, will someone be offended because we aren't teaching them to be self-aware enough and are exploiting them? Should we come down on them like a ton of bricks if they steal something from a store, or do we ignore it because "It's a stage and we don't want to upset their psyches"? Have we become so understanding of people with problems that we can't take a stand on morals and values? If we teach our children four basic values, I think the rest will follow.

1. Kindness and Compassion

This brings us back to Jenny and Alex and the first value to teach children: kindness and compassion. It wasn't that Alex didn't know the value of kindness; he did and he felt bad when his mother confronted him with her disappointment. His friends were another story. When Jenny told the other boys' mothers, they were unconcerned and even a bit annoyed that she brought it up. "It was only horseplay. Don't be such a spoilsport!" said one.

Jenny discovered that it wasn't enough just to tell Alex he should be kind and compassionate, but that she needed to discuss why and to show him the right way to behave. She had a long talk with Alex and explained ways to get out of such a situation should it arise in the future. She also took him to an animal sanctuary (which he later raised money for by doing a sponsored walk) and impressed upon him the importance of humane treatment of animals. Although he still plays with those friends, they have never repeated their cruel actions, as far as Jenny knows. Although she can't change the attitudes of the other families, Jenny hopes that Alex will influence them, rather than the other way around. Her discussions with Alex and having him take the consequences of his actions in a positive way by raising money for the sanctuary were brilliant ways of helping him learn a better way to behave. Jenny did not tell Alex that he was a terrible person, but she did make it clear that what he had done was terrible.

Too often we read of criminals, murderers, and rapists who have at one time been bullies or had killed or tortured animals. I know from my work with young offenders that many were bullies, cruelly tormenting other children, and that no one ever stopped them. In fact, one young teenager said to me that everyone was very understanding of all his problems, but no one tried to develop any kindness in him. Certainly, he had been neglected as a child, but with everyone so careful not to blame him, he felt he could just carry on being horrible.

2. Understanding Consequences

If someone had given the young offender to whom I had spoken cause to think, and there had been consequences to his actions, perhaps the young mother that he mugged would not have suffered a broken shoulder and jaw. The idea of consequences seems to be quite unpopular these days. Why? I think it's because some people feel that there are so many social injustices that no one should be blamed for anything. But I also think that children who develop an understanding that there are consequences to actions are well equipped to deal with life's ups and downs.

Take the case of Daniel Jewell, a British fifteen-year-old who was beaten by three boys and then kicked as he lay on the ground. He staggered home and was taken to the hospital by his father. The doctor said that internal bleeding had left him within ten minutes of death. The boys who beat him had been bullying him for some time, and it escalated into this tragedy. The boys were convicted of grievous bodily harm, sentenced to young offender institutions, and were publicly named by the court.

These are logical consequences to actions, you might say, especially if it had been your child beaten nearly to death. Yet a "training officer" who goes round to schools teaching a "no blame" approach to bullying, stated in a newspaper that "naming the accused is an awful thing to do and is counterproductive." I beg to differ! Why should you keep the names of the offenders, at least of those old enough to know better, secret when they have done something so wrong? Surely, one of the consequences to these actions should be to realize you have done something against the values of the community, and be ashamed. It is shaming to be named in public, but isn't that productive rather than counterproductive? To humiliate and degrade the culprits would be counterproductive. In my opinion that would serve no purpose except to make the offenders even more vindictive. However, a little old-fashioned shame might bring about a change in attitude.

Fortunately, very few of our children will ever be involved in such horrific cases, but we can help them along with their understanding of consequences by our own example and by discussion. If a store clerk mistakenly gives you $5 extra change, it is very tempting to grab the money and run. But this would be an excellent oppor tunity to help your child think about consequences. Say to the clerk, "I think you gave me too much change," and subsequently explain to your child that, otherwise, the clerk might have to put the money back from her own purse or even lose her job. You could also explain that taking the money is stealing and that if everyone did it, the store would have to close. Then ask your child what he thinks. You can at various times expand the discussion to other issues important to you, be it war, the environment, poverty, or whatever. But don't try to do it all at once, or you will find your child running for the nearest exit or hiding under the bed to get away from old moralizing mommy or daddy! And I would be right there with him. No one likes a self-righteous bore.

It's always a good idea to talk about good consequences and to reward children when they do something well, too. It is vital that kids know there are good and bad consequences to actions. When our sons are recognized for outstanding achievements or work, we take them out for a treat. I guess we just have to hope that there are more times we can salute the good than deal with the bad!

3. Honesty

When I asked several friends (all parents) what were the most important values they would teach children, honesty came up more than anything else. If we teach our children about consequences and help them develop a conscience, helping them to be honest should be an easier task. On the other hand, there are so many ways to be dishonest, breaking promises, lying, cheating from someone else's homework, and so on. And it does make it more difficult for us ordinary folks when many of our so-called leaders are setting bad examples with headline-grabbing news about marital cheating, politicians "forgetting" to mention gifts and money, and important people making lots of money from insider trading.

Still, there are ways to help children learn to be honest. When one of my sons, then age seven, took a trinket from a store, I scolded him and marched him back to the store with the item. He begged me not to make him go, but it was vital that he understood the consequences of his actions. I was very careful not to call my son a thief, and I told him that I did love him, but I did not like what he had done. He then knew he shouldn't have taken it. He was miserable and ashamed and vowed never to do it again. Good! I was pretty miserable, too, though I have a dim memory of having done something similar as a kid.

I think we can help kids think about honesty by asking them questions such as:

- Why is it wrong to lie?
- Who is hurt by lying?
- Why is it wrong to cheat on a test or to copy someone else's homework?
- Why is it wrong to steal?

If your child answers, "Because you get caught," that's honest, but you've got a lot of work to do! Explain that:

- Lying, stealing, and cheating hurt other people, but also the person who does it. The culprit has to continue lying to cover up the lies, the stealing, or the cheating, and will probably feel bad inside. Certainly, parents and friends would be disappointed if they knew.
- Sometimes children can't figure out a way to stop because they get into the habit of doing these things, but that you will always try to help him if he needs it. That doesn't mean bailing him out of the consequences, but it does mean you will do your best to think of possible solutions and ways to change behavior.
- Honesty is the best policy. Stick to your principles, but also try not to punish your child if she does tell the truth, even if she has done something wrong. It might be worth skipping the wrong behavior in favor of praising their honesty!

4. Developing a Conscience

I like to think my son developed a conscience because of that little stealing episode, but there is never a guarantee that when our children are out of our sight they will do the right thing. If I could only teach my children three values, developing a conscience would be one. When we were growing up, it always seemed as if a little voice inside nagged at me if I did something wrong. My father told me the voice was my conscience; and a persistent little creature it was. I'm sure I needed it and, luckily, it was reinforced by the teachers in school and by the church I attended.

It certainly seems harder today to help my own children develop a conscience. Here I confess that we don't go to church, except for special occasions like Christmas. My children don't have that tradition, but that is our choice. Also, the teachers seem to be far too busy teaching subject matter to spend time on moral issues. So, for many families like ours we have to take full responsibility for trying to instill consciences in our kids. I will keep working at it—my conscience won't let me do otherwise!

Ways To Teach Values

There are so many things we want to teach our children: fairness, responsibility, courage, humanity...the list goes on and on. But it seems to me that if we start with kindness and compassion, honesty, developing a conscience, and an awareness of consequences, then these other values will naturally follow. The specific ways I can think of to get our values across to our kids are all based on old-fashioned communication.

5. By Example

We can teach values to our children through our own actions. And we can reinforce good morals when we hear about various good deeds, such as people who risk their lives to save others, people who try to help starving children, people who speak out for their beliefs, or people who excel in music, sport, academics, and so on. Stories like this abound in the media every day.

6. By Explanation and Discussion

Don't be afraid to express your approval or disapproval of what is going on, and to explain why. If you give money to a cause, tell your children why you are doing it. Equally, if you do not approve, explain what your values are. Discuss with your children their opinions and encourage them to start expressing their own values.

7. By Using Books, Films, Television

Use books, films, and television programs as a point of dis cussion. In C.S. Lewis's *The Narnia Chronicles,* children encounter love, hate, loyalty, and deception. In *The Lord of the Flies,* the child characters deal with cruelty, loyalty, honesty, courage, and responsibility, as well as countless other values. Little Lord Fauntleroy shows courage, compassion, and kindness and brings out the best in his grumpy old grandfather. And, of course, *Oliver Twist* deals with the larger-than-life issues of child thieves, murder, revenge, and the shining courage of Nancy in saving Oliver from a life of poverty and degradation. If you are religious (and even if you aren't), the Bible has some riveting tales, and you can use numerous other religious books. (See p. 146 for a list of books for teaching values.)

The wonderful thing about books is that they offer heroes and heroines to emulate, villainous actions to despise and distance yourself from, and characters to stimulate thought. And, if you are working through a particular problem with your child, you can always ask the librarian for books about subjects such as lying, courage (*The Diary of Anne Frank* and *The Red Badge of Courage* were childhood favorites of mine), friendship, and so forth. All of the books I have mentioned are also films or television shows, so you can watch them with your children and discuss them if reading is a problem.

8. By Asking "What If?" Questions

Posing dilemmas is another excellent way for children to learn about values. This hit home quite graphically when I asked my children what they would do if they saw someone lying on the sidewalk. Soon after, we were traveling in the car and one of the children pointed out a man who had collapsed on the street, and asked us to drive around again "to see if he was OK." We did, stopped the car, and watched in amazement as people literally stepped over him, presuming that he was drunk. My sons and I got out, went over to him, and discovered that he was having an epileptic fit. Other people *then* stopped and joined in to help when they saw the man was convulsing. Thank goodness an ambulance passed by and we waved it down. We never found out how the man fared, but my kids felt good that they had helped.

9. Be Willing to Take a Stand As a Parent

This is fairly self-explanatory. The best way to teach values is to draw a line in the sand and stick to it. It won't be long before your children know exactly what you do and don't expect of them.

Changing Values

I have not adopted all the values I grew up with. I don't, for example, teach my own children that they will go to Hell without passing Go if they do something bad. Nor do I insist that they kiss all their relatives goodbye so they won't hurt their feelings. My kids' feelings about owning their own bodies are more important to me.

We used to place a value on children being seen and not heard. We also used to "value" children working down mines in and up in chimneys. In some countries, they still value children as slave labor. I recently saw a documentary in which a man said, "Of course we use children to tie the tiny knots in the carpets. They are valuable because their fingers are so small." Another person defended the use of children to make and pack matches for the same reason, in spite of the fact that the children were suffering, going blind, and dying of malnutrition. I felt like hitting the television (I quite often feel like hitting the television, actually). So, I guess it is a good idea to question values, especially if they hurt someone else. This doesn't mean we have to have a moral vacuum, but simply that we should not be afraid to stand up for what we believe and know to be right. It seems to me to be just plain common sense to say loudly and clearly that we want our children to have values, and that we're proud if they do, regardless of whether they are the same values we grew up with. Our values might not be exactly the same as they were in the distant past, but I suspect that my grandmother would agree with ninety percent of what I've written.

One thing that has changed that she would definitely not approve of is pregnant women and old people standing on public transportation while healthy, strong children and young people sit. I always get up and offer a seat, because it was one of the values taught to me. It drives me nuts when children push past to sit down, leaving their elders tottering.

One thing is certain, however: Common sense should always be used with values. I was standing with one of my sons on the bus when an elderly white-haired gentleman at least twenty years older than me got up and offered me his seat. My son looked at me and I wondered what to do. The man was being kind and compassionate. He would have been offended and embarrassed if I had said no. I graciously accepted. I didn't even need to explain it to my son. When we got off the bus, he reassured me that "It was the right thing to do, Mom."

It Sometimes Works

I know we don't always get it right, but we try our best and, once in a while, something happens that makes you feel it was worth it. I will remember until my dying day a Saturday morning just after the James Bulger murder trial had ended. James was the three-year-old English boy who was kidnapped from a shopping mall and murdered by two ten-year-old boys, which caused shock and outrage around the world. I was driving my eleven-year-old son to football and was stopped at a traffic light when the "Don't Walk" sign flashed and our light turned green. Frozen in the middle of the road was a blind man who had obviously become slightly confused. It was single-lane traffic and the driver behind me could not see what had happened. He began honking.

Before I could say a word, my son was out of the car. He escorted the man across the road and jumped back into his seat. In the meantime, the light turned red for us. As we finally pulled out and turned the corner, a taxi driver pulled up next to me and signalled for me to roll down the window. I did so, half expecting to be told off, but the man smiled, handed something to my son, and said, "Have a treat on me. I wish we had a million more like you." As he drove off, my son looked at the money in his hand and asked why the driver had done that. I knew the driver and I were contrasting my son's actions with those of the boys who had murdered Jamie—my son was the same age as they were—but I couldn't say a word. My eyes and heart were too full. Maybe, just maybe, my son had a few good values to see him through.

Perhaps I should have urged my son to give his money to charity, but I told him to keep it and buy a treat. Virtue may be its own reward, but a little reinforcement never hurt.

Ten Important Values

If I had to pick out the most important values that I really hope my children will take through life, they would be:

- Compassion
- A conscience
- An understanding of consequences to actions
- Honesty
- A sense of responsibility
- Courage
- Respect
- A sense of fairness
- Sportsmanship
- Sympathy for others

Have you ever had a "values" dilemma, or have you a great way to teach children a way through the moral maze? Let me know and I will include it in the next edition. And I will use it with my own kids!

Books for Teaching Values

Young Children

Pinocchio	Loyalty, conscience, lying
The Three Little Pigs	Hard work, loyalty, courage
Snow White	Cruelty, kindness, love, loyalty
The Tale of Peter Rabbit	Lying, disobedience, love
The Sneetches	Prejudice
The Grinch	Greed
Horton Hears a Who	Everyone is valuable
The Lorax	Environment
Charlotte's Web	Helping each other
The Wind in the Willows	Kindness, loyalty
Please & Thank You (Richard Scarry)	Manners, consideration

Older Children

Aesop's Fables	Full of tales of wisdom
Watership Down	Courage, environment, evil, loyalty
Little Women/Little Men	Respect, responsibility, caring
The Wizard of Oz	Courage, love, intelligence
The Beech Tree	Love, understanding
The Secret Garden	Kindness, caring, assertiveness
A Christmas Carol	Consequences, kindness, conscience
The Trumpeter of Krakow	Courage
Kes	Courage, prejudice, kindness, caring
Black Beauty	Kindness to animals
The Adventures of Tom Sawyer	Conscience, respect, loyalty, kindness
The Adventures of Huckleberry Finn	Consequences, honesty, prejudice

19

10 Ways to Motivate Your Child to Be a Winner

Have you ever wondered why some children seem to develop certain traits or skills and wished that your child could do the same? "I just wish Will would learn to play the piano. I always regretted that I didn't," or "My children don't enjoy reading, but my nieces and nephews seem to love it," or "Sally is so popular and funny. If only my Judith were like that."

Why do some children seem to succeed, while others with equal ability just get by? It isn't always the brightest or those born into families with power and influence who excel. Just having money or privileges, or even being intelligent, counts for very little if you aren't motivated to succeed.

Here are ways we can help our children to become winners, each in his own way.

1. Share Your Own Interests and Skills

Charlie is an excellent saxophone player. He plays with the school band and has won honors in many contests. Everyone comments on how lucky his parents are to have such a talented son.

Shelly loves science. She has won prizes in school science fairs ever since she first started school. Her science teacher foresees a promising future for her at a top university, and then in the field of research. Maybe she will find a cure for some dread disease.

147

James is the star soccer player in his school. He gets his work done so he can practice his skills every day. No one pushes him; he does it for the sheer joy of playing.

If Lisa has a spare moment, she is either reading a book or writing a story. She is full of ideas and is a bright, popular girl who is seen as a class leader. "Wish we had more like her," her principal commented to her parents.

These four young people have different interests and skills, but they have one important thing in common. Each child has a parent who also excels in or is interested in her child's particular skill. And each child's parent has helped his child foster that skill. A parent's interest and support in a skill or subject can be a very powerful influence on a child.

Charlie's mother loves music and, although she can't play a note, music and singing are common in in Charlie's home. His mother remembers dancing around the kitchen, "Pregnant, singing away to the radio." When Charlie was born, his parents played music to him and sang him to sleep at night. Charlie grew up associating music with warmth, love, and fun. His parents could not afford a piano, much to his mom's regret. She would have loved for him to play the piano. But when an elderly relative died, an old saxophone was found among his possessions, and it was given to young Charlie. His parents had it refurbished and Charlie taught himself to play with a do-it-yourself book. Charlie, now sixteen, plans a career in music.

Shelly's mother teaches science. Shelly's room seems at first glance to be a complete mess, but on further inspection you see experiments going on everywhere. Her mother says, "She was pulling apart toys to see how they worked as soon as her fingers would let her. I was half afraid that I would come down one morning to find her taking apart the refrigerator." But Shelly's mother didn't clean up the messes Shelly made; instead she sat down with her daughter and complimented her on what she was doing. She was always interested in Shelly's experiments. "I didn't try to turn her into a scientist, it just came about naturally," she says.

Jamie's dad played soccer with his local club, and Jamie and his sister were taken to matches from the time they could first walk. The whole family went along and often spent the entire day out with picnics and lots of fun and laughter. Their father spent loads of time just "fooling around and kicking the ball about with the kids." Not surprisingly Jamie and his sister ended up loving the game.

Lisa's parents don't watch much television. When Lisa was little, her parents read to her and let her play with books. Although she is thirteen, Lisa still enjoys cuddling up to her mother or father when each reads Lisa her own books. Sunday morning is an orgy of newspaper reading, with everyone in the family competing to read out the most humorous, bizarre, or interesting story of the day. Debate over issues brought up is often boisterous and good-natured. Clearly, that family emphasis on reading has paid dividends.

None of these parents put pressure on their children. They simply spent time and had fun with their children about what turned out to be a shared interest. No hidden messages like "You'd better do this" were sent—just loads of attention, approval, and support attached to the activities. Try:

- spending time with your children in the activity you wish to encourage.
- making the activity as fun as possible so children will want to do it.
- paying lots of attention to your child when she shows an independent interest in the activity.
- praising and rewarding your children's efforts.

2. Build Your Child's Self-esteem With Praise

"What a big girl!" Two-year-old Sarah's mother scoops up her daughter and gives her a big hug. Sarah squirms with delight. What has brought about this jubilation? Sarah has put her sweater on by herself. The fact that it is back to front and inside out doesn't matter. She feels proud of her achievement; her mother is starting her on the road to high self-esteem.

When Jamie missed an important goal and felt really terrible, his dad's comment was, "Never mind, there's always a next time and you did your best." Jamie still wished he had made the goal, but he knew that his dad still had faith in him.

School results for Lucy were not as good as she'd hoped, but she and her parents knew that she hadn't given it her best effort. In fact, they had had angry words about how her study habits took second place to her desire to go out with friends and talk on the telephone. Lucy was disappointed with the results. Her parents wanted to say "told you so," but bit their tongues and instead said, "We know you aren't happy with what you've done, and we believe you can do better. How can we work together to make sure this doesn't happen again?" They were giving Lucy the message that they knew she had it in her to do better instead of telling her that she was a failure.

Children who feel good about themselves are much more likely to become winners. Building self-esteem is one of the most important things we can do for children, and we can start from the moment they give us that first smile. When we smile back and say to our babies that they are brilliant (even if it was just a burp that produced that smile), they don't understand the words, but they soon get the idea. Of course, it will need to be tempered with kindness and compassion and all those other things discussed in the chapter on values, but a child with self-esteem is ready to try anything.

Try using some of the following messages with your children.

When It Doesn't Quite Work Out

- "Nice try, I'm proud of you."
- "You've really improved."
- "You're doing much better."
- "Great effort."
- "I can tell you've been practicing."
- "You're getting the hang of it."
- "You really stuck to that."
- "You've come a long way."
- "Every day it's getting a little better."
- "Things take time, don't be discouraged."
- "Rome wasn't built in a day."
- "You're learning a lot."

Praise for Achievement

- "Brilliant."
- "Well done."
- "I'm so proud of you and what you've done."
- "Smart girl/boy."
- "Fantastic."
- "You deserve to be very proud."
- "You're a winner."
- "You're a star."
- "You're first rate—couldn't be better."
- "Marvelous achievement."
- "You've outdone yourself."

- "I'm so proud that you're my son/daughter."

I am sure that you have a million things you could say. These are just to get you going. Praise works wonders to build self-esteem. Try it!

3. Encourage Curiosity

"Why doesn't the moon crash into the earth?" asked Tony. "That's a very good question, young man. It's got to do with gravity," replied his grandfather. "What's gravity?" "Well, it's the pull of the earth. It keeps us from falling off the earth and other things from falling down on us," said his grandfather. "But, I don't understand," said Tony. "I've got a great idea, Tony, let's go to the library and find a book that can explain it a bit better." Tony and his grandfather found a book and then did a couple of experiments that were at the right level of understanding for Tony. But, more importantly, Tony's grandfather showed Tony ways to find out information and that everyone goes on learning regardless of age. He fostered Tony's curiosity instead of giving him a perfunctory answer to get rid of the pesky kid. Telling Tony that his question was a good one will also make Tony want to ask more questions.

Encourage children's curiosity by:

- Answering their questions as best you can.
- Saying things like, "I am really pleased you are asking questions," instead of sighing and rolling your eyes.
- Comment to others in front of your children that you love it when they are curious about things, instead of saying "He drives me nuts with all his questions." That is a sure way to stop curiosity dead in its tracks.
- Involve yourself in finding answers with your children—don't just tell them to go look it up themselves. Your involvement makes it more likely that they will ask again, and that their curiosity will grow.
- Never say "Curiosity killed the cat!"

4. Encourage Lots of Different Experiences

Tom loved the science museum. "I finally had to drag him away in order to pick up the other children on time. He burst into tears because there were many more levers, buttons, and wheels to push and turn, and he wanted to do it all. I promised to bring him again next week. I never thought he would enjoy it so much." Tom's father was pleasantly surprised that his son would be so excited about the museum. He thought that it might be too tame after things like amusement parks and computer games.

Children's will expand their intellectual horizons if they have the opportunity to experience as many different activities and interests as possible. By making the effort to get your children to as many different places and activities as you can—exhibitions, museums, plays, movies, concerts, railway journeys, sporting events, and anything else you can think of—you increase their appreciation of life's experiences. Although many children get information about the world from television, and though much of that information is excellent, it is a poor substitute for hands-on experience.

When Jane took her five-year-old goddaughter to a concert for the first time, she was amazed that the little girl thought music came from cassettes. She really did not know that people played the instruments. "I just assumed that somewhere along the way she would have realized this," said Jane. "The good thing is that she now wants to try an instrument, though I do think the tuba is too big for her!"

You need to give your children a variety of things that might inspire them to try something new and different, and that gives them more opportunities to shine and to develop new skills. Perhaps Tom's parents will get him a science-experiment kit for Christmas instead of another computer game, and by doing so they might set him on a different path in life. You never know.

Here are a few ways to widen your child's horizons.

- Find out what is happening locally that might be interesting, and try to arrange to take your children.
- Check for the free or discount days at museums and go with your children and their friends. Make it a fun excursion and take lunch and some treats.
- Look for interactive children's theaters in your area.
- Enroll your child in a pottery, tap-dancing, or cooking class.
- Find out about half-price tickets for plays, and support your local theater groups.
- If your children have never been to a professional or minor league sporting event, take them.
- Watch out for specials from Amtrak or local transportation authorities when you can take your children on a daytrip for a very small price, or even free, with your ticket.
- Get your children library cards and take them often.

- Go to concerts in parks, churches or libraries. Many children have never heard instruments played live.

The more things children try, the more likely it is they will find something they enjoy and that will improve their self-esteem.

5. Help Your Children Assess Their Strengths

"I just don't know what to do for my project," Darren told his mother. Darren's teacher had asked his class to write about what they saw themselves doing in ten years' time. "Let's think about what you like to do and what you're good at, and then see what kinds of things you could do with those strengths," replied his mother. A wise woman, Darren's mom. She was helping him to think for himself and to appreciate his own abilities. Together they made a list of Darren's strengths:

Reading
History
Writing
Thinking of ideas to save the environment
Loving animals
Playing football
Good balance
Good eyesight
Gets along with friends
Likes traveling
Skiing
Swimming
Happy most of the time
Feeding the goldfish
Good hand-eye coordination

When they had compiled the list, they looked up a variety of jobs and activities at the library, knowing full well that in ten years' time lots of other jobs not even thought of today will be possible. Darren thought that being a veterinarian was a great idea because he loves animals, but that his lack of interest in science would probably be a hindrance. The idea of writing and broadcasting about environmental issues was very appealing as was becoming a sports coach, because he enjoys games and likes working with people. He rejected being a travel guide because of his indifference to learning languages, but he thought he might write a travel guide.

Darren eventually decided to do his project on being a broadcaster who played soccer with his local club on weekends. He felt quite good about his project and learned that his strengths and interests now would probably influence what he did in later life.

If children can be helped to realize their own strengths, it can make a difference in their attitudes toward school and other activities. Darren's mother posted his strengths on the front of the refrigerator and noticed that Darren would sometimes pause beside the fridge and read them over with a smile on his face.

Help your children by:

- making lists with them of their strengths.
- posting the lists and updating them when necessary.
- encouraging them to think about their strengths.
- praising the things they do.
- finding examples of people who have used similar strengths to do exciting or interesting things in life.
- giving them biographies of people who have achieved things that you think your child might be interested in.
- encouraging them to ignore any weaknesses they can't change or that don't hinder them. Too often, people focus on what they can't do rather than what they can.

6. Help Your Children Decide What They Want to Accomplish

In the summer, just before the beginning of each new school year, Angela sits down with her children individually and helps them think of what they would like to accomplish that year, academically, socially and in other activities. It isn't a great long list, but it includes goals for the year and sometimes longer term goals such as eventual career plans. One of her children's lists included:

- Get to school on time.
- Get a better grade in French.
- Turn in homework on time.
- Get to know at least one new student.
- Keep my friends.
- Do at least one good deed for someone.
- Improve in gymnastics.

Angela goes over each child's list, listens to concerns, and makes suggestions. She also notes anything that might signify a problem. Because her daughter had mentioned "Keep my friends" on her list,

Angela asked if her daughter was happy about what was happening with her friends. She learned that her daughter was quite worried about starting the new year because she was feeling left out. They decided to invite friends over before school started and the problem was nipped in the bud.

Put the lists in a safe place and go over them once a term to see if your children are achieving the goals, and think about how you can help if they aren't.

Try:

- helping your children think of what they want to achieve.
- discussing with them how to reach their goals.
- helping them set realistic targets. Being elected to the Senate at age eight might be a bit ambitious (although it could be an improvement on some Senators), but visiting local governmental offices and finding out how to go about becoming an elected official as an adult is realistic.
- helping them to break the goal into manageable bits. Saving the whales is a great idea, but perhaps it needs to be done in stages.
- updating their goals with them on a regular basis.

7. Help Your Child Cope with Disappointment

Susan was desperate to get the lead in the school play, but when the roles were announced, she was playing a minor character. She fled the school and ran home, bursting into tears as she came through the door. Her father knew how much she had practiced and rehearsed for the audition and how much it meant to her. He remarked "We all know that there are disappointments and discouraging things that happen in life. I've certainly had my fair share, but somehow it always seems worse if it happens to your child. You want to take the hurt away, take it on yourself instead of on them."

A completely understandable reaction—I feel the same way. But learning to be successful inevitably includes setbacks. If our children learn to deal with these disappointments they will be less likely to be pulled down into depression by life's curveballs.

Susan's father didn't know what to say, so he wrapped his daughter up in a big hug and told her soothingly that he was so proud she had auditioned for the play because he himself would never have had the courage. He didn't care what part she had, it was better than he had ever done in the theater. To his delight, his daughter stopped crying and looked at him in astonishment. Her father was an executive with a large company and was always making presentations, so this was news to her.

Sarah didn't realize that her father had always been terrified of getting up in front of people and even now had to steel himself. He told her about the time when he was in school and had wanted to run for a student election. He practiced and practiced what he was going to say, but he never went through with it—nerves got the better of him. Because he was determined to go into a business that demanded this skill, he had taken a course in public speaking. So, even though he didn't enjoy it, he could do it.

Sarah's father said he didn't know how to help Sarah cope, but he instinctively did the right thing for her. By sharing his own sense of failure at not trying out for the student election, he showed her that people get through these things and are sometimes motivated to change. He also made her feel good that she had been brave enough to audition for the play in the first place, something he had never been able to do. Telling her he was proud of her achievement, even if it wasn't as great as she wished, was like a balm to her.

To help children cope with disappointments:

- accept that it is important and don't say "It doesn't matter." It obviously does matter to your child.
- say you are sorry it happened.
- give them hugs and attention, no matter how big they are. Inside, they feel about two, and they want your support.
- tell them about times when you were discouraged or disappointed, but try to mention how something good followed. No point saying something like, "I never got over what happened." Choose your examples to help your children cope, not to encourage them to give up.

8. Help Your Child Learn to Relax and Enjoy Life

"Jill is always wound up like a top," complained her mother. "If she is like this at her age, I hate to think what will happen to her when she gets out into the real world." Jill's mother is right to be concerned, but the funny thing is she is ten times worse than her daughter and doesn't know it. Guess where Jill has learned her behavior from? (No prizes for right answers, sorry!)

I have a friend who drives us all to distraction. She never relaxes, and wonders why we all make excuses to leave after being with her for less than an hour. She cannot sit down and talk, always finding something to do, like make a fifth cup of coffee, plump up the cushions, fiddle with the cord of the telephone—it's perpetual motion. An hour in her company leaves me feeling slightly more hyper than the the Road Runner. Her most noticeable problem, though, is that she is so busy being busy that she doesn't listen to anyone. She simply cannot relax long enough to engage in meaningful conversation. Sad, but true.

Back to Jill. Why do we care if our children relax or not? Because when you're relaxed you are receptive to other people, your mind is clearer and ready to accept information, your body isn't at war with itself and you can tune into your own feelings and thoughts.

Of course, at certain times your child might function better if he is are slightly tense and the adrenaline is flowing, perhaps before a big game, or before a performance or test. But functioning on that level all the time just leads to burn out and children need to know how to relax. You can help them by:

- teaching them to sit or stand very still.
- asking them to close their eyes and think of something calm, like a clear lake, a sunny meadow, or a peaceful experience they have had (like sitting on Gran's lap and having a story read to them).
- teaching them to breathe deeply, slowly, and calmly.
- asking them to hold the thought that is relaxing them and to focus on it until they feel quite calm and still.
- explaining that they can use this technique whenever they feel themselves getting upset, or before they have to try to do something difficult or of great importance to them.

The ability to relax helps children (and the rest of us) to put aside worries or distractions and to focus on what they need to do.

9. Pay Attention to Your Child's Work and Work Habits

My youngest son came in the door, threw a pile of papers in my direction, and waltzed out of the room. I knew he was dying to talk with me about them, but he wanted me to make a fuss and look at them first, then come and find him to tell him how brilliant I thought he was. It's a kind of ritual in our house—passed down from generation to generation, I think. I used to do the same with my parents and grandmother. I didn't want to appear to be too pleased, but I couldn't wait for the adulation I knew would come. Some papers, I confess, never made it home, but then you can't expect a kid to ask for trouble, can you?

When your kids bring home their work and reports from school, take the time to go over them and read them. Comment about specific things you like and ask them what they think. Make a fuss, put the work on the refrigerator (why don't they make stronger fridge magnets? Papers end up on the floor whenever we take out the milk.), call their grandparents and brag about them, and generally tell them how proud and pleased you are.

When dealing with your children's work habits, ensure that there is a place—not in front of the television—they can do their homework in peace. For some children, it is essential that they have a quiet place; others seem to function quite well in a busy, slightly noisy kitchen. My elder son informs me that he *has* to have music or his brain withers. I'm not convinced, but he is doing fine, so I won't complain...yet.

Ensure that your children have all the information they need to do their reports or homework. Check to see if they need any help, but never do their work for them.

Make sure that your children get to school on time and go with something in their stomachs. A recent study showed that children who eat breakfast function better than those who don't.

Don't come back from vacation three days after the start of a term. It isn't fair for your child to have to start from behind. Try to make appointments with doctors and dentists outside school hours.

Encourage debate and discussion about issues. The dinner table is a great place to bring up subjects that tie into what your children are studying (it's a bad place to bring up biology experiments, however).

10. Encourage Self-congratulation

I know, I know...it's very immodest to encourage self-congratulation. I can just hear you saying, "We'll end up with insufferable little monsters bragging about themselves!" That isn't what I mean, actually, though I see nothing wrong with being able to say, "I did that well." What we're talking about is teaching children:

- to *tell themselves* that they did well or that they can do a brilliant job.
- to practice saying to themselves that they are great, wonderful, fantastic, and that they are going to do it (whatever *it* is).

- never to be ashamed of doing something well.

These are exactly the sorts of things top athletes, businesspeople, actors, and musicians do. They jump themselves up by saying, "This is going to be my best performance ever," or "I'm going to get that commission because I have the best product," or "Today I'm going to win that medal because I deserve it after all my hard work." Sort of like "Watch out world, here I come. I'm a winner!" Try it!

20

The 10 Worst and 10 Best Things You Can Say to Your Kids

Lisa comes through the front door, drops her books on the floor, deposits her sweatshirt on the kitchen counter, steps in the dog's bowl of water, and grabs a handful of jelly beans on her way out of the room. "Lisa come back here." Says her mother. "How could you be so clumsy and inconsiderate? Why can't you do anything right?"

You're on a longed-for vacation. All you want to do is relax by the pool. Then it starts. "Did not." "Did." Whack! "Moooooommmie—he hit me." "Out of my sight, both of you. I wish I'd never had children."

How could we say such things to our kids?

Give me a break. We've all done it. We've all said things we wish we could take back. Let's face it, children can drive you crazy, and none of us says the right thing every time. Of course, we feel annoyed—even murderous— at times and we do make hurtful comments.

Not that the occasional remark will wound them for life, but we'd all agree that it isn't the best way to talk to children or to teach them how to behave. In fact, a barrage of negative comments can destroy your child's confidence altogether.

Marcia still remembers her mother's favorite put-down. "I'm glad I had your sister—you're nothing but trouble." At thirty-five Marcia is nervous, worries constantly, and feels she is worthless. She has been divorced three times and has four children who are all unhappy little creatures. She is still afraid of her mother and cannot stand her sister. Marcia is one of the casualties of parental power gone wrong. Even so, she admits to saying much the same thing to her children as was said to her in childhood...and so the sad pattern continues.

Usually, when we make hurtful comments, it is because we are frustrated and angry, not because of deep psychological problems. But even if it might be a natural reaction to lash out, we need to remember the effect that it can have.

Try asking your friends if they can remember something, said to them as children, that still rankles. Forty-year-old Michael is hurt to this day by his father's comment: "He told me I was an idiot, with such contempt that it really hurt. I still get a tight feeling when I think about it."

Take heart, we all make mistakes along the way. But what we say to our children does have an amazing influence on them. Just think how often we hear ourselves repeating something our parents said to us. If we can break the cycle, our children and grandchildren will be the real winners.

Read on for the ten worst and best things we can say to our children. And see if any of them rings a bell with you.

The 10 Worst

1. "You're So Stupid!"

Parents often say this in exasperation or in panic.

Karen's four-year-old daughter dashed into the path of a car, which screeched to a halt just inches from the terrified child. Karen grabbed her daughter and shouted, "You're so stupid!" Of course, this was blind fear taking over. Karen said she later gave her daughter a hug and apologized, but she had thought her daughter was going to die and couldn't believe it when the car stopped. I doubt her daughter will remember the exact words Mommy used. No real harm done here.

Sara, on the other hand, uses "You're so stupid" as a weapon. Her children hear it frequently and say it to each other and to friends. More important, they believe it. They are downtrodden kids who do badly at school and who feel they cannot win. Surprise surprise... they can't. Inside, they are saying to themselves, "It doesn't matter, I'm just stupid anyway."

"Stupid," "dumb," and "idiot" are such negative words. They destroy confidence and initiative. Children learn to value themselves from those around them. If we tell them they are stupid, they will always feel inadequate.

Sometimes kids do stupid things. (So do we.) Try to remember to respond to the action, not the child, as in "That was a stupid thing to do," not "You're stupid." It helps to have some standard phrase like: "When you do that it drives me up the wall," so you won't blurt out something you'll later regret.

2. "You Could Do So Well, if Only..."

Keith said that his parents were constantly told by his teachers that "He could do so well, if only..." in other words, he had potential. "That meant I wasn't doing enough to please them. But then I never could do enough to please them."

Have you ever noticed that the word *potential* is never used positively? As Keith says, "Having potential is like having an illness. When I was little, I thought I might outgrow it."

If your child has abilities he is not using, don't despair. Just plot. Wait until your child does something you can praise, then say, "You have really improved. That makes me really happy." If you can praise what he does right, you may be able to bury the word *potential,* and he may even finally live up to it.

3. "Why Can't You Be More Like..."

This is never said as a compliment. Think about it—if you want your child to be more like someone else, you want her to be less like herself.

"I was always told to be more like my brother," said Stephanie. "I ended up hating my brother and not feeling good about myself, either. It seemed he did everything right and I was a dud. Sometimes I wished I hadn't been born."

Stephanie's parents should have focused on the behavior they wanted her to change. Why did they want her to be more like her brother? If he was neater, they could have given her specific ideas, such as cleaning up her room. If he was better at math, they could have looked for her talents and praised what she did well. As it was, she just felt generally anxious and was sure she could not live up to anyone.

Stephanie was four years younger than her brother. What probably happened was that her parents forgot how long it took her brother to learn to walk, talk, and so on. It quite often happens that parents make unfair comparisons between older and younger children.

4. "I Wish I Didn't Have Kids."

We may all wish this at least once in a while, but we should never say it. *Never.* It is the ultimate rejection for children and one of the most devastating things for them to hear.

If you do feel angry enough to say this, take a deep breath and say, "Sometimes you make me mad enough to spit." Or use a calmer approach, "When you do that I feel very angry."

If things get to the point that you want to lash out verbally like this, take yourself out of the situation. Leave the room. It's called "time-out for grown-ups" and is a valid way to deal with extreme frustration and the desire to be single and carefree again. (Those were the days, you must admit.) It's normal to feel you want out sometimes, but it's *not* OK to tell the kids! They'll find out on their own one day.

5. "Look At All I've Given Up for You."

Groan! This is a comment most adults remember with a mixture of anger and guilt. In other words: "If you hadn't been born, my life would have been better and I could have accomplished so much. It is your fault that I am a failure." Children, don't ask to be born. Parents are supposed to be there to take care of children, which entails sacrifices. But kids don't need to be told this and are not interested anyway. What can they do about it? Disappear? Some have tried....

Sharon ran away from home when she was fifteen. She could no longer take her mother's continual stream of abusive remarks about how difficult it was having children. "I decided that I would be doing her a favor if I just left." Now married with three children of her own, she rarely sees her parents. "It is too painful. My Mom still pushes my buttons over and over and she doesn't even know she does it. I say to my children that they are the best thing that ever happened to me, and I mean it."

If you have given up a lot for your children (let's face it, who hasn't) and are tempted to tell them so, stop. Don't ever say it.

6. "You're a Liar, a Thief, and a Lazy Good-for-Nothing!"

Seven-year-old Larry took his brother's toy soldiers and then lied when asked about it. "You're not only a liar, but a thief as well," shouted his parents, enraged that a son of theirs could steal and have the audacity to lie about it.

Most kids steal and lie. They learn from it, outgrow it, and move on *unless* we label them. Kids believe what we tell them; if we say they are lazy, thieves, or liars, they begin to think of themselves that way.

Try saying that you don't like laziness, stealing, or lying—attack the behavior, not the child. You can get away with calling your child a "lazy good-for-nothing kid" in jest as long as everyone knows you don't mean it. Humor can forgive a lot—as long as it isn't at your child's expense.

7. "Don't Be Silly, There's Nothing to Be Frightened Of."

Eight-year-old John woke up in the middle of the night, screaming. His dad hurried to comfort him. "There's a monster in the closet, Daddy." "Don't be so silly, there's nothing to be frightened of," he replied.

By saying this, we give our children potentially harmful messages. It's silly to be scared. Is it? Parents know there aren't monsters in the closet, but they are very real to John. It's far better to say, "It's all right to be scared. All children get frightened sometimes. I know there is nothing in the closet, but let's look together." Telling a child it is silly to be scared won't make the fear go away; it may prevent the child telling you about his fears in the future.

By saying that it is all right to be frightened, you are also acknowledging that the world can be a frightening place and that you will support your child through his fears.

8. "I'm Going to Leave You."

You are in a hurry and Lucy is dragging behind looking at the toys in the store. "If you don't come right this minute, I'm leaving," you say and off you go toward the door. Lucy panics and runs behind, crying. The thought of Mommy leaving reinforces the basic childhood fear that you may disappear and never return. Andy, fifty-five, still remembers his mother getting in the car and driving away, just to stop his constant dawdling. It worked—he never dawdled again—instead clingy, whiny, and was terrified to ever leave his mother in case she left for good. Try giving your child a few minutes warning and then giving them the choice of taking your hand or being carried. Bribes will also work: "If you come now, we will have time for a story or a treat."

9. "You Must Always Obey Grown-ups."

A mother wrote to me about a terrifying incident: "I was sitting in the park reading while my three-year-old daughter played. I glanced up to see her being led away by a man. I ran after them and found myself in an isolated place with this man. Knowing we were both in danger, I just chatted with him, took my daughter's hand, and gradually edged away. When I asked her why she had gone with him, she replied, 'He told me to obey him.' I shudder now to think that my insistence on always obeying adults could have had such terrible consequences."

By all means teach children to respect adults, but also explain that there may be times when it isn't safe to obey.

10. "Wait Until Your Father Gets Home."

To set one parent up as the disciplinarian is an awful thing to do, bad both for the parent and the child.

Peter still shudders when he remembers this threat. "Whenever we did something wrong as children, Mom would threaten: 'Wait until your father gets home.' We knew that meant a spanking, and dreaded Dad coming in the door. Imagine living all day with that fear and hating our father because he administered the punishment."

Whatever form of discipline you use with your children (and I am against hitting them), it is better done at the time and by the person who is with the child. If Matthew hits Sam and the punishment is a set amount of time when TV is not allowed, do it while Matthew still remembers what the punishment is for. It is much fairer, it will get the message across, and is kinder to the child.

The 10 Best

1. "You've Always Been a Plus in My Life!"

Tell your children how important they are to you. It's a wonderful thing to hear. For a child to know that she is the best thing to happen to you sets her up for life with good feelings about herself.

2. "Telling Is OK."

"Mommy, Jessica pushed me." "Don't tattle tale," you reply without skipping a beat.

Your child isn't "tattling," she's telling you what happened and wondering what she or you should do about it. She's testing her new-found independence to see how to respond to the world; how should she react if she has been taught not to fight or hit.

Some kids are tattle-tales. But be sure not to ignore real problems. Why do we tell children to be quiet, not to tell about problems, keep the code of silence? It's probably because we were told the same thing when we were growing up. Next time, think twice and say, "Let's see what we can do about this." This will give Jessica some strategies on how to deal with similar situations in the future and show her that you are interested in what is happening to her.

3. "I Am Proud of You, You Did That So Well."

Jenny had just tied her shoe for the first time. "Jenny, that was wonderful," said her mom. "I'm proud of you." Jenny beamed at her mother's praise. It is lovely to think that someone is proud of you. It gives a child the incentive to try anything. Don't be afraid to praise and to praise often.

4. "I Said NO!"

Nancy wanted more than anything to be friends with her children. She remembered how her parents had always been so negative, and how frightened she was of them. Determined not to let that happen with her family, she allowed them everything. She never said no. By the time her kids were teenagers they were rude and demanding, and they wouldn't listen to anyone.

Her children *wanted* and needed limits, they needed a mother with grown-up judgment, not a benevolent older sister. However much they protest, children need guidance. It's great to treat kids with respect, but they need our maturity to put them on the path to responsible behavior. It took some time for Nancy to realize it was OK to get angry and to say no. In fact, her kids were secretly relieved to blame Mom for "not letting me do it." They didn't lose face and were saved from having to act beyond their years.

5. "It's All Right to Cry or Feel Sad or Scared."

While on vacation we were walking behind a young family. Their three-year-old son was wobbling along on a bicycle with stabilizers and fell off just in front of us. He howled loudly. His father crouched down, took him in his arms and said, "That hurt, didn't it? You have a good cry until it feels better." Allow children to cry and to feel sad or frightened. It lets them come to terms with their own feelings, not just our ideas about how they should feel.

6. "It's OK to Make Mistakes."

Well...some mistakes. Being calm when your child spills indelible red ink on a white wool carpet may be beyond most of us, but helping children learn that everyone makes mistakes is not. Some mistakes will have consequences, such as your fifteen-year-old coming in an hour after an agreed upon curfew. She may be grounded for a while, but it clearly isn't the end of the world.

Children will make mistakes growing up. Keep them in perspective, or kids will be so afraid of making a mistake that they won't try anything. So, if your four-year-old picks the rare orchid your husband has been cultivating and presents it to you, smile, keep your cool—and leave town quick!

7. "You're So Smart to Have Worked That Out."

Giving a child the chance to sort things out on his own will give him the confidence to try. Even if your child tries and fails, you can say, "It's really great that you tried. I'm so pleased you did."

8. "You Don't Have to Do Anything."

Nowadays, it seems children have every waking hour filled with "meaningful activities": ballet, art, music lessons, tennis lessons, chess, football training. You name it and children are able to sign up for it.

When my children say they've nothing to do, I reply, "You're lucky." There's nothing wrong with having time simply to think, to wonder. When my sons go to Andrew's house, his mom always has the day planned. First the movies, then pizza, then supervised tennis. It's all right once in a while, but Andrew has his whole life planned for him. It destroys creativity and the unstructured play kids need. When Andrew comes to our house, he loves it. "You don't have to *do* anything here," he says wistfully.

Continually entertaining kids doesn't help them to develop. "Don't *do* anything" might just startle them into their own activity.

9. "I Like You Because You're You."

Wouldn't you love it if someone said that to you, with no "ifs" or "buts"? A child needs to feel that he is "just right" as he is...today, this minute, now. You're also saying that your child doesn't have to prove anything to you; it's enough that he is there.

10. "I Love You."

For children, these are simply the best three words in the English language. As parents, we should use them at least once a day, if not more often.

21

17 Things You and Your Children Need to Know When You Go Out Without Them

There will always be times when you have to or want to go out without your children. If they're young, you leave them with a babysitter or a relative. If they are old enough, you leave them on their own with lots of instructions and hope they don't have wild parties.

Home Alone

How old should children be before you leave them home alone? States all have their own laws, but occasionally you just have to leave your children home alone, regardless of what the law says. How often have you had to run across the street to buy some milk and left your kids for just a couple of minutes? Fortunately, nothing untoward usually happens for most parents. When something horrible does happen, we read the headlines and wonder just how those parents could have left those children alone, even if we've done it ourselves. I talked with a group of five-year-olds in one school and found that fifteen out of twenty of them had been home alone at least once in their lives.

So, I guess there is no set age when it is OK to leave kids home alone. It depends upon where you live and who is nearby and, of course, the maturity of your child. Personally, leaving children as young as five home alone scares me. I worry about things like fires, accidents, or the possibility of intruders when I consider leaving kids at home. So what should kids know about if they are to be left alone?

1. Fire

Practice fire drills with your children and make sure they know exactly what to do and how to get out in case of fire. Seek advice from your local fire department.

2. Emergency Telephone Calls

Practice making emergency telephone calls with your children. Well, don't *really* practice or you will have the police at your door. Use a toy telephone, or unplug the telephone, and then have your kids go through the stations. Explain that the operator will ask them their name and number and which service they need: police, fire, or ambulance. Explain also that they should never make such a call unless it is an emergency and that the number they call from can be traced immediately.

3. Obscene Telephone Calls

Tell your kids to hang up and not to respond to obscene calls, then to immediately call either you or whoever they have as a contact and arrange for help.

4. Intruders

If your children are home when someone tries to break in, if possible, they should try to get out of the apartment or house and go to a place of safety close by, such as a neighbor's. Then they should immediately call the police. Ask your local police department to check your home and give advice on making it as safe as possible.

5. List Contacts

Make a phone list of people your child can contact and put it near the telephone. Also work out what to do if you do not have a telephone, or if it is out of service for some reason. Arrange for someone your child can get in touch with without using the telephone.

6. Answering the Door

If someone your children is not expecting comes to the door, I suggest that they don't answer. If it is a delivery, it can be made later; if it is a friend he can telephone and come again. If there is an emergency involving the police or the fire department, the officers will give your children identification or, in extreme cases, break down the door (to save children from a fire, for example). In most situations, children should simply ignore the doorbell. If someone persists in trying to get them to answer the door, instruct them to call you or their contact and explain what's happening.

7. List Do's and Don'ts

Children need to know what they are allowed to do when they are home alone. Obviously, this will depend upon their ages. For example, you may make a blanket rule that cooking is not allowed, to eliminate the possibility of them burning themselves or the house down. You might ask them not to use the iron for the same reason (if you are lucky enough to have children who are dying to iron their clothes!). Knives and blenders could be off limits. It is not a good idea for children to take baths in case they scald themselves, or use the washing machine because of floods.

You may allow your children to eat foods, such as fruit cereal, and other snacks you put out, that require no cooking. Also, they can watch television, do their homework (yippee), talk on the telephone with their friends, and so forth. If you do have to leave your kids home alone you need to work out the most detailed instructions possible and hope that their common sense will prevail.

Choosing the Right Babysitter

If you are leaving your child with a babysitter, consider the following when choosing someone to babysit for your child:

8. Check Them Out

Be sure to talk to the person who has recommended the sitter, and find out what he knows about her? In a study I recently completed, I found that 48 percent of the male child molesters we interviewed made contact with their victims by babysitting! That certainly doesn't mean that all babysitters are child molesters, just that babysitting is an excellent way for child molesters to be alone with children. Another note of caution, You cannot assume that a babysitter is OK just because she is female. I have, unfortunately, dealt with children abused by both men and women. I am not trying to frighten you into never leaving your child with a sitter, but it pays to know as much as possible about who this person is.

9. Take Care with Babysitting Ads

Never use babysitters from local adverts without taking references, and actually talking to other mothers and fathers who have used this person.

10. Look for Signs of Problems

How do your children react to being left with the person?

- Are they happy to have the person return as a sitter?
- Do they cry when left with the person?
- Do they beg their parent to stay home and not go out?

11. Can She Cope with Emergencies?

Does the sitter know basic first aid, or what to do in case of emergency? Ask the person to tell you what she would do in case of a fire, a child getting burned, or if your child were injured.

12. Get to Know Him

Meet the sitter before you leave your children with him. Make sure you can call the sitter or know where he lives.

13. Use the Element of Surprise

Call or come home unexpectedly to check that everything is all right.

14. Ask the Children

Ask your child about the sitter, even if it is someone you know and like. You need to make sure your child likes the person and doesn't feel unsafe in any way. Since people who molest children often ask the child to keep secrets, you might casually ask your child if the babysitter asked her or him to keep any secrets. This doesn't mean that you have to interrogate your child, just that you be aware of what could happen so you can prevent your child being harmed. In all probability, your child will be quite safe with the babysitter!

15. Leave a Contact Number

Make sure the babysitter knows how to reach you or the person you have designated in case of emergency. And ensure the babysitter knows what to do and who to contact should anything happen to you. Who would come over to take care of the children if you had an accident, for instance?

What to Tell Your Children

Having decided on a babysitter, you can now go out without worrying about anything except giving advance instructions to your children. They may need to know some of the same things they would if they were home alone, but there are two especially important points to remember.

16. Telephone Numbers

Even if the babysitter knows how to contact you, make sure that your children do as well. They should also have another emergency contact—who should they contact if the babysitter gets sick, for example? Even though this is unlikely, better safe than sorry.

17. Arrange a Secret Code

Arrange a code with your children so they can let you know if something is very wrong and you need to come home. For instance, one parent I know worked out with his children that, if one called him and asked how to do a math problem, something was amiss that she couldn't say for some reason, and that he should return home immediately. Fortunately, they have never had to use the code. Something like this would be vital if the babysitter was doing something to threaten the safety of the children.

Go Out and Have a Great Time

We all need to get away from our kids from time to time, if for no other reason than to maintain our sanity. Don't get me wrong, I love my kids. But it is wonderful to escape and have a good time without them. I think it's also good for them to learn to be independent of us. I just want to make sure that they are as safe as possible, and I will certainly let them be completely on their own—maybe in about thirty years!

22

24 Ways to Bribe Your Child

We know, of course, that it is wicked to corrupt innocent children by implying there's a commercial value to every act. How about doing the dishes out of noble concern for your mother? Or taking care of your little sister because you love her? By talking about bribes, I'm not trying to imply that children should never perform selfless acts. I'm suggesting that, by admitting that we use bribes anyway (who hasn't bought a toddler a box of animal crackers so he will stay in the shopping cart while you struggle with the grocery shopping?), we can actually use them even more constructively—and everyone wins!

Would you work—on a regular basis—for no reward? It's certainly true that we do many things in life out of a sense of duty, or out of fear of what will happen if we don't do them, but we work with most spirit when we're highly motivated. We work for money or job satisfaction. So why not, when a child needs motivating, set up appropriate reward "traps"—and turn the sometimes tedious processes of learning and cooperating in to a winning game. If you still think you're not—and never should be—a briber, consider how often we use "negative bribes" such as spanking, not allowing a child to play with friends, taking away a privilege or possession, shouting, sarcasm, counting to three with the threat that something dire will happen, or criticism. These do work, but they only turn kids into "non-losers" as opposed to "winners."

Here, I've included ideas for good bribes, many from my own or friends' experiences. It's important to remember that the younger the child, the more immediate the reward should be. Asking a four-year-old to wait until next week is like asking an adult to wait until the end of next year.

If the word *bribe* bothers you, substitute the word *reward*.

Collectables

1. Stars on a Chart

Children love to collect things just to see how many they can get. The final reward, if there is one, becomes secondary to the game of collecting. Stars can cost you nothing. Letting a small childdraw a colored star in a space on a homemade chart every time he goes to bed without complaining, for example, can be sufficient. Stars have value, provided they aren't given for nothing.

2. Tokens

For an older child, say an eleven-year-old who does not want to do her homework, you could use something more tangible. Agree with her how much time homework should take. Put on a timer and offer her ten tokens for working the for set time. When she gets 100 tokens she gets an agreed-upon reward: a friend to stay the night, a visit to the movies, whatever she chooses that both of you think is worth so much effort.

3. Stickers

Stickers and cards are things children collect and swap, but they do seem to go in and out of fashion. Find out what, if anything, your children are interested in and try to get them special stickers or cards they really want. You might also consider an album to put the stickers in, as another possible bribe.

3. Money

Money is a more controversial bribe. Although adults consider it perfectly acceptable to work for money, many people think children should do things for the joy of it. The problem is that many of the tasks we set children are not joyful.

If you use money with small children, give them lots of little coins each time they succeed. With teenagers, the promise of a certain amount at the end of the task will work better than lots of change. A young friend of ours, Jennifer, bit her nails until they were sore. Her mother offered her $1 for each nail that was a certain length by Easter. Jennifer soon stopped nibbling at her nails and by Easter, when she had $10, she'd broken the habit of biting her nails all together.

Money bribes can teach children to respect your own budget. Learning that money comes through effort helps them understand when you say: "Sorry, I'm broke this month—how about washing the car for love?"

Edibles

With food, it's a case of identifying the "currency" that motivates a particular child.

5. Tangerines

My friend's little boy, Malik, was such a dedicated tangerine-eater that he got through a week's supply in a day. It wasn't such a good idea for my friend's budget or Malik's digestion. I suggested restricting him to one a day, with extras if he did whatever she needed him to do that he found difficult. If a child won't eat breakfast before school, for example, use an extra tangerine as a "carrot" (so to speak). Even young children enjoy planning their own food treats.

6. Candy

Another friend of mine's two-and-a-half-year-old daughter, Nicky, wasn't interested in using the potty. Her mother wanted her out of diapers for a long journey they were taking in a month's time. Nicky could use the toilet when it suited her, but she was a bit lazy. Nicky's mom put a jar of M&Ms, tightly sealed, near the potty and showed Nicky that every time she used it she would get three M&Ms. She was daytime trained in a few days.

M&Ms are also useful for teaching colors. If you pick the right color, you get to eat the M&M. This needs to be monitored, or your children will have no teeth, but they'll know their colors beautifully!

7. Favorite Pudding or Cookies

You may not want to bribe your kids with teeth-rotting candy. Instead, try giving them a favorite pudding or cookies as a snack, rather than their normal snacks. It's not exactly healthy, but it may save you a trip to the dentist.

8. Fast Food or Pizza

Personally, give me fast food or a pizza and I'll do anything (just about). This only works if your children don't have so much McDonald's and Domino's that they are overdosed on them.

Escapism

Children, like adults, will work for "fun." As we all know, fun doesn't always come cheap. It does no harm to explain to kids that you enjoy expensive outings, but they'll need to help you so you can afford the time and money.

9. Movies

Designate specific chores as "movie" jobs—from dusting the banisters to cleaning the table after meals for a week. Before you set up this bribe you have to be careful not to say anything you don't mean. In other words, if you really plan to take them to the movies on Friday anyway, come hell or high water, then it's pointless pretending the excursion is totally dependent on the tasks you give them. Instead, you can invoke moral bribery: "I need you to help me now, if we're going to make it to the movies on Friday."

10. Videos

A trip to the video store and the promise of an extra video can also work wonders. Combine this with the promise of staying up late to watch the videos and you will probably be able to bribe your children for a month.

11. Children's Theater

A special treat for kids that is often as educational as it is entertaining is a trip to a children's theater. If you can't afford a professionally staged play, look into community theaters, too.

12. Museums

Many museums are designed especially for young children. Many other museums are designed for adults, but can be equally educational and fun for kids, such as a natural history museum with its dinosaur skeletons. Most museums charge only a nominal amount, or simply a donation, and they are vast resources for teaching your kids about the world.

13. Books

I think that a book or a gift certificate to a bookstore is the best bribe going. I would do most anything for a new book. I realize that some children would rather have a new computer game, but I don't include this as a bribe because, not only are computer games too expensive, they are mind-numbing, in my opinion.

Extras

Have you ever noticed how angelic children are just before birthdays, Christmas or other holidays? The stocking is, if you like, the best bribe of the year. You can use the Christmas factor to good effect at other times, too. If a child starts wheedling for extras, you should give his desire the importance it deserves and suggest that he might like to work for it.

14. Extra TV

Joan wanted her nine-year-old daughter Emily to play the piano, and she was initially excited. After several weeks, however, Emily said it was boring to practice, and that she would rather watch TV. Joan and Emily worked out an agreement. For every ten minutes that the girl practiced, she would be allowed to watch ten minutes of television. (This only worked because Joan usually restricted Emily's TV time.)

15. Staying Up Late

On the weekends or holidays, one very effective way of getting children to behave is to allow them to stay up late to watch a favorite TV program, or simply to spend time reading or playing. Young children often feel that all the "action" goes on after they go to bed, and so are very excited when they think they are going to be a part of it. (And they'll find out just *how* exciting it really is after bedtime—ha!)

16. Extra Allowance

If you are desperate to get your child to do something and are meeting with little or no success, by all means try a little extra allowance, if you can afford it. Pamela's nine-year-old son had the really nasty habit of burping all the time. His friends encouraged him and laughed whenever he did it, but it had gotten beyond a joke with his parents. The trouble was, he sometimes did it without thinking— great loud belches that were incredibly embarrassing. Once they were to go away on vacation in four weeks, and Pamela really did not want to be stuck in a nice restaurant with a burping son. She offered extra allowance for the weeks leading up to the vacation, so her son would have more to spend when they got to the resort. It did the trick, and the burps subsided!

17. Tapes and CDs

Tapes and CDs are much sought after, but they are a fairly expensive bribe. Try telling your child you will match what she saves toward the CD she wants if she stops fighting with her sister for a set amount of time.

18. Special Clothes

It seems kids always have to have the absolute latest in fashion or they'll be a hopeless outcast. They beg and beg for brand name blue jeans or jackets. Why not use these as rewards for good behavior? Since you have to but them clothes anyway, add a bit to your budget when you think they're deserving of a treat, and get that hat or shirt.

Funnies

19. Ping-Pong Ball in the Toilet

Anything that involves humor helps make tasks lighter. A good, amusing way to encourage small boys to aim straight when they learn to pee standing up is to put a Ping-Pong ball in the toilet as a target.

20. Musical Potties

Musical potties have the same function as the Ping-Pong ball, but at an earlier stage, and they work for boys and girls.

21. Mom Paints Her Face

Children always complain about how Mom makes them do things all the time. They love nothing more than making Mom do something—and the more comical, the better. If you really want your kids to clean their rooms, tell them you'll paint your face like a clown if they do. You'll be Bozo in about a half-hour.

22. Mom Stands on Her Head

I once rashly promised my children that if they brushed their teeth every night for a week, I would stand on my head in the park. It was worth it—just!

23. Get Dad with a Water Pistol

Outdoor chores can be rewarded with outdoor fun. If the gardening is done, and Dad is relaxing in the sun, allow your kids to sneak up on him and drench him with water pistols. Dad may not like it, but you'll both like the clean yard.

In the Name of Love

24. Cuddles

Children need love and affection, regardless of how they behave. It is their birth right. But extra cuddles, or words of praise, show children that their efforts are especially valued.

Grasping Little Creeps

So, if you bribe your children to get them to do what you want them to do, will they turn into nasty, grasping, horrible people? I don't think so. In fact, children are generally more noble and moral than we give them credit for being. They might not need much to motivate them to change or help. And you can't use bribes all the time, anyway. If you find your child won't do anything without a bribe, then you need to stop and reconsider your methods. Use them to get children started, not forever. If a child continually cries or acts out and then demands candy, firmly say no. Otherwise you are rewarding bad behavior. If your children will only be "good" when bribed, then you should have a talk and explain that you will occasionally give them something extra, but they won't know when, so they have to try all the time. Then surprise them. After a while, the behavior will be so ingrained that the bribe isn't necessary. A word of praise will be the best reward.

Helping Others

Remember that children can be motivated or bribed in very simple ways to help others, an important trait to try to instill in children. Every year on the first day of December, my grandmother would bring out the Christmas crib, with all the figures except the baby Jesus. Next to it, she put a pile of short pieces of straw. For every good deed that my sister and I did between December 1 and December 25, we were allowed to place a piece of straw in the cradle. Our reward was an increasingly soft bed for the baby. The one thing we were not allowed to do, however, was tell anyone about our good deeds. They were to be our own little secrets. My sister and I pursued our task with relish, though I confess we did brag once in a while to each other about what we had done. I suspect that a little one-upmanship was also part of the plan. My grandmother was a master of bribery. I will always love her for it.

PART III

Getting Through a Crisis

23

34 Suggestions About What to Do When Your Kids Screw Up

"Your son has been stealing money from children at school. Would you please come in so we can discuss this problem?"

"We have just found out that your daughter has been spreading nasty rumors about another girl and causing great distress."

"Your teacher called me today. You've been skipping school!"

"I'm sorry to tell you that your daughter has been caught shoplifting. Can you come to the police station?"

"I've got a note from your teacher about that homework you said you didn't have last night."

"Your children have been harassing my children, and now my children are afraid to go outside and play."

Rare are the parents who has never had to deal with their children "screwing up." We are lucky if our children are only called to task for such relatively minor problems as not doing their homework. Most of us can cope with such things by monitoring our children, restricting television, grounding, or the like. It isn't a crisis, only a drama that will soon pass.

However, what happens if our children do something that does create a crisis, like injuring another child, being brought home by the police, or being sent home from school in disgrace?

Ten-year-old Jon decided to skip school one day with some older children. They got bored and decided to hang around the local mall.

One thing led to another and they ended up forming a club that you could only join if you successfully shoplifted something costing at least $5. The older children managed to succeed and taunted Jon, calling him a baby and a sissy for not trying to steal. Jon nervously went into a store, was instantly spotted by security staff, and was caught as he left the store. The other children scattered when they saw what was happening, leaving Jon to fend for himself. By the time Jon's parents learned what he had done, everyone else knew as well.

"We were mortified and very angry," his father told me. "Jon let us and himself down very badly. He really isn't a kid who does things like this. He usually does well in school, he has enough allowance, and doesn't want for anything. We've tried to be good parents and teach him right from wrong. We can't understand how this happened."

Jon's parents felt terribly guilty, but they were good parents. You can't be with your kids every minute, nor can you control all the outside influences in their lives. The bottom line is that kids make mistakes, big and small, and you have to figure out how to help them learn from those mistakes. If your children are accused of screwing up somehow, here are some suggestions about what to do.

Keep Calm and Find Out the Facts

This is easy to say and hard to do when faced with awful, embarrassing accusations about your child. Sometimes we react by immediately assuming what we are told is correct. It may be, but until we find out the facts from all concerned, it isn't fair to judge. Things are not always as they seem at first sight.

Helen told me about the time another mother called to say that Helen's ten-year-old son, David, had been rude and hurtful to her son, Max. The mother told Helen that David was spreading rumors that Max had "pooped in his pants." Since Max and David had been friends and she knew Max's mother, Helen apologized profusely. Max's mother wanted David to apologize in front of the class and to admit that he had lied about Max. When Max's mother asked to speak to David, Helen called him to the phone. She heard David dissolve into tears as Max's mother yelled at him for being so horrible to Max. Helen, thinking that David had been naughty, felt he deserved to be told off.

Helen said, "I should have told Max's mother that I would call her back, but I was so embarrassed and annoyed with what David was supposed to have done that I wasn't thinking straight. It was only when I sat down with him that I found out what had really happened. Then I really felt horrible. It turned out that the boys were fooling around and that Max had farted several times, to the delight of all the boys. Everyone, including Max, had been giggling like mad about it. David had said, "You pooped in your pants," which again made them all laugh. Max was not upset. One of the other boys told his mother what David had said and neglected to say how it had come about. This mother called Max's mother and Max's mother called me. The kids were actually fine. The mothers had got it wrong!

"I was angry at myself for allowing David to be yelled at, and furious at Max's mother. Poor David—maybe he probably shouldn't have made the comment, but he was condemned quite unfairly. I apologized to him and still cannot talk to Max's mother. Next time anyone tells me something about David I will look carefully before I leap to conclusions."

It may be that you find your child has done what he or she is accused of, but try to make sure you:

1. Ask (calmly) for as many details as you can.
2. Don't make any rash promises about what you will do.
3. Give yourself a breathing space to take in what is happening. If someone calls you, listen with as little comment as possible, then tell the person you will call back to discuss it.
4. Talk calmly with your child to find out his side of the story.
5. Find out information from other sources, such as other parents, witnesses, children, teachers, and so on.
6. Seek legal advice if your child is in trouble for having broken the law. Unless you have access to your own lawyer, contact an organization such as the Legal Aid Society.
7. Take no action until you have had time to reflect. Cool off, even if that just means taking a walk to clear your head or having the proverbial cup of tea or coffee.
8. Have the best moral and emotional support you can muster for both you and your child.

Act Decisively

Once you have all the information, act as quickly as possible to sort out the mess. If your child has done something wrong, face up to it

and deal with it immediately. One thing that cools down situations is
the feeling that something is being done. Delaying action once you
know the facts will only add angst to the situation and may make it
worse. If your child has purposefully spread rumors, somehow hurt
another child, or stolen from a store, restitution is in order.

9. Your child should apologize to the victim and, if necessary,
   others who were affected by what she did.
10. If your child stole something, it should be returned or replaced
    and the child should make up the cost by doing extra jobs, if
    necessary.
11. You may wish to apologize, as well.
    This is especially helpful if your child has harmed another
    child in some way. At least the victim and her parents will feel
    their needs are being considered.
12. Plan how to accomplish the punishment constructivly.
    There is no point in humiliating your child. The purpose of
    the exercise is to make the victim feel better and to help your
    child learn this is not the way to behave.
13. Tell your child what you expect to happen next, including
    whatever punishment follows, such as restricting privileges.
    If the police are involved, explain what is will happen.
14. Explain that when your child has made the necessary steps to
    correct her mistake, you expect this behavior not to be repeated.
15. Make sure your child knows you don't think he is condemned
    for life and that we all make mistakes.
16. Make sure that your child is not so devastated by what has
    happened that he or she does something drastic, like running
    away from home, or, worse, trying to commit suicide. Even
    young children can make these dramatic gestures, which
    sometimes go tragically wrong. One eight-year-old felt he had
    done something so terrible that he would never get over it. He
    was standing in the road waiting to be hit by a car when his
    older brother saw him and dragged him to safety. Assure your
    child that you love him in spite of what they have done. Repeat
    the old adage: "I don't like what you've done, but I still love
    you."
17. Make sure your child understands what will happen if he or she
    transgresses again. For example, Linda's teenage daughter Shelly
    came home one night well past her curfew. After along
    grounding, Linda relented and let Shelly out again with the

proviso that, if she was late again without good reason and didn't call her frantic mom, her curfew would be pushed back an hour for every five minutes she was late.

18. Don't hastily give out punishments, which turn out to be so severe that you have to backpedal. But don't stick to a punishment you've meted out if it is too severe—be willing to admit that you've made a mistake. (After all, beheading is a little over the top!)

Recently, I received a call from the mother of a five-year-old boy, Blake. She had just come from an emergency meeting with her son's principal. Blake was caught in the toilet with another five-year-old boy. They were touching each other's penises and doing some other, more serious things that were quite inappropriate for their age. She had to act decisively.

Even though the principal was reassuring and said that children do experiment, Blake's mother was very worried about Blake, about the other boy, and about what the other children and parents would think. We went through the process of finding out the facts. It seemed unlikely that Blake was himself abused, given the information about him. He was doing well in school, had never been inappropriately sexual before, was bright, articulate, and well-adjusted. A few weeks before this incident, however, he did find a pornographic video (not homemade and not violent or degrading) that was hidden away. Blake's father had the video from before their marriage and had put it out of sight and forgotten it. At the time, his mother, horrified when her son innocently asked her questions about it, destroyed the video and told her son not to think about it.

It seems Blake didn't forget it but decided to try out some of the things he'd seen. I felt it important not to label Blake as a "sex abuser," nor to have him feel badly about his body, and to be sure counteract any rumors in the school that might start. His mother worried that Blake might have done these things with other children during the two or three weeks since he saw the video. After we talked, Blake's mother decided to:

19. Tell Blake that she loved him but didn't like what he had done.
20. Make sure that Blake understood that sex was not a bad thing, nor was he bad.
21. Ask Blake if he knew why the principal had asked her to come in today. Trying to get Blake's perspective on what had happened

was important. I think he just thought it felt good and that it was naughty—two things guaranteed to spark a kid's interest.

22. Try to find out if anyone had ever done anything sexually to him.
23. Talk to Blake about the video and explain that what he saw was acting, and that people don't necessarily do what they see on film.
24. Explain that he can do things to his own body, but that those things are private and that he should not be doing them with other children.
25. Explain that he would get into trouble if he did sexual things at school with other children. We used the example that teachers don't go into toilets and touch each other.
26. Explain that touching is nice and that it should not be kept secret. Touching privately, at home, by yourself is different from keeping it secret. Abusers often ask children to keep touching secret.

Finally Blake's mother was going to meet with the mothers of the other children to ask their advice, and to explain what had happened before rumors started to fly. She and the other mothers are friends of long-standing, so this would make it easier. In a situation such as this, which could result in a child being ostracized or even asked to leave the school, it is vital to act immediately. Trying to sweep it under the carpet only makes things worse.

Follow-up on Jon

After Jon was caught shoplifting, he was cautioned by the police and turned over to the care of his parents. They also had to go to the school and sort out his truancy and his relationship with the older children. Jon was grounded for several weeks and forbidden to see the other children (who escaped police action because they were not caught, but who were in trouble at school). His parents, with the help of the teacher, encouraged other more positive and age-appropriate friendships. Jon had skipped school once before this incident, but he now seemed to prefer the relative safety of school, even if he still got bored once in a while. Jon came through his experience wiser and more cautious. His parents say they've learned a lot and are now paying much more attention to what is happening to Jon.

If your child has done something wrong, which you have managed to sort out, be sure to follow up your actions.

28. Give your child lots of praise for good behavior.
29. Keep an eye on the situation and ask the school, if involved, to help you.
30. Don't continually bring up the transgression, unless you want to make your child feel guilty and useless.
31. Keep in contact with other parents if more than one child has been involved.
32. If other children have been influencing your child to get into trouble, either forbid contact (if your child is young enough—much harder when they are teenagers) or arrange for contact with them to be supervised, perhaps at your home.
33. If your child has been bullying another child, keep in contact with the parents of the victim to make sure it has stopped. In some cases, the bullying continues, but the bully becomes more subtle.
34. Try to create opportunities for your child to shine—and praise, praise, praise.

Most messes that kids get into are fixable, even if they are a pain for parents to deal with. Reassure your child that everyone makes mistakes, and that even you have made a few—unless, of course, you are, like me, one of one of those perfect people who never has. Hah!

24

38 Ways to Deal With Lying, Cheating, and Stealing

"Tell her I've just gone out—I'm not home," you hiss to your daughter, Vicky. It's your dreaded aunt on the telephone and you know you can't bear to listen to forty-five minutes of the same old complaints about how all her children, your children, and the world in general are going to hell in a handbasket.

"Um...Mom says she's not home just now, Auntie. She's just gone out."

Great! Vicky can plausibly come up with twenty completely false excuses for not cleaning up her room, but she can't handle one lame lie to your aunt. You grab the telephone and resolve to cut her allowance by 100 percent.

"Hello Auntie, how are you? I was closing the front door when I heard the telephone ring and thought I better come back to see who it was. Yes, I know what Vicky said. I told her just as I was leaving to tell anyone who called that I was going to be out for several hours, but luckily I heard the telephone. Lovely to hear from you."

Lovely, my foot. You hate talking to her and will do anything to get out of it. Anything except tell her the truth—that she's a bigoted, silly old cow and always has been. Well, she is an old lady now and you can't hurt her feelings.

Does that make you a liar? Well, perhaps a *kind* liar. Were you trying to get your daughter to lie for you? Yes. Have we all lied, cheated, or stolen occasionally? Of course. But we know it's wrong, and we certainly want our children to be honest. In fact, most of us believe that honesty is the best policy, unless we have to spend two hours listening to grumpy old Auntie.

Why do our children lie, cheat, or steal, and how can we instill in them a sense of right and wrong?

Why They Do It

Children have the same motives as adults for the things they do. They may lie, cheat, or steal:

- because they don't understand something
- to seek revenge
- for personal gain
- to get friends
- to get out of a difficult situation
- because they fear the consequences
- because of peer pressure
- to please someone
- because they want something very badly
- for the thrill of it
- because they get into the habit
- for attention

With luck, our children will pass through the "phases" of lying, cheating, and stealing without harming themselves or anyone else. Most children do go through these phases and come out as honest little critters at the other end. Still, it is upsetting to be told that your little Sarah is a marauding thief or a shameless liar—you wonder where you went wrong.

Let's take the issues one at a time: lying, cheating, and stealing—though sometimes a child manages to do all three at once. Don't despair—in all probability your children will turn out just fine. Here, nonetheless, are some hints to help you through the worst.

Lying

How can you tell if your child is lying? My grandmother only had to look me in the eye to know that I was not telling the truth. I used to think she could see right inside me, and I would turn scarlet at the very thought of lying to her. Not that she ever beat me or struck fear into my heart. No, she would just look at me and I seemed to curl up with guilt. It is no surprise to me, looking back, to see why she could tell I was lying. My red face, evasive answers, and refusal to look at her were rather striking clues. For years, I thought she was Sherlock Holmes, but I guess I was such an open-and-shut case that there was no need for detective work. Mind you, that doesn't mean that I never tried to get away with things! It just means that I did my best not to have to explain it to her.

Although these signs may have other causes, your child may be lying if:

- he shifts around uncomfortably and twist his hands
- she refuses to look you in the eye
- the story he is telling doesn't fit
- she changes the explanation several times
- he seems afraid
- she is vague
- your intuition tells you something isn't right—parents (or grandparents) are usually quite tuned in to their children and know something is amiss.

Of course, if you always overreact to things and your children are constantly frightened of what you will do or say, they might be nervous even if they are telling the truth. It may be that you are always suspicious, or that they have been wrongly accused in the past and therefore feel uncomfortable the minute they have to discuss anything with you. They are afraid and vague because they are so worried.

On the other hand, if you have a good relationship with your children and can usually discuss things openly and in a good-natured manner, the above points are useful clues.

Storytelling

If your child is lying, try to sort out the reasons before grounding him or her for life. A young child may really not know the difference between reality and fantasy. Whenever I work with young children, it is refreshing to see how much imagination they bring to their everyday world. If you ask a group of five-year-olds what they did on vacation, some will always have had the most marvelous adventures, which become even more fantastic as they listen to others. When my son, then age five or six, was telling his friend William about our trip to the Statue of Liberty, Will went one better. His family had been to the Sears Tower in Chicago and had been all the way to California!

He wasn't lying so much as wishing, dreaming, and spinning tales. Wills always came up with inventive stories and still does occasionally. (Perhaps he will be the next Hans Christian Andersen!) He certainly isn't a manipulative liar and should not be branded as such.

One way to handle the child who continually makes up stories is to say: "I understand how much you wish what you say would come true, and wishes are a very good thing. I wish for lots of things." The child knows you know, but you aren't making him feel like a liar. The next step is to bring the conversation back to reality and focus on something the child can talk about without storytelling. For example, you could switch the topic to the wonderful time the child had at the park on the swings, or planning what you will have for lunch—anything that lends itself to a factual-based conversation.

Making Up Imaginary Friends

Many children have imaginary friends when they are young. These friends are fun and a great comfort to children, as well as a handy source of blame. Pauline, age four, decided that her bedroom walls would look pretty painted with rainbow colors, like the painting she did at nursery school. She busily got out her paints and dabbed blue, yellow, red, green, and purple all over one wall. When her mother walked into the room to tell Pauline that lunch was ready, she couldn't believe the mess. She began shouting. Up to that point, Pauline had thought that she was improving the dull decoration of her bedroom. Her mother's reaction convinced Pauline that it was time for her imaginary friend Susie to come out and take the blame. (Many times I've longed for an imaginary friend to shoulder the blame for something I've done, but I guess I'm too old!)

When Pauline's mom settled down, she asked Pauline to explain herself. "Susie thought it looked nice, but Susie's naughty," said Pauline, who was too frightened to own up.

"Tell me what Susie did," asked Pauline's mother. Little by little she coaxed the truth out of Pauline.

"I know you think Susie was naughty to paint on your walls. I understand it is hard to tell me what happened when I was so angry. I'm not angry now, so you don't have to pretend that Susie painted the walls. You can tell me."

Pauline tearfully explained that she wanted rainbows on her walls and that she hadn't meant to do something bad. Her mother told her that she should ask before embarking on interior design and made it clear that painting was for paper, not wallpaper.

Did Pauline lie? In a way, but it was only a brushfire, not a full-scale inferno. By treating it as a learning experience (if you don't include the cost of repapering the wall!), the child won't grow up thinking she's a liar. Thank goodness her mother didn't call her a liar and make matters worse. She took exactly the right view: that her daughter needed to learn the difference between truth and falsehood and that this was an opportunity to help her.

Deliberately and Persistently Lying

Leaving aside the kind of things mentioned above, let's turn to the little artful dodger who is lying his head off. We are talking about the child who sets out to deceive and is making a habit of it. Why is the child doing this? There are many possible reasons, but the most likely cause is a child who is not functioning very well in real life and finds it easier or better to lie. Perhaps the expectations placed on the child are unobtainable, perhaps the child is terrified of parental reaction, perhaps the lying gives him the only relief from an awful life, perhaps lying has become a bad habit, or perhaps it has developed because the child cannot figure out how to stop lying.

Ian was the eldest of five children. His parents were loving but strict. If Ian brought home a poor report from school or got into trouble in any way, the consequences were swift and nonnegotiable. Ian felt he was always wrong and could not succeed, so he started lying to cover up. Of course, he didn't always get away with his lies, but he found that if he stuck to his story and was charming, he could at least get away with some things. Ian could look someone right in the eye and, without a hint of discomfort, tell his parents or any other adult exactly what they wanted to hear.

Ian lied, cheated, and squeaked through school, but everyone loved him. Nothing was ever his fault and he has now come to believe it so strongly that he cannot separate fact from fiction. He is a charming, compulsive liar.

So, how might his parents have handled the situation differently and how can we learn from their mistakes? Remember the story of my aunt's phone call at the beginning of this chapter? It turned out that Ian's parents expected absolute honesty from their children, but that their children saw that they were not always honest themselves. Ian's father, a businessman, was often "not at home" to telephone calls, sometimes stayed home sick when he wasn't, bragged about the deals he pulled on other people to their disadvantage, and took the family out to dinner as a "business expense." Ian was actually learning through example, regardless of what his parents said.

1. Check Your Own Example

If you lie and your children catch you out, admit it and apologize. Explain that, even if someone doesn't always tell the truth, admitting a lie is the next best thing. If you're not a paragon of virtue, handle mistakes in a way that gives a good model for your children to follow.

2. Stay Calm if Your Child Is Lying

Your child may be confused, using fantasy, or scared to death about something. Shouting only makes it worse.

3. Gently Question

Approach your child gently without immediately placing blame. The more forcefully you approach a child who is lying, the more likely it is that the child will cling to the lie.

4. Bite Your Tongue

You may want to berate your child for lying, but you cannot shame and humiliate children into responsible behavior. If a child is continually lying, it is often because of a lack of confidence, and ridicule will only increase her bad feelings.

5. Find Out Why the Child is Afraid to Tell the Truth

A question like: "What is it that you think would happen if this was true?" might elicit the reason why the child is lying. The over-riding concern is often self-protection or protection of a friend, not a desire to be malicious.

6. Change Your Child's Perception of Himself

Tell him "I know that inside you are an honest person and that's why I am so disappointed by your lying. Once we've sorted this out let's work on not doing it again."

7. Tell Your Child You Know She Lied

If you are absolutely positive of the facts, tell your child in a matter-of-fact way that you know she lied. If you saw your child pull the dog's tail, don't *ask* what happened, *state* what happened. If she denies it, don't get into a back-and-forth argument about it; this will only make the child lie more in a desperate attempt to prove innocence. Say, "You go away and think about it. You can even write me a note, if that's easier, and then we'll talk some more."

8. Let the Child Face the Consequences of Lying

If, for example, your child has not done his homework for no good reason, don't write a note letting him out of the situation. A small lesson now will prevent big trouble later.

9. Follow Through

Although it is sometimes easier to let the child off the hook because you are tired, or it just doesn't seem worth it, follow through so that the situation is finished for the child. Forgetting about something or letting it slide sends the message that lying isn't really that bad, after all. For instance, if your child writes you a note, as in point 7 above, sit down and have a chat about it, and decide on the sanction.

10. Let It End

After you have finished dealing with it, do just that: finish it. Don't bring it up again and again or you will end up with a child who is a liar—a self-fulfilling prophecy.

11. "Little White Lies"

Explain that sometimes it is kinder to not say anything, or just to tell a "little white lie" if the truth is hurtful. When a friend of mine had radiation therapy after surgery for cancer, she lost her hair and wore a wig, which made her self-conscious. Every time she came over, she asked if I could tell it was a wig. "It looks amazingly like the real thing," was my reply, though it was obviously a wig. She certainly didn't need me to say something that would undermine her confidence any further. It would have been cruel. So I guess I am saying that sometimes it is OK either to lie a little or be silent. I don't want my children to blurt out truths such as, "You're smelly," or "This is the most boring time I've ever had," at the difficult relative's house. Maybe I'm a coward and you don't agree with me, but I think that there are times when people's feelings are more important than the absolute truth.

12. Negotiate

Don't force your child into lying by being totally unreasonable. Ian's parents actually put Ian in a situation where he couldn't win. He felt the only way to get through life at home was to lie because he couldn't live up to expectations. There was no room for negotiation.

Deborah's eldest son, Chris, was invited to go to a dance club with a group of his friends, but knew from past experience that curfew would be an issue. He wanted to go so badly that he arranged to spend the night at a friend's house rather than tell Deborah he needed to stay out late. She found out from another mother and was ready to turn Chris into finely minced hamburger—until she realized that something was amiss if Chris felt he couldn't come to her with a problem like this. They negotiated, and Chris has never once let her down since.

13. Don't Go Overboard About Small Things

It will make it harder to deal with the more important issues.

14. Consequences

Make sure that the consequences to lying are known, if possible, in advance. For example, "If you lie, then you won't get to watch that favorite television program." Or, "You will have to tell anyone you lied to what you did, and apologize to them." It won't always be possible to set consequences in advance, because each situation is different. But generally knowing what will happen might be a deterrent, if it isn't too draconian.

15. Admit Your Mistakes

Admit if you make a mistake and make amends. If you wrongly accuse your child of lying, apologize, offer to get them a new, more perfect mother or father, and keep trying. No one gets it right all the time—people who say they do, are lying.

16. Get Professional Help if It Is Needed

If your child is older than pre school age and is a compulsive liar, and you've tried everything you can think of, get professional help. There are some underlying reasons why they are trying so hard to lie, and it does take effort to keep up a lying lifestyle. Whatever you do, don't ignore the problem and hope that it will adjust itself in time. It won't. Check with your child's school, your doctor, or a psychologist or counsellor.

Cheating

Kids are bad losers. So are some grown-ups I know. To make sure they don't lose, they cheat. When I first started teaching my children card and board games, their ability to cheat was breathtaking. Cards would miraculously appear from up their sleeves, Monopoly money and property cards mysteriously ended up in their ownership, extra Scrabble letters suddenly popped up from nowhere, and the rules shifted ominously in their favor. If they lost, there were tears, cries of "that's not fair" and sulks combined with threats of "I'm not playing with you ever again." Yet, somehow, both boys have turned into avid and fair game players. At times, I despaired this would never happen and I thought only my children were such horrible monsters. Not true.

All children cheat, especially when they are young. Cheating comes naturally when you want to win, haven't yet learned that other people have feelings and that fairness doesn't just mean fair for you.

The trick is to help them through this selfish stage and to make sure that they don't turn into habitual cheats who get into trouble when they are older. I guess we are trying to give them a sense of fair play.

Start when your children are first learning about games, sports and rules:

17. Explain That Cheating Is Wrong

Always explain that cheating is wrong, because it is not fair to everyone. Try to get children to see that they would not like it if someone else cheated on them. Give concrete examples such as: "If Alan took away your card, would you like it? Would it be fair? Then it isn't fair to take away Alan's card because he doesn't like it." Young children work better with examples than with abstract ideals.

18. Explain the Rules

Explain each rule clearly in terms your child can understand. "Everyone takes seven letters. If you take more, it is cheating and we all know that is wrong. But I know everyone is going to play fair because that's more fun." (I know they may not buy it 100 percent, but keep saying it until they do.)

19. Let One or Two Things Pass

With very young children, you might let one or two things pass. However, it is best to try to stop cheating whenever you see it. Sometimes, a quiet word with the culprit works better than embarrassing her in public. Other times you may have to resort to shoot-out-at-the-OK-Corral-type tactics and call her out on her cheating. Usually, one of the other kids will begin the "shoot-out" and you'll have to mediate.

20. End the Game if Necessary

If it is not clear what happened, the game may have to end. This is unfair to those who weren't cheating, but sometimes it can't be helped. Always follow up this kind of outcome with a discussion, and reinforce your disapproval of cheating.

21. Supervise

If your child cheats and you know it, then supervise any situations with other children as much as possible. Play games with them. Wander into the room where they are playing and observe. Use what you observe to discuss with your child how to behave. Play games alone with your child, and help him model good behavior.

22. Notice and Comment on Fair Play

Give kids lots of praise when they do it right and say how proud you are that they are turning into fair players.

23. Use Tools

Look for books and videos with fair play themes. Use them as a way of showing your children how people should behave.

24. Apologize

Teach your child to apologize for cheating, but don't make it so humiliating that it is counterproductive. A quick "Sorry" is good enough in my books, if it is followed by fair play.

25. What if She Cheats at School?

If your child is cheating at school or in sports, you will soon find out about it, either from the teachers or from other children. First, find out all the facts (as in Lying above). If it is true, then make sure your child apologizes, accepts whatever sanctions are set, makes up for the cheating in some way and then starts again with a clean slate. This may be difficult if all the other children know, and you will need to support your child through the bad times. Let him or her know that you understand people make mistakes, and that you know it won't happen again.

Make sure that your child isn't cheating at school because the pressure is too great. If your expectations are too high, you might be inadvertently pushing your child into cheating. This doesn't mean you shouldn't have expectations. It does mean that you should check with the teachers and your child to set is realistic goals. This is very important. I have dealt with several cases of suicide and attempted suicide of children under the age of twelve who felt completely out of their depth. It's far better to ease off than to have to cope with such tragedies.

If your child is putting pressure on him or herself that leads to cheating, seek professional help. If you feel you cannot cope with what is happening and your child's cheating behavior does not stop, don't ignore it. Get help. (See point 16 in Lying, above.)

Stealing

When young children see something they want, they take it. As far as their little egos are concerned everything *is* theirs. The sun isn't the center of the universe—they are. That is why they get so hysterical when someone takes something that belongs to them. One mother consulted me in a panic because her two-year-old was "stealing" from shops, from her, from relatives, and from neighbors. She thought she had a budding Al Capone on her hands and wanted to fix it before her child fulfilled his early promise! After reassurance that this was quite natural behavior and that she was not a terrible mother, she went home relieved. I wish all my cases were as easy.

Just because small children think that anything within reach belongs to them, doesn't mean we should let them get away with it— not by a long shot. With little ones, we watch like hawks in stores put back ill-gotten gains, and pay for those consumed in seconds. We keep a look out for objects that don't belong to them that have materialized out of thin air in their pockets. And we tell them that those things belong to someone else, even if they don't want to hear it or believe it.

As children get older, say six or seven, depending upon their maturity, we might have to march them back into shops and enjoin them to apologize for taking something without paying. Most kids try it at some time, and we have to make sure they don't get into the habit. It is highly embarrassing for parents to have to do this, but believe me, it is effective.

To help children learn that stealing isn't something you'll put up with, you might want to try some of the following ideas.

28. Express Disapproval

Make sure they know that you think stealing is wrong. If you are clear about this in discussions and show them by example, they will know the ground rules. If you are given too much change in a store, give it back, and then explain why. If you see someone shoplifting, report it. Use books and films to make sure they understand why stealing is wrong.

29. Return the "Goods"

Make sure that if your child steals something, he or she gives it back. It is best to ask him what he thinks he should do. If he doesn't come up with the right answer (i.e., give it back!) tell him. Help him make arrangements to return or make restitution for what he's taken.

30. Meet Your Child's Needs

Make sure you are giving your child enough allowance (within reason, of course!) for his or her needs. It may be that your child cannot go out with friends or manage on what she is given, and that this is the reason for the stealing.

31. Get to the Root of the Problem

Try to find out any other reason why your child is stealing. It may be for the thrill of it, or because of peer pressure. In at least six cases I have dealt with, children were stole to pay off bullies who were threatening them. It could also be some underlying problem, such as unresolved hostility, jealousy, or anger, which requires some counselling. Or it might just be plain, everyday greed.

32. Help Him Stop

Use common sense to help the child stop, whatever the cause. If your child steals because friends are pressuring him to, try to help him get new friends. Or contact the parents of the friends and have a meeting to bring about more parental control. If it isn't possible to change or cut out these friends, arrange supervised playtimes or outings so that your child can't get into more trouble. If your child is paying off a bully, contact the school or the police. If your child needs counselling, contact a local family service organization. If your child is stealing out of greed, arrange for her to do a little community service to get a different perspective on the world. Perhaps a local soup kitchen needs volunteers, or a home for the elderly could do with someone to help weeding or serve dinner.

33. Use All the Help You Can Get

If you are really desperate because your child continues to steal no matter what you try, contact your local friendly police officer—the one who goes into schools if your community has this service—and get some advice. Sometimes a talking to or a little reality therapy goes a long way when it comes from someone in authority.

34. Use Her School's Resources

Work with the teachers and staff if your child is stealing at school. If the other children know about the stealing, your child will be labelled a thief, which will make it more difficult for him to have friends. Other parents might not want your child to come over to their homes. You may try talking with one or two other parents and explain that you are dealing with the problem and would appreciate their support. You may find them quite understanding. Perhaps the teachers could help by choosing books or projects around themes such as people changing their behavior, forgiveness, or not being judgmental. The lessons should not be obviously aimed at your child, but it is a positive way to give kids a second chance.

35. Don't Provide Temptation

Make sure that you don't leave money lying around. This might tempt your child into more stealing.

36. Share Your Stories

Tell your child about a time you took something. Relate the consequences and what you learned from it. It helps kids to know that everyone makes mistakes and that they are not condemned for life.

37. Praise Your Child for Good Behavior

Let him know that you believe he is capable of not stealing and that you are proud of him for trying so hard to stop.

38. Reward Honesty

Too often we focus on what children do wrong, instead of what they do right. So look out for little acts of honesty and give lots of praise. When your children bring you change from shopping or give you something they found, make a fuss and tell them they are wonderful.

Fortunately, most children do not turn into compulsive liars, thieves, or cheats. They dip briefly into these vices and quickly learn it isn't the right way to behave. Some children, I am told, never do any of these things and are little saints, though I've not met one. For those of us who don't have saints for children, I think the best things we can do to help them grow up to be good, honest adults are:

- to keep their transgressions in perspective
- to catch them being good
- never to label them as thieves, liars or cheats
- to be patient, firm and loving
- to set a good example

Setting a good example means that if you get stopped for speeding, you should tell the officer that you knew you were speeding and admit that this isn't the first time you've done it and that you were just lucky not to be caught before. And you have to talk to your aunt when she phones, instead of pretending not to be home. Now *that's* what I call honesty.

25

10 Things to Do When Your Child Is in With a Bad Crowd

What can you do if your child chooses friends you hate? Or worse, if you spot your round-faced, dewy-eyed pre-teenager hanging out with a bunch of shaven-headed, multi-earringed weirdos who make the rival gangs of your youth look like Boy Scouts? It's a situation all parents face sooner or later. Unfortunately, we seem to be facing it sooner with younger and younger children. Should we live with "the gang" or take drastic action.

Here she is at last, the girl your just-turned twelve-year-old has waxed lyrical about for the past three weeks. "She's just great," your daughter said last week. "Some kids don't like her, but they're just jealous because she is so popular with the boys. She's got some really *rad* friends."

"Invite her over some time," you said.

She arrives in black fishnet tights, heavy white makeup, frizzy bleached hair, and a skintight miniskirt that even you wouldn't have dared wear in the sixties. This is your innocent twelve-year-old daughter's new best friend. (Did she say her name was Lolita?)

Suppressing a desire to giggle and scream at the same time, you offer your hand. Fingernails from hell come toward you, each one a different color and an inch long. Perhaps you're only dreaming. Muttering something about finishing your report for the office, you retreat to the bathroom and close the door.

Where did you go wrong? Oh, for the days when you invited her friends over and served jello and cookies....Then you remember your neighbor's boy, David.

David was such a lovely kid when he was small, but he fell in with the wrong crowd at just this age. He refused to go to school, stayed out late, got into trouble with the police for shoplifting, and caused your friend to age ten years. Whatever happened to him? Was it a modern-day Alcatraz he ended up in? Oh, that's right, he's married now, with a little girl of his own. He's a dentist or something like that.

OK, maybe you're overreacting, but the truth is that Lolita is here, now, in your daughter's bedroom. What does your ordinary, nice child see in her?

When I was twelve I did well at school, helped around the house, and was a goody-goody. My friends were the stalwarts of the school, until Denise came into our class. Denise, it was rumored, knew how to French kiss. I desperately wanted to learn how the French kissed, and I thought Denise was wonderfully grown-up. I looked up to her. I loved her. My parents did not. I was attracted to Denise for the same reasons today's kids are attracted to "unsuitable" friends and gangs.

To Test Values

Because then they'll find out what they really believe in. David, now the dentist, went with the gang for kicks. It was fortunate that his gang didn't do anything worse that might have affected him for the rest of his life. His parents were farsighted enough to stand by him and not label him a thief. Ultimately, he discovered that his family's values were more important to him than the gang's.

To Act Grown-Up

We adults drink, maybe smoke, and stay out late having a good time. We tell our kids to wait until they're grown up to do these things. Then we are shocked, hurt, or angry when we find our kids trying out these things "before their time." The gang tells them they are already grown up, and proves it by doing all the forbidden things that adults enjoy. Even to be on the fringes of a group that tries drinking and smoking is exciting, especially if you think you're more grown up than your parents think you are. With Denise and her gang, I once tried smoking. My career as a *femme fatale* was, however, short-lived; I somehow dropped the lighted cigarette into my blouse. It is hard to look cool while dancing around beating at your breast and screaming.

To Meet Emotional Needs

Eleven-year-old Andy was so shy he could hardly look people in the face when he talked to them. He was bullied and had no friends. So his parents were delighted when Andy started hanging around with a group and getting telephone calls. Delighted, that is, until the principal called to tell them that Andy and his group had been picking on the younger kids.

Horrified, they confronted him. Andy fiercely defended his new friends and said they were only playing. But at their meeting with the principal, his parents found out that Andy had become one of the ringleaders of the gang. Andy was striking back against all the slights and hurts he had received over the years. In a gang, he felt safe enough to vent his anger. With the right group of friends, he might have found a more positive way to express himself.

To Be Accepted

Being accepted by their age group is vital to children. It gives them the structure and safety to make mistakes, to develop their personalities, and even to become a little humble (we wish!).

A good group helps reinforce the values parents like; a bad group can make life intolerable for us. To be accepted, kids will do almost anything, including experimenting with illegal drugs, which seem to be available even to elementary school children in some areas. Kids may also try alcohol, cheating, smoking, vandalism, and shoplifting. If the gang does it and you want to be in the gang, you do it.

At my son's school, the teachers were shocked when they found out about the activities of a ten-year-old boy. Over the weekend he invited some other boys to his house. They drank all the alcohol they could find and accidentally set fire to the carpet while lighting up his father's cigars! Don't ask me where his parents were, but I am just thankful that my son wasn't there. I can only hope that if he had been, he would have left, but I will never know.

I think we have to keep it in perspective. Were these some of the things you tried in order to be accepted by a group: clothes, hairstyles, bad language? The dangers of drugs and solvent abuse that threaten our children probably seem a world away from the danger many of us faced. Feel for them.

To Experiment

When they only experiment by growing penicillin cultures on discarded snacks under the bed or never hanging up their clothes, you're lucky! When they experiment by getting into the wrong crowd and try illegal drugs or driving around in stolen cars, you're not. And then, of course, there's sex.

Thirteen-year-old Jenny looked and acted nineteen. She attracted the attention of some older boys, who invited her into their gang. She was flattered by the attention and by being told that she was "sexy." The young girl soon found her status in the gang depended on having sex with the leader. When Jenny's parents heard what was happening, they intervened. Jenny had been having some other problems, and the family did need some help, so this did not come as a bolt out of the blue. Long often heated discussions followed and Jenny was subsequently kept in and forbidden to see the boy or the gang. She did sneak out once or twice, but it was more to test her parents' resolve than to get back in with the crowd. Her parents could have called the police, because the older boy was breaking the law by being sexually involved with Jenny, who was under age at the time.

Jenny later told her parents that she was secretly glad to be able to blame them because she just didn't know how to get away. She needed help. And that's usually where parents come in. Don't be put off by your children's protests that they are grown up and can handle whatever happens. They aren't and they can't.

There are some strategies you can try when you are worried about your kids" friends. Some may work and some may not, but at least you'll have done your best.

1. Invite Those Awful Friends Over

It may get on your nerves having Lolita, Jungle Jim, and Monosyllabic Bill around, but better to have them where you can see them than out of sight but always on your mind. Impossible though it may seem, you may even grow fond of them once you get to know the people behind the horrendous exteriors.

Suggest places to go, like bowling alleys, movies, clubs, and swimming. So much of the malaise children exhibit is due to being at a loose end. Those kids who seem to have the easiest passage as teenagers, are often the ones with lots of interests, many developed from an early age: music, art, drama, sports. Kids look for excitement, which can lead to car stealing or shoplifting, or can be channeled into something more useful.

2. Try to Withhold Judgement

When I brought my friend Denise home, the only comment I remember was Dad saying he cared too much about me to let me go out dressed like her. His comment was not against her so much, just protective of me.

Denise let down her guard with us. My parents did not hesitate to say what they thought and felt, but they never made it seem as if they were judging. No one ever said how much they liked Denise, but no one ever said she was a terrible person, either.

3. Help Them Set Limits

Often, teenagers are afraid to hurt someone's feelings or do not want to look foolish in front of others. Then they end up in dangerous situations. If you can help them decide their limits in advance, they will be in a better position to make judgments about what to do. Talk to your children about what they'd do if they were with a group that wanted to get drunk, take drugs, shoplift, sniff glue, crash a party, and so on.

4. Help Them Stick to These Limits

The old "My mean old Mom won't let me..." routine is useful whenever they're asked to join in something they think is dubious. (I don't mind the mean, but I object to the old!) We shouldn't be put off by our children's rebellious poses; they may complain, but many are secretly grateful to be able to place the blame on their parents.

5. Tell Them to Trust Their Intuition

Often, children, particularly young teenagers, do not trust their own feelings and judgment. They often go along with bad ideas so they won't appear silly in front of friends.

Max was talked into having a party while his parents were away for the evening. His friends said they would help clean up and that his parents would never know. Everything went well until a group of troublemakers crashed the party. Max knew immediately that he should get help, but thought that by handling the situation himself he would appear to be a big man in front of his friends, and that his parents wouldn't find out. The troublemakers began to beat up the boys, molest some of the girls, and wreck the house. Finally Max called the police. If Max had trusted his initial judgement not to hold the party, or even to get help right away, none of this would have happened.

6. Arrange a Code

Regardless of whether you love or hate your child's group of friends, arrange a code that can be used to rescue her from any situation.

Twelve-year-old Heather was at a party where drugs and alcohol were available. She had lied to her parents about where she was (she was supposed to be spending the night with a friend) and she needed rescuing. She hadn't expected to be confronted with this. She and her dad had worked out a code to be used in case of emergency. Her parents would know that she needed them to get her if she called and asked, "Has Pat called me?" Dad had promised her he would pick her up any time, night or day, with no questions asked.

She decided to give it a try and it worked;—she told him where she was, and he came, collected her, and restrained himself from asking anything. Soon after, Heather gave up this gang of friends. Her dad will never know for sure if it was his nonjudgmental attitude that helped her break away, or whether she just outgrew them, but the code certainly didn't hurt.

The hardest part for her parents was sticking to "no questions asked." It was better, though, than Heather not calling from a potentially dangerous situation. It would have been even better if Heather's parents had telephoned the parents of the friend Heather was supposed to be staying with, even though some kids consider this "checking up on them." Well, so be it—we do need to talk to another adult if our kids are going to be in someone else's care. For that matter, what if we need to contact them in an emergency and find they are not there?

7. Find Time to Be Alone With Them

Try to establish a time with your child when just the two of you can talk privately. If possible, do this away from the home so that you have a neutral place to talk. Perhaps you can go to a cafe for a hot chocolate or coffee, or even out to lunch. You don't have to bill it as a time to talk, but that is usually what ends up happening. I've noticed that when our family is traveling or eating out together, our children seem to be much more willing to talk than at home. I guess it's because the lure of the television, telephone, and other distractions are missing and it frees them (and us) to focus more on one another.

8. Encourage Interests

It is possible that your child is stuck with this crowd because she can't find other children with common interests or skills. Find out what is available that your child might like to get involved in, and that could also open up other friendships. Music, sports, martial arts, dance, computers—there are many possibilities either at school or within your local area. It may be a pain to organize, but it is worth the effort if it gives your child a way out of the crowd she is in now.

9. Give It Time

The policy we usually have to follow when our children fall in with the wrong crowd is simply to wait it out. Nerve-wracking and heart-stopping though this may be, it almost always works. The group just outgrows itself and no longer meets anyone's needs. Kids drift off, find new friends, leave school, or move, and suddenly the problem has resolved itself.

10. Get Tough

You need to make your position quite clear when your child is in real danger from a bad crowd. I am sure Denise wouldn't have been welcomed into our house if she had been using drugs. If your children are in danger, it goes without saying that your first responsibility must be to them.

The first line of defense is to know the signs of gambling, drug, alcohol or solvent abuse. I know it seems impossible to have to consider this with children, let alone teenagers, but we must. I never really thought I had to worry about any of this stuff until my children were older, but that's not true any more. A recent survey of 5,000 children in elementary school showed that almost 40 percent of four-year-olds and 93 percent of eleven-year-olds knew about drugs. In the same survey, 53 percent of the eleven-year-olds felt that drugs could be good for them. More comforting was that 90 percent also knew that there was a potential harmful effect of drugs. Our children often know more than we think they do, and some are being offered drugs and others are already taking them before the age of eleven. If your child exhibits signs of drug abuse or gambling, forget the "It'll soon pass" attitude and take action. Get involved, and call on experts.

Symptoms of Possible Drug or Solvent Abuse

- inexplicable personality change
- frequently changing moods
- becoming secretive, vague, or withdrawn
- alternately very drowsy or hyperactive
- paranoia
- slurred or slow speech
- paraphernalia left around, such as burnt foil, needles, pipes
- glue on clothing
- red eyes, spots, red nose, jerky movements
- stealing, lying

Signs That Your Child Might Be Gambling

- money disappearing from home
- truancy
- possessions disappearing or being sold
- lying
- bloodshot eyes
- behavior that is aggressive or completely withdrawn

If you think your child's crowd is into drugs, stealing from shops, or skipping school, then forget the nonjudgmental, sit-back-and-wait attitude. Here's what to do.

- Keep an adult perspective and don't feel it is necessary to get on the same level as your children or teenagers by acting "cool." They have enough of the other point of view from their group.
- Don't be afraid to say that using drugs, shoplifting, skipping school, and gambling are wrong, that you disapprove wholeheartedly, and that you will ensure that it stops. Talk about your family standards and values. Tell your child that it doesn't matter to you if her friends and their families have different standards. Explain that you expect your child to uphold your family standards.

Children may rail against this outwardly, but often it gives them the inner strength they eventually use to break away from the gang.

- Get it together with parents of other members of the group and agree rules, allowance rates, and any other guidelines that make it harder for your children or teenagers to say "but everyone's doing it."
- Keep communication open, because although you are worried and angry, the more you withdraw, the more they will—a downward spiral.
- Use a last resort if your child is in extreme danger and you need to get him out of the situation. Ask your parents, in-laws, or other relatives to let him move in for a month. Or take your child out of school and educate him at home, with the help of your school district, if possible. This does place quite a burden on you. In extreme cases, consider moving to get away from the gang once and for all.

None of these solutions will work, though, if your child really needs whatever the gang provides. Sometimes it is just bad luck that the child ends up with a wild and weird group. Other times, a child has a very real problem and the choice of group reflects that.

If all your efforts fail, it's time to seek professional counseling to try to unravel things before they get worse.

Take Heart

Children need to break away, change, grow, and find their own paths. Groups help them do that. Sometimes even the wrong crowds help them find their own values, which turn out not to be a million miles from your own.

We laugh about my childhood friend Denise now—she and I together, that is! Through our friendship she grew to adopt the values of my family. Now she complains about "kids today." I used our friendship to find out if I wanted to keep those very same values. I did. And I just hope I have a tenth of the patience my parents showed me when, and if, my two boys get into the wrong crowds or bring home a Lolita Liz or Acid House Annie as the latest girlfriend.

26

16 Things to Do About Lost Children

"How many of you have ever been lost?"

The assembly of 300 children became a sea of waving hands.

"How many of you have never been lost?"

Four hands shot up.

Amazing? No. Ask any group of children and you will be hard-pressed to find many who haven't been lost.

Six-year-old Alan keeps his hand up, urgently seeking attention. "Mrs. Elliott, Mrs. Elliott!"

"Yes Alan?"

"My mom got lost in the shopping center. I looked up and she was just gone. Moms shouldn't go off that way—it scared me." The older children giggled. Sooooo sophisticated, at ten!

Then everyone wanted to tell their stories. It seemed that getting lost was the most common thing that ever happened to kids, and the one thing that caused great anxiety. In fact, ask your adult friends.

"'We were at the park and I suddenly realized that my mom had disappeared. I was absolutely terrified. The trees became attacking giants, the wind was swirling around, ready to take me off. Even the passing people looked sinister. I was only four, but I can still remember that awful, sinking feeling of being alone." Lynn is twenty-seven years old but the look on her face is still of being four and lost. This feeling of absolute panic is one parents will know well.

Discovering your child is lost ranks amongst the ten worst things a parent dreads, and it is one of the ten most likely things to happen while you are raising children. I don't know a parent who hasn't lost a child at one time or another. Luckily, most children are found safe and none the worse, apart from fear, within minutes. The rescuer is usually another parent, who recognizes the signs of distress only too well.

We took our children to a large amusement park in Florida and were getting lunch when I noticed a little boy, about age three, looking very forlorn. He was walking slowly around the huge cafeteria, one foot carefully placed in front of the other, as if he was measuring the edge of the room by the length of his feet. He carefully scrutinized every table as he walked past, and kept anxiously looking at people going by with their families. He reminded me of a caged animal. Something wasn't right. I watched for a few minutes to see if anyone came up to him, but no one did. Finally, I approached him, knelt down next to him and asked, "Where is your mommy?" His eyes filled with tears and he gulped, "I don't know." He just collapsed into my lap and threw his arms around my neck. I comforted him, told him we'd find his parents, and asked my husband to contact the cafeteria manager. I tried to turn over my new little friend, Miles, to the manager, but he wouldn't let go. I guess he had decided that I wasn't a stranger, but the manager was. After the public announcement, a frantic, crying woman came rushing in, followed by an equally distraught father and endless other relatives, and Miles was safely back in the bosom of his family. I wonder how long he wandered around before I stopped, and how many people had not picked up the signs? It scared me, because you hope that your child will be helped by a kindly adult should he get lost, and that people will not just turn away. I guess we have to rely on the goodwill of people and give our children some suggestions to follow just in case. But what can we do to arm our children if they get lost? How do we give them strategies without scaring them to death?

1. Arrange a Meeting Place

When you take your children to any public place, arrange a meeting place. Most of us now do this automatically, whether in a store, shopping center, park or restaurant. Our local shopping center is the ideal place to get lost—with lots of eye-catching displays and distractions. The most noticeable feature is the large water fountain, so we always tell the children, "We will meet you at the fountain if we are separated from each other." We say it every time we go to the shopping center, so our kids interrupt to say "I know" or "Boring." Good! I drum it in to those little heads until it is second nature.

2. Give Instructions About Public Transportation

The same goes for public transportation. Helen was getting on the subway with her baby in a carriage, shopping bags, and her three-year-old, Peter.

"I let go of Peter's hand for all of thirty seconds. When I turned to gather him in, the doors closed with him on the outside and me inside. Both of us started crying and screaming, but the train pulled out just the same. I got off at the next stop, with a kind woman who came along when she saw what happened. We ran across the platform, waited for what seemed like an age and got on a train going the other way. We ran back to our original platform, where a group of adults was comforting my very distressed son. I grabbed him and held him close and just wept with relief."

Give your children very clear instructions about what to do if you are separated on a bus or train. You may decide to tell the child to wait at the stop or platform until you come to her. Or you might want her to stay on the bus or train and tell her to talk to the guard or driver, and ask that she be accompanied to the end of the line, where you will arrange to meet her.

3. Accepting Help From Strangers

What about accepting help from people you don't know? This is a dilemma. What if the woman who helped Helen had offered to hold the baby and told her to go and find her son. Well-meaning though she may have been, Helen did not know if it would have been safe to leave her child with her. She was a complete stranger. In a recent case, a woman claiming to be a store detective assured a mother that she would look after the children while the mom went back into the store for a refund. The "detective" kidnapped the baby, who was eventually found safe, thank goodness. We warn children about strangers, but we, too, can become unwitting victims of a kindly face. Most people are genuine, but you never really know. So, always keep your other children with you if you have to look for a missing child. Peter, however, was obviously being helped by a whole posse of kind strangers.

The best advice we can give children is not to talk to strangers if they are on their own. However, if they are lost or need help, tell them they can ask a person who works behind the counter, a police officer, or a person with children for help.

But explain to children that they don't have to hold hands or go anywhere with the person. They can tell the adult that they promised to stay where they last saw you. This relieves them of having to go off with a stranger. Obviously, in the case of my little friend Miles, he was too young and frightened to keep his distance. He just wanted a mommy figure to hug him, and help find his real mommy.

How Adults Can Help

My husband said he'd have felt uncomfortable had the child flung himself into his lap, because he was worried about being seen as a child molester or kidnapper! My husband would help a child in distress but would try to keep the child at arm's length. Unfortunately, this is not an uncommon feeling amongst men because of all the media coverage about child abuse, so I understand how they can feel this way. But I think it is sad, both for men and for children. A well-meaning adult can help lost children by:

4. Offering to get an announcement made or getting a couple of other adults to go for help while he stays near the child.
5. Talking to the child reassuringly.
6. Not offering to hold the child's hand or forcing the child to hold yours.
7. Giving comfort if the child climbs on your lap or grabs your hand.
8. Not taking the child away from where you find him or her unless absolutely necessary, or you could be accused of kidnapping.
9. If possible, calling the parents or waiting until they arrive.
10. Not taking the child somewhere in your car.

What Parents Can Teach Their Children

11. Teach children their full names, addresses, and telephone numbers.
12. Teach children how to use the telephone.
13. Teaching children that they can dial the operator to call home, or they can call 911 or other emergency services without having to use money.
14. Get a friend or relative to wait by the phone if the child is missing for any length of time.
15. Contact the police if you are worried and your child isn't found quickly. Better safe than sorry.

16. Hug them tightly when they are found. Don't yell or scold
    them—they are frightened enough.

Helen says, "The fifteen minutes it took to get back to Peter were the
longest in my life. I am just so grateful that everyone was so helpful."
That is the real message—most people will help and comfort a lost
child, and you are soon reunited with him. The world isn't such a
bad place, after all.

27

53 Things to Do About Bullying

"Bullying is part of human nature, something children must learn to cope with if they are to survive the rough and tumble of everyday life." This can be a hard line to swallow for parents of tender five-year-olds; little ones often find the playground jungle a sinister place at first. At least, though, five-year-olds usually tell their parents about events and people that worry them. The further they go up the school, the more likely it becomes that your children will suffer in silence; either that, or they reveal so little you're not sure how seriously to take it.

Should you root out the problem make an unholy fuss if you find your child is being picked on? Or is it usually best to leave children to sort this kind of thing out between themselves? Bullying is an abuse of power, which has the potential not only to cause short-term misery, but can lay the foundations for adult aggression. After all, versions of the playground heavies and their victims are reenacted in living rooms and boardrooms daily.

1. Know Who Bullies

Before discussing some of the things you can do if your child is being bullied, or if your child is being a bully, let's briefly look at who the bullies are. The stereotype of the big, mean, nasty boy is one that usually comes to mind when the word bully is mentioned. The reality is that bullies can be any shape or size and that girls are as capable of bullying as boys. The kids who frequently bully do seem to share some common characteristics. They often:

- feel inadequate.
- are bullied themselves within their families.
- come from families that extol the "virtues" of bullying.
- are victims of some kind of abuse.
- don't know how or are not allowed to show feelings.
- are not succeeding in school.
- feel no sense of self-worth.

There are also bullies who are self-confident, spoiled children who have always had their own way, expect it as their right, and are prepared to bully to get it.

Then we have the children who may bully others once in a while because they have some sort of upheaval in their lives, such as the birth of a baby, the death of someone they love, rejection from a friend, being the victim themselves of bullying, a run-in with a family member or a teacher, boredom, or a whole host of other problems that lead them to lash out at another child.

2. Understand What Bullying Is

Bullying is the use of aggression with the intention of hurting another person. It results in pain and distress to the victim. Bullying can be:

Physical	pushing, kicking, punching, hitting, or any use of violence
Verbal	name calling, sarcasm, spreading rumors, nasty teasing
Emotional	excluding, being unfriendly, tormenting, using racial taunts, threatening, or making rude gestures

3. Know the Signs of Bullying

Parents need to be aware of the signs that a child might be being bullied. If your child shows some of the following behaviors or signs, you may want to ask about bullying. Children may:

- be frightened of walking to or from school, or change their normal route to school
- not want to go on the school bus
- beg you to drive them to school
- be unwilling to go to school or feel ill every morning
- begin skipping school
- begin doing poorly in their schoolwork

- come home with clothes or books destroyed
- come home hungrier than usual (the bully has taken lunch money)
- become withdrawn, start stammering, and lack confidence
- become distressed and anxious, or stop eating
- attempt or threaten suicide
- cry themselves to sleep or have nightmares
- ask for money or begin stealing (to pay the bully)
- refuse to say what's wrong (frightened of the bully)
- have unexplained scratches, bruises, and so forth
- begin to bully other children or siblings
- become aggressive and unreasonable

If your child does show some of these signs, then ask him if bullying is a problem. Be direct. Say, "I think you are being bullied or threatened and I'm worried about you. Let's talk about it." If your child doesn't tell you immediately, say that you are there and willing to listen, night or day, when he is ready to talk. Then keep a watchful eye—kids can become quite desperate when they are being bullied, and do dumb things like run away or take an overdose because it all seems so hopeless to them.

4. Try to Understand Why the Bully Does It

Bullying is intended to humiliate the victim, and most bullies know exactly what they are doing. Bullying makes them feel powerful and in control. There are times, however, when the bully doesn't realize how much harm she or he is causing. Perhaps she goes along with the crowd and says hurtful things without thinking through what she is doing. Perhaps she bullies because she is secretly frightened that, if she doesn't, she will be the next victim. Perhaps she bullies because she is bored. Whatever the reason, it is no comfort to the victim, whose life has been made miserable.

5. Recognize If Your Child Is a Potential Victim

In my experience, most victims of bullying are sensitive, intelligent, gentle children who have good relationships with their parents. They don't come from families full of conflict and shouting, so when bullies come at them, they don't quite know what to do. They frequently ask why someone would want to bully them—they've done nothing to deserve it and they haven't been treated this way before. The sad fact is that, from the bully's viewpoint, they make excellent targets because they are nice and won't fight back. They might even cry, a bonus for the bully. If you could point out one "fault" of these victims, it would be that they are too nice! In a school that doesn't tolerate bullying, they have no problems.

There are, however, some children who seem to get bullied everywhere—at school, parties, activities, clubs—you name it and they are bullied. These are the children who seem to invite bullying, and almost thrive on the negative attention they get when they are bullied. It is as if the bullying confirms their opinions of themselves that they are worthless, and deserve what is happening to them. These children may have problems that are very similar to the problems of the bullies mentioned above. Or they may have been bullied right from the day they started school and never recovered their confidence. Whatever the reason, they seem to go through life as perpetual victims.

6. Understand the Harm of Bullying

Over the years I have dealt with hundreds of letters and telephone calls about bullying. Children tell of fear, threats, violence, bribery (money or candy being extorted by bullies), sexual attacks, ostracism, and racial attacks. Each letter or telephone call represents a small personal tragedy.

I have talked with parents whose children have run away, continually skipped school, turned to drugs and solvents, become withdrawn, angry, or aggressive, failed in school, and even committed suicide because of bullying. It is a heart-wrenching experience to try to help parents cope with the unnecessary and senseless death of their child, when you know that, had someone taken effective action, their child would still be alive. The parents blame themselves, which is understandable.

But most bullying is school-based and, if the school knew about the bullying but did nothing to stop it, the schoolis to blame. Schools can do many things. If they don't, parents should suggest they adopt the following approaches.

7. Crack the "Code of Silence"

Bullies depend on a code of silence for their success. It is based, of all things, on honor ("It's wrong to tell on someone") or on fear ("Don't tell anyone or I'll beat you"). Either way, it prevents children from telling when they have been bullied or have seen someone being bullied.

To crack the code of silence, schools should be encouraged to become "telling" schools. The principal should makes it clear that bullying is unacceptable and that bullies will not be tolerated. The children have an *obligation* to tell if they are bullied or see bullying take place. They also need to ensure that the adults do something when they are told. Adults have an obligation to *act*. For this approach to succeed, children must be able to rely on a sympathetic and helpful response if they do tell. In this way, they learn that speaking out will make things better; keeping quiet will make things worse. Experience has shown that bullying is much less likely to happen in schools that have a clear policy against bullying.

8. Set Up Student Helpers

The idea of using students to help others is as old as teaching itself. I used this method more than twenty-five years ago when I had a classroom of thirty-four children in Florida, and a few of the older children were making it their business to bully the younger ones.

At the start of the school year, assign new students an older "helper" who acts as an adviser, protector and mentor. Usually, older or bigger children pick on younger or smaller ones *who are alone*. This approach eliminated that problem, and the older children took pride in helping "their" charges. Of course, I had to prepare the older children and instill in them a sense of responsibility, but that wasn't difficult. If a helper was a problem, we didn't allow him or her to be in the program. The competition to be good enough to be a helper was immense, and quite a positive force in the school.

We also set up student helpers who were chosen anonymously by the children and teachers as "people you would most likely seek out to talk to about a problem." They were the "natural helpers" in the school. We gave them some extra training and they become the liaisons for children who felt they needed more help solving a particular bullying problem and felt they wanted someone to go with them to get help from teachers. We made sure the student helpers had a place and time to talk with the children, and privacy to do so. It was a bit of extra time and trouble for all of us, but the results were excellent. Some schools are still using the student helpers with great success.

9. Set Up Bully "Courts"

As with the suggestion about setting up student helpers, I have always found that one of the most effective deterrents to bullying is other kids. In other words, if bullies can be made to feel that their behavior is unacceptable *to the other children,* they will be much more likely to change than if they are simply told by adults to mend their ways. To bring this form of change about, schools can try:

- setting up bully "courts," in which bully and victim are brought together, with a teacher and perhaps the parents, to discuss the causes and effects of what has happened.
- ensuring that the courts are part of a whole school policy, within an atmosphere in which bullying is stripped of any glamour and clearly condemned as wrong. These courts can change a bully's behavior and make the children feel they have a direct involvement in stopping bullying. If the school doesn't wish to set up courts, it is still a good idea to use them as a role palying exercise followed by discussion.

How to Help the Bully

Sometimes it is possible to help a bully by recognizing that she, too, is a victim; perhaps unloved or mistreated at home, or making up for a feeling of personal inadequacy by dominating others. In these cases, treating the underlying cause may also eradicate the bullying. For example, a child with an otherwise poor school record who is encouraged to work hard and excel at some particular subject—art, photography, computing—may in the process gain enough approval to stop bullying. If parents of the bullied can take a sympathetic approach toward the parents of the bully—acknowledging that any of us could find ourselves a parent of a bully one day—there's more likelihood of cooperation than if they feel accused.

In practice, this sort of bridge building is not always possible. Bullies, as I have said above, are very often children who are bullied at home; they may be punished for their own weaknesses (such as bedwetting or something as minor as putting a sweater on backwards), so that they come to see weakness in others as something to be attacked and despised. It is almost a form of self-hate, a diagnosis that will be of small comfort to the mother of a bullied child. Reforming the behavior of a chronic bully is not easy; power may be the only language she understands. When schools organize meetings to discuss the problem of bullying, it is usually the parents of the victims who turn up.

However, if you find yourself as the parent of the bully and are in despair over what to do, approach the school and try to:

10. Remain calm.
11. Find out the facts.
12. Talk to your child to find out if he is upset, or perhaps has been bullied and is lashing out as a reaction.
13. Find out if your child realizes that she is bullying and hurting someone else.
14. Talk with the parents of the victim, if possible, to set things right and to avoid the bullying carrying on.
15. Work with the teacher and show you are concerned.
16. Talk to your child and explain that, whatever problems there may be, bullying is not the way to solve them.
17. Work out a "behavior plan" and reward good behavior.
18. Arrange a daily or weekly report from teachers so you can work together to change your child's behavior.

How to Help the Victims

Sometimes parents and teachers have to work around bullies by teaching their children how to cope with threats, and how to avoid attracting them in the first place. Some children seem more prone to bullying than others. This may result from factors beyond their control that sets them apart from others: the color of their skin, for example, or some striking physical feature, such as being above or below average height. Or it may be that, if they are repeatedly bullied, children start acting like victims. If this happens, parents can take steps to help overcome the problems. Children can be helped to learn some techniques.

19. Walk tall and straight, in a confident way, rather than hunched over, looking scared and uncertain.
20. A timid, shy child can, as a game, practice looking in the mirror and saying "No" or "Leave me alone" in a clear voice, looking into their own eyes as he says it. A firm rebuff will often deter a bully who is looking for signs of weakness and acquiescence.
21. Role-playing. I have used this with great success in schools, and it is something you could try at home with your own children or groups of children. Act out the threatening situation and practice responding calmly but firmly. This type of imaginative play can also help defuse some of the anger that builds up inside children who are persistently bullied.

22. Ignore the bullying. Pretend not to be upset and turn and walk quickly away.
23. Use humor. It is more difficult to bully a child who refuses to take the bullying seriously. This is especially useful with verbal bullying. However, it could make a situation worse if your child is being physically threatened or confronted by a large group of bullies who might get violent.
24. Avoid places where bullying usually occurs.
25. Try to stay with groups of children, if possible. Bullies usually pick on kids alone.
26. Respond to taunts by saying the same thing over and over. This is called the broken record approach. For example, to a chant such as "You're ugly," respond with "Thank you." Then keep saying it over and over: "Thank you, thank you." It gets rather boring for the bully after a while.

    In order for children to feel confident using some of these ideas, you may want to help them to practice and to come up with other ideas. Also, try to give your children confidence by:
27. assuring them that the bullying is not their fault.
28. telling them that you love them and are 100 percent behind them.
29. encouraging them to join groups outside school. Suggest groups such as Cub Scouts, Brownies, Boy or Girl Scouts, clubs, theater or music groups, gymnastics, martial arts clubs—anything which might give your child a chance to develop their talents or new friendships.
30. teaching them relaxation techniques.
31. inviting individual children over to play.
32. helping them to stop any bad habits that might be contributing to their being bullied (such as biting their lips or making strange faces because of nervousness).
33. seeking professional help, if necessary.

Approach the School

Your child may beg you not to talk to the teachers, which will place you in a difficult position. If the bullying is happening at school, the school needs to do something about it. You can certainly try to work it out with your child alone, if that is what you both think is best, but rarely does that solve the problem. Try to talk with your child about who would best deal with the problem at school, and then work out a plan together. Whatever you do, don't ignore the bullying; it will most likely get worse, or even lead to your child trying something desperate to get away from it.

If you are going to approach the school, try these steps.

34. Call and make an appointment with the teacher. Don't just show up, especially if you are angry, as it will start things off on the wrong foot. It is unlikely that the teacher will be able to see you without an appointment, anyway. If it is urgent, say so when you phone, and ask for a meeting within the next couple of days.

35. Bring a written record of what has happened to the meeting. Also have copies of any letters you may have written to the school, and details of any telephone calls. This makes it easier to remember and to check on facts, if necessary.

36. Listen to the school's explanation. Say that you want to work together with them to stop the bullying. It is always better if there is cooperation between the parents and the school.

37. If you feel unsure about the meeting, or if there has been any antagonism between you and the school, bring along someone else who could be a witness to what is said.

38. Make out a short list of points you want to cover in the meeting, and use it as a reminder.

39. Ask to see any policy the school has developed about dealing with bullying.

40. If the problem has not got out of hand yet, ask that the children work together on a solution. This is a particularly good approach if your child has been part of a group, that has somehow fallen apart. When this happens, the children usually have some residue of good feelings that can be used to resolve the bullying. The best outcome in your child's view may be that she makes up with her old friends, or that they are at least sympathetic and stop bullying.

41. If the problem is sustained bullying from someone or a group with no previous friendship with your child, and it cannot be resolved as above, the school should:
    • ensure your child is safe.
    • investigate what has happened.
    • interview the victim and bully separately.
    • interview witnesses.

Depending upon the situation, they should take appropriate action such as:

- obtaining an apology.
- informing the bully's parents.
- imposing sanctions.
- insisting that anything that was taken or destroyed be returned or replaced.
- providing support and a safe place, if necessary, for the victim.
- ensuring that the bullying stops by supervising the bully.
- giving the bully help to change her behavior
- letting you know what is happening.

42. Set a mutually agreed time limit for the action to take place. If you feel that the bullying has not stopped or nothing you agreed upon is being done, make another appointment with the principal.
43. If the bullying still continues, contact school superintendent.
44. If that doesn't help, think about contacting your school board. Complain in writing. Begin your letter with, "I am writing to make a formal complaint..."
45. If the matter is still not deal with, and is extreme enough, you may wish to bring in the local media. Make sure that this is all in the best interests of your child.

Each district has its own procedures—this is just a general guide. You will have to find out what happens in your own.

Last Resort

If you feel that no one is helping and that the situation with the school has become impossible, try one of the following ideas.

46. Get a Sick Note From the Doctor

If your child is really stressed, keep him at home until you can sort things out

47. Remove Your Child From That School and Find Another

If at all possible, find one that which has a strong policy against bullying. In some cases I have dealt with, the child who was the victim of bullying in one school thrives and has no problems in the new "anti- bullying" school. One can only conclude that it wasn't the child who had the problem, but the school that allowed it to go on.

48. Home Schooling

Think about educating your child at home. In most localities you can find organizations that give advice and support for homeschooling.

The great majority of bullying cases never reach these later steps. And most schools now do seem to want to deal with bullying, but you may be unlucky.

What if the Teacher or Staff Member Is the Bully?

Some of the most difficult cases I have had to deal with has been when a teacher or a staff member is reported to be bullying children by picking on them, humiliating them, or taunting them. If you discover that your child is being bullied in this way take the following steps.

49. Talk With the Teacher

Express your concerns. Perhaps your child has misinterpreted something that was said or done, and it can be straightened out without a fuss.

50. See the Principal

If you feel the situation is beyond this kind of repair, and that you cannot speak to the teacher or staff member, see the principal and explain what has happened. In some schools you have to go through the principal to make an appointment to see teachers, anyway.

51. Keep a Log

Keep a written record of the incidents and how they have affected your child. It may be that the teacher is unaware of what she is doing and that the bullying will stop. But it may be that the teacher's way of dealing with children is not suited to your child (or any child) and that the teacher needs to be talked with and shown more positive ways of interacting. Whatever the reasons, if the teacher is bullying children, then it should be stopped immediately.

52. Move Up the Ladder of Bureaucracy

If the bullying goes on, get in contact with the superintendent or whoever is appropriate in your district. Follow the steps laid out above. At all stages, keep written records and, if you can see that it is necessary, bring along someone as an independent witness to meetings.

53. Change Schools

If, ultimately, it doesn't stop and all avenues fail, then try your very best to find another school.

End the Conspiracy of Silence

One thing's for sure: Bullying is one of the hardest social problems your children have to deal with. It has probably been made harder by the conspiracy of silence about it bred into us by our stoic forebears: Don't be a tattletale or the handle-it-by-yourself ethos. This tacit approval of bullying is one inheritance we needn't pass on to the next generation...and our children need not suffer in silence.

28

26 Ways to Help Your Children Deal With Divorce or Separation

When I was nine, my best friend Celeste found out that her parents were divorcing. Celeste was the only child in the entire school to have this happen to her and the shock was enormous, not only to her but to all of us, the teachers, and the community. It was spoken of in whispers.

Today we no longer speak in whispers about divorce or separation which is Not surprising, considering that something half of marriages end in divorce. That figure doesn't even include partners who live together and then separate. Exact figures are impossible to determine, but at least several million and probably more children are affected by these breakups—certainly, many more than when Celeste had to cope.

The shock for children is still the same as it was for Celeste all those years ago. I was counseling ten-year-old Marilyn, who told me about how she found out her parents were splitting. She was seven at the time.

"I'll never forget the day my mother told us. My younger brothers and I were playing outside when she came out and asked us to come indoors. She was crying and said she had some bad news. I was terrified. My father was waiting for us. With us all sitting there, my father said he was leaving and divorcing my mom. She was sobbing. All of us kids started crying, too. I asked him why. After a long silence he said that he had fallen out of love with Mom and in love with someone else.

"I screamed 'No!' and ran out of the room. My six-year-old brother ran after me. My youngest brother sunk deep into the sofa and cried his heart out. It was like a bad scene from a film and everything was in slow motion. My mother came after us and hugged us while we all sobbed.

"I was crushed. I hated my father for causing this pain. I wanted to help my mother, but I was too upset and angry. I guess I was too little to have been of much help, but I really did want to make her stop crying and become our happy Mommy again. I knew lots of kids who had stepparents, or who commuted between their parents, but I never, ever thought it would happen to me.

"It was awful when Dad left. I couldn't believe that we would never be a family again. I missed him, but I hated him, too. You know, I never heard my parents fight so the whole thing was a shock. I went over and over in my head how I could have prevented it happening. I decided that maybe I should have cleaned up my room or not fought with my brothers. Maybe I should have got better grades at school. I also thought that, if I promised God I would be good for the rest of my life, He might organize it so they would get back together. All I wanted was for things to get back to normal. For a while, I made a secret pact that I wouldn't eat and I would get so sick they would have to put me in hospital. Then my parents would come to visit me and promise to get back together to save me."

Her parents didn't get back together. Marilyn is coping. Her father has remarried; he and his new wife are expecting a child. Her mother is working full-time and occasionally goes out with friends, but she doesn't have a boyfriend. Marilyn no longer hates her father; she and her brothers see him on weekends. They like his new wife, but they are torn by loyalty to their mother and are worried that she is lonely.

Marilyn's story is not unusual. I suppose she is lucky that she is loved by both parents and has maintained contact with her father. Often, the parent who leaves home ends up leaving the family, or is pushed away. One study showed that over 50 percent of noncustodial fathers had completely lost contact with their children within five years of their divorces.

Children are not consulted about the breakup of their families.

They usually have no control over who gets custody and how often they see the noncustodial parent. Some divorces occur because one parent is trying to protect the children from the abuse of the other parent. More often, divorce happens because parents are trying to protect themselves. They think that "It's better for me and it must be better for the children." Often that's true, but sometimes it isn't better for the children. That doesn't mean that parents should stay together in an intolerable situation only for the sake of the children, but they should not kid themselves that their children will thank them for divorcing or separating.

Telling Your Children

In my opinion, Marilyn's parents did the right thing by together telling their children that they were divorcing. My concern, however, was that it turned into such a dramatic scene. All the children I have seen can remember in great detail exactly what happened when they were told about their parents splitting up. While it is understandable that everyone will be upset, try your best not to fall apart when telling the kids. It also may be better to tell them over a period of time, but that will depend upon how old they are and how much the two of you can work together.

Before you do anything, it might be a good idea to go to the library or bookshop and get one of the many books that are available on the subject of divorce and children. There seem to be hundreds of them. Keep in mind that many have been written by parents who have themselves been through divorce, so you may or may not agree with all the advice they give. But it might help you avoid pitfalls that others have fallen into.

From what children have told me, the following suggestions seem to make it easier for them to adjust.

1. Plan in advance what you are going to say. Agree to keep personal blame out of it.
2. Tell them together, if possible.
3. Tell them the truth. Whatever you do, don't gloss over the fact that the marriage or relationship is over. That will only prolong the suffering, and they won't trust what you say later.
4. Give them time to adjust. For some, like Marilyn, the news comes out of the blue.

5. Allow them to let out their feelings, even if they are very angry. This is not the time to scold them for their rudeness. You may just have to "take it on the chin" and bite your tongue. This is far better for them than forcing the anger inside where it will eat away at them.

6. Try to stay calm. It is reassuring for children to think that adults are still in control when their world has been turned upside down. If you cry and carry on it won't help them. Avoid quarrelling and laying blame.

7. Turn your attention to the children, and be as cordial to each other as you can under the circumstances.

8. Talk about what will remain the same. Kids will wonder if they will be moving, whether they will go to the same school, what will happen to pets and possessions, and so forth.

9. Reassure them that you both still love them. If possible, explain that they will still see both parents.

10. Reassure them that it is not their fault. Make sure they know that nothing they did was responsible for the split.

11. Answer their questions as frankly as you can. If you don't know the answer, say so.

12. Be patient. Things do get better with time. Children are resilient. With your help, they will cope.

How Children Are Affected by It

If you have to divorce or separate, children will be affected in different ways. Some will be relieved because the constant tension at home will finally go away. Others will be distraught. A few will seemingly take it in stride. Whatever reactions they show us, I have found that most children are negatively affected by these three aspects of divorce or separation.

- They are lonely and feel isolated. Attention and affection that would go to them is diverted away because parents are struggling with their own emotions and needs.
- Children use a stable family life as a base and a model for their future relationships. If this base is unsettled it can make them unsure and distrustful about forming close relationships with people.
- Children are often used as part of the cannon fodder of disintegrating relationships. They are pulled one way and then the other

by parents trying to gain their loyalty. They may be asked to prove their love by rejecting or vilifying one of their parents—an impossible choice for most kids.

If you can address these issues, it will help your children in the long run. Obviously, you cannot help breaking up the family base, but you can talk about it and help your child see that not all relationships end this way. If there is any way you and your ex can form a friendly or at least tolerable relationship, it usually helps the children enormously.

Reactions

Children react in different ways to a family breakup. They may:

- withdraw.
- cling to both parents.
- become irritable.
- become aggressive.
- be sad and cry.
- do badly at school.
- blame themselves.
- play one parent against the other.
- grieve.
- run away.
- stop eating or even try to commit suicide as a means of getting parents back together.
- get sick.
- become angry.
- feel guilty and responsible.
- be bullied by other kids using this as an excuse.
- feel bitter.
- start acting out and refusing to obey.

Some children will show none of these signs, improving because the previous situation was so bad; the divorce has made it better. Others will take all their pain inside so they can protect their siblings or their parent. To help make it better:

13. Tell Your Children as Much As Possible

The kids I've talked with really resented not knowing what was happening. One boy said that his parents presumed he wouldn't understand and so didn't explain things. As a result, he imagined all sorts of things and worried unnecessarily. "They thought that, since I was only five, I was too young." Kids usually cope better when they aren't kept in the dark.

14. Answer Their Frequent Questions

Children will ask the same questions again and again, but it is not to get attention or to drive you nuts. They need to be told for reassurance. Answer in a matter of fact way and try not to get annoyed.

15. Try to Provide Stability

Spend as much time as possible with them and try to keep their routine as it was. If they are acting out, it is probably to test that there are still limits out there. Allow some leeway, but don't let them get away with things. If they do, it will only increase their anxiety. They need to know you're still in charge, which will give them stability.

16. Get Help if Necessary

If things are not going well, get professional help. Sometimes it is too much for you and the children to cope alone. As I mention in the next chapter about grief, there are times when it is easier and safer to talk with someone outside the family. This is not a reflection on your parenting skills. The reality is that you might be too close to what's happening to be able to help effectively. Of course, you may wish to get help, too, through this difficult time.

Afterward

You will have many things to work out regarding the children. I see far too many children who have parents who hate each other. They are lost little creatures and need lots of help. I suspect there are lots of children out there who have gone through a divorce but don't need professional help precisely because their parents handled things so well. The parents may well hate each other, but somehow they have managed to put their own needs aside and help their kids. Maybe they are just good actors! In any event, try to make it as easy for your kids after the split as you can.

17. Work Out Custody Agreements

Try to agree access before the court battle. Seeing both parents is very important to most children.

18. Let Kids Have a Say

Give children as much input as possible, depending upon their ages. One seven-year-old girl told me that she was furious because no one asked her if it was all right for her to see her father only once a week. It was not all right, and she showed her anger by withdrawing from everything—school, home, friends. She came to my attention when she deliberately walked in front of a car to try to kill herself. Of course, this was an extreme case, but so much could have been avoided had she thought anyone cared about how she felt and what her needs were.

19. Provide a Stable Environment

Give them stability, even if it is in two separate places. Have a routine for each home, and make sure your children feel equally welcome in both your homes.

20. Allow Access to Mom *and* Dad

Seeing both parents is important. The children need to make sure each parent is OK and coping. It makes them feel more secure and less stressed if both Mom and Dad seem to be happy, or at least getting on with things.

21. Curb Your Anger

Bite your tongue when you want to criticize your ex. Children may agree with you now but form a completely different opinion later on, and then blame you for turning them against the other parent. You cannot win by undermining your children's love for their other parent.

22. Involve the Kids

Involve children in custody arrangements, but not in nitty-gritty details. I firmly believe that a person independent of both parents needs to talk with children and find out who they think they would like to live with. The courts might decide against the wishes of the children "for their own good," but it is time we stopped treating kids like communal property with no voice of their own. The CD player doesn't care where it ends up. The kids do, and usually with good reason.

23. Don't Battle With Your Ex

Don't fight every time you pick up or drop off the children. If you can't stand your ex, then stay out of the way when he arrives to collect the children.

24. Don't ask children to spy on and report back on your ex.
25. Don't question children about what they did. Tell them you'd like to know, but don't dig at them to tell you.
26. Accept the loss your children feel. Sympathize with them, even if you wonder why you ever got involved with your ex in the first place.

Children are often so badly affected by the breakup of families, it is worth doing everything in your power to try to avoid a split, if possible. In hindsight, many people i know wish they had worked it through. But if it isn't possible, don't despair. For some children, the divorce or separation turns out to be a blessing in disguise. Parental fighting frightens kids. And children can and do adjust to new situations. Some are happier either with one parent or in a new stepfamily. And bad effects seem to get better with time, especially if you are sensitive to your children's needs.

My friend Celeste says now that she wishes her parents had been more tuned in to how she felt about their divorce, but in the long run it was best for all of them. But Celeste was determined not to have her children go through what she did, so she and her husband have worked hard to avoid the pitfalls and to create a happy marriage and stable environment for their children. So far, they have succeeded wonderfully.

There are zillions of books and articles about stepparenting and merged families. I suggest another trip to the library or bookstore.

29

45 Suggestions to Help Children Cope With Grief

Six-year-old Eric and eight-year-old Dennis lost their mother, Carmen, to cancer when she was only thirty-four. They and her husband, Robert, were devastated. Carmen was a friend of mine, a fellow teacher, and one of the most beautiful and kindest people I ever met. After the funeral and the initial shock, Robert turned all of his attention to helping his children adjust to their terrible loss. But the children also made it their business to help their father. I'll never forget Robert telling me that one of the boys took his hand in the car on the way to the funeral and said, "We'll get through this together, Dad." And they did. But it wasn't easy for any of them.

Most children will experience the death of someone they love: grandparent, friend, relative, parent, or sibling. I remember my first experience of death, when my great-grandmother died. I'll never forget having to approach the coffin and being lifted up to kiss her goodbye. She looked strange and cold; I started to wail. Nonetheless, I had to do as I was told. No one comforted my sister or me. We hid under a table and discussed how horrible it was that she would never make us her delicious cakes again and how awful it was that we had to kiss her. Worse, we decided it wasn't fair that we were stuck inside, and we slipped outside to play. Were we callous and unfeeling or just working things out for ourselves, as kids often do? No one took the time to tell us anything, so I guess we just handled it as best we could. Looking back, we were lucky that we didn't have the kind of trauma that Eric and Dennis had—the death of someone young and vital to our well-being, such as a member of our immediate family.

First let's turn to the question of dealing with the death of pets, something that affects every child who has ever had a pet of any kind.

It may seem insensitive to mention the death of pets in the same chapter as the death of parents or siblings and friends, but often the demise of a pet is a child's first experience with death. I certainly wish now that my first encounter with death had been with a goldfish, gerbil, or another pet, instead of a person. I think that my sons have been fortunate because their first experience of death was with their hamster, Hammy (such an original name, I know). This, at least, gave me the opportunity to help them learn about death in what I consider a fairly nontraumatic way, though they thought it was pretty terrible at the time. My younger son found Hammy and came running in crying that Hammy was dead because he had forgotten to feed him that morning. Not so, of course. Hammy died because he was, in hamster terms, old. My son didn't believe me and continued to say that Hammy would still be alive if he had fed him.

1. Explain What Has Happened

If your pet has died of old age, explain how all creatures have a time to be born, to live, and to die. If possible, try to prepare your children in advance for the death of an aging pet, so it won't come as such a shock.

If your pet has died as a result of an accident or illness, talk about how some things happen that we can't change, no matter how much we wish we could. We will perhaps be angry and sorrowful and miss the pet, but there is nothing we can do except remember the good times and how lucky we were to have such a wonderful pet.

2. Arrange a Funeral

We buried Hammy in a shoebox, complete with flowers and a moment of silence. Allow the children to organize the formalities, if they wish.

3. Talk It Over

Discuss the children's feelings and let them cry. Eventually, my son accepted that he wasn't responsible for the death of our hamster, but he was still sad for several weeks. We talked about his sadness and how it was all right to feel that way. My son decided that Hammy was now a spirit roaming freely around the hamster universe, which made him feel better.

4. Consider a Replacement

Get a new pet when the time is right. After Hammy, we decided that if we were going to have all this hassle, we might as well have a proper pet. After several months of careful planning, we got a lovely chocolate-colored cocker spaniel and thought up another original name—Hershey. He is only seven now, but I have told both boys how long spaniels usually live, and hope that we don't have to deal with his death for years and years to come.

Although it is difficult and sad for children to have to come to terms with the death of a pet, it is far more horrendous to have to deal with the death of a person they know and love. Whether that death is accidental or sudden, or due to a long-term illness, children will usually respond with denial, anger, and shock.

Children's reactions will depend upon their age and the relationship to them of the person who has died. Children under the age of five usually have difficulty accepting the finality and reality of death. They will use the term without really understanding what it means. One four-year-old girl I dealt with wanted to know when her older brother was coming back from his funeral. She worried that he was cold and hungry, and she wanted her mother to set a place for him at the table.

Under Fives

With children so young, explain death in simple, concrete terms.

5. Say that the person is dead, which means he or she won't be coming back.
6. Say how sad you are. Don't be afraid to show your own feelings.
7. Explain that it isn't anyone's fault. Young children sometimes think it wouldn't have happened if they had somehow acted differently.
8. Don't say the person has gone to sleep, is away on vacation, or other euphemisms. You may find young children terrified to go to sleep or go away on vacation because they think they'll die.

9. If you have a religious belief, talk about what you believe has happened to the person who has died. If you think he is in heaven, in the stars, or is a spirit, use this belief to help your child.
10. Answer your child's questions. Be direct and as honest as you can be. If you don't know the answer, say so.
11. Explain that death means not breathing, eating, or feeling pain anymore. It also means not being frightened, worried, or angry.
12. Encourage your child to talk about the person who has died. Ask the child to remember as many nice thing about her as possible.
13. Keep photographs of the person who has died. Help the child remember what the person looked like, and how the person acted, laughed and talked, and so on.

Be prepared for the young child's lack of understanding. He may ask to go out to play after finding out someone has died, then come in and ask where the person is. Or the child may ask the way to heaven, or even pack some belongings and set out to find the place where the dead person is. After a time, you may think that the child finally understands, only to have him or her saying "Mommy has been gone long enough now. When is she coming back?"

When I was five, a little girl in our class died in a fire. Though we were all told that the child was dead, several weeks later I asked her brother when she was coming back to school. He was only six or so and replied, "Don't know." Neither of us really understood what it was all about.

Fives to Tens

As children grow older, they better understand that death is irreversible. They are interested in what happens to people after they die, and may draw lots of pictures of tombstones and skeletons. When Carmen died, one of Eric's teachers became very concerned because he was drawing a picture of his mother in her grave. The teacher thought it was macabre and unnatural. On the contrary, it was a normal, healthy way for Eric to come to terms with what had happened. Eric's father accepted this and did not react with disgust or horror, as some parents have when their children depict death in this way.

When talking about death with children this age, you have to be a bit more sophisticated.

14. Give them as many details as they ask for about what happened. They are not being weird by asking, they are trying to put the death into their own framework.
15. Tell them you understand if they try to deny what happened, but that it really is true.
16. Agree that it isn't fair. Tell your kids that you, too, wish it weren't so, but that sometimes things happen that aren't fair.
17. Don't respond with anger if the child seems to be apathetic or doesn't seem to care. Sometimes this is the only way kids can cope for a while. If the child did love the person and this continues, think about getting professional advice to help the child unblock her feelings.
18. Encourage memories. Display photographs and talk about the person.
19. Don't be afraid to cry and show your own feelings. This will give your child permission to express her feelings, too.
20. Answer questions and try to put fears to rest. Children at this age realize that they, too, could die and it is frightening for them. This is especially true if a brother or sister has died.
21. If one of your children has died and another child asks for the dead child's room or belongings, don't be shocked or angry. This, too, is a natural reaction, and the child does not mean it in a cruel way. The child may be seeking comfort in his or her sibling's possessions, or be thinking that somehow this is a way of maintaining contact.

Be prepared for the child of this age to react with anger and aggression. But you may also be surprised at how empathetic and supportive they can be. While this may be a way of keeping the death at a distance from them, it can also be an excellent way for them to cope. As Robert found with his children, they gained strength by supporting him when he was low, just as he became stronger by helping them. By all means, allow children to do something to help. Preparing a family snack or adding their own comments to any letters you might be writing might help them and you. If the person who died is a parent or sibling, your child may wish to help in planning the funeral or choosing the clothes for the deceased. Or, if you are sorting out the person's belongings, it might be therapeutic to let the child help, if he wishes to. You could tell the child you are about to clear the room, and give him the option of helping.

Tens to Teens

Older children will respond to death with much more understanding, and will delve into the "meaning" of life and death. If the death is in the family, they may try to take on the responsibility of dealing with the funeral, and of phoning people, in order to take the burden off others, such as parents. They may suppress their own feelings so they don't upset others. They are very aware of how final death is.

22. Give them as much detail as possible about what happened.
23. Allow them to help make arrangements.
24. Be willing to discuss the more abstract and philosophical aspects of death.

25. Watch for Morbid Signs

Beware of them becoming morbid about death in general and relating it to themselves. "What's the point of living anyway, if we're all going to die?" Statements like this should be followed up and discussed, in case they are indications of suicidal thoughts.

26. Be Prepared for Them to Be Angry

One boy of thirteen, when told his father had died, raged against his mother, saying it was her fault and he hated her. He didn't, but she was the safest person he could vent his anger and frustration at, though he was quite contrite later.

27. Be Aware of Apathy

The child may react by going about her normal routine and showing not much emotion at all. This is one way of temporarily keeping the reality at bay. But it could also be that the child did not really like the person who died, even if it was a member of the family. One fourteen-year-old boy whose father committed suicide said that he was so relieved he wouldn't have to put up with his father's disapproval anymore that he was glad his father had died.

28. Be Aware of Behavior Changes

The child may react by doing badly at school or acting up in an uncharacteristic way. For example, if a parent dies, a child may test the limits that the other parent or guardian sets. This is usually just to make sure that there are still limits, since the world as the child knew it has changed.

Specific Suggestions for All Ages

When helping children to cope with grief, you can do several things to make it easier for them. If the person who has died is a friend of your child's, at least you probably won't have the intense personal grief of your own to deal with, as well. If, however, the person who died is in your family, this often makes it more difficult for you to help your child.

If a parent has died, children will start to worry about the slightest thing happening to their remaining parent. They may ask questions like, "What will happen to me if you die?" or become hysterical if you get sick or come home late. Sometimes, children even have this reaction if the parent of another child dies. Three families from the school I was working at were killed in the Paris airplane crash of a DC 10. For months afterwards, children not only continued to mourn the loss of their friends, but many were fearful for their own families.

One of your children dying is the worst tragedy a parent can experience. But, far too often it also means that other children in the family become casualties of the death of their brother or sister. They may feel that they should have died instead, or that the dead child is being turned into a saint who never did any wrong. That makes them feel angry, and at the same time guilty for thinking such thoughts.

Whoever has died, you may want to try some of the following approaches when trying to help your children:

29. Tell your children you know it is difficult for them to see you so upset. Explain that you know they are upset, too. Tell them you are trying to cope and that you love them very much.
30. Talk about the person who has died and try to remember the good and bad things.
31. Don't put the person who has died on a pedestal. Never make your other children feel they must take his or her place.

32. Tell Your Children That It Is All Right to Laugh and Enjoy Life

This is important even if you can't join in at the moment. One nine-year-old I talked to said that his home had turned into a place of gloom and dreariness—no one was allowed to joke or laugh for fear of offending the memory of his sister.

33. Give Your Children Permission to Be Angry

Express your own anger, if you feel it is necessary or helpful. If the person died as the result of suicide or through an accident that seemed to be her fault, it is a natural reaction to be angry with the person. If someone else was responsible, it is also natural to be angry with that person. Bringing out these feelings can be an important part of coming to terms with the death.

34. Tell Your Children That You Are Glad They Are Here

Another child I counselled tried to commit suicide after his older brother died because he felt that being dead was the only way to gain his mother's love. She, of course, did love him, but was beside herself with grief and could not reach out to him.

35. Let Everyone Grieve

Give members of your family the right to grieve in their own ways. Just because someone is not crying all the time, it does not mean he is not grieving. Everyone grieves in his own way.

36. Prepare Your Children

If it is likely that someone is going to die, prepare your children as much as possible. It may still be a shock when the person does die, but it will not come as a complete surprise.

37. Allow Goodbyes

If possible, allow your children to say goodbye to the person who is dying or who has died. This will depend upon your religious beliefs and on the age of the child, but I think it is easier to cope with death if you've been able to say goodbye. One mother I know shooed her children out of the hospital room just as their father was dying to save them from the pain. But they wanted to be with him and resented not being there at the end.

38. Keep to Your Routine at Home as Much as Possible

When a death has turned the world upside down, it is comforting for a child to have meals, bedtimes, and so on much as before.

39. Realize Seasonal Difficulties

Holidays, birthdays, and anniversaries may be particularly difficult, especially in the first year. Some families go away at these times because they can't face being in the home where they are surrounded by memories of the person. Others stay put and fondly recall past holidays, or invite lots of people over. Still others go to the grave of their loved one or have a religious service of remembrance. One family, whose fourteen-year-old son died, said the first Christmas was so impossible that next Christmas they are going to volunteer to help in a soup kitchen for the needy. Give some thought as to how you are going to deal with these times, but also try to make them as fun as possible for the children, who will not want to think that every holiday is going to be hell from now on.

40. Get as Much Help and Advice as You Can

Get it from friends, from your children's teachers, and from books. Words like those at the end of this chapter are often comforting if they fit in with your beliefs about death.

41. Get Help

Seek professional help for you and your children if you or they are not coping. Sometimes it is easier to talk with a counsellor, even if the person is a stranger. Children may feel more comfortable talking about their grief to someone who won't be hurt by their pain. It doesn't mean that children don't want to confide in their parents, only that an outside view and support may be more helpful at times.

42. Help Your Children Find Their Own Group of People to Support Them

It might be too much for you to cope with everything. The list of people can include aunts and uncles, family friends, teachers, and others.

43. Go Out With Your Children

Do something different and fun together. Start creating new memories for them and for yourself.

44. Don't Try to Shield Your Children From Grief

You might think you are protecting them, but you aren't. They need to grieve and to share in the sadness.

Children will need your help and support to deal with grief, and they will respond best to honesty and lots of love and understanding—just like adults.

By the way, Robert married one of his son's teachers and both boys have grown into wonderful young men of whom their father and stepmother are very proud. Carmen would have been proud of them too.

45. Some Helpful Words

Canon Henry Scott Holland wrote this many years ago, and I find it comforting. Perhaps you will, too.

Death is nothing at all...I have only slipped away into the next room. I am I, and you are you. Whatever we were to each other, that we are still. Call me by my old familiar name. Speak to me in the easy way which you always used. Put no differences into your tone. Wear no forced air of solemnity or sorrow. Laugh as we always laughed at the little jokes we enjoyed together. Play, smile, think of me. Let my name be ever the household name that it always was. Let it be spoken without effort, without the ghost of a shadow on it. Life means all that it ever meant. It is the same as it ever was. There is absolutely unbroken continuity. What is this death but a negligible accident? Why should I be out of mind because I am out of sight? I am waiting for you for an interval somewhere very near...just round the corner. All is well.

32

10 Parents Tell Their Worst Regrets

The perfect mother or father? I've never met one! We all make mistakes with our children. But we can learn from the things we do wrong and hope that it hasn't damaged our children beyond repair. I know I was a much better mom by the time my second child came along. Mind you, my older boy often tells me that I let his little brother get away with murder!

Most of us eagerly devour "expert" childcare manuals in the hope that we'll learn to avoid the pitfalls of parenthood. I read every one I could get my hands on, and they did help, as I hope this one will. But I also think that chatting to as many other moms and dads as possible, and learning from their experiences, is invaluable. So, I am ending this book with words of wisdom from those who have been there. See what you make of other parents" regrets about bringing up their children.

1. Let Them Be!

"I loved it when people told us how well-behaved and angelic our children were," says Kate, mother of two girls, now twenty-one and twenty-four. "It's true, they were good—but at a price they are now paying. Both my girls are perfectionists and worriers. I'm sure that's because I was always anxious about them making a noise or not having good manners. Now I think the girls missed out on being children."

She's Right

I remember how much fun we had as children, getting our hands dirty and our hair wet—even if my mother told us off for being "naughty." Being exuberant and making a mess is a natural part of a child's development. Of course, there are limits. I reached mine when my son created a mud mosaic on my kitchen floor. Did I admire my child's artistry? No way! Turf them out dressed in old clothes and let them get as dirty as they like outdoors.

2. Listen to Them

"I was enormously busy when the children were little—what with running the house and doing part-time teaching," recalls Jackie, mother of three grown-up children. "But the best advice I ever had was to stop everything when the kids needed to talk. I remember once when I was doing a quick cleaned up before friends came round for dinner, my eldest son got out of bed and came into the living room. I told him I was too busy to chat, but a friend who'd arrived early shooed me off, saying the meal could wait. She was so right. It turned out that Tom couldn't sleep because he was having trouble at school. Thank goodness he told me."

Listening Is the Key

The best time to start listening is when kids are young. Remember that they'll often try to slip in something that's really bothering them when you're busy—it's as if they're scared of facing up to it. Sometimes it's hard, but try not to say, "I'm busy, tell me later." "Later" can be a long time for children, and they may get the wrong message: You don't think what they have to say is important. Five minutes could prevent a minor worry from becoming a major problem.

3. Don't Force Them to Eat

"My worst mistake was to make food a big issue," says Dan, father of two sons. "Once, we made James, then only six, sit at the table in front of a plate of uneaten peas. He refused to eat them; we refused to give in. Hours went by. Food became a silly power struggle that only made both the boys fussy eaters...and James hates peas to this day."

Creating Problems

As Dan discovered, being too strict about nutritious food can backfire. Instead of appreciating good food, kids will often get uptight at mealtimes and can even be at risk of developing eating disorders later in life. I know it's easy to get impatient when it comes to educating our kids' tastes, but so what if he goes through a phase of only wanting potato chips? He'll grow out of it.

4. Turn It Off!

Single mom Jill's life was so fraught that television seemed a godsend. "I'd just started running a freelance business from home and I was so grateful when the little ones were quiet that I let them watch TV, often for much longer than I'd intended. I've come to think that's one of the reasons they get bored so easily now. They seem to need the constant stimulation that television provides. They can't entertain themselves, and they don't like to read or play games. I am trying now, though. I turn off the TV for several hours each day."

Give Them Something Else to Do

Hard as it is, Jill is now putting her kids on the right track by rationing TV each day. At first, it might be necessary to stimulate kids" inventiveness by giving them versatile props, such as drawing materials, or by playing a game with them. If your kids have turned into zombies and can't cope when their TV is turned off, tell them they can be bored if they want, even stare at the walls if they like! Don't feel obliged to entertain them. You can rest assured that they won't sit in silence for ever.

5. Tell Them They're Great

"I told everyone else how wonderful my kids were, but I never told them," says Patrick, a father of two. "I guess I assumed they must know it and I didn't want to make them big-headed. If anything, I underplayed my pride in them, which I now think was a big mistake. My compliments were always conditional. I'd say, 'I'm pleased you've got a good grade in math, but why isn't it higher?' or, 'Well done for washing the plates, but why have you left the pans?' I wish I had praised them without reservation and told my kids that they were great."

Praise Your Kids Often

We all love compliments. Now, Patrick's daughters love to hear their dad say how much he thought—and thinks—of their achievements. The only caution: Don't send your adult friends into a catatonic state by going on and on about your kids. There's nothing worse than continually hearing how well someone else's are doing—especially if our own aren't as successful!

6. Ask for Help

"I was too reserved to ask for help," says Liz, an outstanding office administrator—before she gave up her job to have children, now twelve, eleven, and seven. "I lived in a street full of people I knew, and my parents were only twenty minutes away, but looking back at the early years I think it was pride that made me tell myself I should be able to cope on my own. As it was, I remember being constantly exhausted."

Pride Mustn't Prevent

Liz is right to notice that it was secret pride that stopped her from asking for help. It's a pity, because it's important for children to know their grandparents, and that little bit of extra help might have relieved some of the early stress for her. Still, she finally saw the sense of not being Supermom and now has a network of other mothers and relatives who all help each other. She thinks the kids are a lot easier to live with; the funny thing is, they seem to think the change is in her!

7. Make Time for Cuddles

"They grow up so fast. Where did the time go?" Debbie shakes her head in amazement that the eldest of her four children has already left home. "I miss the cuddles, the kisses on their little noses, the hands clasped tightly around my neck. I wish I'd spend more time giving them cuddles, and being there for them. You think you have all the time in the world and suddenly they are eighteen. I stopped cuddling when they were about five and starting school because I felt it would toughen them up."

Show Your Affection

Hugging and cuddling children is one of life's greatest pleasures. We do have to hold back when our kids signal they are not in the mood for a cuddle. They'll push you away with an "Oh, mom..." if it doesn't feel right and, of course, you should never embarrass them in front of their friends. But I reckon there is never a right time to stop showing affection. After all, we Moms and Dads enjoy—and need—those hugs as much as kids do! And holding kids physically close can actually make them more independent, because they'll feel secure in your love.

8. Trust Your Intuition

Linda, who has an eleven-year-old son, telephoned me at my office to ask advice. "Gavin's been quiet and moody for more than a week," she said. "Yesterday, he told me he was fed up at school—though he wouldn't tell me why—and said he didn't want to go. I thought I had to make him face up to the problem, whatever it is, and go to his classes. When he came home, though, he was in tears and he looked terrible. This morning he doesn't want to go to school again. I'm at my wits' end."

We Know Best

Linda may have rung me for advice, but she didn't need me to tell her what to do. All I had to say to her was, "What do you think is best for Gavin?" "Well..." said Linda doubtfully, "he's so upset I think he really might do something stupid, but he has to go to school." "Leaving school aside, what do you really think would help Gavin?" I asked. Linda paused. "I really want to keep him home for a few days and get him to calm down enough to feel safe. I want to find out why he's so unhappy."

Linda already had the answer. Her son's welfare was more important than forcing him to go to school. She called back later to say that Gavin had finally blurted out the truth about a group of bullies at school. Thank goodness she hadn't forced him to go back into an intolerable situation. Her instincts told her what to do—protect her son when he was vulnerable. I told her she was lucky Gavin had shown some symptoms to alert her to the problem. Some children don't, as I have seen all too tragically.

9. Don't Organize Too Much

"My worst mistake was that the children never had a free moment," remembers Anna, the mom of two teenage daughters. "They had swimming lessons, sports, trips to museums—when anything was going on in the community, they were signed up for it. I organized them to death. I thought that fun had to be planned and that children left to their own devices would stagnate. My kids don't have much self-confidence now, and maybe it's my fault that I have to prod them to do things."

Use Imagination

Anna's kids might have had more self-confidence if she had encouraged them to come up with their own ideas, or just let things happen spontaneously once in a while. OK, there might be failures some days. But letting them have the freedom to find out what they want to do is how they will learn to organize themselves and become self-starters.

10. Write It Down

"If only I had scribbled down even a few of those great moments," sighed Marilyn. "The other day, my nine-year-old asked me when he first walked and I couldn't for the life of me remember. You think you'll remember everything your children do. I thought that every momentous event would be sealed in my memory forever. Hah! By the time my eldest was only two, I already could not tell you when he walked, the cute little things he did, or the date of his first tooth."

Favorite Stories

Marilyn told me this when we were both in hospital—me with my first baby, she with her third. I took it to heart, bought a blank notebook, and jotted things down. Sometimes I waxed eloquent; other times it was a quickly jotted, misspelled mess. Those books were my children's favorite bedtime reading for years! Even now, my teenagers will listen with rapt attention to a day in the life of them, age three or four. So, Marilyn, wherever you are, thanks for telling me your mistake.

Happy Families

If you recognize yourself in some of these scenarios, don't worry. We have all made at least one of these mistakes, and perhaps much worse ones. But if anything touches a raw nerve, don't torment yourself with guilt. The good news is that it's never too late to change the way we do things and improve our relationships with our kids. Be positive, keep a sense of humor and stay cheerful. No child wants a woe-is-me parent! And be prepared to experiment to find the changes that might suit your family. Remember, kids are resilient. We can't go too far wrong if we tell them often how much we love them, and how lucky they are to have us as parents!

Index

MANAGING
PROFESSIONAL PEOPLE

MANAGING
PROFESSIONAL
PEOPLE

*Understanding
Creative Performance*

Albert Shapero

The Free Press
A Division of Macmillan, Inc.
NEW YORK

Collier Macmillan Publishers
LONDON

The Free Press
A Division of Macmillan, Inc.
866 Third Avenue, New York, N.Y. 10022

Collier Macmillan Canada, Inc.

Printed in the United States of America

printing number

1 2 3 4 5 6 7 8 9 10

Library of Congress Cataloging in Publication Data

Shapero, Albert.
  Managing professional people.

  Bibliography: p.
  Includes index.
  1. Professions.   2. Personnel management.   I. Title.
HD8038.A1S53 1985   658.3′044   84–18728
ISBN 0–02–928870–3

To Gitel

To Gitel

Contents

Introduction

THE MANAGEMENT of creative workers has become the most critical area faced by managements in both the private and public sectors. Without a great deal of fanfare, creative workers, or, more strictly, professionals, have come center stage in the United States and in the rest of the developed world. Quantitatively, professionals now surpass all other categories in the work force of the United States. Qualitatively, professionals have a disproportionate effect on all aspects of our society, as the researchers, designers, decision makers, and managers who define and direct much of what is done in society. The quality and extent of what is accomplished in the foreseeable future have become a function of the ability of managements to harness and channel the efforts of creative workers. The difference in success between one effort and another, one organization and another, increasingly depends on whether management understands the differences between the management of professional activities and the management relevant to the assembly line.

An early definition of the term *profession* was "a particular order of monks, nuns or other professed persons" (compact edition of the *Oxford English Dictionary*, 1971). More recent is the definition "a vocation in which a professed knowledge of some department of learning or science is used in its application to the affairs of others or used in the practice of an art founded upon it" (ibid.), and a *professional* is one who "belongs to one of the learned or skilled professions" (ibid.). Social scientists use the term profession to denote "occupations which demand a highly specialized knowledge and skill acquired at least in part by courses of more or less theoretical nature and not by practice alone, tested by some form of examination either at a university or some other unauthorized institution, and conveying to the persons who possess them considerable authority in relation to 'clients.' . . . Such authority is carefully maintained . . . by guildlike associations of the practitioners . . . which lay down rules of entry, training, and behavior in relation to the public . . . and watch over their professional status" (J. Gould and William A. Kolb, eds., *A Dictionary of the Social Sciences*, New York: The Free Press, 1964).

In modern society a professional is usually someone who has completed the equivalent of at least a baccalaureate degree that has the number and mix of courses certified by some professional society. The members of the profession identify themselves in terms of their profession and have expectations of status and treatment on the job that are clearly different from those of people in skilled and unskilled trades and blue-collar and white-collar work. Because of the status attributed to the professions, occupations constantly attempt to be identified as professions by restricting entry through special educational requirements, examinations, licensing, and the establishment of a code of ethics. Furthermore, would-be professions are marked by calling for "more professionalism" and institutionalizing what is considered professional and nonprofessional behavior in the occupation.

To be a professional has very positive social connotations, and members of a profession identify strongly with their profession even when there is an apparent conflict between employer and profession. It is quite in character to call on professionals to "blow the whistle" on an employer when the employer is seen as doing something in conflict with the standards of the profession or contrary to the public good. The word *profession* still carries something of its earlier definition as a religious "order," and the more narrow definitions used today of clergy, medical doctors, and lawyers (the so-called free professions) characterize what all professions reach for.

Where once professionals were few in number relative to the total working population, today they are far more numerous relatively and absolutely. The proportion of the work force that can be designated as professionals is steadily increasing. In 1979 (*Statistical Abstract of the United States,* 1979), over fifteen million workers were classified as professional and technical workers as compared with a little over eleven million in 1970 and approximately seven and a half million in 1960. In 1979, professional and technical workers constituted just under 16% of the total work force as compared with 14% in 1970 and a little over 11% in 1960. If we admit managers and administrators to the ranks of professionals, the numbers go up to twenty-five and a half million and 27% in 1979 as compared with nineteen and a half million and 25% in 1970 and fourteen and a half million and 22% in 1960.

By all measures professionals make up the largest single category in the work force of the United States, surpassing those classified as "craft and kindred workers," "operatives" of all kinds, "service workers," and "clerical workers." Further, the numbers shown above refer only to those employed in industry and do not include the substantial number of professional workers to be found among the self-employed, who numbered over six million in 1979. The self-employed include those physicians, lawyers, other health professionals, and consultants of all kinds who work by themselves or in group practices. The list of those classifiable as professionals includes architects, accountants, engineers, scientists of all kinds, doctors, dentists, nurses, pharmacists, lawyers, designers, librarians, computer specialists, editors, journalists, managers, clergy, dieticians, advertising specialists, statisticians, and on and on.

There are many reasons for the growth in the professional

work force, among which are (1) the steep growth in technology requiring specialists, (2) the growth in large organizations requiring the services of many technical specialists, and (3) the sharp increase in the number of educated people who generate a demand for professional status.

Ours is the era of the "knowledge society" or of the "information revolution." Increasingly our society and economy are shaped by special bodies of knowledge, and by those who possess them—these are the professionals, and their management is the subject of this book.

HOW PROFESSIONAL ACTIVITIES DIFFER FROM OTHER ACTIVITIES

Mapping the world of work in terms of the types of activity carried out and the types of human resources required, the results can be roughly depicted as in Figure I–1. Work activities can be distributed along a dimension of increasing uncertainty. At one extreme are those activities that are denoted by being essentially routine. They are predictable, stable, and specifiable. Consequently, they are relatively easy to plan and budget. They lend themselves to long-run operations. All of the conditions describing routine activities tend to make them process-dominated. To meet the conditions of predictability, stability and specifiability over time managers must understand and control the process.

At the other extreme of the dimension are the activities that are most unpredictable, those that can be described as one-of-a-kind. One-of-a-kind activities are essentially unspecifiable or predictable and are least amenable to the arts of estimation and budgeting. Such activities are inherently human-dominated, for when one is unable to predict the nature of a process one inserts a human, a substitute for oneself, to do what is needed within the unpredictable context. If it is to be done at all, a one-of-a-kind activity will be dominated by a human.

The types of human resources required by different kinds of work activity are distributed along a dimension of knowledge

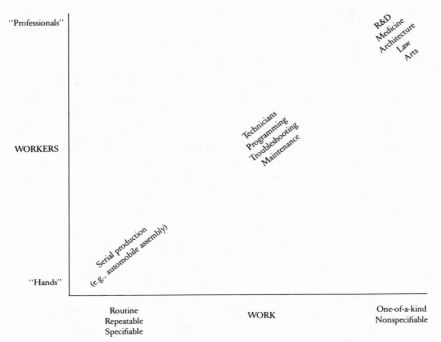

FIGURE I-1. A Map of the World of Work

required and decision-making. At one extreme of the dimension are found those referred to as "hands," those who essentially perform motor activities with a minimum of autonomous decision-making. At the other extreme of the dimension are those referred to as "professionals," who have a special body of knowledge and who are called upon for significant judgment and decision-making in carrying out their work.

Exploring the map, it is easy to locate all work activities and the kinds of management they require. In the corner of the map, where routine activities performed by "hands" are located, we find serial production activities typified by the automobile assembly line, parodied by Charlie Chaplin in the classic movie *Modern Times*. At the other extreme corner of the map, where one-of-a-kind activities performed by "professionals" are located, are a host of diagnostic, consultative, prescriptive activities characterized by the knowledgeable transformation of information from one form into another. In the center of the map are those activities clustered under such terms as "semi-professional" or "technician activities"; these include equipment maintenance, trouble-shooting, programming, and other jobs combining high motor skills with special knowledge.

There is an implicit assumption in most writing on management that management is the same for all activities. However, any close examination of both successful and failed managerial practices quickly establishes the fact that the management appropriate for assembly line operations is inappropriate to professional activities, if not downright harmful. Managing the routine activities exemplified by an automobile assembly line includes:

1. The layout of the entire process before beginning operations with all subprocesses specified
2. Decision as to how each part of the process is to be done, including all input and output characteristics
3. Where humans are to be used in the process, the requisite human and physical characteristics are specified and distributed, including dexterity levels, non-color blindness, physical size restrictions—for example, during World War II, the Douglas Aircraft Company used human midgets to work on aircraft nose-wheel assembly and inspection operations because they were of a size to ride the wheel up into the fuselage conveniently
4. The development of very explicit job descriptions in which the requisite human activities are distributed and clustered into human-sized packages to which are assigned titles, compensation levels, and positions in the organizational hierarchy
5. The hiring of people with the requisite skill and physical characteristics and in appropriate numbers to operate the process—testing and other forms of measurement are used in this step to make sure that those hired "fill the bill" of specifications
6. Training those hired to perform the work required to the specified standards

7. Developing and applying incentives of various kinds to assure performance of the work required by the process in the appropriate time
8. Continuing supervision of the process to assure that it is being performed as specified; the techniques that fill management magazines are clustered here, including flextime, suggestion systems, piece rates, production prizes, quality circles, and foreman training in interpersonal skills; production line quality control is dedicated to measuring and taking steps to assure that the process works within the prespecified limits. Personnel practices are used to assure that the assemblers will maintain their quantitative and qualitative production within prespecified limits.

The qualities that are most desired in assembly line activities are dependability, predictability, and steadiness. About the last quality desired is creativity. The creative assembler is the person who puts the proverbial soda bottle in the automobile door to rattle and tantalize the owner. The creative operator in the middle of a petroleum refinery can be a dangerous person if the urge to try out something new finds expression in new valve settings.

By contrast, when it comes to the one-of-a-kind activities performed by professionals, the management described for assembly line activities is clearly inappropriate. First of all the process cannot be specified. Any professional who has taken over a project or patient or operation in mid-stream knows that the first thing to be done is to change the way the process is conducted. Changing the process is not a product of the perversity and egotism of individuals. It is simply that to reach a specified output from a specified starting point each professional carries out the process differently. After the desired results and the general kind of human capabilities required are given by the manager, the professional doing the job is in control of the specifics. To intervene is to slow and confound the process.

For professional work, management must hire someone

with the requisite general capabilities, and then let go of the details of the process. Anyone who has had experience as a professional or manager of professionals has heard the exasperated response given to detailed supervision, "Look! Either you're going to do it or let me do it!" There is really no way successfully to apply the personnel practices appropriate to mass production to the management of professionals. As long as the process cannot be specified in detail it is not possible to spell out the specific requisite skills and to train people for them. In the context of professional work, job descriptions are at best glittering generalities; "Do science in a scientific manner, and answer the phone in the absence of the boss."

All routine, specifiable tasks are theoretically automatable, and it is no accident that robots are replacing people on the automobile assembly line. On the other hand professional work is unspecifiable, it is dependent on situation and problem, and requires the judgment, ingenuity, and creativity of an individual possessing a particular body of knowledge. Whenever a professional is doing routine and specifiable work you can be sure that it is nonprofessional work, e.g., the physician giving shots, the engineer doing routine testing, the professor administering multiple-choice tests, the accountant doing set-piece bookkeeping.

The techniques developed for managing assembly lines are not appropriate to the management of professional activities. Most management literature is written to explain and advise on the management of routine and specifiable jobs, and is consequently inappropriate to the management of professional activities. In their efforts to improve performance, professional societies often advocate the use of so-called modern management techniques by their membership, and many consultants with business administration backgrounds have sincerely sold their repertoires of techniques appropriate to General Motors to organizations concerned with professional activities. In most cases, the attempts to apply techniques developed for the routine and specifiable to professional activities make little difference since, according to Shapero's Second Law, "No matter how you design a system, humans make it work anyway." Elaborate job description systems are devised that have little effect except to encourage political skirmishing. "New" organizational structures are elaborately installed, such as Matrix organization. ZBB, MBO, OR, Quality Circles, and Theory Z (courtesy of the Japanese who learned their management techniques from the Americans), are sold, installed, modified, and forgotten in rapid sequence. In some cases the application of inappropriate management techniques to professional firms has been disastrous, particularly for smaller firms that lack the resources to survive large perturbations.

If professional activities are not specifiable and humans make all systems work anyway, why should we even bother to talk about "management" of professional activities? The foregoing is a good question, and the answer is definite: we can do far better than chance, and we can do far better than depending on the natural skills and expensively acquired lessons of experience. A better understanding of what is known about the nature and management of professional activities can provide us with the knowledge and tools to do more than cut and try, and systematically to improve the overall performance of the professional activities for which we are responsible.

The available literature is scattered throughout several fields under a variety of classifications. It is the purpose of this book to bring the available data together and to organize it in terms of the processes and structures critical to this particular world of management. The information used here is drawn from such diverse areas as information science, the diffusion of innovations literature, personnel research, advertising research, the history of science and technology, the psychology and sociology of creativity, the history of art, the physiology and sociology of age and aging, labor economics, organization behavior, and the psychology of work, as well as the traditional fields of business administration and the occasional offerings to be found in trade and professional journals of the professions.

This book is concerned with the management of professional activities in organizational contexts. It is intended for use by those charged with managing professional activities in large and small firms, whether they are primarily concerned with professional outputs (as is true of architectural and other design-related firms, advertising, consulting, the health professions, and the like), or serve as functional parts of organizations delivering non-professional products and services (such as the R & D, design, and advertising functions in an industrial or consumer products company). The book is also aimed at that broader category of professional activities called "management," and is concerned with providing useful information for the management of managers.

1

Hiring: The Most Important Management Decision

THE PROFESSIONAL WORKER is *the* critical resource in any professional activity. All other resources, without exception, are far down the list in terms of importance in the achievement of professional outputs. Further, the most important management decision in the conduct of professional activities is hiring. All other decisions have far less effect in determining the capabilities, productivity, quality, and quantity of output achieved by a professional organization than the apparently simple task of hiring.

The importance of the hiring decision cannot be overemphasized. Professional activities are person-dependent, and consequently the quality of the work produced is dependent on the qualities of those hired. It is possible for management to influence the quality and quantity of output of those hired, but management is severely constrained by the capabilities and outlooks of those hired. If one hires well, the chances are that the organizational output will be more than satisfactory. If one hires badly, no matter what management techniques are used (aside from early firing), chances are the output will be less than desired.

Professionals are not "replaceable" in the interchangeable-parts sense of the word. Though two professionals may have the requisite professional capabilities to accomplish a particular task successfully, each will perform that task with a different style and approach. Two physicians treating a patient with a given disease will each go about it differently. Two actors playing the same role or two musicians playing the same composition can each produce satisfactory but different interpretations. Two professors teaching the same course from the same textbook and syllabus will produce different experiences though both meet all criteria for acceptance. Anyone who has had to take over a project from someone else has gone through the painful process of realizing that one cannot just continue one's predecessor's work but must restructure the approach to fit one's own style.

The importance of hiring is further amplified by the evidence that (1) quality of performance persists through time, and (2) a relatively small percentage of those hired are responsible for a disproportionately large percentage of both the best and worst performance.

The Persistence of High and Low Performance

A demonstrated persistence in high and low performance on the part of professionals underlines the relative importance of the hiring decision. What you hire in the way of performance quality essentially determines the level of performance you will have to reckon with in the absence of heroic management efforts. If you hire carelessly or poorly the probability is low that you will be able to "correct" the situation by professional development programs, management techniques, or on-the-job therapy. In a rare longitudinal study of the job performance of professionals, Price, Thompson, and Dalton (1975) measured the performance of technical professionals in an industrial laboratory at two points in time separated by nine years. They

TABLE 1–1
Performance Ratings of Professionals in an Industrial Laboratory
at Two Points in Time Nine Years Apart

AGE IN SECOND ROUND (1960)	NUMBER IN GROUP	1960 RANKING	1968 RANKING		
			High	*Medium*	*Low*
31–40	124	High	63%	28%	9%
		Medium	20	45	35
		Low	10	35	55
41–50	129	High	45	45	10
		Medium	45	37	18
		Low	9	24	67
50+	58	High	55	35	10
		Medium	33	33	33
		Low	60	30	10

SOURCE: From Price, Thompson, and Dalton, 1975.

found a strong tendency for those judged "high" performers in the first round to be "high" performers in the second round, and those judged "low" performers tended to persist as "low" performers (see Table 1–1). There was little migration from the "low" to the "high" category or from the "high" to the "low" category over time. Only those judged to be "medium" performers in the first round showed any progression or retrogression, with one-third moving up and one-third moving down in the second round.

A Few Account for a Lot

Small percentages of the work force account for the best and worst performance. This is an example of Pareto's law, or Pareto's principle, which holds that, in social and economic affairs, many relationships can be expressed as a straight line on a double-log diagram; or, simply, a few of the x's account for a large percentage of the y's. Among some management practitioners it is known as the "eighty-twenty" or "ninety-ten" rule. Typically, 80% of an inventory's costs are attributable

3

to 20% of the items, or 12% of the Californians account for 75% of the alcohol drunk in that state.

Interviews with managers in the fields of R & D, architecture, publishing, academia, engineering, and the performing arts provide evidence of Pareto's law. Those interviewed state that 80–90% of the best output of their organizations can be attributed to 10–20% of their people, and, conversely, 80–90% of the disasters to another 10–20%. Any manager can name the people in each extreme category and remember the former employees, by name and accomplishment, who were at the extremes. A manager of one of the best industrial R & D organizations in the world told me that over half of the laboratory's successful developments were attributable to one of the twelve hundred fifty members of the laboratory.

The Pareto law effect in professional activities provides an opportunity to achieve powerful leverage on the quality and productivity of an organization. Relatively small improvements in hiring can achieve very large improvements in performance. If 80% of the outstanding work accomplishments are attributable to 20% of the workers, and 80% of the disasters are, similarly, attributable to 20% of the workers, a systematic improvement in the numbers in either limited category can have a disproportionate impact on the organization's performance. The trick is to identify and hire in the high-performing category and to identify and make sure not to hire those in the other extreme. To overcome hiring mistakes always takes too long and is too expensive in terms of damge caused, managerial time lost, and feelings hurt.

Hiring Can Be Systematically Improved

Since hiring is the most important management decision in professional work, anything that improves the quality of hiring can determine whether professional efforts succeed or fail, clients and customers are satisfied, the organization is exposed to liability suits, and whether managers' jobs are fun or are miserable chores.

Is it possible to do any better than we are doing at the present time just using our instincts and our experience as guides? The data available from a variety of sources leads to the unequivocal conclusion that it is possible to achieve significant qualitative and quantitative improvements in the hiring of professionals. The evidence, however, brings conventional hiring practices into serious question, and a manager who wants to improve hiring must be ready to challenge many popular and cherished personnel practices.

CRITERIA FOR HIRING OF PROFESSIONALS

What does a manager explicitly or implicitly look for in a professional being considered for hire? What should guide how he or she seeks potential hires? What should he or she expect of them? Any group of experienced managers can easily reach a consensus on two or three obvious criteria, but other criteria are relevant:

1. Capability for high technical performance
2. Ability to enhance group performance
3. Initiative-taking capability
4. Potential for development and renewal over time
5. High probability for retention
6. Creativity

Capability for High Technical Performance

Technical capability is the *sine qua non* when hiring professionals. The ability of a professional to perform the job competently comes before all other considerations in hiring, and much of the hiring process is taken up with efforts to determine a potential hire's professional competence. To demonstrate their abilities, architects, artists, and advertising professionals maintain a portfolio of paintings and drawings. Academics list their publications by title and publication to establish their research

5

competence. Other professionals list patents, projects, descriptions of positions attained, and places of employment (a matter of competence by association).

From the evidence provided by a potential hire a manager attempts to deduce something of the qualitative and quantitative professional output to be expected from the candidate. Given a choice among apparently competent professionals the tendency is to hire the person one "likes" in terms of some gestalt or overall judgment. Given the pressures of a tight labor market the tendency is to hire whoever comes through the door, despite personal likes or dislikes, as long as the individual is above some minimal threshold of technical capability. Civil services attempt to hire on "objective" grounds of technical merit as a matter of principle, implying that this is the only way to obtain equity. Unfortunately, in many cases the criterion of technical competence is the only one applied, and it is too limited a basis for so important a decision as hiring.

Ability to Enhance Group Performance

Experienced managers worry about the interactions of a potential hire with the rest of the work group, the net impact of the potential hire on the overall performance of the organization and on the energy and time of the manager. Experienced managers often cite "the potential effect of an individual on group performance" as an even more important criterion than that of technical competence.

On the negative side, a candidate may be considered in terms of potential for causing interpersonal problems within the group. A frequent question in the mind of an employer is, "Will this person be a problem?" A technical genius who manages to enrage the clients, insult colleagues, and make disproportionate demands on the time of management can generate a net loss for an organization. A potential hire with two doctorates and a distinguished list of publications whose behavior on the job may cause an exodus of other competent people is a threat rather than a find.

6

Initiative-Taking

Almost by definition, a professional is someone who can act independently while bringing a body of special knowledge to bear in a work situation. "We would like someone who is a 'self-starter,' " is the common way managers describe this initiative-taking capability. Professional work depends to a great extent on the self-direction of its workers, unlike the world of routine work.

The notion of "the span-of-control," developed in the context of production management, refers to the number of subordinates a manager can supervise directly. Traditionally, management authorities held a span-of-control of five to eight subordinates as the number that could be effectively managed. For routine production tasks the number was increased to ten or fifteen. When it comes to professional activities the concept does not make the same kind of sense. In production work the process dominates, and the manager can be aware of the entire process and specify the tasks of each subordinate. The manager deals with a relatively small set of circumstances, the only limit being the capacity of the manager to observe and keep track of operations.

In professional work the process is in the heads of the professionals, each of whom, legitimately, approaches the task somewhat differently. In professional work, the manager cannot directly control the details of the process. Control of professional activities depends on the capabilities and motivation of the professionals carrying out the work. Consequently, control consists in eliciting from employees a propensity to initiate requisite actions without their being constantly directed by a manager who cannot know whether the professional sitting with feet on desk is loafing or doing the kind of thinking that makes the difference between success and failure. Given competent, initiative-taking professionals, a manager's span-of-control in professional work can be as high as fifty. With one incompetent professional the span-of-control quickly becomes one, since the manager will have to do the job of that individual until he is replaced by someone else who is competent.

7

Potential for Development and Renewal Over Time

Managers often forget when hiring that beyond current needs and conditions will be future projects and changing technology and environments. It is expensive to hire and integrate new professionals into an organization, and it is difficult to fire old employees. Furthermore, among the most painful problems faced by a manager of professionals is the so-called plateaued or burnt-out individual: the person who has contributed well for years, has reached a high salary level, but who is not performing adequately anymore. The thoughtful manager considers what will happen beyond the current set of tasks when considering a potential hire. It makes good sense to hire those most likely both to maintain their current capabilities and to develop new capabilities to match new needs.

Retainability

"What is a good turnover rate?" is a question managers frequently ask. The only sensible answer is, "It all depends." If you have technically competent professionals who are good to work with, who are initiative-takers, and who develop themselves to meet new demands, the answer is, "A turnover rate of zero is just fine." However, if your professionals are incompetent, miserable as colleagues, inactive, and resistant to change the answer could be, "A turnover rate of 100% is called for."

If you have hired a desirable professional who meets all the criteria for hiring, you should want to keep that desirable worker in the organization. At the time of hiring it is useful to consider the likelihood of retaining the promising candidate.

Creativity

In some professional fields such as advertising, R & D, the performing arts, the plastic arts and architecture, employers consciously seek out people who are "creative" in the belief

8

that such individuals will give their organization a competitive advantage.

MEETING THE CRITERIA FOR HIRING

It is possible to identify and rank a set of criteria for hiring professionals that describes what is wanted in terms of work behavior, but the key difficulty is to know if a candidate for hire meets any or all of the stated criteria for hiring. Experienced managers often express reluctance to go through the hiring process because of past unhappy experiences. Typical comments are, "The best interviewee I ever encountered turned out to be the worst paranoid I ever had to deal with. It was only after the fact that I learned an intelligent paranoid will give you all the responses you want in the interview situation," and "I look upon each candidate for hire as a potential disaster, a destroyer of my peace of mind, a disrupter of my department."

How can you determine whether someone has the desired capabilities and characteristics? In an assembly line situation, it is possible to determine quickly, through straightforward testing, whether an individual has the necessary motor skills and intellectual capacity. In the case of a professional, determination of the requisite capacities is far less straightforward. The high turnover rates for professionals indicate the difficulties encountered.

Hiring the Experienced Professional

When hiring an experienced professional some formal and informal record is available on which to base judgement. Sometimes there is physical evidence in the form of a portfolio, a listing of publications, citations, or news items. Witnesses of the past work of the potential hire such as employers, co-workers, or clients might be contacted for evaluations. The data on the application form can be checked for accuracy and evaluated. Interview information, and sometimes test results, are also available.

9

Despite the abundance of conventional wisdom on hiring, there is relatively little useful data on the relationship between information available at time of entry and subsequent performance on the job. It is common for an experienced manager to state that after many years of hiring he can determine who is going to do well on the job. The available data suggest that the confidence expressed is misplaced. How then can a manager tell what he is getting in the way of potential performance? What is the relative utility of the various kinds of information available at the time of hire? What specific information relates to work performance identified as desirable?

Information available at the time of hire. Typically, at the time of hire, managers make use of a variety of sources of information about the candidate. The data in the resumé and application forms, the portfolio of past work, and references show something about the demonstrated performance of the potential hire. Testing, interviews, and references reveal applicant characteristics considered relevant to the work situation.

The interview. The available data on interviewing throw doubt on the validity and reliability of interview information as an indicator of how an individual will perform on the job. Interviewing can be improved somewhat by training interviewers, by clearly structuring the questions to be asked, and by using a series of different interviewers. Nevertheless, the results of these improvements are minimal, and their implementation tends to trap the interviewer into justifying personal judgments and strongly held biases.

Despite research demonstrating the low validity and reliability of the interview in hiring, it remains the dominant method for evaluating candidates. The dominance of the interview in hiring decisions is remarkable in view of its limitations. If only one hiring tool could be used, 80% of those hiring would choose the interview (Martin et al., 1971). According to the same study, 90% would hire individuals on the basis of an interview even if negative information was received from other sources.

Authorities on interviewing consider the interview to be a social situation affected by the nature of the transaction, and the perceptions the two actors in the situation have of each other and of the task at hand. The interview is an obtrusive process in which the interviewee is a conscious part of the game. The interviewee's responses are affected by embarrassment at ignorance, fear of consequences, liking for the interviewer, physical condition (a severe cold can make a significant difference), and self-perception (we prefer to see ourselves in ways that may not represent the way we really are).

Different interviewers get different responses from an interviewee. Interviewers unconsciously indicate which responses are more acceptable to them, and the interviewee is likely to try to provide these responses. If the interviewer, just to make conversation, mentions having been an athlete in college, the respondent will attribute a constellation of values and preferences to the interviewer and respond accordingly. In the interview process managers tend to identify with interviewees who are most like themselves. Several studies have found that the decision to hire is made very early in the selection interview.

In effect, the interview, usually a matter of an hour or less, is like the passing of two ships at sea. Each ship presents its best side and all of its flags. Friendly signals are exchanged. Little is learned about the cargos buried in the hold, possible destinations, changes of course, responses to emergencies, or past engagements.

The application form and the resumé. The application form and the resumé are intended to provide an employer with enough biographical information to (1) determine whether an individual meets the minimum, formal requirements for hiring (e.g., a degree in the appropriate discipline or the requisite license), (2) provide the interviewer with indicators worth following up, and, less frequently but more importantly, (3) provide biographical data and experience data that might be used to predict performance on the job. The forms used by different organizations ask very similar questions and in recent years have been modified to remove data concerning race, sex, age, and religious and sexual preferences.

Since biographical data shown in the application form or resumé is important to whether an individual is even considered, the validity and relevance of the information found in these biographical forms should be evaluated in relationship to potential performance on the job.

In the instances where they have been systematically used, biographical data have been found to be of greater validity than those obtained by other carefully constructed selection procedures. It is reasonable to infer that if an individual has succeeded in the past in a work situation similar to the one being applied for, he or she will most likely do well in the future. The behavior of an individual is reliable over time, and past performance is the best predictor of future performance. The question to be asked is whether the past situations are those the individual will encounter in the future. The less variation between past and predicted situations the easier it is to predict. With the inherent variation in professional work, good matches between past and present are hard to come by, and only an ability to deal with variation may be relevant.

There is a question of whether applicants lie in presenting their biographical data. One study of 112 applicants for jobs in a police department (Cascio, 1975) found a high correlationship between the application information provided and fact. Another study found significant distortions in both biographical data and in responses to a standard personality test, the MMPI, on the part of respondents. In a study using the application forms of aerospace scientists and engineers, my colleagues and I were informed by personnel people that they found differences between application forms data and data provided by the same applicants in security forms serious enough for termination of individuals already hired.

Testing. A potential hire's characteristics and skills are tested to predict work-related behavior. Thus, for a mechanical assembly job, a mechanical aptitude test might accurately predict how an individual will do on the assembly line. A test is essentially a sample of a person's behavior under particular, and inevitably limited conditions, and the test situation hardly represents the real work context. Consequently, the art of testing is to identify critical behavior patterns and to develop probes that might validly and reliably predict them on the job.

First, for a test to be useful, it is necessary to develop a clear understanding of the requirements of the job. Without clear-cut criteria against which to match test results it is not possible to construct a relevant test or to determine what the test results mean. Second, tests must be selected or developed that can be related to the job criteria. Third, the tests must be shown to be valid and reliable. Finally, any program of testing must avoid violations of privacy, feelings of equity, and legality.

Tests used in hiring can be broadly classified as aptitude tests, achievement tests, and motivation tests. Aptitude tests attempt to measure general intelligence, job-related intellectual aptitudes, motor skills, and personal decision-making competence and interpersonal skills. Achievement tests essentially measure what the individual has learned, as compared with the aptitude test which measures the individual's ability to learn (Schneider, 1976), and includes performance tests for craftsmen, paper and pencil tests on occupational knowledge, and behavior in simulations (e.g., the in-basket test for managers). Motivation tests include personality tests and measures of interests. Personality tests operate on the premise that certain personality variables differentiate successful from unsuccessful work behavior. Interest tests compare the interests of the candidate with the measured interests of successful performers in the field.

Tests can be valuable in the hiring process when done carefully with due regard to their relevance and with a clear understanding of their limitations. Every serious review of the testing literature underlines the limitations of applying generalized tests to specific situations and the consequent need for tailoring a test to the specific job and organization. The great majority of work on testing has been done with clerical and blue-collar occupations where the work varies little compared with professional occupations. To develop valid and reliable tests is an expensive process, and, if undertaken, it must be assumed that the jobs will remain relatively unchanged over time. Consequently, we find that most of the testing data available refer to large and relatively stable corporations such as Sears, Standard Oil of New Jersey, AT&T, and 3M.

13

Testing often reflects the biases of personnel departments and managers. For example, there is the strong feeling that "general intelligence" is somehow related to job performance (Landy & Trumbo, 1980). However, the only proven utility of such tests has been to predict the success of young children in school work (Schneider, 1976). There is no real agreement on what general intelligence is and whether what is measured by general intelligence tests is related to specific occupations.

The one developed area of testing relevant to professional work is that concerned with managerial performance. Managers are professionals, and managerial activities share the unpredictability and variation typical of other professional activities. One review of work on prediction of managerial performance from aptitude test results (Campbell et al., 1979) concludes from work done in the largest corporations that some very specific aptitude tests, such as those for verbal and abstract reasoning, do provide useful predictors, and that even general intelligence tests predict performance in forecasting and budgeting but not in sales or interpersonal relations. A great deal of work has been done with the in-basket test, in which a series of simulated job situations are presented to the person tested, who is then judged by a panel of managers and/or personnel professionals. Though good results have been obtained with this test, questions have been raised about the difficulty of obtaining reliable results with different panels of observers and about the expense and time required for the process. Questions remain concerning the relevance of the exercises to the particular jobs for which they are used as predictors.

References, formal and informal. References are usually required in the hiring process. Written references and letters of recommendation are hardly worth the paper they are written on. One study of written references found they tended to leave out any negative information. A study of the validity of different types of references found some correlation between references from supervisors and acquaintances and subsequent performance and absolutely none between recommendations from personnel officers, co-workers, and relatives and subsequent performance (Mosel & Goheen, 1959).

Recent court cases have even made a request for references a question of invasion of privacy, and many organizations (including universities) will not give any kind of reference without written permission from the concerned person. Some organizations will not take the chance of a lawsuit and will not give any kind of recommendation even with the express permission of the person being considered.

Informal references made face-to-face or over the telephone are far more productive of relevant information, bringing closer the connection between requester and provider and minimizing the threat of loss of confidentiality which is inherent in a formal document. More importantly, spoken communications are orders of magnitude richer than the written language. Because of hesitation, emphasis, and intonation, it is almost impossible not to provide significant information in spoken language (see Chapter 4, "Managing Information"). If someone writes, "This man is a good worker," the message seems clear. The same individual, over the phone, might respond with a long hesitation, followed by a rather toneless, "This man is a good worker." The phone response alerts the listener, and all kinds of suspicions fill the mind. The same words produce different messages in the two forms used.

Technical Competence

Technical competence in a professional may be associated with degrees received, years of experience, nature of experience, promotions, honors, salary level, and evidence of specific outputs. The resumé and application blank are useful in identifying these quantitative extrinsics, but less useful in providing qualitative information, except in the case of honors. Even "portfolios" may be of questionable value. As one newspaper editor put it, "A sheaf of articles in a portfolio may mask the extent to which the applicant's writing was improved by a good editor."

In large organizations, structured wage and salary rules make it difficult to differentiate between the average and the very competent. Promotion policies are such that rank cannot generally be assumed to be directly related to technical competence. It is hard to know from the record whether two parallel "one year" experiences are equal: did one consist of forty hours a week of routine activities while a second was sixty hours a week of diversified, developing experiences?

To obtain some notion of the qualitative aspects of an individual's technical abilities requires combining the information found in the resumé and application blank with that obtained through conversations with people who have had the opportunity to see the applicant's work, such as former employers, colleagues, clients, and professors. It is necessary both to evaluate the source of the reference to determine if it is to be taken seriously, and to go into enough detail and depth to get a rounded idea of the applicant's ability to respond to a variety of problems and situations.

Other considerations related to technical competence are encompassed in the questions, "Is it better to hire a generalist or a specialist?" and "What is the relationship of age to performance?"

The generalist versus the specialist. Unless a specialty is defined very broadly (a contradiction in terms) it has a limited lifetime. A tidal wave of new information floods each profession every year. New techniques, new concepts, new data, new equipment, and new interpretations are the norm in medicine, engineering, management, advertising, and social work. Specialties are quickly made obsolete by technical events—anyone practicing a profession for more than five years need only think back to what was central in the practice five years ago compared with the present. Note a few of the changes: the impact of the small computer and the silicon chip, of new drugs, and of recent environmental concerns.

There is nothing sadder than professionals in a specialty that has been abruptly made obsolete. What happened to electronic tube specialists once semiconductors took over? The narrow specialist is most valuable in the short run, saving much time and uncertainty, but who can predict that current specialties will accommodate to new technology and problems? A sur-

16

vey of industrial R & D groups found that one-half of them were engaged in fields of research different from 10 years ago and that over a fourth had changed from five years ago (*Industry Week*, 1982).

Though any specialist can retrain for another field, there is a very human resistance to change from a field in which one has made a large investment. One study found that Ph.D.'s were least amenable to shifts to new enterprises or fields while those with the master's degree were the easiest to transfer and had the best record of success. The resistance of those with Ph.D.'s was attributed to their personal investment and to a socialization process they go through in a particular narrow slice of a technology which makes it difficult for them to transfer to another field. Anyone with a Ph.D. is as able as (if not more able than) a master's degree holder to learn and do new and different technical work. Yet the generalist may be a far better bet in the long run.

Age and technical competence. (See Chapter 5, "Technical Obsolescence, Burnout, and Staying Alive.") In general, professional competence increases with age. Measures of performance used in the relevant studies included annual order-of-merit rankings used for salary evaluations, unpublished reports, published papers, scientific contributions, and overall helpfulness as judged by peers and supervisors and patients. On the average, performance increased with age, peaking in the mid and late fifties. The probable explanation for the decline after age fifty is social-psychological rather than a matter of technical know-how, and is probably a manifestation of what is now referred to as the "middle-age" or "mid life" crisis.

The evidence clearly shows a gain in contribution and utility with age and experience. With a few exceptions, such as in the field of mathematics and in some areas of basic research, competence persists and is enhanced by experience. With experience, competent individuals gain in knowledge and ability. For example, creative people tend to remain creative throughout their careers. If the employer can find someone who has demonstrated creativity in the past, the likelihood is high that the individual will be creative in the future. Despite a general tendency to assume that a recent university graduate has command of "the latest," the evidence is that the competent older worker is more useful than the competent younger worker, and certainly a better bet than the unproven younger person.

Ability to Enhance Group Performance

An individual can substantially affect the way a group operates and the subsequent quality and quantity of the group's professional output. In terms of technical contribution, in addition to direct labor, an individual brings access to an "extended family" of information sources that are part of his or her personal professional network outside the organization.

Beyond the strictly technical professional aspects of work an individual professional can make a substantial contribution through many kinds of social and professional interactions that include: helping new and younger people; helping to create a positive atmosphere during tough or pressure-filled times; a willingness to work through the night to finish something on time without being asked; dealing well with clients or other groups; and, not least, making only limited demands on managerial time.

Information. The information made available by an individual is a function of (1) what is "in the head" of that individual, (2) what can be obtained by that individual through interaction with others within the organization or through social and professional circles to which he or she belongs, and (3) that individual's ability and willingness to communicate with others.

Some idea of an individual's information potential can be gathered from the number and variety of the candidate's personal periodical subscriptions and book buying habits, and the interest the candidate takes in company information offerings and facilities, and in professional society activities.

Comments by former co-workers and supervisors on the role played by a candidate for hire as a source or even as a "pusher" of information provide a good indication of that individual's potential as a contributor of information to others in a group context. A contributory characteristic is, for want of a better term, "niceness." When asked, "With whom would you prefer to work?" respondents in both a non-profit laboratory and a commercial electronics R & D division singled out those to whom they turn for technical information (Shapero et al., 1978).

The interpersonal capabilities of a good communicator are indicated by access to large, extended networks of professionals outside the immediate organization. Typically, a good communicator is in frequent contact with others in various fields and thus brings much more information to an organization than others.

Interpersonal capabilities. The ability to deal with others is recognized as a prized ability in all organizational contexts. When asked by the author, "What is the one thing you wish you had learned in college?" a majority of a one thousand managers and professionals responded, "Dealing with other people," "Interpersonal relationships," "The psychology of dealing with others." Though recognized as desirable, a candidate's interpersonal competence cannot be determined with certainty. A mild correlation between judgements of interview behavior and interpersonal competence has been reported, but the connection is uncertain. Informal references are more useful and accurate indicators.

Disproportionate demands on management time. Anyone who takes a disproportionate amount of management time is a serious drain on an organization. When asked, "What is the worst management experience you have had in the last nine months?" managers frequently answered, "A good worker quit!" Often a competent, desirable employee quits because the manager of the organization has not provided the feedback everyone needs. The good worker is often a person who seldom comes to the manager's office or his attention out of pride in being able to function without constant supervision. Nevertheless, everyone wants to know that management is aware of his or her presence. When there is no feedback, an individual may either create situations that will demand managerial attention or quit. Thus, any individual who takes up a large amount of management time and keeps managers from spending some of that time with others in the organization can be costly in terms of turnover.

KEEPING COMPETENT PERSONNEL

The undesired loss of competent personnel is costly to an organization in both direct and indirect terms. The obvious direct costs are those expended in the hiring and entry processes. Hiring costs include advertising, recruiting travel expenses, time spent by key personnel interviewing, testing and physical examination costs, costs of generating new records, moving expenses, and special inducement expenditures (bonuses, housing allowances, etc.). In addition to direct employment costs there are the entry costs that include orientation and training efforts that can range from formal courses (i.e., orientation sessions, security instructions, etc.) to non-formal orientation efforts such as learning where and how to get internal information, how to get something done within the system, or the location of the nearest sandwich shop.

The estimated costs of hiring a professional for one distributed-data processing company were more than $9,000 for a hypothetical $18,000 a year position, with higher salaried positions entailing higher hiring costs. The same study estimated that training costs were close to $16,000, including direct support to the new employee during the first few months and learning-curve costs. The costs were based on careful surveys of managers and calculations from actual company data (Jindal & Sanderberg, 1978). In another study the total cost of hiring a manager was estimated at $25,000 and $30,000 in 1973 (Hall & Hall, 1976).

The extensive literature on the subject of turnover (Price, 1977) points out that the major factors affecting turnover are organizational and managerial, though there is also considerable evidence relating personal factors to voluntary turnover.

In studies of technicians and engineers (Bassett, 1967), scientists and engineers (Farris, 1971; Shapero et al., 1965), it was found that voluntary turnover is related to age. In general, younger employees are more likely to leave than are older ones. The new college graduate has little information upon which to judge whether a job is a good one, and it is not unusual to hear a young professional say, "I didn't realize until now how good a job I had."

The institutional source of a prospective employee is also somewhat related to turnover. It was found that aerospace scientists and engineers from government stayed with the hiring organization for a longer period of time than those from industry (Shapero et al., 1965). Several other studies show that nongovernment organizations have higher turnover rates than government organizations (Price, 1977).

"Extreme" personality characteristics have been related to a tendency to voluntary turnover. Individuals who manifest such traits to a lesser degree show a higher degree of retention (Meyer & Cuomo, 1962; Farris, 1971).

One study compared retention of high vs. low performers among scientists and engineers (Farris, 1971) and found the personal factors that predicted stayers and leavers were the following:

> High performers stay, low performers leave, when importance is attached to the opinion of colleagues outside the organization and to maintaining contacts outside the organization.
> High performers leave, but there is no difference for low performers, when there is high professional orientation.
> There is no difference for high performers, but low performers stay, showing independence.
> Both stay at the same rate in the case of older employees.

Summarizing the data on personal characteristics related to retention, we see one more argument for hiring the older competent worker, that age is negatively correlated with voluntary terminations. Other important personal characteristics associated with high performers include lots of contacts outside the organization and a high professional orientation.

What is a good turnover rate? Ideas about turnover are often based on the notion there is some utility in maintaining a certain amount of movement in and out of an organization, reflected in the question, "I understand our turnover rate is below 6%, and isn't that bad?" Taking the notion to its practical conclusion, you would fire people to maintain some assumed "correct" failure rate. One Los Angeles electronics firm had an arbitrary policy in the 1950s, of firing 10% of the work force every six months. "Keeps everyone on his toes!" was the president's claim. It was true, all of the best personnel were on their toes and in their track shoes, and the company's turnover rate was on the order of 90% per year. One by-product of firings that reach visible percentages is that the workers you want to keep become uncertain of their place and also leave.

There is no correct turnover rate. For an organization made up of high performers who have a great deal of initiative, who are dynamic in maintaining their technical capabilities, who are good communicators, and who get along well with each other, with clients, and with strangers, a good turnover rate is zero. On the other hand, for an organization full of low performers who are aggressive, constantly demanding managerial attention, uninterested in personal development, and in constant conflict with everyone, a turnover of 100% in six months may be a very sensible rate.

The tenure vs. voluntary termination data raise questions about the value of continuing education being made available for all professional employees. The five-plus year employee is the least likely to leave voluntarily. Should you spend much money on continuing education for employees in their first two years with the organization since they are the most likely to leave or should you spend heavily on continuing education of the five-plus year employees for the highest amount of retained knowledge per dollar expended?

Geography, streams of migration, and turnover. The movements of professional workers to a particular geographic location are strongly correlated with well-trodden general migratory pathways. If a professional is hired in consonance with established migratory patterns (i.e., from within the local area or from "upstream" on an established flow to the area of hire), there is a higher likelihood that the individual will stay with the hiring organization than if he is hired from outside the established patterns. Hiring from "downstream" in the migratory flow patterns results in higher turnover except in the case of individuals who come from the area originally and are returning.

Using the personnel records of thirty-five thousand scientists and engineers, it was found that geographic movements between jobs correlated with the general population migration pattern into each area studied with correlation coefficients on the order of .98 (Shapero et al., 1965; Draheim et al., 1966; Howell et al., 1966). In other words, the geographic origins of the scientists and engineers in a city correlated with those of the general population as shown by the Census data on migration. The professionals studied followed general streams of population migration as old as the country, including one southern and one northern east-to-west flow, a traditional south-to-north movement, with a steady counterflow to Florida from the northeast and midwest. Thus, it was found that a Boston engineer would not move from Boston to a missile company in Denver. A scientist would move from St. Paul to Seattle or to Denver, but would not go to Tucson. In the 1950s a missile company in Orlando, Florida, advertised for technical workers to fill twenty-eight hundred positions and got over sixty thousand applications from the northeast.

A study of new college hires who stayed more than five years in a large Dallas electronics company showed the same patterns. Despite following the prescribed personnel practices, the new hires who remained with the company for five years or more reflected the long-term historical social migration pattern. A personnel manager in Colorado remarked, "It has taken me a long time to learn that we have wasted a lot of money trying to hire engineers from Boston [off stream], and it has taken me another block of time to learn that hiring people from Los Angeles [downstream] is like putting them in a revolving door; they're soon on their way back down there."

Trying to hire someone living "upstream" in a migration flow pattern has a higher probability of being effective, even without great economic incentives, than offering a job to someone living "downstream" with an economic premium attached.

Responsibility

One of the most desired and least understood of the characteristics desired in a professional employee is variously called "initiative taking," "self-starting," "enterprise," and "leadership." What managers seek is the ability and desire to take responsibility, to show spontaneity in doing the work to be done, and to initiate actions rather than to wait to be told what to do next.

One source of data would seem to be the large body of studies on leadership, but apart from goal-setting the leadership literature is primarily concerned with setting tasks for others. A more useful source of information on initiative-taking is found in studies of entrepreneurship that use locus-of-control. Locus-of-control is the perception by an individual of where control over his or her life is located: whether control is within the individual and "internal," or is in outside forces or persons and "external." Thus, the more one perceives control to be within, the more that individual is judged to be "internal"; and the more one perceives oneself as controlled by luck, chance, or other people, the more one is judged to be "external." The relationship of measures of locus-of-control to initiative-taking comes from the suggestion that to take initiative, one must feel able to influence events.

There are several paper and pencil locus-of-control instruments. Two of the most widely used are those of Rotter (1966) and Levenson (1972). The latter measures have been quite widely used, and some of the more interesting and relevant results include the following:

1. Entrepreneurs, managers who are more entrepreneurial than others, and entrepreneurs who survive are far more internal than the general population.
2. Managers who are internal are promoted to a greater extent than those who are not, and attach less importance to salary, job security, and retirement.

3. People who have high internal scores have more information and make better use of information than others.

Creativity: The Most Elusive Virtue

When a manager wants a potential hire to be creative, it implies that he places a high premium on new and different solutions to problems and on uniqueness in outlook. Creativity, thus defined, is the essence of professional work. A manager expects a professional to bring a specialized body of knowledge to unique solutions of unique problems. Creativity is particularly identified with certain professions which consciously seek out more of this quality in their hiring practices. In professional activities associated with the performing or plastic arts, creativity is a leading personnel dimension, as it is in such professions as architecture, research and development, publishing, planning, some aspects of engineering, management, and education. (In advertising, as in other fields, there is the formal title, "creative director.")

A number of theories attempt to explain creativity, and some tests have been developed to gauge an individual's creative ability. However, there is still no valid or reliable method of predicting creative behavior on the job other than evidence of such behavior in the past (see Chapter 6, "Creativity").

Creativity is often sought by a potential employer who, in practice, really does not need it. This is the case in the architectural or engineering-design organization looking for someone to be a detailer. In such cases, the requirement for "creativity" is a cultural trapping of the profession, not a requirement of the job. Asking for a creative person in a situation where creativity will in fact be penalized is bad management, and is costly to the organization.

THE "PURE" CASE: THE NEW GRADUATE

Once a professional has accumulated some work experience records of performance are available. In the case of the new college graduate there is little in the way of a relevant work record: this is the "pure" case. Consideration of the pure case vividly illustrates the gap between what little is known in a systematic way about effective hiring and the actual hiring practices of personnel departments and managers.

Much of what is published about hiring newly minted college graduates is based on the experiences and reports of college recruiters and college placement officials, whose information is severely limited. Typically, two hundred to five hundred companies recruit at any campus, and these are primarily large companies that recruit from several campuses. Considering the fact that there were more than sixteen million companies in the United States in 1983, of which 1% had five hundred or more workers (this does not include nonprofit organizations or government organizations that do college recruiting), this represents a very limited sample of the total number of employers of professionals in the country.

When considering the new college graduate, recruiters are faced with the question how to determine the future work performance of someone without a record of professional work.

Essentially, recruiters and managers turn to the following in judging a new college graduate for hire:

Grades, in the form of an overall measure such as Grade Point Average (GPA) or in terms of grades in selected courses considered more relevant to the job; seen as indicators of relative technical competence and of motivation and ambition

Extracurricular activities, particularly sports and leadership positions in organizations

Appearance (grooming, clothing, demeanor)

Personality, attitudes, outlook on life

Personal goals

Interviewer intuition about the person, which encompasses judgments of future potential, maturity and communications ability

The evidence shows no valid or reliable relationship between any of the above and subsequent performance on the job!

26

Grades

The measure most widely used for evaluating new college graduates is grades. Grades are considered in terms of their absolute number value (e.g., 3.8 out of a possible 4.0), or of the class ranking they indicate (e.g., in the upper 10% of the class). Some recruiters look at grades received in the last two years of college, reasoning that they are more indicative of the mature individual's capacities or that they show a significant trend. Some recruiters consider grades in courses that are specifically relevant to the interests of the hiring organization.

Because of the wide use of grades as a criterion for hiring, there have been many studies of the relationship between university grades and subsequent performance in the working world. The literature is practically unanimous in its conclusion that there is *no* measurable relationship between grades in school and performance on the job. There is even some evidence of a negative relationship between good grades in school and creativity in science and engineering.

Studies of the relationship between grades and subsequent performance have been done with physicians, Navy divers, entrepreneurs, MBAs, managers (male and female), engineers, teachers, nurses, psychiatrists, and ministers. An extensive longitudinal study of MBAs from a prestigious school did find grade point average related mildly with compensation at the five year and ten year points (Williams & Harrel, 1964), *but the GPA used was for grades in the second year of the MBA program, since it was found that the overall GPA was not a good predictor.* The second-year included more optional courses, and it seems that grades in optional courses were far more predictive than overall scores! It is difficult to fathom the significance of optional courses over the rest. Could it mean that required core courses have little relationship to work situations? Some employers agree that grades are not important, though they do consider them. One study found that 53% of the personnel managers agreed that grades did not predict job performance (Drake, 1973).

The subject of grades is emotionally loaded. For a professional, grades have been critical to parental approval, positive teacher feedback, honors, choice of university, scholarships, and acceptance to professional school and/or graduate school for at least sixteen years. Consequently, it is difficult for many to accept data that show little or no relationship between grades and subsequent activities, and this influences the hiring process.

The critical point is that school and the workplace are different environments requiring different behaviors. In school there are fixed problems to be solved, well-known patterns of problem-solving and performance measurement (examinations), relatively mild sanctions, and very benign schedules. A student is seldom "fired" for turning in a late paper or for doing below-average work. Professors are judged by the way their students evaluate them rather than by some external and inflexible criterion such as net profit.

The data on how professionals spend their time, on the other hand, paint a picture of activities marked by meetings and interruptions and a constant demand for improvisation. In the typical work situation few can go one half hour without interruption. The typical professional spends between 35% and 50% of the time in meetings and 15% on the telephone. A major complaint of engineers and architects is professional under-utilization. The information required on the job is never available in neat and ready form. The problems are messy, the deadlines are changeable and abrupt. Several problems must be dealt with simultaneously, and the criteria for evaluation are vague and changing.

School grades measure performance in school-related activities, so college grades correlate with high school grades, and graduate school grades correlate with undergraduate performance. Thus, college grade averages were found to correlate with grades made in basic science courses in medical school, but neither correlated with clinical performance (Hammond & Kern, 1959).

Inflation of grade-based entrance requirements to universities may screen out many who have high potential for distinguished performance. The Dean of Admissions of Harvard College identified fifty graduates of the Class of 1928 who had achieved distinguished careers, and examined their credentials at the time of admission to Harvard. He found that two-thirds of the fifty would have been turned down for admission by the standards used at the time of the study (1958), which were considerably more lax than those applied today (Livingston, 1971).

It must be remembered that every college graduate is a member of a segment of the population already differentiated on the basis of cognitive capabilities. University graduates, particularly the products of professional programs, are highly competent when it comes to cognitive and intellectual capabilities. The classification of school performance (A to F) to differentiate within a population that is already quite capable does not provide significant information. The last person in the class, graduating with a degree in engineering or architecture or medicine, has met rather high standards set by accreditation organizations, and must be considered intellectually capable.

Extracurricular Activities and Leadership

Extracurricular activities, particularly as officer of an organization or as team captain, are sometimes seen by managers to indicate qualities of leadership which are relevant to professional work. The presumptions seem to be that school activity leadership is an indicator of job-related leadership, and that leadership is inborn or the product of a set of traits that will manifest itself in any context. Research shows that effective leadership depends not only on the qualities and attitudes of the individual designated as leader but equally on the work situation, including both the environment and the work to be done. The leader who is appropriate for an automobile assembly line is not likely to be appropriate for an advertising agency project, and the latter is unlikely to be appropriate for an agricultural experiment station. The effectiveness of top executives is found to be limited even between companies in the same industry, as each company has its own particular environment produced by its unique history, organization, and culture and demands a unique combination of leadership skills and approaches (Shetty & Peery, 1976).

Though one study (Williams & Harrel, 1964) showed a correlationship between earnings five years after receiving an MBA and offices held as an undergraduate, the mass of available evidence suggests that extracurricular activities are of little use in predicting effective leadership in a work situation. The same study found no correlation between extracurricular activities in graduate school and earnings.

Appearance, Grooming, Clothing, Demeanor

With the possible exception of an individual who insists on bizzare dress or hair style, there is no measurable link between appearance during a job interview and behavior on the job. Nevertheless, the literature on how to prepare for a job interview stresses appearance and demeanor. The applicant is advised to dress in a particular way, to be sure to give a firm handshake, and to look the interviewer straight in the eyes. When surveyed on the importance of job applicant characteristics, recruiters, students, and faculty all gave appearance a very high ranking. On a scale from one to seven ("very important"), recruiters ranked appearance fifth out of fourteen items with a score of 5.55, students ranked it fourth with a score of 5.79, and faculty ranked it first with a score of 6.19 (Posner, 1981).

Recruiters do place emphasis on appearance, and it behooves the would-be hire to recognize this predilection. However, there is no plausible relationship between appearance and the quality or quantity of professional work. When recruiters are asked why they give weight to appearance during the job interview, typical answers include: "It shows the applicant is serious, and has respect for the company," "A neat appearance indicates an orderly approach to work," "It's more professional." Good, bad and indifferent students all tend to "dress up" and sport fresh haircuts when interviewing, and the incompetent look as barbered as the competent.

Clothing and appearance are primarily functions of the style of the times, and anyone can easily assume acceptable external packaging. The only thing appearance tells the interviewer is the extent to which the interviewee is in tune with current style. Appearance has no relationship to professional performance, except in positions where there is a need to impress selected audiences, as in sales.

Interview Behavior

The interview is the primary vehicle by which a recruiter or a manager makes determinations about the personality, attitudes and outlook on life of the graduate who is a potential hire. The interview also serves as a means for making assessments about appearance and grooming, and about whether or not the interviewee communicates well. During the interview the potential hire is queried about personal goals, ambitions, and motivations, all of which are considered important to the hiring decision. It is during the interview that the interviewer forms opinions about the personality of the potential hire, and makes judgements about how he or she will fit in with the company and what kind of potential he or she has.

Personality, Attitudes, and Outlook on Life

It is the rare sociopath who goes to an employment interview intending to present other than the best front that can be mustered. Few college graduates lack the minimum intelligence required to fathom what is wanted in an interview. The potential professional hire quickly understands how to respond in an interview. Some interviewers take pride in tricking interviewees into revealing themselves in response to trick questions or several drinks, but these methods reveal little.

The question of which personality attributes can be correlated with performance on the professional job has not been answered. Few data show one or another attribute to be required for the successful performance of medicine, architecture, science, engineering, law, or the ministry. Furthermore, it is doubtful that any particular personality attribute can be discerned through the interview process.

Goals, Ambitions, and Motivations

In view of what is known about the dynamics of the interview process, it is surprising that among the questions most frequently asked of the new college graduate are, "What are your five-year goals? Your ten-year goals? Your long-term goals?" The ostensible purpose is to elicit some real notion of the intentions, ambitions and motivations of the potential hire. The interviewee will always contrive some rational answer to the question. After the first interview, the answer to the question is carefully constructed and modified in preparation for subsequent interviews. What would the interviewer (or the reader) come up with if asked to specify five-year or ten-year goals? Few professionals could answer the question. Few find themselves doing later what they expected at time of graduation. What can the inexperienced college graduate imagine of the possibilities "out there?" The future is crowded with a host of interacting unknowns and unknowables, not least of which is a genuine lack of knowledge about situations not yet experienced. TIME Magazine once reported the statement of a forty-year old dentist who complained, "Some damn fool nineteen-year old decided I would be a dentist all my life!"

Fit with Organization; Future Potential

Judgments as to fit and future potential are almost universally made during interviews. In the initial interview, the interviewer exercises intuition based on observations and interviewee responses. When a candidate is interviewed more than once at a firm, the interviewers arrive at a consensus as to whether the candidate is "one of our kind." Once the decision is made, supporting information is sought from references and the school record.

Differences Between Schools

Some organizations place a great deal of emphasis on particular schools, preferring the graduates of some over others, and sometimes offering higher entering salaries to graduates of the preferred schools. They assume that the favored school's graduates will perform significantly better than those of other schools for a number of reasons: the selectivity with which the school admits its students, the presumed excellence of the educational environment (good faculty, fine facilities, and high standards), and the high expectation level of the student body.

There is little evidence of a relationship between the school attended and performance on the job. One study, using salary data on thousands of scientists and engineers in the aerospace and electronic industries (Shapero et al., 1965), found that graduates from prestigious schools (e.g., MIT and Harvard) obtained somewhat higher compensation than graduates from other schools, but that the data were influenced by the fact that many companies offer higher entering salaries to graduates from prestigious schools. Most company wage and salary systems take considerable time to overcome an initial salary advantage, and differences may not be erased for years. Thus, a study relating quality of electrical engineering graduate schools and salary showed an initial advantage for "prestige" schools that disappeared with time. Another study found initial salary advantages associated with grades disappeared with time (Martin & Pachares, 1962). Another study concluded that academic achievement and quality of institution attended were poor predictors of both job retention and salary progression (Schick & Kunnecke, 1981).

EFFECTIVE HIRING

The Hiring Process Itself and Subsequent Performance

The channel through which someone is hired and the way the new hire is put to work are far more predictive of subsequent performance than any indicators obtained from interviews, application forms, tests, and assessment center procedures. The data relating subsequent salary increases (a very good indicator of an organization's judgment of individual performance) and retention (a good indicator of individual satisfaction with an organization) to channels of recruitment and first work experiences within the organization demonstrate this.

Channels of Recruitment and Subsequent Performance

A channel of recruitment is the route by which an individual comes to an organization. Channels of recruitment include:

Employment agencies
Advertisements (in newspapers and trade and professional journals)
Company recruitment (college recruitment, professional meeting recruitment)
Self-recruitment (through friends or acquaintances, knowledge of company's work or reputation, perceived advancement opportunity)

As can be seen in Table 1–2, the great majority of professionals in organizations are hired through self-recruitment channels. Over two-thirds of the professionals working in three major missile companies in three widely separated locations were hired through self-recruitment (Shapero et al., 1965). The relevance of the data shown in Table 1–2 to other time periods and industries is shown by other studies such as that of Azevedo (1974) which explored the utilization and effectiveness of different channels of recruitment in terms of frequency of use by scientists and engineers and effectiveness in gaining employment in a time of economic downturn in the industry (see Table 1–3).

Azevedo also found that over two-thirds of the successful strategies used were methods of self-recruitment. The distribution between use of reference networks and direct applications differed from what was found in an earlier time period: 31%

TABLE 1–2
Sources of Professional Employees (Channels)

CHANNEL OF RECRUITMENT	CURRENTLY EMPLOYED N = 3045	TERMINATED N = 413
Placement service	5.1	14.3
Advertisements	14.6	25.4
Newspaper	10.6	19.1
Magazine	2.2	4.4
Trade journal	5.1	14.3
Company recruitment	7.6	10.9
College	4.8	10.2
Other	2.8	0.7
Self-recruited	70.9	44.6
Friend or acquaintance	51.1	28.6
Company reputation	17.0	12.1
Advancement opportunity	2.8	3.9
Other	1.9	4.9

SOURCE: Data from Shapero et al. (1965).

TABLE 1–3
Jobs Yielded by Job Search Strategies (Channels)

CHANNEL	HIGH-EMPLOYMENT YEARS	LOW-EMPLOYMENT YEARS
Placement service (State, private, outplacement, college alumni, executive recruitment)	15.7	16.1
Advertisements	14.5	15.5
Newspaper	10.5	8.9
Professional journal	2.0	4.8
Trade journal	2.0	1.3
Employment newsletters	0.0	0.5
Self-recruited	67.4	66.7
Friend, relative, or acquaintance	26.9	32.1
Direct application	40.5	35.6
Other (Includes professional meetings, job shops)	2.4	1.3

SOURCE: Data summarized from Azevedo (1974).

came through friends and acquaintances and 36% through direct application, as compared to almost 52% and almost 20% in the earlier study. The shift in percentages is attributable to differences between "good" and "hard" times in the industry, with "hard" times raising the incidence of direct applications.

Subsequent surveys of a large variety of professional groups by the author show a remarkable persistence in the frequency of use of the different channels of recruitment among architects, librarians, consulting engineers, surveyors, medical research professionals, and computer professionals in state positions covered by Civil Service regulations.

The effectiveness of self-recruitment channels is demonstrated in several ways. The data in Tables 1–2 and 1–3 clearly show the effectiveness of self-recruitment channels, which generate two-thirds of the professionals found on the job and two-thirds of the jobs for professionals seeking work. In terms of who stays (a measure of satisfaction on the part of both employer and employee), a comparison of the data on channels of recruitment with the data on those who terminated shows striking differences. Self-recruitment channels were responsible for 70.9% of those on the job as compared with 44.6% of those who had terminated. The typical personnel recruitment channels such as placement services, advertising, and college recruitment were the sources of the majority of terminated employees: 14.3% came through placement services compared with 5.1% of those on the job; advertisement produced 25.4% of employees terminated as compared with 14.6% of those on the job; and for college recruitment the figures were 10.2% as compared with 4.8%.

Another important measure of the effectiveness of various channels of recruitment is the correlation of average salary increases with channels of recruitment. It was found that those who had come through self-recruitment channels received significantly higher increases than those from other channels (Shapero et al., 1965). Those who applied directly received the highest average annual increase, $92.50 a month, and those who came through a friend or acquaintance, $71.84 a month. The professionals who had come through advertising channels averaged between $54.98 and $64.64 a month, college recruits averaged $58.66, and placement service hires $53.66.

The source of recruitment of research scientists was found to be strongly related to subsequent job performance, absenteeism, and work attitudes. "Individuals recruited through college placement offices and, to a lesser extent . . . via the newspaper were inferior in performance . . . to individuals who made contact based on their own initiative or a professional journal/convention advertisement" (Breaugh, 1981).

A less frequently used recruitment source worth mentioning is co-operative education. Co-operative education rotates a student between on-the-job training and the university classroom on a systematic basis. An evaluation of recruitment sources for R & D employees at the NASA Langley Research Center at Hampton, Virginia, found that former co-op students significantly outperformed professionals obtained from other sources (Jarrell, 1974). The former co-op students had a lower turnover rate and received more awards for exceptional performance than did others.

Former co-op students are self-recruited since the decision to go to work for an organization is a matter of choice by the former students. In the Langley case, about 30% of the co-op students accepted employment offers from Langley over a seventeen-year period.

Self-Recruitment and the Power of Social-Professional Circles

Why do self-recruitment channels do so much better than channels that dominate formal personnel department practice? The most likely answer is provided by the effects of expectations on behavior. The expectations generated by norms arising from association with a social-professional circle or network, and their activation by the manner of entry into an organization, go far to explain the effectiveness of self-recruitment channels.

A norm is a standard accepted and shared by members of a social group and to which members of the group are expected to conform. A group requires the existence and maintainance of norms if it is to exist for any period of time. Given the norms of a particular group, one can predict with some confidence the behavior of an individual identified with that group.

Norms are enforced by a group in both positive and negative ways, ranging from physical harm and withdrawal of approval to rewarding acceptable behavior. Some norms are maintained by "identification" and "internalization." Identification occurs when an individual defines himself with others and acts in a way that will gain acceptance by those others through meeting their norms. Internalization is the most powerful way in which norms operate, and occurs when an individual defines himself as one who acts by those norms and does so without surveillance by or reference to anyone else.

In our complex society each individual is a member of a bewildering variety of groups: work, social, neighborhood, ethnic, religious, professional, school, and former work groups. Consequently, each individual incorporates and maintains a variety of norms not always similar or even synchronized. One of the ways in which the uniqueness of an individual is achieved is by a particular mix of the norms and values of the many groups with which he identifies.

The groups or social circles, professional and otherwise, with which we identify are crucial to our lives. They are vital to effective job search, crucial to how we get information and even determine to whom we get married. In answer to the question, "How did you meet your spouse?" the same channels of "recruitment" patterns are found: "We met through friends," or "I heard about her and sought her out," or "We met at a church social."

Though few of us are conscious of how dependent we are on our social circles, we consistently turn to them for important personal and work-related information. We are very careful how we act in our social-professional circles. We conform to their norms or are dropped from them and thereby cut off from information essential to professional performance and development. Members of the academic social-professional circles called "invisible colleges" know about research in their field as early as two years before publication. They receive profes-

sional recognition, invitations to take important roles in conferences, journals, and societies, and receive desirable job referral
through their circles. Those who break with the norms of the
circle by such behavior as never contributing information with
colleagues who share with them are dropped from the circle.
The sanction is not imposed by a formal decision, rather by
a kind of withering of one's umbilical connection to the circle
(Price, 1977).

An individual hired by an organization through referral
by a friend or acquaintance (through a social-professional circle)
agrees to an implicit "contract." The new hire feels obligated
to live up to the expectations of the person who did the referring, and, thus, is directly controlled or influenced by the standards of that person. The employer reinforces these
expectations by attributing to the hire the standards and outlook
of the person doing the referring or the circle to which he or
she belongs. Consequently, consciously and unconsciously, the
new employer makes evident what is expected of the hire.

An individual coming to an organization through an employment agency forms expectations as to what is expected
from the agency's interviewer. The individual feels no obligation to the agency since the transaction is commercial and carries with it no strong notions of the standards and expectations
of the organization being entered. Just the opposite occurs with
self-recruited individuals who come to an organization because
of its reputation. They have high expectations and do far better
than those coming through other channels.

Entry into the Organization and the First Work Assignments

The first assignments a professional worker receives have
a powerful and lasting effect on his or her subsequent outlook
and performance. The effect of first assignments is particularly
relevant to the newly graduated professional but applies, to
some extent, to any professional entering an organization. First
assignments establish powerful expectations. Anyone who has
worked on a construction crew or in a factory can attest to

the short time it takes to learn an expected and acceptable rate of effort. In a matter of hours the new worker learns that to work too fast is to be a "job killer" or "rate buster," and to work too slowly is to "shaft your buddies." Every newly graduated architect learns with amazement on the first job how fast drawings can be produced.

First assignments are critical to the subsequent performance, promotions and pay increases of an employee. Challenging early assignments have been shown to be related to strong early performance, and to the maintenance of performance and competence throughout a professional's career. Early challenge has been found to be effective in professions as diverse as engineering and the Roman Catholic priesthood. When a new worker is expected to perform at a high level he or she does, and, as a consequence, is rewarded and given more challenging work assignments which continue to reinforce the desired performances.

When an experienced professional is hired into an organization, the effects of first assignments are not as clear as with new professionals. Good performance persists, and if one hires an experienced professional who has been competent it is likely competent performance will be obtained. However, the majority of professionals judged as middling in performance can make substantial shifts upward or downward, depending on management actions. In the latter case, the first assignments of the incoming professional can be vital. What the new hire is assigned to do, and who he or she is assigned to work with can effect the subsequent performance of even an experienced worker.

How to Hire: Practical and Operational Implications

The research on hiring professionals leads to two inevitable conclusions: (1) there are obvious ways to systematically improve the hiring of professionals both qualitatively and quantitatively, and (2) the elaborate structure of conventional hiring practices is ineffective for hiring professionals.

Why Conventional Practices Persist

Despite their relative ineffectiveness, classified ads and employment agencies are used as the prime sources of professional hires by 70–80% of 188 large national firms surveyed. What can explain the use of ineffective and costly practices that many experienced personnel professionals readily admit are hit-and-miss?

Several elements interact and reinforce current professional hiring practices. First is the existence of a large establishment with a strong, vested interest in current practices. The establishment is made up of personnel departments, personnel professionals, academics offering personnel courses, consultants, and suppliers of such paraphernalia of personnel work as tests. The present personnel establishment arose in response to the needs of a large, growing industrial manufacturing sector, predominately concerned with routine and predictable work. As a consequence, personnel practices applied to professionals have been drawn from a large, elaborate, and comfortable matrix that was useful for production work.

Another factor in the continuation of current practices is a remarkable lack of systematic evaluation of their effectiveness. There is little evidence of efforts by corporate personnel departments to determine what does or doesn't work when it comes to hiring professionals. With rare exceptions, such as the longitudinal studies conducted by AT&T, companies do not relate data on subsequent performance of professionals to the data used at time of hire.

Conventional practice also can persist because they are bypassed in actual practice. How is it possible that two-thirds of the Civil Service professionals we interviewed had been hired through self-recruited hiring channels despite legal mandates? Typically, an experienced manager asks a colleague to recommend a good engineer. Then the manager calls a long-time associate in the personnel department to ask, "I've got someone really competent I want to hire. How can I do it without going through a month of procedures and three interviews with inappropriate applicants?" The associate replies, "Easy! Hire that engineer as a part-time or temporary worker, and after five and a half months (be sure it is less than six months) we'll process a Change-of-Status Request which will make it legal."

Concentrate on the Hiring Process Rather Than the Traits of Individuals

You can do far better concentrating on elements of the hiring process than on the apparent characteristics of the individuals being considered. To illustrate, if you hire at random from a university graduating class, and concentrate on establishing high expectations in the new hire through a challenging first assignment that entails working with your best professionals, you will get far better long-term performance than by hiring from the top of the class and putting the new hire through a company training program. To put a newly graduated professional into a training program is to delay entry into realistic work situations, and is a continuation of not-yet-ready-to-start expectations far longer than is useful.

Remember, there is no relationship between grades in school and performance on the job. As I have written elsewhere:

> It should be clearly pointed out that people at the top of the class are not less competent than the rest of the class. However, there is little to say they'll do better. There are thus good arguments for hiring from the bottom of the class. Those at the top have been conditioned in a special way by those of us in academe. We encourage them to aspire to join us on Olympus where they can drink nectar with the gods. Their expectations are very high both as to what they will and won't do and as to what they expect in the way of rewards. On the other hand, according to the starting salary data, those at the bottom of the class start out costing a lot less, and as I've pointed out, on average they perform just as well as the class brains. Finally, as Ben Franklin said in talking about a not dissimilar situation, "You'll find they are Oh so grateful." [Shapero, 1977]

Use personal reference networks. Use personal networks to identify good potential hires. Good performers tend to be associated with social circles, professional or otherwise, that maintain high norms of work behavior. The old adage "birds of a feather flock together" could be restated: "birds that flock together become of a feather." Watch for the identity of the group through which the individual is referred, since all of us are members of many groups with differing norms and values. Working through your immediate and extended professional social circles, the probability is high you will obtain accurate information about potential hires, and you will get value judgments not available through any formal channels. Information obtained from someone you do not know personally but to whom you are referred by someone you know will still be of high quality.

Concentrate on effective channels of recruitment. Concentrate on "self-recruitment" channels. Hires who come to an organization because of its reputation or through friends and acquaintances are the best performers on the job. Over the long term, it is possible to enhance the flow of high-quality applicants by a program of institutional advertisements (as opposed to employment advertisement) and other public relations activities that convincingly portray the organization as having high professional standards, valuing high-quality work and productivity, and having an appropriate environment. One national research organization ran ads in technical and trade journals with pictures and quotes of great scientists (e.g., Newton, Einstein, Kepler), and in very small print at the bottom of the ad gave a name and number to call for anyone interested in being associated with an organization that valued such people. Similarly, a major aerospace company once took the complete middle spread of several major newspapers to list over four hundred titles of papers written by its technical staff, and to invite those who were interested to request copies and to apply for work in an organization that put such a high premium on technical papers.

Maintaining good public relations pays off over time. A good reputation makes it possible to obtain the quantity and quality of professional manpower desired when needed, which is often hard to do under the immediate pressures of a large project or contract. One caveat should be noted: the institutional advertising and public relations must be realistic rather than fanciful. One company that advertised the glories and pleasures of its professional environment harvested a sharp increase in

43

professional turnover made up of angry employees who contrasted the advertisements with their daily realities. The ads were put up on bulletin boards all over the company with appropriate graffiti.

Enlist friends, acquaintances, relatives, former colleagues, former professors, people met at technical meetings, friends of friends as sources of referrals of potential hires. Using one's own contacts to stir up potential hires is a good way to generate a flow of first-quality potential hires. Most managers will say, "But I do that." Of course they do. That is why such a high fraction of professionals are hired through the channel of "friends and acquaintances," but the process should be systematized. It is a preferred means and should be given precedence in time and resources.

Use professionals already working in the organization to identify and bring in people they know. Many organizations circularize their employees, but few design the effort in terms of what is known about good hiring. It is important to focus on your best performers for candidates. Chances are good that someone referred by a high performer will also be a high performer. Similarly, the professional referred by a low performer has a good probability of having the same standards as the person doing the referring. It is safe to assume the high performer will judge the person he recommends by his own standards. In any case, if you personally ask employees to recommend someone like themselves you have paid a high compliment, which provides positive feedback reinforcement even when it doesn't result in hires.

In times of high demand for professionals, as during the missile buildup of the 1950s, some companies rediscovered an idea invented several times: offering a bonus or fee to employees for every qualified person they referred who was hired. Engineers were in great demand, and the competition was fierce. The situation was exacerbated by the policy of the government to pick up all personnel costs. Large salary increases and promotions were used to attract qualified people. Inter-company pirating was rampant. One missile company sent twenty-three engineers to recruit at an engineering convention and only three returned, all the others having been hired away. In that environment more than one company came up with the idea of paying "bounty" to their own employees for bringing in engineers. Paying bounty did not work well. The practice resulted in poor hiring. By paying the employee for bringing in a candidate the act becomes a commercial transaction rather than a personal responsibility, and the feeling engendered in the employees can be expressed, "If you hire the person I bring in, it's your responsibility. I'll bring in as many people as I can, of all kinds, and leave the evaluation and judgment to the company."

Maintain a program of summer jobs for students, participate in cooperative education programs, and use intern programs for effective, low-risk means for obtaining high performing professionals. The summer employee, co-op student, and intern come to work under conditions in which organization and nascent professional can look each other over without commitment or risk. The managers in the organization can affect the performance of the individuals by the assignments given and the people with whom the individual is assigned to work. Meanwhile, the student becomes familiar with the company and its ways, and can make an informed judgment about the desirability of working there.

Summer jobs, co-op programs, and internships are very popular with students. The best students are anxious to obtain professional experience and seek out such opportunities. One consulting engineering firm in the Pacific Northwest attracts summer students with the promise that they will work directly with the firm's principals—and with no pay! Hands-on programs in architecture, engineering, and business schools are oversubscribed. There is one caveat to be noted. A hands-on program that doesn't put the students to work doing genuine, challenging work will create strong negative reactions. Participants in programs that use them as clerks or that let them study rather than work take home and circulate a poor image of the company. The student employees don't come back, and the organization gets a bad image among other students.

Set high expectations on entry. Locate the new employee, particularly the new college graduate, in a group of individuals with very high standards of performance. The performance

45

of those in the new individual's immediate work environment and their response to his behavior will establish what is expected and strongly influence the individual's behavior. Once set, it takes a long time and a great many different experiences to change the effect of the early expectations experienced by the new employee.

Many organizations undertake the mistaken practice of putting a "young tiger" into a group in need of livening up. Chances are that instead of an enlivened group, the results will be a dead "tiger" or early turnover of the new hire. Group norms are powerful and persistent, and it is extremely difficult to change them. To enliven an organization it is better to build up clusters of high performers, centers of excellence, while allowing low-performing groups to shrink by attrition or to be broken up.

Give the new employee a first or early assignment that is challenging, and make it clear that high performance is expected. It informs the employee of standards and expectations of the organization. A useful way to "save" an employee who has performed well in the past, but who appears to have plateaued, is to put the employee in a lively group and give a demanding assignment that helps evoke earlier standards of performance.

Hire with the flow of streams of migration. To increase the numbers of employment offers accepted and of workers who will stay with the organization, managers should: hire from within the immediate area; hire from upstream; when hiring from downstream, hire people who came from the immediate area (the "return home phenomenon").

To set up a facility in a new geographic area an organization should first draw upon members of the organization that originally came from the area, and should "map" the historic migration patterns affecting the new location as a guide for its hiring efforts. The choice of geographic points of recruitment can make a substantial difference in whether desirable professionals will come to work or stay with the company.

To illustrate the migration path effect, when Huntsville, Alabama, was bustling with space and military work, a large number of contractor and subcontractor organizations set up facilities in the town. Many had large demands for scientists and engineers and expended much on recruitment. One organization needing two hundred professionals placed an advertisement in the local newspaper intending to attract people from other local government and contractor facilities. The advertisement was answered by a large number of applicants from the North, and all the positions were filled. The applications came from Alabamians who had migrated to the North and were ready to return home, a classic pattern. They had obtained the advertisement from relatives who wanted them to return or from their hometown newspaper which they continued to receive.

Similarly, on publication of news of plans to build a plant in Northern Arkansas, a business machine company received over two thousand applications from people who had lived or vacationed in the area, and who wanted to settle there.

Put teeth into the probation period. Hiring is the most important management decision made, and the probation process should be considered a critical element in the hiring process. Firms with more than a handful of employees almost always have a probationary period after hiring. The probation period varies from one month to three months, and is a time when employees can be fired without recourse and even without explanation. Probation is a period in which employees' performance can be assessed before they enter the permanent work force.

Frequently, probation has been a matter of negotiation between union and management to establish a point beyond which an individual is considered a member of the work force with all the protection of the union against layoff. Many organizations have a probation period for all employees, professional and nonprofessional, and it is made clear at the time of hire that such a period must be undergone before the employee is considered a permanent hire.

Despite intentions, few organizations make serious efforts to fully carry out the probation process. In most cases, probation is a perfunctory processing of paper work except in the most flagrant cases of incompetence or behavioral disturbance.

As with the human body, organizations cannot afford to

"ingest" individuals who can seriously affect their ability to achieve high performance. The criterion for probation should be, as with the body, "when in doubt, spit it out." A probation system should establish criteria and operational procedures for evaluating new hires, and for letting people go who do not meet the criteria. Firing is the most painful experience a manager goes through, but there is an important trade off between the short-term difficulty of firing and the long-term costs to everyone of an unsuitable employee.

A useful probation system should include the following:

1. Probationary criteria based on an organization's experience
2. Procedures for making the new hire clearly aware of the probation process, and the criteria used
3. Procedures for probation review applied, where possible, by someone who did not do the hiring, to keep the person who did the hiring from rationalizing the unacceptable performance of the new hire

Organizations suffer from functional amnesia when it comes to their hiring experiences. Few organizations record and review their hiring experience in relationship to subsequent performance. Every organization, even the smallest, should record what was perceived in the new hire in a way that it can be retrieved for comparison against performance. In the absence of the data, subsequent comparisons will be distorted by later impressions.

Low and high performers should be identified and their characteristics and hiring processes (including who recommended them or hired them) compared. Efforts should be made to identify any existing patterns. Efforts should also be made to identify the kinds of organizational events associated with the loss of high performers.

Take Advantage of the Errors in the Conventional Wisdom

Conventional wisdom on hiring is embodied in many personnel practices that have no measurable relationship to the professional performance desired. Consequently, many opportunities are available to enlightened management to gain a competitive advantage in hiring excellent but untapped human resources. The two largest groups of competent and relatively unsought human resources are (1) new college graduates who are not in the upper echelons of the class, and (2) older professionals.

A good opportunity exists for hiring excellent newly graduated professionals, by focusing on the lower two thirds of the class. First, the largest corporations, consulting organizations and government agencies concentrate on graduates with high grade point averages, making it difficult for any single organization to compete successfully for them, bidding up their starting salaries, and giving the candidates an unrealistic notion of what awaits them in the work place. Second, those with the highest grade averages are socialized by their professors to take advanced degrees, to aspire to become academics. The "good student" is asked by the professors, "Have you thought about graduate school? Would you like a recommendation for a fellowship?" The student with lower grade averages is not better (or worse) than the high GPA student on the job, tends to be far more ready to enter fully into the work force, and is happy to be sought out.

The validity of the assertion that there is no relationship between grades in school and performance on the job is easily checked by any organization with more than a handful of professional employees. Any management can rank its employees in terms of performance from highest to lowest, and then check the school records of the employees against their rankings. If the grades scatter, as in all probability they will, it will demonstrate that grades and performance are not correlated.[1]

Older workers are another relatively untapped source of excellent professional manpower. Older workers perform well,

---

[1] In response to a large number of challenges to a column expressing the point about the lack of relationship between grades and performance on the job, each of the challengers was asked to make the check described here with the assurance that if they disproved the statement the evidence would be published and the statement retracted. No disproof was received.

and bring many other positive attributes to their work. In many cases, the financial situation of the older worker is such as to make them desirable employees. Their children are finished with college, their houses are paid for, their retirement has been partially provided, and they are less likely to make job decisions on the basis of marginal differences in salary. Older workers are not amenable to being underpaid, but are more likely to put a premium on the quality of the work environment, the chance to keep up professionally, and the congeniality of colleagues than on "career opportunities" and promotion.

Some older workers prefer to be hired on a part-time basis or on a part-of-the-year basis so they can take advantage of long vacations to travel or pursue other interests. As a consequence of the predilection for part-time employment, nominally retired professionals are useful in handling the peaks and valleys of project/contract work without the trauma of hiring and firing employees. Some organizations hire "emeritus" professionals on a contract basis so that both parties are freed from a host of procedural and regulatory burdens such as deductions and fringe benefit calculations. Many managements have independently "discovered" the use of older professionals as part-time employees, and are unanimous in praising their capabilities, work performance, and attitudes. Many see the older professionals as good influences in their organizations.

SPECIAL CASES

Special situations in hiring professionals to consider include (1) hiring minority workers and women, and (2) hiring in a seller's market when business is good and professionals are scarce.

Minority Workers and Women

Organizations are concerned with the representation of minority and women professionals in their work force both because of government regulations and a sincere desire for more equity. In spite of persistent and expensive efforts the results have been uneven. There are many reasons for the poor showing to date. Sometimes demographic situations make the task virtually impossible. One nuclear power facility on the Ohio River, ordered by the government to increase the number of black professionals on its staff, found it impossible to convince black engineers to move to an area where less than 2% of the population is black. Another severe limitation can be the absolute numbers of designated professionals available. Though 43.3% of all professional and technical workers in the United States are women, only 2.9% of the engineers, 10.75% of the physicians and osteopaths, and 12.4% of the lawyers and judges are women. The 43.3% figure was achieved by including professions where women predominate: i.e., nursing, 96.8%, teaching, 70.8%.

A more painful dilemma is expressed by the black woman director of minority hiring in a major state agency who said, "We've tried our damndest to hire competent black professionals, but we haven't done well at all. Very few have applied despite the good salaries and conditions offered, and the quality of those who do apply has been poor. What can we do about it?"

As with any professionals, if you want competency, go to competent people for references. If you want good referrals of black, Latin-American, or women professionals, go to competent people and ask them for their recommendations. If you are trying to hire competent black engineers use all of the social-professional circles you have access to and turn to the most competent black professionals of any kind you can contact (physicians, teachers, ministers, social workers) for their recommendations. (The government agency minority recruitment director had to find a way to get referrals into and through the civil service procedures.)

Taking a longer view of the problem, an organization should hire minorities and women for summer work or cooperative-education programs, thus building a long-term flow into the organization. Where a geographic area has very few minority or women professionals in the population, an organization can take advantage of historic migration patterns. By using census data on migration for the past decade, it is possible to identify (1) from where minority professionals in the area have migrated, and (2) the areas to which minority members have been migrating from the local area. Streams of migration all tend to have a two-way flow. The two-way flow was demonstrated in the 1970s by a reverse migration from the North to the South of blacks who had previously migrated to the North, and particularly of those who had achieved professional and technical skills.

No approach to hiring minority or women professionals will have any lasting effect if it is not paralleled by subsequent practices that reinforce the intentions of the organization as expressed in its hiring program. The power of the new hire's expectations is even more important in the case of minorities and women. The organization that hires minority workers in response to governmental pressures, and then proceeds to expect them to perform poorly, generates a self-fulfilling prophecy. Under such conditions, employees will perform as poorly as expected or will leave at a high rate. Those who leave will convey the organization's expectations to the general community, affecting subsequent minority hiring. It would be better to initiate no special minority hiring program if no special attention is paid to initial assignments and locations.

When Business Is Good and Professionals Are Scarce

Professional work tends to be done in terms of projects. The project format typifies research and development, construction, advertising, the performing arts, consulting, and architecture, to name the most obvious. Furthermore, many professional fields have very sharp fluctuations tied to socioeconomic conditions such as booms, slumps, and variations in building, and in the patterns of government expenditure.

As a consequence of the "lumpiness" of project work, many organizations often experience precipitous and simultaneous demands for the same kinds of professionals. Under such "sellers' market" conditions it is important to consider what attracts professionals to one organization over another. Too often, it is assumed that outbidding other organizations is the key to successful hiring. Thus, in the 1950s period of missile buildup, competing companies bidup the salary level of scientists and engineers in the aerospace industry to twice the average for all scientists and engineers in the United States.

Many noneconomic factors influence the employment decisions of professionals. Geographic migration patterns have been discussed. Other clues to the job decisions of professionals come from studies showing that professionals place a high premium on professional challenge, interesting work, reputation of the organization, professional climate, opportunities for professional growth, and recognition.

A final note on hiring in good times: An organization can adopt a long-term stance that assures an adequate flow of good people when they are needed. A long-term stance reflects the view that it is important to maintain at all times the kinds of communications relevant to good hiring, even when the situation is bleak. The best channels of recruitment are those least amenable to being turned on and off with a budget. It is easy to turn on advertising, employment agencies, and recruiting campaigns with a budget, but budgets cannot generate and nurture the social-professional networks and reputations so effective in producing good hires. The latter are maintained by encouraging publication, attendance at professional meetings, and maintaining a host of informal contacts with other professionals in the field on the part of an organization's professional staff, during times when those contacts are not needed.

2

Motivation

A GREAT RE-EXAMINATION of American management practice has been stirred by the success of the Japanese in world markets. Though some cry, "Foul! The Japanese are unfair!," most attribute Japanese success to higher productivity and search for the sources of Japanese advantage. Among the factors credited have been lower wages, more automation, more focused R & D expenditures, and, most of all, better motivation on the part of Japanese employees and managers.

Much effort has gone into explaining Japanese industrial motivation. Credit has been given to Japanese culture (for its homogeneity, devotion to nation, etc.,); guaranteed lifetime employment and its subsequent benefits in terms of long-term vs. short-term decisions (i.e., R & D expenditures, lower wages, acceptance of innovation capital investment, long-term cost-benefit analyses); and Japanese management styles (e.g., consensus decision-making, and worker participation as exemplified by quality circles).

Most of the attributions are without much substance or are relevant only to a limited segment of Japanese industry.

Guaranteed lifetime employment applies to less than twenty-five major corporations and not to the 75% of the Japanese work force found in small companies. There is little long-range planning, in the U. S. industrial sense, in Japanese companies. There is a great deal of competitiveness in Japanese society and industry. Many, of the admired worker-participation methods, such as quality circles, have American roots, and were introduced to the Japanese by American efforts through the occupation authorities and U. S.-sponsored productivity centers. Quality circles, an admired feature of Japanese management, derive from work simplification programs and quality control methods that were the hallmark of much of U. S. industrial practice four decades ago. The most useful clue to the Japanese success is found in motivation.

Motivation is certainly one of the most frequently mentioned concerns of U. S. managers. One often hears them complain, "If we could only motivate our people . . ." or "Workers are not motivated the way they used to be." Yet, as with quality control, it is the United States that has always dominated the subject. American scholarship and thinking pioneered and still leads the field of motivation research.

Historically, managers have been concerned with the morals and morale of the workers since the feudal relationship between the lord of the manor and his serfs. However, serious interest in understanding what influences the behavior of workers and how to use that knowledge did not begin to develop until the early 1920s. In the 1930s the field took off with a tremendous increase in the space devoted by management texts to behavioral concerns, and textbooks of the period bristled with such terms as "adjustment," "status," and "social environment." In the 1950s the terminology showed a preoccupation with "informal groups," "roles," "job satisfaction," "work performance," and "work motivation." Through the mid-1970s the term "motivation" was second in frequency only to "leadership" in management texts: in twenty-eight textbooks it was mentioned 611 times, compared with 860 times for "leadership" (Aronoff, 1975).

It must be pointed out that when managers complain that "the workers are not motivated" they are dead wrong. There is no such thing as a sentient human being who is not motivated. It is impossible not to be motivated. Even to lie in bed and refuse to move is a motivated inaction. When a manager says that someone is not motivated, what she or he is saying is that the individual is not motivated to do what the manager wants that person to do at the time and in the manner that the manager deems appropriate. What the noncooperating individual is showing is not lack of motivation. He or she might actually feel a strong motivation to do something to frustrate the manager or to accomplish something counterproductive to the needs of the employing organization.

The complaint of the manager about motivation should be reinterpreted to read, "How can I get these others to do what is in the interests of the organization rather than what they might do if left to their own devices?" The problem is one of work motivation, and the manager must find ways to effectively influence the behavior of those managed. Work motivation is central to what managers do since most management work consists of influencing human behavior, and in professional activities the proportion of management work devoted to influencing human behavior is much higher than for other kinds of work.

Except for rather infrequent events—such as when a contract is bid for and accepted, a project is launched or terminated, a campaign is undertaken or completed—the management of professional activities is primarily concerned with influencing the behavior of the professionals doing the work of the organization. Managers spend the bulk of their time listening, evaluating, encouraging, defending, criticizing, coaching, and advising—in other words, responding to the needs of or influencing the behavior of subordinates. The more the work of an organization is human-centered, the more the manager must be an influencer of human behavior. In organizations primarily engaged in professional activities, the work is almost entirely human-centered, and thus the manager is primarily a work motivator whether consciously or not.

In a sense, every chapter in this book is concerned with influencing human behavior or motivation, whether we are discussing this directly or are considering incentives, evaluation, creativity, technical obsolescense, burnout, information-communication, or hiring.

Incentives are institutionalized influencers of behavior. Incentives (such as compensation, for example) are used to elicit kinds of behavior other than might have been chosen in the absence of incentives (Gellerman, 1968).

Evaluation is another way of influencing future behavior. In evaluation the manager provides verbal feedback of judgments together with instructions, advice, and suggestions.

Creativity, technical obsolescence, and "burnout" are human processes, relevant to professional work, that can be influenced to some extent by the actions of managers.

Information-communication behavior is a vital work-related activity that can be influenced significantly by managerial actions.

Organization structures and processes are concerned with configuring, channeling and affecting the ways people in the organization relate to each other in carrying out their work. A good deal of what managers do with organizations has to do with the effects of their actions and of the organizational structure on the work of their employees.

Hiring, too, engages us in a discussion of motivation and the influencing of human behavior. As was underlined in the chapter on hiring, the most effective means of hiring positively influences the behavior of those hired (i.e., the use of networks, the importance of first assignments and locations, etc.).

Thus, the subject of motivation is the logical place to begin consideration of how managers can go about achieving influence over worker behavior through incentives, evaluation, organization, and so forth. A manager needs enough information to feel comfortable in dealing with the subject from a rational, data-based perspective rather than from hearsay and gut feeling. An understanding of motivation, of the dynamics of influencing behavior, provides the manager with the knowledge from which specific means of influencing employee behavior can be developed.

Drawing upon the growing pool of research data on motivation, and particularly on work motivation, the process of work motivation is mapped below to help managers find a useful path through the maze of factors identified as influencing work place behavior. The "map" is eclectic in that it draws upon various theories and upon empirical studies, and is designed to identify for the manager what can be influenced in the work situation, and what important factors are outside that situation, and outside the reach of the manager. The map also helps identify which factors are more important than others in influencing the work behavior of professionals, and identifies available motivational tools.

MOTIVATION IN GENERAL AND MOTIVATION IN THE WORKPLACE

The word "motivation" is used to describe goal-directed behavior, as differentiated from reflexive behavior such as the blinking of an eye or the knee-jerk reaction to a knock on the knee which are unconsciously activated. According to one definition, motivation is concerned with:

> how behavior gets started, is energized, is sustained, is directed, is stopped, and what kind of subjective reaction is present in the organism while all this is going on. [Jones, 1955]

In the work situation, motivation is narrowed to questions of work performance: the starting, energizing, sustaining, directing, and stopping of behaviors relevant to the work situation.

When researchers in the field of work motivation, such as organizational behavior specialists and industrial psychologists, write about motivation, they are concerned with the "whys" of an individual's motivation to work. Behaviorial scientists raise questions like: why does an individual choose to work for one employer rather than another, or prefer one task to another? why does an individual choose to initiate a particular piece of work? why does an individual put as much effort into a task as he does? why does an individual complete an effort or even come to work every day?

When managers refer to motivation, they are concerned

with the "hows" related to an individual's motivation to work: how to get an individual to work for his organization rather than another, or to prefer an assigned task to another? how to get an individual to initiate pieces of work chosen or preferred by the manager rather than others? how to get an individual to put a desired level of effort into a task? how to get an individual to complete an assigned effort and complete it on time. How to get an individual to come to work at the appropriate times?

AN ECLECTIC MODEL OF WORK MOTIVATION

A number of theories have been developed to explain work motivation. Each of the theories offers a plausible framework which a manager can use to derive operational clues, but to limit one's perspective to any given theory deprives one of what can be gained from other theories and from the many available empirical studies. To make more of the available information available in a form that can guide managerial efforts to understand and affect motivation, a simple model has been developed (see Figure 2–1) to depict the factors that affect an individual's motivation in the work place. The model is "eclectic" in that it draws upon both a range of available theories and empirical studies. In addition to the eclectic model, the major work motivation theories are discussed from the viewpoint of the manager of professionals.

How an individual's work motivation is affected is described below in terms of an Expectations-Motivation-Performance-Experiences-Comparisons -Expectations cycle embedded in three overlapping fields: the work motivation field of the individual, the work situation, and the larger environment. The primary or central field is that of the individual, and within it is embedded the motivation cycle. At work, the individual's field is surrounded by the work situation which includes the organization, the physical facilities, and all of the conditions of work such as tools, materials, assignments, resources, rules and procedures. The larger environment encompasses all of the world outside

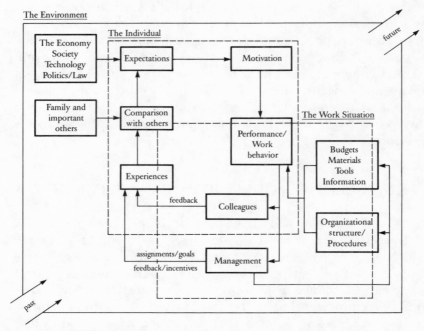

FIGURE 2–1.   Work Motivation of the Individual

work that is significant to the individual and includes family, friends, other significant people, political and economic factors, technology, and law.

The Work Motivation Cycle and the Individual

Work behavior begins with *expectations.* What we expect to happen affects what we are motivated to do. The individual starts with a set of expectations about what will occur as a result of various work-related and social actions. It is the individual's expectations that are transformed into those predilections that we usually refer to as *motivation:* the propensity to move, the tendency to act in a particular manner or to work at a certain rate, to volunteer or withold suggestions, to express or hide enthusiasm, to act creatively or "play it by the book," to put in extra hours or not.

Motivation leads to *performance:* performance of the work to be done, as well as social and other behavior in the work place. Once the individual has done something in the workplace, several kinds of feedback—both external and internal—are received: the responses of managers, colleagues and clients, personal feelings of pleasure or displeasure at the outcomes, and other formal and informal signals of all kinds. The sum of all these kinds of feedback is the work *experiences* of the individual, which determine whether one feels that one has done a good job, is appreciated, or had a bad day.

Work experiences, however, do not occur in a vacuum. The individual is part of a work group, an organization, a profession, and a social group. Consequently, to be able to evaluate one's experiences, to decide whether they are good or bad, getting better or worse, the individual compares them with those of others. By making *comparisons* of one's experiences with those of others, an individual determines whether the treatment received is "fair," or should be protested. Most important, by evaluating what has been experienced as a result of the way one has performed, and by comparing it with what happens to others, expectations are re-examined, and, where it appears required, modified.

It is a dynamic cycle, constantly in action, constantly being modified. A change in the work situation, including what happens to others, leads to a change in the results of comparisons, changed expectations, and changed motivation.

From the viewpoint of the manager, it becomes apparent that exhortations to "change your motivation," or "change your attitude," are superficial and likely to be ineffective. The actual way motivation is changed is far less direct. Motivation is affected by what happens daily on the job, what happens to others, by rules and organization, and by the availability of all those other elements that go into doing the work, among which are the reactions of colleagues and what the manager says and does directly.

An examination of the cycle suggests where the manager can and cannot act directly on work motivation. The cycle begins with expectations which immediately suggests that the manager might help establish initial expectations and continue to affect them through a variety of actions. Realizing that the individual's experiences are partly a product of reactions from others and that those of the manager are the most influential suggests the importance and power of a frequent flow of managerial feedback to the individual. The alert manager can gear salaries and conditions to those of comparable individuals and organizations and can make sure the comparative data are freely available.

The Work Situation

The work situation is the domain of management, and it is the field in which the manager has most control. Managers determine the form of organization, the facilities to be used, the work rules and procedures, and the formal system of rewards. Managers make the work assignments, allocate resources, assign the schedules, and determine who works with whom. It is through manipulation of the work situation that managers have their greatest impact on the motivation and subsequent work behavior of the professionals that work for an organization.

The performance of an individual can be described in the form of an equation:

$$P = M \times A \times N$$

where P = performance

M = motivation

A = ability

N = necessaries (resources, information, budgets, organizational structure and procedures)

The job performance of the individual is the result of an interacting mix of the individual's motivation and ability, and of the availability and quality of the items necessary for performance of the work to be done. All of the elements are relevant, and all can be affected—one way or another—by management.

Availability of the necessary situation elements is almost

completely in the hands of management. Ability and motivation cannot overcome a lack of instruments and technicians. An organization's structure and procedures can make it difficult to get the timely decisions, resources, or information that can be crucial to whether work is performed well or not. Examples abound of the negative effects of various kinds of organizational structures or bureaucratic procedures on a firm's ability to carry out effective research and development or to deliver construction projects on time.

Further, the highest motivation cannot overcome an individual's technical incompetence. The inherent and acquired abilities of a professional combine with motivation to affect work performance. Management can affect technical competence and abilities by providing for technical updating, and by enabling the individual to continue developing personal professional skills and knowledge through a variety of means (see Chapter 5, "Technical Obsolescence, Burnout, and Staying Alive").

The manager, by all counts, has the most influence, directly and indirectly, in determining the nature and quality of an employee's work experiences. As has been pointed out above, the manager determines the employee's resources, information, organizational constraints, assignments made, goals set, as well as providing feedback in terms of approval, criticism, rewards, incentives, and recognition.

The manager affects work motivation indirectly by locating the professional employee physically and socially (organizationally) in a particular environment. Where and with whom one works closely has a distinct influence on one's work motivation. Assigning a new employee to an established group means the employee will be given all kinds of direct and indirect signals by members of the group as to what they consider good work behavior. Thus, assigning a new employee to a group with a low output rate is likely to set the new person's expectations to a low level of performance. Research has shown that a new employee's values tend to converge over time with the values of those already in the organization at time of entry (see box, "The Power of Expectations").

THE POWER OF EXPECTATIONS

The psychologist R. Rosenthal created a furor in research circles in the early 1960s when he found that the attitudes of individuals carrying out an experiment affected the way rats performed in running mazes. Using rats drawn from the same strain, he presented one group of experimenters with some of the rats with the explanation that they were specially bred for brightness. He assigned them the task of teaching the rats to run a maze. With a second group of experimenters, and rats from the same strain, he explained that the rats had been bred to be poor at running mazes, and he also assiged this second group the task of teaching the rats to run a maze.

Right off, the rats believed to be smarter did well, and the rats thought to be dull did very badly, sometimes refusing even to leave the starting position. Students who thought they had brighter rats found their subjects to be more pleasant and more likeable than those who thought they had dullards.

Rosenthal's results raised a lot of laughter as well as furor. Why did the rats act as they did? What did this mean to all the data based on rat experimentation? One could picture laboratory rats asking each other, "Hey, what's the hypothesis?" and knocking themselves out to prove it. Could it be the experimenter projected expectations that affected the performance of the subjects? What might the same kinds of expectations mean in human situations?

The Environment

The larger environment encompasses all the institutions, persons, and events significant to the individual and the work situation. The larger environment includes family, peers, and other significant people; the economic and political situation; and what is going on in technology and the profession. The way family and peers perceive and react to the work an individual is doing, to his or her position and pay, and to the employing organization has an influence on the individual's expectations and subsequent performance. Working for an organization held

In 1968 Rosenthal and Jacobson created similar kinds of expectation conditions in an elmentary school in South San Francisco. They told the teachers they needed further validation for a new kind of test to predict academic blooming or intellectual gain in children. They used what was then a new standard intelligence test unfamiliar to the teachers. Before school opened the following fall, using random numbers, 20% of the students were arbitrarily designated as potential "spurters"; about five to each classroom. The names of the so-called spurters were transmitted to the teachers casually at the end of the first staff meeting in September, and the students were subsequently tested and retested three times throughout the year.

The children whom the teachers were led to expect to show the greatest gains did show the greatest gains: the designated spurters showed the greatest increase in total IQ, in verbal IQ, and in reasoning IQ. At the end of the first year the greatest gains were made by those in the first and second grades. At the end of the second year the greatest gains were among the fifth grade spurters.

Those designated as spurters were judged by the teachers as having a better chance for success in later life, as being happier, more curious, more interesting, more appealing, better adjusted, more affectionate, and less in need of social approval than other children. Among the undesignated children who gained in IQ during the year, the more they gained, the less favorably they were perceived.

in high or low regard by the general public does have an influence on work performance. There is a long-term value for an organization in projecting a positive "image." It attracts desirable applicants, offsets their decisions to accept other positions, their decisions to come to work or be absent, and their on-the-job performance.

The general economic and political environment has an impact on the expectations of the individual professional. Most obviously, in hard times expectations shift in the direction of concern for security. In hard times it is important to keep professional employees attuned to the condition of the company with regard to the economy. In times when professional employees are in demand, there is a different weighting of incentives than when work is scarce. In recent years the legal environment has become more influential in the work situation with increasing exposure to professional liability and requirements for hiring minority and women workers. Professionals are acutely aware of what is happening in the legal environment and it influences their expectations. It is vital that management convey to its employees how the organization will respond to new legal requirements, in terms of hiring, promotion, rewards, and treatment.

Perceptions of what is going on in the world, economically and politically, and of what is going on with others in the same profession in other companies influences an individual's expectations and are a major cause of comparisons of work experiences. When times are bad economically and unemployment is high, an individual's perceptions of the relative value of work experiences will be influenced by that fact, and professionals may lower their expectations. When times are better and it is easy to find other positions, the standards will change. One is constantly comparing one's work experiences with what is happening to others in the same organization, as well as with what is happening to peers in other organizations. An individual may be happy with his or her work experiences until they are compared with those of professionals in other organizations. The results of such a comparison may produce greater job satisfaction or disgruntlement.

A manager cannot significantly affect the larger environment that operates on the employee but can take the existence and influence of that environment into account. Since individuals are constantly comparing their experiences with those of others, it is important the manager be aware what comparisons are being made. The most obvious comparisons are concerned with salaries. This is recognized by managers, and enlightened organizations survey the general salary climate to see how they stack up. Comparisons are also made of promotion policies, special bonus arrangements, the experiences of colleagues who have gone into business for themselves, technical content of work, and degree of autonomy.

Managements usually recognize the importance of the environment in deciding where to build facilities. The nature of the locale in which an organization is situated affects the employment decisions of professionals, and their subsequent decisions to remain with an organization. Thus, the availability of educational, cultural, and recreational offerings in a community should be of interest to managers. When there is a shortage of professionals in a given field, some organizations will deliberately locate facilities with an eye to gaining a competitive advantage in hiring or to retaining desired professionals. During the defense system buildup of the 1950s, major facilities were located or relocated to the "sunbelt" states (i.e., Florida, Arizona, Colorado, California) to keep and attract scientists and engineers. One major company, Contral Data Corporation, built a facility in a rural community in Minnesota because of the predilections of its key computer designer.

The Past and Initial Conditions

Each individual comes to the work situation with a set of purposes, drives, needs, and attributes—the product of whatever moves humans in general and of the individual's particular biological and historical past. The individual's past manifests itself in the work situation as a collection of talents, skills, and knowledge called "ability," and as a collection of expectations as to how the organization and the work to be done relate to the individual's purposes, drives, and needs. An individual prefers one organization to another because of some perception of what future experiences can be expected in that organization in terms of rewards, personal growth, interaction with others, image, etc. When hiring, the manager is really trying to match the products of the past, as expressed in the apparent abilities and attitudes (expectations) of a candidate, with his own perceived need in the workplace.

The individual professional comes to the hiring process with expectations formed by what has been learned about the organization from relatives, friends, or publications. Initial expectations motivate the individual to go through the hiring process, and, during that process, to act in ways that are a product of those initial expectations. An individual's experiences with the hiring process, and the explicit or implicit employment contract that results, are the first test of initial expectations. Far more powerful is the first operational test of expectations in first assignments and first interactions with managers and colleagues.

First experiences on the job in an organization have an influence on later performance that is very difficult to change. An individual's entry into an organization and its impact on subsequent performance suggests a number of important implications for managers.

Feedback from the Manager, Evaluations, and Incentives

No matter how we try to create organizations that are flat in terms of hierarchy and informal in terms of authority, the hierarchical model is so deeply ingrained that a manager has to work very hard to play other than an authority role. There have been many attempts to create "dual ladders" in organizations that give equal status and pay to individuals going up either the managerial or professional track, but research has shown that no one believes the two are really equal after a few months in the organization. Managers, in the end, control the real sources of power, the budgets, and the organizational structure. Managerial power is exemplified by the fact that managers have the power to decide whether to end the dual ladder system and how to fund it.

What the manager says and conveys through actions has an influence often far greater than intended. An inadvertent remark by a manager can lead to interpretations by others of organizational policies diametrically opposed to what was intended by management. How a manager reacts to the work or comments of an employee is interpreted as the way the organization views what has been done or expressed, and helps form the expectations of the employee.

The daily feedback received by the professional employee is a constantly reinforcing set of experiences with much more influence than a once-a-year or once-every-six-months formal evaluation. The daily feedback from a manager can generate a movement in the work motivation cycle that will determine what happens at the time of a formal evaluation. Frequent positive feedback and coaching establish and maintain expectations that motivate the professional to perform in a way and at a level that evokes more positive feedback, thus exercising the work motivation cycle over and over again in the direction of desired performance. Managers who do not actively exercise the cycle over and over again, and who remain remote from the day-in, day-out work situation, can hardly expect to seriously influence work performance with evaluations only every six months or a year.

Humans are so in need of feedback from the environment they will generate it even if they have to do something quite counterproductive to get it. An example we instinctively understand is the apparently atrocious behavior of a child to which we typically respond with, "He's only looking for attention!" In the work situation, where frequent feedback is not supplied by the manager a worker will give more credance and weight to feedback from colleagues, from gossip, from the smallest signs to be found in memoranda, or from the actions or inactions of managers.

WHAT CAN A MANAGER AFFECT?

The work motivation model highlights ways managers can systematically and effectively influence the work motivation and resulting performance of the professional employee.

The New Employee

The lasting effect on subsequent performance of the way the individual enters an organization suggests a number of important guidelines for managers:

1. Establish realistic expectations as to the work to be performed, the conditions of employment, and the reward system. (A chance to provide a clear understanding of

what is expected on the job without great risk is one reason summer hire programs are so successful in producing good hires.)

2. Treat the first assignment given a professional as the important event it is (this is almost never done). Make sure the first assignment is a demanding one, and that the first people the newcomer works with are your best workers. The professional's first assignment and colleagues provide important experiences that have a long-term effect on a newcomer's expectations.

3. Be chary about establishing or using long-term training programs for new, entering professionals. Unless done extremely well, a formal training program is a good way to establish the wrong set of expectations in new hires. A training program puts a new hire right back into a school situation, in a student role, and delays the appropriate work experiences. Seen in its proper light, a tough first assignment with high demands on quality, quantity, and delivery time constitutes a very effective training program more in consonance with the model of work motivation than a training program.

4. It is important that initial conditions and experiences are not out of line with what happens to others. Perceptions of equity are very important to each of us. We are always comparing our experiences with what we think others are experiencing. It is amazing to find how many managers believe the salaries and work arrangements negotiated with individuals can be kept confidential. All workers find ways to learn what others are getting, and professional workers tend to be more ingenious than most at doing so. It is not necessary to publicize every individual arrangement, but don't operate on the assumption that they can be kept secret.

Give Motivation a Fighting Chance

Professionals start out with a higher level of positive work motivation than most other workers. Their work has high status in society, and by its nature professionals have more opportunity than most to do things that are interesting and varied. It is the responsibility of the managers of professionals to provide the conditions and where withal that will let the naturally motivating force of the work itself operate.

Motivation cannot overcome the lack of the "necessaries" to do the work. Management is responsible for providing the budget, equipment, materials, time, information, and organizational arrangements to accomplish the work assigned. Making it impossible to achieve good work performance by denying the means for success results in both internal and external negative feedback and lowers expectations. It also generates resentment and feelings of inequity.

Provision of the wherewithal to do the job is obviously required of the manager. Not quite as obvious are the many actions the manager can take with regard to the provision of "necessaries" that significantly enhance work performance and, eventually, motivation. This can be illustrated in the area of information. There is much that managers can do to obtain large improvements in the flow of information (discussed in depth in Chapter 4, "Managing Information"). Designing organizational structures, procedures, and physical arrangements to encourage and increase communications—particularly informal communications—among an organization's staff, and between the staff and professionals outside the organization, will result in improved performance. The manager can hire people who are good communicators, design physical facilities and organizational procedures to promote information exchange, provide liberal budgets for telecommunications, travel, and publications, and encourage coffee-klatsching and reading, all of which not only encourage the exchange of information but also result in the kinds of experiences that lead to high expectations and high motivation.

By encouraging and even requiring the professionals in an organization continually to upgrade their professional abilities, and by providing them with the means for professional development, management can upgrade work performance. Even more effective in the development of the professional abilities of the staff is a conscious effort to broaden and deepen their professional experiences through the progression of work assigned them.

Feedback

The vital part played by managerial feedback in motivating and shaping the performance of the professional cannot be over-emphasized. The manager is the most important source of the feedback that reinforces or modifies expectations, subsequent motivations, and performance.

Management should recognize the role played by feedback, in affecting motivation and that the part played by the manager in providing that feedback is the critical first step to consciously influencing the motivation of the professional worker. This should force a certain amount of unwelcome but necessary self-consciousness on the manager in dealing with those who report to him.

The importance of feedback is recognized in all organizations by a number of formal mechanisms, and the manager is the primary channel for formal feedback. The forms of feedback include the universal, patterned, performance evaluations scheduled on an annual or biannual basis (discussed in Chapter 3, "Performance Evaluation"). Another form of feedback is the salary review, which is often coupled with the performance review. The whole spectrum of nonsalary incentives are other forms of feedback to the professional, many of which are governed by procedures and written instructions.

Formal means of feedback are important, but the informal feedback received by the professional can be far more effective in shaping, directing, and motivating work performance. Formal feedback occurs too infrequently, and, because of its very formality, becomes ritualized and generalized. Professionals want management to be interested in what they are doing, and to comment on it regularly. They don't like to be told how to do the job but want and expect reaction to what they are doing.

The colleagues one works with are also major sources of

feedback on work performance. The individual's new peers will be giving feedback day-in, day-out. Assigning a new, lively person to a low-performing group probably won't raise the standards of the group; the reverse usually results because of the power of the feedback from the group on the individual. It is usually better to break up the low-performing group and reassign its people to higher performing groups.

Management should consider the value of their five-year plus employees. On the order of 85% of all the professionals that voluntarily leave an organization have had a tenure of less than five years. Those that remain more than five years are most likely to stay much longer and, in the main, determine the operative value system of the organization. Whatever new management policy is adopted, if it is in conflict with the prevailing value system of the majority of the professionals in the work force, it will have a hard time succeeding. Managers should measure the prevailing value system to gain an understanding of what predominates in order to do better hiring, make better assignments—and also to ensure that the values are in consonance with the values of management.

The values of the existing work force exert a powerful influence on what happens to professionals who join the organization. Newcomers to an organization go through a process of socialization if they are to become effective members of the group, and, if they don't, they are isolated or pushed out by social pressure. As Brim defined it (1966), socialization is "a process by which individuals acquire the knowledge, skills, and dispositions that enable them to participate as more or less effective members of groups and society." Socialization is a lifelong process. An individual is socialized to his or her profession, and, within the work situation, an individual is socialized to the organization. In a study of the socialization process in a research and development organization, Dewhirst (1970) found the values of the majority of professionals who were new to the organization converged with those in the organization by the fifth year.

The manager's own work performance and behavior become a model that gives the people reporting to him a number of signals as to what is expected. The manager who comes in early will find that most of his people begin to come in early. The manager who reads at work will encourage others to read at work. The way a manager spends money on a trip sets a standard that is noted by all under him.

Taking Comparisons into Account

Individuals compare the feedback and rewards they receive with their efforts. Further, they make comparisons of their rewards, treatment, and situation to those of others within and outside the organizations for which they work. They compare salaries, promotions, perquisites, and general treatment. If inequities are perceived, the individual will act to reduce the inequities by asking for different treatment or by a change in performance.

Alert managements frequently survey salary and other work-related conditions for professionals in other organizations and modify their own practices to either minimize differences or skew them in favor of their own organizations.

The feeling of equity is important within an organization. It is impossible to keep salaries secret for any length of time. Professionals in organizations eventually learn the relative salaries of others, and will make personal comparisons. Managers should have a rational, defensible system for distributing rewards, and be prepared to use it to explain differences.

Affecting the Greater Environment

The manager can have little direct effect on the larger environment of the professional. It is possible, however, to influence how the organization is perceived by the world outside and thus indirectly affect the expectations of candidates for hire, employees, and important people outside the organization. Development of an organization's positive public image has a number of benefits, including an effect on the motivation of its employees. An organization perceived by the general public, or the professional public, as being a good place to work, a place where a professional can develop, an organization that has high professional standards, a company that emphasizes advanced technology (and/or quality, integrity, etc.), attracts and keeps the best professionals. A good public reputation increases self-recruitment and assures a flow of good professionals when general demand rises.

Develop a policy for active public relations. An appropriate program should encompass policies on attendance and exhibits at professional meetings, advertising in professional media, contacts with universities, and community relations. A well-designed public relations program is a concrete way to help develop the kind of high expectations that result in high initial motivation in new hires. Institutional advertising in professional and trade journals that feature desired values are particularly effective.

A steady flow of high-quality publications, public appearances, and press releases about the professional accomplishments of an organization can have a variety of positive side effects, ranging from increased sales to ease in obtaining resources when they are needed. There are many examples of the potential effects of good public relations. In one case, a newly hired controller of a West Coast electronics firm initiated a policy of issuing press releases whenever anything of positive technical value occurred in the firm. Every time one of the staff gave a paper at a professional organization a press release was sent out. The technical staff was thus given very positive feedback as to the way the organization valued their technical activities, and there was an increase in the number of good applicants for positions in the company. Furthermore, appearance of the positive company news created a public awareness of the company, and the price of the company's stock doubled on the stock market! (It should be noted that an effective public relations program cannot be built on "hype." Advertising that portrays a false image can backfire in very direct ways.)

Diversity

Diversity enhances productivity of professional workers: diversity of projects, of functions performed, of people communicated with. Using as a measure of productivity "overall-usefulness"—in a development context (rather than the more science-oriented measures, "scientific contribution," "papers," and "unpublished reports" used by Pelz and Andrews)—it was found that higher productivity was associated with the following (Pelz & Andrews, 1976):

> Spending half or less than half of one's time in technical work increased productivity; productivity dropped precipitously as the percentage went up.
>
> Those with no areas of specialization were very productive, surpassed only by those with three; those with one area of specialization were least productive.
>
> Performance was highest for those engaged in five different R & D functions, and lowest for those engaged in only one.

Deliberate steps should be taken to encourage and assign diverse tasks, including a number of projects, a mix of administrative and professional work, and a mix of functions. Encouragement should be given to the development of a number of specialties. The manager who frowns on diversity in the interests of short-term efficiency generates signals that tell the professionals to narrow their perspectives. The consequences will be loss of those very productive people who naturally seek diversity and a long-term drop in productivity among those who remain. Of course, there are times when all attention must be concentrated on a crash program, but they are rare and should not set the style. At the least, the manager should smile upon efforts to achieve diversity, and at best should deliberately take steps to generate it: (1) don't always give an assignment to the person who has done that kind of thing before; (2) deliberately assign some nonprofessional work to technical people; (3) give professionals some administrative assignments; (4) occasionally make assignments that put an individual into another group, temporarily or permanently; (5) don't let the inertia and comfort of group managers or the professionals themselves keep you from enhancing diversity.

Diversity also enhances creativity, which may also influence productivity. One definition of creativity is the ability to make associations between widely separated items, and the more widely separated the items are that you can associate, the more creative you are. An increase in the diversity of input made available by participation in different kinds of activities and functions can significantly raise the probability of making creative sense out of that input.

A question that may be raised by the data is whether or not it is the "nature" of people to seek diversity or whether they will be more responsive to diversity if management deliberately provides it. Whatever the answer, stimulation of diversity is good for any capable professional. Professional work is not linear and repetitive in the manner of production-line assembly. When a professional is plateaued or stymied on a given project, a switch to another project or function or task is refreshing and energizing, and often permits the first project to work itself out below the level of consciousness.

Merit Salary Increases and Promotion

Merit salary increases and promotion to higher rank are the most often used and most expected forms of incentive. Both managers and professionals rank merit increases and promotion first and second in terms of their value. A major reason for this is that they are almost the only formal, explicit incentives used by organizations and, therefore, they make up the perceived spectrum of incentives. There is abundant evidence that professionals are moved by many incentives other than pay and promotion, yet there is little evidence of efforts to broaden the repertoire of formal incentives offered.

Merit pay rewards are unequivocally more motivating than non-merit pay rewards—e.g., piece rates as opposed to hourly pay, merit reward rather than seniority—and all organizations claim to use merit reward policies of one kind or another. There are, however, significant differences between organizations in the effects of their pay systems, and what companies claim is often different from what is perceived by their employees. When employees see themselves as above-average in comparison with their peers, and yet do not get above-average pay increases in one period (since not every individual will be judged above-average every time), the overall effects can be negative. And negative effects of merit pay rewards have a more lasting effect than positive ones.

As a consequence of all their difficulties, no matter what management's intentions pay practices tend to become routinized, to follow a "least trouble" pattern. When performance declines, an employee's salary is almost never reduced, and though subsequent increases are kept to a minimum, the differences between the lowest increase and the highest is often not very large. When performance is really high, it is seldom rewarded adequately. There is a strong tendency to keep the whole salary structure moving together without letting anyone's salary get "too far out of line." This is easier on the manager and on the personnel department. It takes a great deal of continuing effort and an ability to accept large variations in pay structure to keep a merit pay system in line with performance, and, thus, actually working as an incentive.

The more a merit pay reward can be linked to specific performance, and the shorter the time interval between performance and reward, the stronger the effect of the reward. Bonuses given to reflect specific accomplishments are far more effective than merit salary increases given at fixed intervals to reflect overall past performance. Unfortunately, it is often difficult to find explicit events that occur frequently enough to fit into a bonus scheme for professionals. It is easier to reward a salesperson whose sales can be measured monthly. However, where and when bonsuses can be used, they are very effective. One company that designs and installs automation systems rewards its project managers and key project personnel with substantial, on-the-spot, money bonuses for delivering a successful system on or ahead of time. An Air Force missile project office made a point of issuing nonmonetary awards to groups and

individuals working for the company being monitored whenever something outstanding had been done. The awards were
carefully given, were treasured by the recipients, and were effective as incentives.

Promotion into management is used as an incentive because
(1) professionals aspire to management even though they often
don't respect it or like to practice it, and (2) management is
hard put to think of other meaningful ways to reward its best
professionals. Too often, the result is the proverbial "We lose
an excellent professional to gain an incompetent manager."
All of the signals in the environment, both within the organization and in the larger world outside, indicate that it is desirable
to be a manager. Management is associated with power, pay,
and perquisites. (This is more true in the United States than
in Europe or Asia where Engineer or Architect are honorific
titles preferred by managers.) As mentioned above, the "dual
ladder" system has been tried, without much success, to keep
professionals from aspiring to management positions. The results so far indicate that the method is ineffective.

Inventing Incentives for Professionals

We need to invent more incentives because our available
set is surprisingly limited and insufficient. Relevant data are
available on what professionals respond to and what motivates
them—the data should be intelligently acted upon. In addition
to aiming for high quality and quantity in professional performance, the new repertoire of incentives should have among
its major goals reinforcement of the professional's desire to
do professional work rather than to go into management, and
encouragement of the individual's efforts at personal professional growth. The author has experimented successfully with
an incentive as simple as a budget for books, journals, and technical meetings that increased over time and according to performance, and that was completely within the discretion of the
individual. This technical materials incentive works and is easy
to administer and justify.

Another longer-term incentive that meets all the relevant

criteria is the accrual of time and money for each month the professional does satisfactory work on organizational projects until some given time period has been accumulated—say, three or four years. Then the accrued time and money can be used for any project the professional proposes as long as it is approved by a committee of peers (not managers) using a very broad, but accountable definition of organization interest (i.e., meets accounting criteria for legitimate business expense such as "internal research and development"). The catch is that if the professional goes into management he or she doesn't qualify for the incentive—it is not available to managers.

Incentive Programming

The ideal incentives are those tailored for the specific individual and are flexible over time. It would, of course, be impossible to conduct a completely individualized incentive system for an organization of more than a few people. It is still possible, however, to come much nearer the ideal than is commonly done.

Within a given suborganization or group, the manager can go a long way toward individualizing incentives other than pay and promotion. This will depend on observation of the individual professionals to see what it is that moves each one— a matter of daily and but thoughtful interaction, and of a conscious effort to learn about the individual. The kinds of incentives that can be applied include assignments made (to provide diversity), recognition, chances for personal growth, and chances to do something different and even risky without penalty.

The younger professional is more moved by money than is the older professional; with time, other incentives become more powerful. These priorities can be taken into account by an organization's formal incentive system. For example, if a large group of professionals is asked to choose between incentives such as a large salary increase or a chance to go to school for an additional degree with only regular salary increases, there will be a split in the responses. If that same group is given a choice between work that will lead to promotion and work that will accrue money and time for a project, there will again be a division among the choosers. Similarly, if a group of professionals is asked to choose between a pay increase and a chance to work for the company in Europe for two years, their responses will be different. Basic differences in outlook, as represented by the examples, inform an organization as to the pattern of incentives that would motivate each group of choosers. Each choice reveals something about the kinds of incentives that an individual responds to. It is feasible to develop an individualized incentive program that takes the effects of time and at least two kinds of individual outlook into account, and that isn't hopelessly complicated.

3

Performance Evaluation

Hiring is the most important decision made by the manager of professional activities, firing and disciplining are the most painful, but performance evaluation may be the most difficult. Performance evaluation exemplifies one of the persistent characteristics of the management of professionals: it has to be done, and there is no neat, objective way to go about it.

For a great many managers of professionals, the task of performance evaluation and salary review is distasteful and dreaded. Once or twice a year, managers are required to conduct performance evaluations of each of the individuals working for them, and to determine how to divide up the budget allocated for salary increases. Despite the counsel of theoreticians that performance evaluation and salary reviews should not be linked, there is no serious separation of the two.

When it is time for formal performance evaluations, the manager is faced with a stack of forms to be filled out and a limited pot of money to be divided up among the professionals in his or her organizational group. In making these evaluations, most managers are caught between conflicting pulls. The individual professionals want to be evaluated—they want to know how they are doing. Higher management wants a rational distribution of rewards that will assure a high level of performance, and that can be justified to organizational insiders and such significant outsiders as stockholders, bankers, and clients. Personnel departments and employee organizations prefer evaluations that result in a minimum of complaint and provide a rational basis for personnel decisions such as promotions, development programs, and transfers.

Complicating the task of performance evaluation for the manager of professionals is a feeling that both manager and subordinates are professional peers. There are also distasteful questions. What might the manager have done to improve the performance of individual professionals in the period under review? To what extent were the matters being evaluated in the control of the manager rather than of the individual professional? To what extent was the individual's performance a matter of unavoidable circumstances?

Performance evaluation is inherently a difficult task, particularly when it comes to professional activities. How do you evaluate one-of-a-kind activities? What can you compare them with? Typically, more than one discipline is represented in the professional organization, no two of the professionals are doing exactly the same kind of work, and all are working on projects that have never been done before. It is also not unusual in professional work that different professionals in an organization are working for different internal or external clients with varying objectives and standards.

While most routine activities are directly measurable in terms of output such as product or activity counts, most of what professional do is not measurable in neat, direct terms. While routine activities can be standardized in terms of time requirements, it is impossible to establish a rigorous time standard for professional work. How does one predict and estimate the time to produce a movie the like of which has never been produced? How does one predict and judge a rare surgical procedure on an individual patient with a unique physical system and a unique personal history?

Take the example of a group of medical doctors. How would

you compare their individual performances? Would you judge them on the basis of cures per head? Opinions of patients? Opinions of other doctors? Attitudes and personality? Some other criterion? When the author presented the preceding choices to a broad audience, 29% opted for record of cures, 29% for the opinions of other doctors, 21% for the opinions of other patients, 7% for attitudes and personality, and 14% for other criteria. Despite the foregoing responses most people judge their doctors on the basis of attitude and personality. There is little possibility of obtaining a record of cures or other doctors' opinions.

One could choose any of the criteria for picking a doctor, but none would leave one truly satisfied. How can you compare a doctor whose specialty is oncology with a pediatrician? The possibilities of cures for cancer cannot be compared with those for children's diseases. On what basis are the opinions of other doctors formed, and how do we obtain them? What can be said about the objective value of opinions of patients? No one has established a significant relationship between the personality of doctors and their medical competence.

The same dilemmas are found in any professional field. Despite a host of efforts to find an objective way to measure as widespread and historic an activity as teaching, there are still no satisfactory tools. The efforts of teachers and professors are judged on the basis of highly questionable student evaluations, peer opinions, or supervisor judgments. The same dilemmas are found in research and development, advertising, engineering, architecture, and the performing and plastic arts. In some professional fields the marketplace and history eventually judge whose work is acceptable or great, but this does not help the manager who must make judgments long before the marketplace or history render their final determination.

DILEMMAS IN EVALUATING PROFESSIONAL WORK

There are many dilemmas in evaluating performance in professional activities. Some difficulties are due to the non-comparability of work among professionals. There is the problem of dealing with highly uncertain subject matter in which the approach taken and the level of effort are unquestionably good, but the undertaking results in failure. Even the definition of "good" performance is not an open and shut case.

Noncomparability

The work of two professionals is hard to evaluate because the problems they work with and the way they go about dealing with those problems are not strictly comparable. No two professionals deal with exactly the same problem despite the fact that the problems dealt with fit into some definable category. Whether it is pulling a wisdom tooth, designing a tract home, or doing a parametric analysis for a weapons system design, no two problems are ever quite the same. Though pulling most wisdom teeth is rather routine, each person's body is somewhat different, and for some the difference is significant. Patients certainly want the dentist to recognize and treat them as if they were unique. Though the basic design of a tract home may be something less than a design breakthrough, no two sites are exactly the same, and the architect is required to take variations into consideration. A particular analytical technique may be the stock in trade of an operations researcher doing a parametric analysis, but each situation requires different assumptions, weightings, and data preparation.

No two professionals attack the same problem in exactly the same way. Though both professionals will come up with satisfactory or acceptable results, their approaches will vary, often radically. Style is important in professional work, and each individual develops a particular style and way of doing things.

The Effort and Approach Were Good, But the Project Failed

There are many reasons why a professional undertaking can fail despite superb efforts and impeccable approaches. The project or case being undertaken may simply be intractable, or the timing may be off. Research and development and medicine are replete with examples of problems undertaken in good faith by responsible, intelligent people, that were inherently intractable. Leonardo da Vinci, unquestionably one of the great geniuses of all times, left notebooks full of feasible inventions that could not be realized in his time because of the state of technology. Chemistry was given a great boost by the many alchemists who were consumed with the problem of transforming grosser metals into gold—something that is finally possible (but not economical) through the use of atom smashing equipment. Cancer, schizophrenia, and the common cold have been subjects of very large research efforts but have not as yet been defeated. Would we have denied Leonardo a merit salary increase or give a negative performance evaluation to the dedicated and competent medical research workers working on cancer?

By its very nature, professional work is beset with high uncertainty. There are unknowns and unknowables. The unknowns are amenable to research, and with time, money and effort can be diminished. Then there are the unknowables for which there are no parallels or precedents. Take the case of the drug Thalidomide. It was developed as a tranquilizer, and was demonstrated to be very effective. Years after it had been on the market an insightful medical practitioner saw a relationship between the use of Thalidomide by pregnant women and the subsequent birth of children with crippling deformities. Now it is widely understood that pregnant women should take no drugs at all (at least not in their third month). There was no way to know about the effects of Thalidomide on pregnancy before the damage had been done. There is no way to know the combined effects over time of much of what we ingest and daub ourselves with until time has passed and someone is astute enough to perceive the relationship. When dealing with unknowables, we have the choice of doing nothing new or going ahead. How should the scientists who developed Thalidomide be evaluated with regard to performance?

Another virtual unknowable is what someone else is doing in the same area of work. In many cases, one worker doesn't know that someone else is doing something that will impact on what he or she is doing, while the second person may very well know about the work of the first. In science there is a rich history of simultaneous discoveries, but what credit is given to the individual or group that publishes second? A fascinating case study of a scientific race in which one side was aware of what others were doing but didn't take their work into account is the discovery of DNA, which resulted in Nobel laureates for Crick and Watson, who published first. Would you give two-time Nobel Prize winner Linus Pauling a bad performance evaluation because they beat him? At one time, Stanford Research Institute had an outstanding radio tube research group which lost all purpose with the advent of semiconductors. What do you do with fifty tube research and development experts in a semiconductor world—and how do you evaluate their performance?

In the case of the development of new products or services for the marketplace, the company that enters the marketplace first often gains great advantage over later entries. The development of new products and services is usually shrouded in secrecy, and in many cases there is no knowledge in one organization of what other organizations are doing in the same field. How should the professionals who developed and brought the product or service to the marketplace second be evaluated? Their efforts were crowned with success in terms of development of the product, but they were a failure in the marketplace for which the product was developed.

Short-term Failures But Long-term Successes

The "success" of creative efforts in many professional fields depends on the opinions, tastes, or acceptance by others. A case can be made that the more an innovation differs from what already exists in form, fit, or function, the more likely it will have a hard time getting adopted. Hence, many of the innovations and works of art now recognized as among the world's greatest did not gain acceptance for decades. There is a rich history of scientists, writers, composers, artists, and inventors whose works were not appreciated during their life-times and of others who received broad recognition in their own times but are forgotten today. In many instances an excellent product comes onto the marketplace too early for its acceptance, a good example of which is the Cord automobile. Cord stopped production in the mid-1930s because of a lack of market acceptance. Later the Cord was hailed as an example of outstanding design, and limited production was resumed in the mid-1970s.

A significant fraction of the professional work force is engaged in industrial activities aimed at generating new products and services. Extensive efforts are made to identify and measure the potential for such new products or services to determine whether they should be developed and what their chances are for success once developed. Nevertheless, a substantial number of these products are failures in the marketplace, some of them despite their technical excellence and the talent and dedication of their developers. Hundreds of millions of dollars were invested in computer developments during the 1950s and 1960s that had to be written off because the market was not ready for the products. In the 1980s the market is burgeoning. The Edsel automobile is a well-known example of a product that failed in the marketplace. Yet it was technically sound and is a collector's item today. How shall we evaluate the performance of the technical professionals who developed the computers of earlier decades and the Edsel?

What Is Good Performance in Professional Work?

Finally, the greatest dilemma in evaluating professional work is to agree upon what is considered good performance. Nearly half the Nobel laureates believe they were awarded the prize for work that was not their best work. Whose judgment of performance is more valid, that of the committee that awards the prizes or that of the creative professional?

In production work, emphasis is on delivery of a product or service that is minutely specified. In professional work, however, a professional who delivers something other than what was specified may be rated highly and even honored. Fleming, credited with the discovery of penicillin, was engaged in research that had nothing to do with the discovery of an antibiotic. The accidental observation of the effects of mold on bacteria in some laboratory preparations was the beginning of the penicillin story. In many laboratories the appearance of mold might have been considered indicative of sloppy work, and someone would have been reprimanded. Fleming was knighted. Fleming was evaluated and rewarded for something he wasn't working on. How would his work have been evaluated before his great discovery?

The British story of the discovery of radar is another instance of great results that were not sought and that had nothing to do with the task assigned. In the 1930s a group of technical professionals was given the task of testing the popular notion of a "death ray" that could knock down aircraft. The group beamed electrical energy at test aircraft, and found that they were getting an echo on their instruments. Someone perceived the possibilities of using such echos to identify and locate aircraft for purposes of defense. The project goals were shifted, and the radar was developed that is given much credit for the survival of Great Britain when it was bombed by the Germans in World War II. Though he didn't achieve what he was charged with doing in the first place, Robert Watson-Watt, too, was knighted for his efforts. In professional work, achieving something other than what was intended can subsequently be judged as superb performance.

The Final Dilemma

Evaluation of the performance of professionals is something that has to be done, but there is no nice, objective, systematic way to do it.

WHY EVALUATE

If there is no objective way to evaluate the performance of professionals, then why do it? The most immediate reason for conducting formal performance evaluations is that implicit and explicit evaluations are made whether formalized or not. Where formal evaluations are not conducted, implicit evaluations will be assumed, and what managers say and do, even casually, will be interpreted and weighted as organizational evaluations. Formal performance evaluations serve both the individual professional and the organization in several additional ways.

From the Viewpoint of the Individual

All individuals want to know how they are doing from the viewpoint of the organization, which means from the viewpoint of management. When people are not informed how they are doing, they will find ways to push the system to get some response. Some will push the system for a response to the point of quitting. It is not exceptional to have a key professional give notice of taking another job. The manager, caught by surprise, asks, "Why? You're one of our best people. Can I get you a raise?" only to get the explicit or implicit response, "You never told me! It's too late now." In the absence of explicit, formal evaluations, an individual will assume an evaluation and it is likely to be negative.

Formal evaluations are needed by every worker and are markedly important for professionals. Since professional work is nonroutine and inherently uncertain, professional workers have no ready, objective measures they can use to inform themselves how well they are doing. As a result, the professional has a need to receive some judgment or evaluation from respected others. The most individualistic of artists and authors needs formal feedback from other artists, authors, gallery owners, critics, publishers—from *someone*. They need to determine if the direction of their work is acceptable, even if only to get a negative response with which to disagree and reaffirm their current direction and efforts.

Interaction with people in management is essential to high performance for most professionals in organizations. Where managers show an interest in a project and take part in decisions about the project with the professional, peformance is high. Pelz and Andrews (1976) found that, with a few exceptions, performance was highest where project decisions were shared by the professional and his or her chief. Next in ranked performance were situations where decisions were made mainly by the chief or by the chief and other executives, rather than by the professional. Interestingly, performance improved if the decisions were made by higher executives rather than the professional's immediate supervisor. The exceptions were the scientists and engineers who had a strong interest in breadth of research rather than in depth and detail (those generalists again). The latter did better making project decisions by themselves. A study of 223 medical sociology projects (Gordon & Marquis, 1963) came to similar conclusions. The study of medical sociology projects found that twice as many projects were judged highly innovative when the project director had an administrative superior who took some responsibility for the project and influenced the project funds and design, as compared with projects with no administrative superior or in which the superior dominated the project.

The picture that emerges from the research shows the professional responding to managerial interest and decisions concerning the work being done. The data also indicate that the input that works is concerned with the direction and design of the project, but not with the internal conduct of the project. Though autonomy is appreciated, there is an advantage to and a need for the expressed interest of management in the work that is being done. Performance evaluations ensure that management formally reviews and responds to what the individual has been doing.

From the Viewpoint of the Organization

There are several organizational reasons for conducting formal performance evaluations, and the need for formalizing performance evaluations increases with the size of the organization.

In small organizations the continuous interaction between manager and professional worker may be sufficient. Management is not an impersonal entity in the very small organization. The professional worker gets constant and immediate feedback and has a clear idea, daily, of what management thinks about the work. In larger organizations, there is far less contact with management. Uncertainty as to how management feels about things requires means to make sure that the individual professional gets a formal indication of those feelings. Organizational reasons for performance evaluation include the following:

Feedback on performance
Compensation administration
Promotion decisions
Identification of development needs
Human resources planning
Validation of hiring and selection procedures

Feedback on Performance

From the viewpoint of management, performance evaluation provides an opportunity for coaching, encouraging strong performance, and strengthening weak performance. In terms of the expectations–motivation–performance–experience–comparison–expectations model of motivation, formal evaluation provides management with a powerful platform for feedback to the workers. The formal evaluation is also an important input for comparisons by the individual to judge his or her position vis-à-vis others in the organization. In large organizations, formal performance evaluation is also used to assure that the individual does get feedback periodically, something often avoided by managers.

Compensation Administration

Performance evaluation is used as the basis for merit increases in salary. It provides an equitable and justifiable basis for compensation bonuses, raises, and perquisites. For managers and personnel departments it is important that the reward system be justifiable and orderly for purposes of organizational governance. A formal performance evaluation system allows the manager to draw upon or point to "the system" as a reference point in compensation judgments. The increase in recent years of laws concerned with compensation and hiring practices has underlined this role of formal evaluation systems. Much recent job-related litigation has been concerned with questions of equity with regard to sex, minority status, and age, and a clearly enunciated and practiced evaluation system is a basic legal defense for an organization.

A cautionary note should be inserted here about the limits and dangers of formal personnel systems. Orderliness can be carried too far. Management's drive for uniformity and consistency also leads to rigidity and a tendency to forget what the work is all about in an effort to maintain the internal management systems. Some organizations would rather lose their most productive people than disturb the established "wage and salary system." A case in point is the company that lost its top salesman because it wouldn't let him earn any more bonuses—after he had earned the permitted amount by the second month of the year—because it would disturb the established system. Another example is the company that lost the head of its most profitable acquisition by insisting on making the head change from his hard-won, familiar, debugged computer system to one used by the rest of the company. It never occurred to higher management that it could "translate" his reports into the predominant format—neatness became more important than performance.

Promotion Decisions

Performance evaluation provides a systematic basis for key personnel actions such as promotion, transfer, firing, and layoff in times of cutback. The formal performance evaluation system contributes a modicum of objectivity to many personnel actions. By establishing criteria for promotion and incorporating those

93

criteria in the formal performance evaluation system some rationality can be introduced into the promotion process. It can incorporate what an organization has learned about who makes a good supervisor, and it informs the individuals about its priorities and where they fit with regard to chances for promotion. Formal evaluations can be a useful means for determining an employee's potential to be a supervisor or to undertake a new and different kind of responsibility.

Transfers, firing, and layoffs can also be rationalized, justified, and explained, offering a greater sense of equity to all in the organization. Formalization of performance evaluations contributes a little to offsetting unconscious systematic biases concerning race, color, religion, appearance, school tie, and the like. (Nothing short of sanctions can overcome conscious biases that will find a way to deliberately color the evaluations given.) Again, the results of formal evaluations are vital on those occasions when an organization is accused or sued on questions of bias or prejudice in personnel matters. Of course, a formal evaluation system also provides managers with an out when they have to perform distasteful personnel actions such as firing. The manager can take refuge in the rules of the system, implying that the system is responsible.

Identification of Personnel Development Needs

Performance evaluations are a useful means for identifying the development needs of the individuals evaluated and of the organization as a whole. A well-designed performance evaluation process should supply systematic grounds for determining what kinds of courses and experiences might help the evaluated individual. The aggregate of evaluations can help determine the developmental needs of the organization as a whole. The results of evaluations can be used as the basis for education policies and program development. For example, if ineffectiveness in a particular technical area shows up in several evaluations, it may indicate a need for training in the area of deficiency. If the performance evaluations show that many of

the professionals are having problems in dealing with people—
a common problem in some professions—then a special program may be called for.

Intelligent use of the evaluations provides valuable information on the manager's developmental needs. Systematic discrepancies in the evaluations of given individuals made by different
managers can indicate a need for a program to bring managers
to some common consensus on criteria for evaluation. Systematic evaluation errors tending to rate everyone high or low
can also be identified and called to the attention of the manager.
Existing and incipient organizational problems can be identified
by a perceptive reading of the aggregate of evaluations. If many
evaluations in a group are significantly lower than previous
ratings, it may be indicative of a serious problem in the group
similar to a sharp increase in turnover rates that should be
looked into. It could indicate a problem with the manager, a
work situation problem, a salary system discrepancy, or some
environmentsl problem needing attention.

Human Resource Planning

Performance evaluations help identify personnel gaps in
the organization. If the evaluations show that many of the professionals in an organization are lacking in some particular specialty, such as computer aided design, it might indicate a need
for a training program and/or the need to hire someone who
is proficient in the area of deficiency. Evaluations are also helpful in determining what should be done with regard to the
loading and distribution of human resources in an organization.
They can indicate where personnel are overloaded, and where
there is slack.

Validation of Hiring and Selection Procedures

Though not done by most organizations, performance evaluations are an excellent means for validating and improving hir-

ing and selection in an organization. Performance evaluations help determine whether an organization's hiring criteria make sense. For example, with regard to the use of grade point averages as a significant criterion for hiring the new college graduate, if subsequent performance evaluations show there is or isn't a significant relationship between subsequent performance and grades, the results should be used to inform the hiring process. Similarly, the worth of different channels of recruitment can be determined. An organization can measure the relative value of "porthole" hiring (hiring right out of college), hiring at conventions of professional societies, advertising (including personnel ads vs. institutional ads), and hiring through reference networks. In the same way, evaluations of managers can provide useful information on the value of the promotion policies of an organization.

EVALUATING

Formal evaluation or appraisal systems are widespread in industry. Surveys of R & D organizations made in the 1960s found that between 79% and 87% of all of the organizations surveyed used formal systems. A survey of manager appraisal systems made in 1977 found that 74% of the organizations used formal systems to evaluate their managers. The need for performance evaluation is clear and widely recognized. Doing such evaluations is another matter. It is a highly problematic undertaking for several reasons.

First, because evaluating means placing a value on something. A value is a concept of the desirable, and when evaluations are made someone or something is being judged or appraised from the viewpoint of what the organization considers desirable. Performance evaluation is the act of judging the desirability of someone's actions, behavior, or characteristics from the viewpoint of the organization. Many organizations and managers have never thought through what it is they consider desirable, what importance to give the various values they hold. There is a tendency to adopt a system that is in general use and operate it without considering whether the values incorporated in the system represent those of the organization.

Second, few managers think about whether they want to use the performance evaluation as a way to elicit future behavior, as a way to judge past behavior, or as a combination of both. The tendency is to just evaluate, but judgments of past behavior should be used as a starting point for the improvement of future behavior. The problem can be stated in terms of something as familiar as school grades. If someone started as a high A performer, but by the time of evaluation is performing barely above a B level on some arbitrary scale, should the grade be an A, or a B with some advice on improving performance?

All present methods of performance evaluation are limited in their application because of common, systematic sources of error. Nevertheless, since some method of evaluation will have to be used and will probably be a variation of generally used methods, it is important to understand both the nature of these methods and the common sources of error.

Errors in Evaluation

To be useful, a method of performance evaluation must be both reliable and valid (Szilyagyi & Wallace, 1980). By reliability is meant that the method must be consistent and stable. Consistency is achieved when two different people make an evaluation—or two different methods are used—and the results are the same. When a method is stable we mean that the same performance evaluation instrument or evaluator gives the same results over time.

Reliability. Many factors can affect the reliability of a performance evaluation method. Some factors are situational.

The time of day can affect an evaluation, but even more important from the viewpoint of professional activities is the phase of the project being worked on. Many professional activities have a long time constant, and it is hard to judge performance en route to the completion of the work. A cancer is considered cured if after five years there has been no recurrence of the disease. Aircraft development takes ten years. How can we reliably judge performance on a cancer research project or an aircraft development project every six months or year during the life of the projects? Another problem with long-term projects is that their objectives may shift due to changing circumstances or to discoveries made during the course of the work. The original justification for the British effort on the Concorde SST aircraft was that it would bring together distant parts of the Commonwealth, such as Australia and England. By the time the project was completed, far different goals and criteria applied. The British discovery of radar illustrates a change of objectives due to what had been discovered en route.

The evaluator's mood, physical health, or general mental health at a given time can affect the content of an evaluation. There are times when we are more tired, more impatient, or more inclined to be generous and lenient. Mood can be a function of personal circumstances that have nothing to do with the evaluations being made, the time of day, or the day of the week.

A given evaluation may also be affected by the previous evaluation of someone else. If the previous evaluation was of someone with very superior or inferior performance, the contrast can affect a subsequent evaluation.

Evaluators vary and are subject to systematic errors based on their tendencies. The three major categories of evaluator error (Landy & Trumbo, 1980) are leniency errors, halo errors, and central tendency errors. Some evaluators are systematically lenient or harsh in their ratings. Given the same group of individuals to evaluate, the lenient evaluator will consistently give better than average ratings and the harsh evaluator will give lower than average ratings. Halo errors occur because of a generally good or bad impression the evaluator has of the individual being evaluated. The good or bad "halo" persists despite the actual performance record of the individual. For example, if the evaluator has a good general impression of an individual who has not performed well in the period under review, the performance will be explained away as "due to circumstances beyond his or her control." Central tendency errors result from a propensity to avoid extremes at either end of the performance spectrum. A particular case of a directional tendency in evaluations occurs in the military, where ratings tend to drift to a narrow band at the top of the rating spectrum.

Inadequate definitions of what is meant by good or bad performance can cause disagreement between different evaluators. The problem is easily demonstrated by asking a group of managers to check off which of the following describes someone who is prompt:

1. One is always early or exactly on time.
2. One is always within five minutes of the required time.
3. One is always within 15 minutes of the required time.
4. One is always within a half hour of the required time.

It is surprising to see how much variance there is between managers within the same organization. This variance can lead to serious disagreements. The person who chooses the first description is assured by someone who chooses the third that a particular worker is very prompt. After some experience with the individual who is consistently ten minutes late, the first manager feels the second manager has misled him. If the first manager says something about being misled, there may be sincere indignation and conflict.

Another source of unreliability is disagreement between methods. It has been found, for example, that interview ratings usually differ from formal, written ratings. Which method is more accurate?

Validity. By validity it is meant that a method is well grounded and actually represents what it is supposed to represent. To be valid a method of performance evaluation must accurately represent the nature of the work and the behavior that pertains, and should not include irrelevant considerations. Validity becomes more of a problem as we go up the occupational scale from simple motor tasks to professional work. With routine, repeatable, simple tasks, it is relatively easy to depict the dimensions of the work and to determine the relevant behaviors. A line assembly job can almost always be described completely and each part of the process delineated. The quantities and qualities of output expected and the requisite skills and behavior can be described and measured. In the routine case, performance is standardized and quantifiable. As we move up the occupational scale to the work of, say, a maintenance trouble-shooter, validity becomes somewhat harder to establish, and when we come to the work of a professional it is very difficult, if not impossible.

Lack of validity is perhaps the greatest inadequacy in methods for evaluating the performance of professionals. Since professional work is concerned with one-of-a-kind outputs, for the purposes of performance evaluation the work dimensions and the appropriate behavior have to be depicted at a level of abstraction that can encompass many different projects through time. How can we depict the work of an editor, a medical research professional, an architect, or a lawyer in a way that accurately reflects the job's key dimensions and requisite behavior, and that applies to other professionals in the same organization? The research question, project, or legal case worked on during the period under review is different from the one worked on the year before and different from those being worked on by others. The higher the level of abstraction used in describing the work and the behavior required, the more difficult it is to deal in anything but very broad generalities.

All professional work faces the same problems of validity. How much easier it would be to measure professional performance in such terms as "copies sold per book per month," or "number of valid findings per page per publication per year," or "sold square feet of buildings designed per month," or "number of dollars per days in the slammer per client per year." Instead, all of the problems delineated above apply and, since performance evaluation has to be done, managers often retreat into any method that measures some apparently appropriate traits, process behaviors, or mutually developed general objectives whether they are valid or not.

Some Widely Used Methods

The three basic methods of performance evaluation are (1) those based on objective performance data, (2) those based on personnel data, and (3) those based on judgment.

Evaluation methods based on performance data are not usefully applied to professional activities. All of the problems with evaluation of professional work already described militate against the development of objective performance data: noncomparability, good methods but failed output, short-term failure but long-term success, and the question of what is good performance.

Methods based on personnel data are used only with hourly, lower-level workers and concentrate on such variables as attendance and length of time with organization. Methods based on personnel data are clearly of little use in evaluating professional performance.

All the methods used to evaluate the performance of professionals are based on subjective judgment. Despite great variety of methods and the many kinds of efforts to increase the "objectivity" of the methods used, they all essentially and eventually depend on judgment.

Methods of Evaluation Based on Judgment

Rating scales. The majority of rating scales are basically graphic scales in that they present the evaluator with either a set of traits or of job dimensions and a set of graduated valuations to be checked off against each trait or job dimension. Typically, a trait-based rating scale might include such traits as job knowledge, judgment, attitude, quantity of work, quality of work, communication ability, and an overall evaluation. A rating scale based on job dimensions for a professor might include key job dimensions such as research, public service, and teaching; for a professional in a contract research laboratory it might include proposal preparation, field research, laboratory research, report preparation, dealing with clients, presentation, and the helping of colleagues. For each trait the evaluator might be asked to pick a valuation from a graduated list that best corresponds to the person being evaluated, such as "excellent," "good," "satisfactory," "fair," or "poor." Some rating scales attempt to spell out briefly what is meant by poor, fair, satisfactory, good, and excellent. For example, in the case of the contract research activity, the ratings for the work dimension item, "proposal preparation" might be spelled out as follows:

Poor = Does not do any proposal preparation
Fair = Helps in proposal preparation but needs heavy editing
Satisfactory = Helps in proposal preparation and input is useful
Good = Prepares good proposals that have moderate success
Excellent = Takes initiative to prepare good proposals that have a high rate of success

Many organizations combine evaluation of both job dimensions and traits in their performance evaluation systems. To illustrate, one large organization's rating form for scientific and engineering personnel had an array of four levels of job dimension performance and twenty traits to be considered in answering general questions concerning the individual (Krantz, 1964). Each of the job dimension performance levels clustered several statements concerning performance. Level one, the highest performance level, had the following kinds of statements:

The employee and/or his unit have made some extremely valuable contributions . . . results achieved far exceed those normally expected of the great majority of engineers or scientists of comparable education or experience . . . exhibits a high degree of creativity or ingenuity in producing useful, practical, often unique solutions to problems . . . gets things done well with established deadlines and at minimum cost . . . consistently productive . . . uses time effectively . . . good teamwork and enhances work of other groups . . . all have high regard for ability . . . personal shortcomings are minor and have virtually no effect on ability to achieve results.

Level four, the lowest performance level, had the following kinds of statements:

The accomplishments of the employee and/or his unit have been limited . . . work accomplishment tends to be erratic or inconsistent . . . frequently too much time, effort, and money devoted to projects . . . unimaginative and routine . . . often goes off onto unproductive tangents which could be avoided by better analysis . . . work often has to be rejected or redone . . . others have some doubts about competence . . . unless performance improves serious questions concerning continued employment.

The traits included for consideration were the following:

Job knowledge
Accuracy
Safety
Attitude
Initiative
Industry or drive
Decisiveness
Judgment
Analysis
Ability in meeting associates and public
Effectiveness in relating assignments to other activities
Profit and cost consciousness
Effectiveness in presenting facts or ideas
Flexibility
Creativeness and resourcefulness
Handling of confidential information
Effectiveness in relating assignments to other activities
Maintaining high morale
Effectiveness in training and developing subordinates
Effectiveness in delegating

There are two main criticisms of rating scales. The first is concerned with selection and definition of the traits for a particular job. There is little evidence of a significant relationship between particular traits and performance of a given professional job. Many so-called traits are really a function of the job situation rather than something inherent in the individual. Consider the traits "flexibility," "decisiveness," "attitude," and "industry or drive" from the above listing. The traits sound desirable enough, but what do they mean exactly, and how, exactly, do they apply to doing (for example) architecture? Are those traits inherent in the individual or are they a product of the job situation? What kind of initiative might be expected in an organization where the management gives little leeway for it?

The second major criticism of rating scales is that they are subject to lenience (and strictness), halo, and central tendency errors. To overcome the tendencies of the evaluators some organizations use the method of "forced distribution" of ratings. In the forced distribution method, the regular rating techniques are applied, but the evaluator is required to distribute the ratings according to some fixed rule. A common example of forced distribution is used in education when a class is "graded on the curve." When forced distribution is used in performance evaluation, the evaluator is required to place some fixed percentage of those evaluated into each of three or four categories (e.g., one fourth in the lowest category, etc).

Though forced distribution helps overcome evaluator error tendencies, it creates a special problem of its own. It requires the evaluator to rate people in each category without regard to how intrinsically competent they may be. Forced sorting can destroy the morale and performance of a high-quality performance team, lower the expectations and consequent performance of good workers, may result in the loss of competent people. The U.S. Air Force introduced forced distribution ratings for officers, which resulted in the loss of very competent, expensively trained pilots who were put in the lower evaluation categories regardless of their absolute capabilities and performance.

Behaviorally anchored scales. Behaviorally anchored scales (BARS) are a relatively recent development in performance evaluation. BARS is a rating method that attempts to overcome some of the problems inherent in conventional rating systems. The scales used in BARS have anchor points directly relevant to the jobs being evaluated. The BARS method combines job analysis and the critical incident technique in generating its scales.

To develop a BARS requires that the dimensions of the job are determined by groups of supervisors and experts in the area of work being considered. Relevant dimensions might include such things as job knowledge, relations with others, motivation, and supervision required. Once the dimensions have been agreed on, a large number of critical incidents are generated by supervisors and experts. Critical incidents are specific descriptions of effective, average, and ineffective work behavior relevant to the job. Another group of supervisors and experts is then asked to individually sort the critical incidents and assign them to the job dimensions. Only those incident assignments that receive a high consensus (e.g., 60–90%) are retained. The panels are then given the remaining incidents with instructions to locate them on a scale of one to nine, ranging from very good to very poor. Finally, the results are edited and checked for agreement.

BARS is considered by psychologists to be the best of the current appraisal instruments. The scales are behavioral and cast in terms of reference used by supervisors and employees. Actual descriptive incidents are used to describe when someone is considered a one or a nine. A lot of the uncertainty and vagueness encountered in the use of such terms as "very good" or "very poor" are done away with. There is some evidence that the scales need not be as job-specific as first assumed; some of the scales are common to a number of jobs. BARS have been used to evaluate some kinds of managers, professors, and, to a limited extent, engineers. The rating process lends itself to providing feedback to the employee. However, developing BARS is expensive and tedious. Studies comparing BARS with other carefully developed rating scales or checklist methods have been inconclusive, and suggest that the large amount of time and expense required to develop BARS may not be warranted.

Checklists. The checklist method presents the evaluator with a set of statements about work behavior. The evaluator is required to check those items on the list that best (or least) describe the performance of the person being evaluated. Depending on the particular kind of checklist method used, the items checked by the evaluator are compared to reference profiles or are summed up using a weighted key to give the individual a final ranking. The values of the profile or the weightings are not available to the evaluator and are scored by the personnel office of the organization.

The checklist is made up of very specific characteristics of job behavior such as:

Can be counted on to help colleagues

Never volunteers to assist others

Needs very little explanation or support once assigned a piece of work

Needs repeated explanations of assignment from management

Checklists are useful in making the evaluator think in very specific terms about what the professional actually did at work, thus overcoming much of the fixed tendency problem. The major obstacles to using checklists, however, are that they are quite costly to develop, and, in professional activities, they can seldom be kept current with what the professionals actually do. To develop a good checklist requires the expenditure of much time and effort on the part of management and professional staff.

A valid and reliable checklist requires the development of a long list of statements describing both effective and ineffective work behavior. The statements have to be scaled by a number of independent judges who must reach a relatively high consensus. To develop a relevant profile or set of item weights demands the extensive calibration of statements with the performance of the kinds of workers to be evaluated. Separate checklists have to be developed for each job or job family.

Though expensive to develop, checklists can be very useful as long as the work being performed does not change substantially. In the case of professional work, change is inherent, and it is difficult to develop a checklist that will be appropriate for a length of time that makes it worth the expense of development. Another criticism of checklists is that they do not lend themselves to providing feedback to the person being evaluated, particularly when the manager doesn't know how items are scored or weighted.

As with rating scales, checklists are prone to evaluator bias, and forced choice methods for checklists have been developed to overcome that bias. In a forced choice checklist, statements (usually four) about work behavior are clustered, and ten to twenty are developed to describe each job or job family. Each cluster contains both favorable and unfavorable statements. When doing a performance evaluation the evaluator is required to choose that statement from each cluster that is most (or sometimes least) descriptive of the behavior of the person being evaluated. Only one of the positive statements and one of the negative statements actually discriminates between favorable and unfavorable performance. Both the manager and employee do not know which statements are significant, and so neither the manager or employee know whether the evaluation is favorable or unfavorable until it has been scored by the personnel people. It has been reported that despite its complexity and apparent statistical nicety, the results of forced choice checklists are no more valid than those of graphic scales. Because of its disadvantages, the forced choice checklist method is not widely used.

Employee comparisons. Employee comparison methods, which have been in use since World War I, compare employees with each other on one overall measure or on a number of specific dimensions. The primary methods of performance evaluation through employee comparisons are ranking, paired comparisons, and forced distributions.

Ranking requires the evaluator to array those being evaluated from best to worst along either one overall or several individual dimensions. Sometimes, to make it simpler for the manager with several employees to evaluate, alternation ranking is used. In alternation ranking the manager is instructed to pick the best and worst employees and set them aside, and then to repeat the process with those remaining until all employees have been so paired.

Paired comparisons require that each person is compared, one at a time, with every other employee. The evaluator is required to choose the better of the two in each comparison. Final ranking is done in terms of the number of favorable pair rankings each individual obtained. In addition to all of the weaknesses of straightforward ranking, paired comparisons take an inordinate amount of time with a group of any size. The number of comparisons that have to be made can be calculated by the equation,

$$N = \frac{n(n-1)}{2}$$

where N = number of comparisons
$\quad n$ = number of people to be evaluated

As can be quickly calculated, the number soon becomes prohibitive. With a group of five, the number of comparisons is only ten. With a group of ten, the number of comparisons is forty-five, and with a group of fifteen, it becomes one hundred five.

Forced distribution requires the evaluator to assign each employee to a scale category in each dimension being appraised. Forced distribution methods have already been discussed in connection with rating scales. Ranking introduces a variation in that each individual is ranked within the category to which he or she is assigned.

Employee comparisons have the apparent advantages of being relatively easy to do, of forcing the evaluator to differentiate between the individuals being evaluated, and of helping overcome the leniency and central tendency biases of the evaluator. Comparison methods have several weaknesses. Ranking does not give any indication of the distance between the ranks. The two top-ranked people may be very close in performance while the next person is far below them, yet they would simply be ranked one, two, and three. Where one overall dimension is used, comparisons do not give any information on components of the individual's performance, and, thus, are not helpful for improving performance. Comparison methods are not comparable across groups or locations and so are useless for promotion or overall development purposes. Where more than one dimension is used, comparison methods tend to suffer from halo tendencies. With comparisons it is quite likely that an individual can improve performance significantly without getting a change in ranking if everyone moves up, at a consequent loss in incentive.

Essay. In an essay evaluation the evaluator is required to write an essay describing the performance, traits, and behavior of the employee including his or her strengths and weaknesses. In some organizations the essay can be written any way the evaluator wants to write it. In other organizations the evaluator is provided with guidelines that require comments to be made under specific headings, such as job performance, technical effectiveness, leadership ability, quantity and quality of work, potential for promotion, and development needs. One survey of how major corporations evaluate the performance of managers found that 37% of them used an essay method (Conference Board, 1977).

One value of the essay method is that it provides a three-dimensional view of the individual being evaluated, even when it follows a set of guidelines, permitting the evaluator to add observations not easily included in a standardized format. The three-dimensional quality of the essay makes it an excellent vehicle for giving feedback and coaching to the person being evaluated. Another value of the essay method is that it forces the evaluator to spend more time consciously observing the people to be evaluated.

A difficulty with the method is also one of its virtues. It requires the evaluator to spend a great deal of time composing the essay, and few managers are likely to want to spend the necessary time. Other weaknesses of the essay evaluation method are that it is very subjective, it does not permit easy comparisons of employees for other personnel purposes, and it subjects the person evaluated to the writing ability of the evaluator. The evaluator who writes poorly can do harm to a career.

Critical incident technique. The critical incident technique is not so much a performance evaluation technique as it is a method for collecting good data to provide the basis for an accurate essay evaluation. The critical incident technique requires the evaluator periodically (e.g., once a week or once a month) to record incidents of an employee's work behavior that represent the individual's best performance and the performance most needing help. The method requires explicit rather than general records. Examples of best performance incidents might be, "stayed late to help out on a rush proposal without anyone asking him to do it," or "helped new engineer get settled in and oriented her on the project." Examples of incidents of ineffectiveness or needing help might be, "missed schedule on delivery of drawings—needs help in getting organized for timely delivery," or "Criticized secretary severely in front of several other people—needs to learn how to deal with nonprofessional staff." Not acceptable would be unspecific comments such as "was uncooperative" or "was cooperative."

The incidents are collected in a notebook, and at the time of review they provide material for an essay or become the basis for ratings using one of the rating techniques. In some organizations notebooks are issued for the purpose and categories for classifying incidents and recording them are provided. The categories might include productivity, interpersonal relations, etc. The collected incidents also provide a basis for explicit periodic feedback to the employee.

One of the benefits of the critical incident technique is that it makes the manager really observe the people who will be evaluated. It is very easy for a manager to become caught up in the daily flurry of improvisations, meetings, telephone calls, and interruptions, and suddenly to realize at evaluation time that the employee was seen every day but not observed. The critical incident technique forces the manager to stop and observe those for whom he or she is responsible—the beginning of really doing the management job. Where there are a large number of employees reporting to a manager, the technique makes sure that everyone comes to the attention of that manager. Another benefit of the technique is that it provides a sound basis for the more frequent, informal feedback that is essential to coaching and shaping work performance long before formal performance evaluation is called for. A manager can sit down for a cup of coffee with an employee and say, "I want to thank you for pitching in and picking up some of the load on that rush presentation last month, it really got us out of a bind." This has much more effect than saying every twelve months, "Your work has been between 'good' and 'very good' this year." It also makes it easier subsequently to make less positive comments, such as, "And, by the way, you've been having trouble getting reports in on time. Is there something we can do to help you?"

The problem with the critical incident technique is that it requires a serious shift in how managers observe their employees. In some cases it can become a matter of "breathing down the necks of the employees." If handled badly, the notebook can become the classic "little black book" in which all missteps are recorded, which is not the purpose of the technique at all. Some companies that have used the technique gave it up because it required too much record-keeping on the part of the manager.

Even where it is not part of the formal system, the critical incident technique is useful for informal feedback purposes. In fact, the technique is widely applicable to other purposes than performance evaluation. It is an excellent method for identifying and measuring many kinds of phenomena. The technique was developed in World War II to determine and measure problems with aircraft instrument panels. Several hundred pilots were asked to identify the worst problem experienced with an instrument while flying. The great majority identified the altimeter as their worst instrument problem. A subsequent experiment found that 14% of the pilots tested made errors of one thousand feet or more when reading the instrument, and corrective steps were taken. In the same way a management can identify critical areas that need correction in an organization.

Try a critical incident technique experiment with your family. Start each dinner with a round of, "What is the best thing that happened to you today?" and see how it changes the tenor of the evening.

Management by objectives. Management by objectives (MBO) is not strictly classifiable as a method of performance evaluation, though it is used widely as such. In fact over 50% of major corporations surveyed in one study cited MBO as the method used to evaluate the performance of their managers (Conference Board, 1977). MBO is a management system sometimes referred to as management by results, performance planning and evaluation, work planning and review, charter of account-ability, individual goal-setting, group goal-setting, and participatory goal-setting (Szilyagyi & Wallace, 1980). In each of these systems of management there is (1) participation of both management and employees in setting performance goals at every level throughout the organization, (2) agreement on the criteria to be used to measure and evaluate subsequent performance, and (3) a requirement for periodic reviews of progress towards the goals, at which time performance is appraised, goals are modified, and coaching is supplied. The emphasis on periodic reviews links MBO to performance evaluation.

MBO is attributed to Drucker (1954) and Odiorne (1965), both of whom emphasized an orientation toward results and participation of employees in the setting of goals. The idea was that participation would lead to responsibility for achieving the desired results on the part of those who participated. The goal-setting approach received theoretical support from Locke (1968), who postulated that an employee's conscious goals regulate his or her work behavior. Locke's laboratory studies and subsequent field studies give strong support to his theory. The implications of Locke's theory (Wexley & Yukl, 1977) fit nicely into the MBO approach. They are as follows:

1. Specific performance goals help maintain individual motivation and guide individual behavior.
2. Goals can be assigned or set jointly, but joint setting is recommended.
3. Goals should be set at levels that are perceived by the employee as challenging and possible to accomplish.
4. Feedback is required to determine progress and to modify goals where needed.

MBO achieves many different useful purposes. First, it makes managers plan, with all the attendant benefits of planning. By planning and setting objectives it helps focus management efforts on achieving those objectives and on helping employees reach their personal objectives. Setting objectives helps managers rationally set priorities and avoid stimulus-response behavior. MBO aids in focussing performance evaluations since there are operational goals and criteria against which individual performance can be compared, and there is a focus on what manager and employee need and can do to reach the objectives. MBO is attractive for evaluation of the performance of professionals since it is individualized and, thus, concentrates on the specifics of what each professional is working on rather than on vague generalities.

Some of the general problems with MBO include a short-term orientation at the expense of important long-term considerations and a concentration on output measures such as production, costs, and profits, thereby ignoring important process measures such as employee development, turnover, and morale. MBO requires constant monitoring to make sure that objectives are not deliberately set low for easy achievement and that it doesn't encourage activities that artificially or destructively inflate output reports.

As a performance evaluation method, MBO has certain difficulties and disadvantages. Developing meaningful and reasonable objectives for each level of the organization and each individual is very difficult and requires considerable training, effort, and time. It is extremely difficult to integrate all the individual sets of objectives into a sensible whole. It is very easy to slide into a mode of generating very general objectives or objectives that don't quite meet the criteria of being challenging and attainable. The system is sensitive to being arbitrarily dictated from above, thus diminishing the degree of participation. MBO is so individualized in terms of standards that it is difficult to use the system for allocating salary increases or for promotion.

Studies of MBO effectiveness have raised serious questions about its value. A review of 185 studies of the effects of MBO on employee productivity and/or job satisfaction (Kondrasuk, 1981) came up with mixed results. The review found that the more sophisticated the design of the study of MBO effectiveness the less support there was for it. Since studies of goal-setting strongly support its effectiveness, the mixed results on MBO may be a comment on the difficulties encountered in establishing and maintaining a comprehensive goal-setting system. A review of ongoing industrial MBO programs found that the successful programs were those where MBO had become the way the company conducted all aspects of its business. Where companies used MBO only for performance evaluation, compensation purposes, or management development there was less satisfaction with the approach (Wikstrom, 1968). Many of the studies of MBO effectiveness make the point that it requires strong commitment and continuous monitoring on the part of top management. Some point out that MBO works well while top management is strongly interested, and goes downhill sharply when top management's interest shifts (Ivancevich, 1974). Similar results have been shown for the effectiveness of organization development (OD), which leads to the conclusion that almost any method works as long as top management focusses on it, and that any method will decline when top management loses interest.

Group methods. Group evaluation methods represent a variation in who does the evaluation rather than in the technique of evaluation. Group evaluations of the performance of an individual shift the evaluation process from the individual's supervisor to others. The groups of evaluators that have been used in such evaluations include the organizational peers of the individual to be evaluated, the subordinates of the individual, and persons outside the individual's immediate work organization. None of the group evaluation methods are widely used, despite some positively reported efforts for peer assessments in military and industrial settings.

Peer assessments include peer-ranking, peer-rating, and peer-nomination. Peer-ranking requires all members of a group to rank all other members of the group from best to worst. A variant of peer-ranking asks each member of the group to partially rank one person by naming one person in the group who is better and one who is worse than the individual being evaluated. Peer-ranking, peer-rating, and self-ranking have been used by research-oriented organizations where the individual works quite autonomously and the supervisor is not familiar enough with the individual's work to appraise it. Organizations such as Bell Laboratories, the Battelle Research Institute, the Rand Corporation, and the Brookings Institute have used peer- and self-evaluation (Szilyagyi & Wallace, 1980).

Peer-ranking suffers from all of the disadvantages of ranking methods already pointed out. In addition, peer-ranking puts each individual doing the ranking under conflicting pressures. If the evaluation is too critical, is a colleague being harmed? If the evaluation is too lenient, will it elicit a negative judgment from management? If the evaluation is too laudatory, does it affect the relative ranking of the evaluator? There has been little research on peer-ranking, but interviews with professionals who have participated in peer-ranking strongly suggest that it is resented by those who have to do it because of the dilemmas the evaluator faces. As one of those interviewed put it, "It's just a way management gets off the hook. They can blame whatever evaluation they make on us. Management is paid to do evaluation. Let them do it!" Peer-rating is subject to all the criticisms of rating schemes, and, in addition, puts pressures on those who do the ranking.

Peer-nomination is a method of evaluating individuals for promotion. In the peer-nomination method, the evaluators are asked to nominate members of their group who are outstanding in general or who are outstanding in terms of some performance characteristic or personal trait. Studies of the peer-nomination method have concluded that it is fairly reliable and accurate in separating the best workers from the worst in a group, but that it has little utility in terms of feedback (Kane & Lawler, 1978). Another criticism of the method is that it does not help discriminate between those defined as outstanding or best.

Evaluation by subordinates can give managers some important feedback not usually available to them. It provides a manager with some information on how subordinates perceive him or her and can be useful in suggesting ways the manager can improve performance. However, as a method for the manager or the personnel department to use for purposes of promotion, transfer, or compensation, it is fraught with political overtones. Managers feel threatened by formal subordinate evaluations that are used by others, and there is little evidence that the method will be used widely. One form of subordinate evaluation is student evaluations of professors. There is much argument as to their reliability and effectiveness, but in any case, unlike the industrial situation, the professor does not have to continue to live and work with the students who do the evaluating.

Evaluation by people outside the immediate work organization includes evaluations by the personnel department, outside consultants, and assessment centers. There is some evidence that outside evaluations might be useful for promotion purposes because the outsiders can be more objective in identifying and evaluating the characteristics, skills, and experiences of a firm's employees. The argument is that the judgment of others in the same work unit may be clouded by personal relationships with the individual evaluated and by feelings of personal comparison.

The Evaluation Interview

The evaluation interview is difficult for both the evaluator and the evaluated individual. When a large sample of managers was asked by the author (using the critical incident technique) to specify their worst managment experience in the previous six months, evaluating their subordinates ranked high among their answers. Where it is not required, managers will tend to avoid giving postevaluation interviews. In fact some students of the subject claim that managers will not give such interviews unless there are strong control procedures to make them do so. There is a strong emotional buildup in both the evaluator and the individual employee. The employee enters the interview on the defensive since he or she is being personally judged, while the manager enters the interview rather uncomfortably, especially if the evaluation includes criticisms or questions concerning the work of the individual. The situation has elements of confrontation where one individual is in a subordinate and, therefore constrained, position.

A consensus holds that performance evaluation is nevertheless useful, since every individual should learn where he or she stands with the boss and the organization, and therefore the manager ought formally to deliver the results of the evaluation. The consensus holds that the evaluation interview provides an opportunity for constructive criticism and coaching. The evidence, however, suggests that the evaluation interview can have lasting negative effects, and that the manager/evaluator should be conscious of the relationship between the way the interview is conducted and the subsequent feelings and performance of the person evaluated. A study of GE's comprehensive performance appraisal process (Meyer et al., 1965) found that:

1. Critical comments during the interview, rather than resulting in improvement, create defensiveness and have a negative effect on subsequent performance.
2. Praise has little effect on performance one way or the other.
3. The great majority of employees (82%) see their manager's evaluation as being less favorable than their self-estimates.
4. There is a nonlinear relationship between the number of negative comments made during the interview and defensiveness on the part of the person being evaluated— defensiveness goes up faster than the number of negative comments.

Some of the implications of the GE study are that comprehensive, formal, annual performance evaluations are of questionable value, they are a threat to an employee's self-esteem, and they can harm relationships between manager and subordinate. A further implication is that negative comments should be fed back to an employee in limited doses throughout the year and not all at once at the time of the formal evaluation interview.

The results of the GE study also suggest that, since you have to follow the rite of the annual review, it should be handled carefully, and that criticisms should be saved for informal daily and weekly feedback sessions when the emotional charge is far lower. The way the performance evaluation and feedback are handled is important. One study has shown that satisfaction with the company and with the supervisor are tied closely to satisfaction with the performance evaluation and feedback system (Landy et al., 1978). It can be seen that one of the attractions of MBO is that it provides explicit, measurable goals and criteria available to both manager and employee, and minimizes the vague threats to self-esteem that are inherent in some of the other evaluation methods.

From the Viewpoint of the Manager of Professionals

Once again, the major point to be made about performance evaluation for professionals is that it has to be done, but there is no objective, reliable, and valid way to do it. Performance evaluation is demanded by each individual and serves many organizational functions so that there is no escaping the task. However, the difficulties and discomforts of the task can be substantially ameliorated in a number of ways.

1. Develop a performance evaluation system that finds a comfortable fit in your organization. Since there is no correct method, the field is wide open for pragmatic, eclectic approaches. Many of the formal systems have elements that can be usefully combined. Some organizations have combined BARS and MBO to take advantage of the useful features of both systems. Don't "buy" an evaluation system off the shelf, and, if you do, take the time and make the effort to modify and redesign it until it fits. Be very conscious of the inherent problems in all performance evaluation methods, and design around them. In general, not enough organizations take an experimental, trial and error approach to their own system.

2. Treat the formal evaluation system as only one part of a comprehensive feedback system in which frequent, informal feedback sessions bear the brunt of the coaching and criticism effort. Let the formal review come as no surprise. Do not let the formal review become the draining emotional experience it is in the majority of instances.

3. Use some form of goal-setting, whether an approach as comprehensive as MBO and its variations or something far less formal and hierarchical. People perform better against goals than in the absence of goals. Shapero's fourth law is, Organiza-

tions and individuals that plan do better than those that don't, *but* they never follow their plan. Goal-setting and planning make everyone more outward and forward-looking and broaden their horizons and awareness.

4. As an individual manager, use the critical incident technique whether it is part of the formal system of the organization or not. The technique makes you observe the people who work for you in a constructive and thoughtful way, and it can help improve one's general management capabilities.

4

Managing Information

PEOPLE AND INFORMATION are the essential resources in professional activities, and it is the task of management to bring those resources together in a way that will raise the probability of relevant and good results. All managers are clear on their responsibilities for obtaining the best people they can, motivating them, and organizing them to do the work of the organization. Managers are far less conscious of their responsibilities regarding the information resources used in their work. Even where they know that information is important, they are unaware of the available data on how people get and use information and of what can be done about managing the information-communication processes in their organizations.

Successful management of the information resources in professional activities begins with a clear realization of the following general rules at both the organizational and individual level:

Anything that improves the quality and quantity of information available to a professional organization, and/or improves its ability to receive, process, apply, and transmit information, will improve that organization's productivity.

Anything that improves the quality and quantity of information available to a professional and/or improves the professional's ability to receive, process, apply, and transmit information, will improve that professional's productivity.

Once responsibility for management of information is consciously accepted, a manager can find sufficient data on the information-communication behavior of professionals to translate the general rules into systematic management applications. The available data suggest management actions with regard to the individual professional, the organization, physical facilities, and the transmission of information.

INFORMATION-COMMUNICATION ABILITIES ARE CENTRAL TO PROFESSIONAL WORK

With few exceptions, professional work consists of transforming information from one state to another. The few exceptions include the surgeon, sculptor, and dentist who not only need skills with information, but also require motor skills to translate what they perceive and interpret into physical results in the form of operations, objects of art, and dental operations.

To illustrate the information-communication character of professional work, consider the medical doctor's activities. A patient calls her doctor and reports that she has a fever, a headache, and an upset stomach (information input). The doctor replies, "There's a lot of that going around" (the result of information inputs previously received from others). The doctor asks, "Are you allergic to antibiotics?" and the patient answers, "No" (another information input). The doctor asks for the telephone number of the patient's pharmacy (another information input), and, drawing upon what she has heard from other medical practitioners and drug detailers, what she has read recently, learned in medical school, and personally experienced (previous information input stored in her head), the doctor diagnoses (integrates the information) and prescribes (a transformation of information received and integrated into an information output). If the patient gets better or dies it is the end of the transaction, but if the patient calls again and says she is still suffering the doctor will tell her to come in. What ensues is another round of information activities. The patient is weighed, her temperature and pulse are taken, and she is observed. The patient's records are reviewed. Then the doctor prescribes again or sends the patient with her records to a specialist who iterates the information-communication process in its general form.

Similarly, the engineer translates design objectives and specifications into plans and reports using varied input from handbooks, catalogs, and reports. The lawyer translates the client's stated problems into briefs and trial statements drawing upon the extensive records of previous litigations as well as information specific to the case at hand. One can readily see the parallels for accountants, design professionals of all kinds, teachers, advertisers, and other professionals.

The importance of information-communication behavior to professional work can be demonstrated in a number of ways. The Pelz and Andrews (1976) studies of productivity of scientists and engineers show a strong correlationship between productivity and the number and variety of work-related conversations an individual has with colleagues within and outside the organization. The Pelz and Andrews data paint a picture of professional productivity being enhanced by frequent exchanges with other professionals. It is a picture that is directly in contradiction with that of the traditional "bull of the woods" production management view that "If they're talking, they ain't producing."

Using one of the Pelz and Andrews measures of productivity—"overall usefulness," as applied to Ph.D.'s in development labs—it was found that productivity rose sharply when the average contact with colleagues went from weekly to semiweekly and remained far above the fiftieth percentile when

TABLE 4–1
Time Distribution of
Professionals and Managers

ACTIVITY	TIME SPENT (%)[a]
Meetings	35%
Speaking on the telephone	14
Reading	16
Dictating, writing	14
Other secretarial interface	5
Observation	7
Personal breaks	3
Thinking, planning	7
	101%

SOURCE: Data collected by author, previously unpublished.
[a] Self-estimates.

the average contact increased to daily. Similarly, productivity rose with the number of close colleagues in one's group (the number of people to interact with), being highest when the number was fifteen to twenty. In terms of the number of colleagues outside one's group but within the organization with whom a professional exchanged information, productivity went up until the number reached ten to nineteen and thereafter declined.

Another very direct measure of the importance of information-communication behavior in professional work is the amount of work time spent in such behavior. As can be seen by the data on the use of time by two thousand managers and professionals, they spend well over 80% of their time in information-communication activities. The data in Table 4–1 are estimates made by managers and professionals studied. An actual time-study made of a group of managers and professionals, using a self–time-study instrument, found systematic discrepancies between their self-estimates and the actual time spent in various activities (Vorwerk, 1979). Those studied spent more time in information-communication activities than they thought. It was found that they consistently underestimated time spent in meetings (closer to 50%), and overestimated the time spent in reading and thinking.

In contrast, Allen (1977) reported that engineers on twelve development projects allocated 77.3% of their time to analysis and experimentation, 16.4% to all communication (including literature use, 7.9%) and 6.3% to other activity. However, no breakdown was made as to how the analysis and experimentation time was spent in terms of communication with others through informal and formal meetings with one or more people.

A strong case can be made that anything that improves the quality and quantity of information available to a professional and/or improves the professional's ability to receive, process, apply, and transmit information will improve that professional's productivity. This is not to denigrate the importance of creativity or other professional capabilities. In fact, creativity illustrates the relationship of information to other professional capacities. Creativity is widely defined as the ability to relate remote bits of information—the more widely separated the items that one can relate, the more creative one is. Koestler (1964) describes the creative act as taking the contents of two drawers in one's mind and dumping them together on the floor. The capacity to impose or recognize a relationship is central to the creative act, but without the presence of information from different sources the act cannot take place.

Information-communication abilities and acts are relevant to a wide range of managerial activities in a professional organization and affect all of the following:

Hiring
Individual performance
Individual growth
Team capabilities and growth
Dealing with subordinates
Dealing with other parts of an organization
Dealing with vendors
Dealing with clients
Dealing with banks, insurance companies, other professionals
Dealing with the government

Learning from What People Actually Do

The ability to handle and communicate information has been an important—probably the most important—survival mechanism of the human race. As a consequence, nearly all humans are superb information handlers. The ability to make it through any given day is a testimony to human information-communication competence. Witness the morning rush hour on the freeways of any major city. Thousands of half-asleep humans pilot tons of steel at breakneck speeds through unpredictable, intricate patterns with a minimum of accidents. Each of the drivers is receiving and processing a very large number of signals, making sense of them, and responding in meaningful ways.

Observing and measuring how humans actually get, respond to, and use information can provide us with data relevant to the management of professionals. Information-communication behavior is pervasive to all human activities, and data about such behavior is to be found in a wide range of fields. The data most directly related to the management of professionals comes from a large number of "user" studies concerned with how scientists, engineers, medical, and other professionals get and use work-related information. Other relevant data are found in studies of the diffusion of innovations, studies of advertising and propaganda, studies of attitude change, and in the history of science and technology.

Studies of diffusion of innovation are concerned with how innovations are adopted by their potential users. The diffusion studies are particularly relevant to questions of how new ideas, processes and materials are recognized and accepted, and are important to the maintainance of professional capabilities, and to the marketing of the products of professional work. Advertising, propaganda, and attitude change studies are relevant to an understanding of how information is perceived and how it influences those who receive it. The historical record provides data on the relationship of information to the creative process and can lead to an understanding of how information-communication processes affect the fate of professional activities and their products.

From the viewpoint of management, information-communication behavior is usefully described in terms of the following:

1. Sources and channels of information
2. Contexts
   a. Nature of work
   b. Physical location
   c. Attitudes of management
   d. Logistic or nutrient needs
3. Individual differences
4. Two-person communications
   a. Effects of sources
   b. Two-person bonds
5. Social-professional circles and networks

Whenever two or more individuals or organizations are engaged in an endeavor, the quality of communications has an important effect on the outcome. The quality of communication is least important when the endeavor is routine and concerned with highly specifiable items. When someone has need of a standard item, communications can often be effectively carried out using a teletype machine. All that is needed is a sentence that includes a catalog number. Where the endeavor is unique, complex, shot through with the uncertainties and anomalies that characterize professional work, then the quality of communications becomes critical. In professional work it is often difficult to convey important ideas or observations that deal with abstractions, new concepts, or complex, new shapes from one person or organization to another.

Sources and Channels of Information

Think of your own experiences. How did you come to the company you work for? What were the channels through which you heard about it? Did you come to the job through an employment advertisement, an employment agency, college recruitment, through the information or recommendation given you by a friend or relative? Where did you get the most important bit of work-related information received in the last three months? Did you find it by accident or did you get the information from a book, memo, report, trade-press publication, or journal? Did you get it from a salesperson, from a colleague over the telephone or over a cup of coffee, or did you get it at a meeting, in a class session, or by overhearing it?

Sources of information include people (interpersonal), documents (including publications, film, computer displays or printouts), personal files, memory and observations. Channels are divided into formal and informal channels. Formal channels and sources are those formally committed to the transmission of information, including books, journals, reports, data systems, classes, meetings, conventions, and exhibitions. Informal channels are those involving person-to-person interactions such as informal conversations (e.g., over a cup of coffee, over the phone, in the halls outside a convention meeting) and correspondence, and they require drawing upon oneself (memory, files) and on information found by chance (e.g., the book next to the book I was looking at while browsing through some apparently irrelevant materials).

Without question, the most important source of work-related information for the professional (and probably for everyone else) is other people, and the most important channels are informal ones. Reviewing several studies of channel utilization by scientists and engineers, Bodensteiner (1970) found that informal communication channels were used far more than formal ones: an average of 55% of the time vs. 45%. It was also found that informal communication channels were used 65% of the time for the transmission of information. Further, studies that explored how respondents happened to use the formal sources and channels they reported, found that much of the time they had been recommended by someone using an informal channel. Among the informal sources and channels, "found by accident" is reported 18% of the time—that is, the information was found when the respondent was not specifically looking for it. "Found by chance" is reported so consistently that Menzel (1958) speculated that the "accident is no accident."

Use of informal channels is not an example of resistance of humans to innovations in the field of data retrieval but is something more fundamental. A number of studies found that the use of informal communications is associated with professional productivity (Pelz & Andrews, 1976; Parker et al., 1968). Informal transmission of information by colleagues, and by colleagues of colleagues, is characterized by other elements not available or only partly available in formal channel modes of information transmission; i.e., participation in stating the question, value judgments, and richness of communications (discussed below in the sections on the two-person information system and the social-professional circles.)

Informal channels and interpersonal sources are preferred by high performers in professional work, and when they use formal sources they tend to be what librarians call "ephemera," e.g., proceedings of meetings and technical reports. A survey of the information behavior of technical professionals working for the RCA corporation (Jenny & Underwood, 1978) measured differences between high and low performers (those in the upper and lower thirds of the three thousand engineers included in the study). The survey found that high performers drew upon far more sources of information, and valued informal sources and channels of information far more, than the low performers. Neither group placed highest value on technical journals or libraries: the low performers made no mention of them at all, while the high performers placed them in fourth and seventh place respectively. The low performers assigned highest value to standards, handbooks, and catalogs. The high performers assigned highest value to conference proceedings, papers, and conventions and meetings.

In a study of winners of the *Industrial Research* magazine award given to the one hundred most significant technical products of the year (IR 100) for the years 1970–1974, Goldhar (1971) obtained data on three hundred cases and found that informal and interpersonal sources and channels dominated as having produced the "greatest stimulus" and "greatest value." Informal sources accounted for three-quarters of those reported and informal channels for 73% of the channels.

Studies of how professionals divide their time between the formal and informal literature in their field (Allen, 1977) emphasize again the relative importance of the informal over the formal. Engineers spent about three times as much time on informal literature (unpublished reports) as on the formal literature (books, journals, and periodicals). Even the methods used for obtaining the formal literature were dominated by informal methods, which were used 73% of the time by the engineers and 63% of the time by the scientists studied. The formal methods included personal library search, search by a library assistant, and technical abstract search. The informal methods for obtaining the formal literature included "on desk" or "in personal file," "borrowed from a colleague," or "other." The only formal method used by the scientists was personal library search. Interestingly, Allen reports that an analysis of technical solution quality vs. the kind of information used showed the higher-rated solutions were based on written sources far less than were lower-rated solutions: 4% vs. 16%.

The data on channels of recruitment (discussed in Chapter 1, "Hiring: The Most Important Management Decision") provide another measure of the importance of informal sources and interpersonal channels of information. The recruitment channel that provided the greatest number of professionals was referral by a friend or acquaintance. With the exception of those who were self-recruited (which often meant they heard about the job from someone they knew), those who were referred by a friend or acquaintance received the highest raises and stayed the longest.

Channel use plays an important role in the effectiveness of communications between two organizations or between client and contractor. The channel used is of particular concern when there is trouble associated with the matters being communicated. One study of the way communication channels were used in communications between clients, contractors, and subcontractors in R & D projects related the use of different channels to various events (Bodensteiner, 1970). The research found:

1. A significant increase in telephone and face-to-face communications was recorded every time there was any kind of technical or contractual uncertainty, which diminished as the uncertainty or problem was resolved.

2. There was no similar increase in written communications. There was an apparent trade-off between face-to-face and telephone communications. The data further suggested there were fewer periods of uncertainty or trouble and they were of shorter duration where there were more frequent face-to-face exchanges. No one seemed to write to communicate, only for the record.

Bodensteiner's findings (1970) and the previously described data on the superiority of informal communications channels can be explained in terms of "richness" of communications. Written communications are far less rich than voice-only (telephone) communications, which, in turn, are far less rich than face-to-face communications. The more complex, abstract, or sensitive the message, the greater resort to richer forms of communications. It is no accident that we get most of our important information from informal (i.e., face-to-face and telephone) communications, or that when there is a problem on a project we switch to the next richer channel. Richness also pays off in terms of effective problem-solving. Experiments comparing effectiveness of problem-solving using ten different modes of communication found the time required decreased with an increase in the richness of the mode of communication. Face-to-face was faster than voice alone, though the two were quite close, and both were far faster than written or typewritten modes.

Richness of a particular mode or channel of communication results from the number of symbols each provides for use. In the written English language there are twenty-nine significant symbols that can be manipulated with twenty-six letters and three significant punctuation symbols. In spoken language there are an estimated thirty-two symbols (phonemes) to be manipulated with accent, pitch, pauses, and intonation. Face-to-face communication has all the symbols of spoken communication plus a large number of nonverbal signals in the form of gestures, body language, and eye position.

There is a tradeoff between telephone and face-to-face in communications between organizations and within organizations. When people are located on the same floor, face-to-face communications make up 80% of their exchanges. When two different floors are involved, face-to-face exchanges drop to one-third of all communications and telephone communications make up the difference. Bodensteiner (1970) also noticed the tradeoff and suggested that it was influenced by the difficulty of travel between organizations (i.e., weather, distance, accessibility).

The tradeoff is not surprising, since telephone communications are about as efficient as face-to-face communications in terms of exchanging information. The substitution of the telephone for face-to-face contact is affected by whether those communicating have previously met face-to-face. "The use of video for conferences is helpful to people who have never met. The act of seeing one another's expressions contributes to communications. Once the first meeting has occurred, however, video is no longer necessary, and phone conversations become just as revealing" (Goldmark, 1973). Once having met people we talk to them on the telephone as if we can see their faces.

Written communications are the smallest fraction of all communications within an organization—something under 5%—while face-to-face and telephone exchanges are used on the order of 75% and 20+% of the time respectively. Even when organizations are separated geographically, written communications make up less than 15% of all the communications between them (Bodensteiner, 1970).

Written communications are used when a large amount of information is to be transmitted, when a large number of recipients are going to receive the same message (e.g., notice of a meeting), and when accuracy of detail is important (e.g., when a lot of numbers are involved and when a record is desired). A telephone discussion may be followed by "I'll send you a note to confirm what I've just said." One of the signs of trouble within an organization is a sharp increase in written correspondence, particularly memoranda written "for the record." A large number of internal written communications signifies that people are writing for all to know what they told you, to cover themselves rather than to communicate.

Spoken and written language are different forms of communication with different ways of handling the same information.

Written language requires "good English"—good spelling, punctuation, and grammar and good sentence and paragraph structure. It is hard to write correctly and harder to write well. Spoken language, even when grammatically correct, is completely different from written language. In spoken exchanges, sentences are not finished. Thoughts are not completed. More than one subject is discussed in the same exchange. Half sentences, affirming grunts, different subjects all make sense in spoken language. Nothing can make one squirm more than to read from a transcript: though it all made sense when presented, it reads atrociously. Words spoken take on a different meaning than when written. Hesitation, intonation, and inflection all enter into the spoken message, and cannot be captured by the written language, thus obfuscating the meaning of the transaction recorded.

Contexts

The type of information used and the sources and channels employed vary with the context in which the work is conducted. Contexts include the nature of the work being done, environmental elements such as physical location and physical barriers, the attitudes of management, the size of the work group, and the nature of the information needed. From the viewpoint of management, an understanding of the relationship between context and information-communication behavior provides a guide to decisions affecting budgets for publications and physical facilities, and the role the manager has in eliciting desirable information-communication behavior.

Nature of work. There are variations among information-communication behavior patterns by profession and by the kinds of functions for which the information is to be used. Information-communication behavior varies between research and applications work, basic and applied research, academic and nonacademic work, and corporate and professional practice, thus the management of information must vary accordingly.

As would be expected, professionals engaged in research and/or academic work make more use of professional journals than those engaged in applications and nonacademic work. Practioners tend to get more of their work-related information from colleagues, reports, salespeople (vendors, medical detailers, etc.), and the trade press.

Written communications are more likely to be used by technical professionals working on basic research projects than by those working on applied research projects. Basic researchers are more likely to need information from professional colleagues working in different locations, even different countries, and are seldom under the time pressures faced by applied researchers.

The problem of the logarithmic growth of the formal journal literature has been overstated and is based on an idealized rather than an actual view of the role of the formal journal literature in professional life. The majority of professionals work in the world of applications and make little use of the journal literature. Journal publications are used primarily by research professionals and academics. The flood of journal publications is a response to a market demand that has nothing to do with potential users of new knowledge. The writer of a journal article is the primary market for the publication. The journal article is the means by which the author establishes "property rights" to the findings presented. Publishing second earns no Nobel prizes. Journal publication earns the academic author promotions and tenure since it is truly "publish or perish" in academic life.

Physical location and physical barriers. Who communicates with whom and the frequency of their communications is affected strongly by an organization's physical arrangements. The distance between the work locations of two individuals, which is determined by management, has a considerable effect on the frequency of their work-related communications. The probability that two persons will communicate on professional matters drops sharply with the distance between them. The probability of two persons communicating at least once a week drops sharply from just about 0.98 at a separation distance of six feet to half that at fifteen feet, and keeps dropping with distance, practically disappearing at fifty feet. (Allen, 1977) Any physical barrier that impedes easy access on a given floor will have a similar effect. Individuals will sooner walk one hundred feet to communicate with someone on the same floor than walk up twelve stairs to talk to someone on the next floor, even when the stairwell is adjacent to their desks.

Within organizations there are frequent moves of groups and individuals organizationally and physically. When professional personnel are moved to new locations, the pattern of interpersonal communications changes accordingly. Within as short a period as four months after a move, the patterns of communication on work-related matters shift as much as 46%, with people turning to those physically nearest to them even though they had not turned to them before (Shapero et al., 1978).

It is a familiar professional experience to have a good, informal, communicative relationship with another professional who works in the same office. The relationship is both professional and social and results in having lunch together frequently, playing chess together, and the like. Then comes an organizational move which separates the two colleagues physically and organizationally. Within a very short time the relationship attenuates to the point where they wave at each other when they meet accidentally, and promise to "get together pretty soon," but they seldom do. People tend to fall into very fixed patterns of movements in their work life, walking the same path to coffee, going to the same places for lunch, and talking with those nearest to them physically.

Attitudes of managers. Motivation is important in any consideration of information-communication behavior. If the individual professional is motivated to want information, to value information, and to want to share information with others it will make a difference to his behaviors and consequent productivity. In the same way, the professional who has learned that active participation in information-enhancing activities will be penalized is hardly likely to seek out and exchange information in such a way as to enhance productivity.

The attitude of managers toward such information-communication behaviors as reading in general, reading on the job, informal exchanges, coffee breaks, and attendance at conferences and professional meetings is an environmental element that affects the behavior of professionals. If management gives negative feedback with regard to them, the activities will not occur or will be seriously diminished. On the other hand, the manager who reads on the job, calls attention to interesting material, participates in informal exchanges and coffee breaks, and encourages attendance at professional meetings will elicit more productive communications. A general management policy that recognizes and rewards the desired communication behavior can have a positive effect. Managers shouldn't make the mistake of their German colleague who was described by one of his employees as "believing so much in the importance of the coffee break that he had the coffee delivered to everyone's desk so they wouldn't be interrupted by all those people."

The information need being satisfied. The kind of information needs to be satisfied can be divided into what may be termed "logistic needs" and "nutrient needs." Logistic needs occur when the kind of information wanted is known, but its content isn't known. Examples include the following:

> We want the name and telephone number of the vice president for marketing of the United Astrology Corporation.
> We want to know the magnetic properties of a particular alloy.
> We want to know what is available in the way of certain kinds of components with characteristics that fall within given limits, their costs, the companies that make them, and whom to call to order them.
> We want a list of everything available in the literature on the disease, multiple myeloma, and then abstracts.
> We want material on the design of stairways.
> We want to know what information retrieval systems contain information on agricultural economics.

All of the above are logistic needs, and are the kinds of needs satisfied by a library search, and by the use of handbooks, catalogs, and well-organized filing systems. Logistic needs are ideally suited for fulfillment by a mechanical retrieval system.

Nutrient needs for information are satisfied by information where it is not known when it will be used. The expression "nutrient needs" (for want of a better term) is used to denote the flow of information needed by the human animal to maintain and develop itself. Nutrient information is required by professionals to maintain themselves and to grow professionally. Every event experienced by an individual, and every significant input of information is registered somewhere in that individual's memory. All of us have had *dejà vu* experiences, recognizing some place we have never been before because it evokes some memory from our large storehouse. No two individuals have the same store of information, not even identical twins, and it is our unique stores of information that distinguish each of us from every other individual.

When faced with a problem, a nonroutine question, or a creative opportunity, we consciously and unconsciously draw upon our unique store of information. A design professional faced with a design problem might draw upon something seen in a trade magazine a year ago, a previous design experience, something learned in a course, a paper heard at a convention, a personal experience with equipment while working on a summer job, and something seen as a child while fishing with an uncle. All of these stored memories come together in some complex, and as yet unexplained, way to form a new design concept.

The notion of information as a nutrient generates a number of inferences. Given equal capabilities, the larger and more varied the store of information in an individual, the greater probability of a creative solution. The more one's store of information is exercised, the easier it will be to avail oneself of all parts of that store. The notion of stored information from previous significant experiences suggests that more importance should be given to feelings than is often assigned them. Our feelings are evoked by experiences with past events. Though we cannot always assign labels or rational explanations to those feelings, they represent uncatalogued information in our store. Though we should not take precipitous actions on the basis of our feelings, we should also not ignore them. Our feelings are a basis for intuition, and are important to inductive thinking and pattern recognition.

Individual Differences

There are, of course, individual differences in information-handling capacities. There are differences due to age, experience, and training. Various cognitive capabilities, such as short-term memory, change with age. In general, however, the information-handling capabilities of almost all humans are so good that, from the view point of the manager of professionals, most individual differences are insignificant.

There is one exception, an individual who has been labeled variously in the literature but who all agree plays a central role in the information-communication process. That central figure, who will be referred to here as "the high communicator," has also been variously referred to as "the technological gate-keeper" (Allen, 1966); "the scientific troubador" (Menzel, 1964); "the information specialist"; (Bernal, 1958; Hodge and Nelson, 1965); and "the special communicator" (Holland, 1970).

Whatever the label, all are agreed on the existence of individuals who play a special part in facilitating and increasing information flows into, within and from an organization. The high communicator is primarily identified by the relatively high frequency with which he or she is cited by others as the person they go to for information. These high communicators raise the total information capabilities and content of an organization. The majority of studies about high communicators have been concerned with scientists and engineers, but the findings about technical professionals are pertinent to other professionals. Among the characteristics of the special facilitators of information are the following (Shapero et al., 1978): High communicators:

Read considerably more than their colleagues
Read more sophisticated technical journals than their colleagues

Participate more frequently in professional meetings and
conferences than their colleagues

Play a pivotal role in professional social circles

Have and use more personal contacts outside the organization than their colleagues

Have more intraorganizational contact than their colleagues

Use more technical specialists within an organization than
their colleagues

Maintain close communication with other high communicators in their organizations

Are high technical performers

Present significantly more papers at professional conferences than their colleagues

There is more than one kind of high communicator. No
one is a high communicator for every kind of information in
the workplace. In research and development, high communicators have been differentiated with regard to three categories
of information: project-task information, state-of-the-art-infor-
mation, and research-laboratory technique information (Holland, 1970; Shapero et al., 1978; Myers & Huffman, 1982). It
is not surprising that the high communicator for project-task
information tends to be a first-line supervisor and more likely
to be a person who communicates a lot with others outside
the organization. The high communicator for state-of-the-art
information is more likely to be a producer of both published
and unpublished papers and to read more technical journals.
The high communicator for research-laboratory technique information is more hardware-oriented and has more patents.

Differences among high communicators are associated with
the institutional contexts in which they work: differences in
technology, institutional purpose, organizational structure, and
organizational history. For example, the high communicator
in a twenty-year-old, nonprofit, contract-research physical sciences laboratory will have a different profile than one in a profit-
making, hardware-development electronics company that is fifteen years old (Shapero et al., 1978).

As might be expected, in the hardware-oriented electronics

organization, the high communicator is likely to have more patent applications, more communication with outsiders, will read more unpublished papers, have more years of technical experience, go to more meetings and receive more awards. High communicators differ from other professionals in the extent and intensity of their information-communication activities, but there are logical differences among them depending on the kind of work they do and the kinds of organizations for which they work. We would expect patents to play a larger role in a hardware organization and to make more sense in the laboratory-research technique than in the state-of-the-art function. We can easily understand the greater importance of writing reports in a research organization.

Two-Person Communications

The two-person exchange is the basic unit in communications. Communication implies a sender, a receiver, and a message. Even when we speak of mass communication, a large number of two-person exchanges with one source and many receivers is implied. In addition to the factors already discussed, two-person exchanges are affected by the receiver's perceptions of the source of the message and by experiences with previous exchanges between sender and receiver.

Effects of sources. Communication is concerned with the transmission and *reception* of information. Effective delivery, which means effective reception, is the main goal of communication. The management of professionals wants to be sure that messages transmitted will affect the recipient's behavior in the direction intended. Whether the intention is to affect work-related behavior, or to be assured that employees (including the managers themselves) are updated professionally, or to raise the likelihood that clients and prospective clients will be affected by its messages, management has to be concerned with effective reception.

A major influence on whether a message will be accepted and acted upon is the receiver's perception of the characteristics of the source of the message. Research has identified three source characteristics associated with the transmission of messages which are effective in terms of persuasion, attitude change, and diffusion of innovation: source credibility, source attractiveness, and power (McGuire, 1969 and 1973).

Source credibility. The same message sent by two persons, one perceived as credible and one as not credible, will be received and remembered equally by a recipient, but the effect of that message (i.e., attitude or opinion change) will be far greater when sent by the credible source.

The credibility or believability of a source depends on his or her perceived expertise and objectivity. The more the source of a message has professional or social authority, the more the recipient is likely to accept and use the transmitted information. Most professionals quickly check a source's degrees, rank, place of work, publisher, and/or school attended before deciding whether and how to listen to or read the information presented. A lecture on the history of architecture by someone identified as a very intelligent butcher will not be taken seriously no matter how good the content of the material.

Advertisers have long understood the effect of credibility on target audiences. Hence the advertisements with a man in a white laboratory coat with a stethoscope dangling around his neck urging the use of a particular headache remedy. When medical associations protested the ads, the stethoscope and white laboratory coat were removed and a microscope substituted.

The status or prestige of the source of information affects the believability of the information, particularly if the status of the source is seen to be higher than that of the recipient of the message. Status and prestige are associated with expertise, among other things. Another element in the perception of the credibility of a source is perceived objectivity. Sources are believed to be more objective when they are seen as having nothing to gain as a result of convincing the recipient.

Something can be learned from the data on source credibility and the use advertisers have made of them. When transmitting important information to clients, prospective clients, higher management, and other branches of an organization thought should be given to who is transmitting the information. This is intuitively sensed by many, but it should be considered more systematically. Thought should be given to the credibility of the messenger in the eyes of the recipient—the best messenger may not be the person most readily available or the one with the highest rank.

If a management is serious about bringing new professional information into the organization, it should consider sending its most respected (credible) people to professional meetings. They are the ones most likely to be listened to when they return, raising the likelihood their information will be used. Proposals for projects provide a good example of where credibility is achieved in terms of the biographies of the proposed staff that accompany them. When an organization making a proposal for work feels it needs more credibility, it can often obtain it by engaging consultants with the requisite credibility—a way of "renting" credibility.

Source attractiveness. Attractiveness here means being likable, admired, and/or similar to the recipient. People tend to agree with those they like, and on learning that someone they like feels negatively towards an idea or object, people will tend to share that dislike. One will adopt a position taken or urged by a liked or admired source to enhance one's own self-esteem by identifying with the source. The use of popular and admired figures from sports and entertainment is a staple of consumer advertising. Naming lines of clothing after popular figures has resulted in significant increases in sales.

Factors that influence likableness in the work situation are suggested by the literature on interpersonal attraction (Berscheid & Walster, 1969) and social exchange (Chadwick-Jones, 1976). The factors include the following:

Propinquity: the closer two individuals are located to each other physically and socially, the more likely they will be attracted to each other and the more likely they will select each other as information sources.

Reciprocity: we like those who cooperate with us in attaining rewards for ourselves, those who like us, and those who give us something. A benefactor is liked better when the recipient has a chance to reciprocate and disliked when there is no chance to reciprocate (Gross & Latane, 1974).

Similarity. Similarity is associated with liking. In addition to being more likely to accept and be influenced by someone who is perceived as likable, an individual is more likely to seek out such a source for information. Conversely, individuals will go out of their way to avoid going for information to someone who is unlikable or who makes them pay an unacceptable psychological price (Shapero et al., 1978).

Substantial evidence suggests that individuals are influenced by messages from sources similar to themselves. The more the recipient perceives the source of the message as being like him/ or herself, the more he/or she will be influenced by the message. The more someone perceives another to be like him/or herself the more it is assumed they share common tastes, standards, and goals.

For example, making use of the data on similarity, advertising on television is becoming more and more regional. The same advertisement, shown in different regions uses people with local accents and appearances. Television advertising increasingly uses "ordinary-looking" people who are similar to a larger audience (like you and me). Ads for computers and laboratory equipment show someone who is a business person or a scientist, give the individual's name, title and company, and statements about satisfaction with the advertised equipment: an example of using similarity for effective message transmission.

As with credibility, management can make use of the data on source attractiveness in many situations. For one thing, it is possible to enhance and shape the flow of information in a laboratory by use of what is known about the effects of propinquity in making office assignments. Putting a development group next to the people responsible for marketing will result in more marketable developments. Putting an R & D group next to a university will result in more publications. Putting an electronics group next to a materials group will result in more exchange and understanding between the two groups. Sending research people to spend some time with salesmen in the field can change the research man into an "attractive" source of information for the field people and vice versa, enhancing the useful flow between the two functions.

A thoughtful matching of the characteristics of whoever is selected to transmit information with those of the intended receivers will raise the chances of the transmission being successful. An ideal choice is someone who is both credible and similar to the intended receivers. For example, if one is mounting an effort to increase the number of minority applicants for a summer intern program, it would be ideal to send someone from the organization who is both a respected professional (for credibility) and who is from the same minority group (similarity). The intelligent manager in charge of the marketing of professional services studies the background and characteristics of those being contracted and sends someone who might have the best chance of being listened to.

The two-person bond. Two-person communications are affected by the history of past communications between the individuals, and their experiences with past exchanges affects the impact of subsequent exchanges. A relationship established over a series of exchanges creates a two-person bond which has a particular strength and which carries with it a set of norms and expectations that do much to determine the attention paid and the value placed on a message sent between the two persons. Knowledge of how two-person bonds operate with regard to information can be employed in many useful ways to enhance the flow of work-relevant information in professional activities. This knowledge is useful in maintaining and increasing the general flow of professional information into an organization or to an individual while simultaneously developing positive relationships with outside organizations and individuals.

A two-person bond begins when "liking" or "attraction" is established by some initial exchange between two persons. Two persons communicating for the first time generate a relationship that has a potential for becoming a continuing bond between them. The initial level of liking is in large part a function of similarity between the two individuals. The more the two persons share in the way of values and characteristics the more likely they will like each other if the context and the situation provides the opportunity.

Subsequent strengthening of the bond occurs as a result of propinquity, reciprocity, and shared experiences, and in their absence the bond weakens and disappears. If there is no physical propinquity, the bond depends on the number, variety and value of the subsequent exchanges (reciprocity). A continuing and growing relationship comes from a series of exchanges of information interlaced with social and professional exchanges of many kinds. The professional exchanges include invitations to lecture or give a paper, recommendations for jobs, recommendations of potential hires, and consulting. Social exchanges include anything from a Christmas card or a drink to invitations to be a house guest.

The length of time between exchanges affects the strength of the bond (and the liking). The strength of the bond weakens with the length of time between bonds, unless there have been so many exchanges that the bond takes on a permanent high level of strength, the kind that occurs with childhood friends. When two "old" friends meet again, it is often as if they are picking up a conversation again in the middle.

There is a norm of reciprocity in exchanges: exchanges must be reciprocal, and they cannot become too unbalanced. When exchanges between two persons become too unbalanced the bond cannot be maintained. Reciprocity does not imply a *quid pro quo*. *Quid pro quo* exchanges are commercial transactions, and each has a one-transaction life. Each of the parties is quit of the other once the exchange has been made, and another "deal" may be negotiated when needed. Bond-strengthening exchanges just happen naturally in context.

Two simple experiments that anyone can try will demonstrate the dynamics of two-person bonds for the readers, and, incidentally, strengthen some of their own social-professional bonds.

In the first experiment, mail some interesting professional material to a selection of people you have met professionally more than a year ago. Draw the names from your address list or collection of cards. Attach your card or a very brief scribbled note to the material. Keep a record of the returns in the following weeks. I sent a copy of a paper I had written to forty people drawn rather randomly from my files. Within ten days I received a number of letters conveying thanks for the materials, stating that they were glad to hear from me, and some filled me in about themselves and what they were doing. Within a month a number of articles, papers, and a report, accompanied by cards and notes, were received from the target group. Within three months a call was received from one of the addressees asking me if I could be included in a proposal for a major piece of research work.

Try a second simple experiment that strengthens bonds. From your address list draw three names of people you have not talked to in over a year. Call each of them, and tell them nothing more important than that you have been thinking of them or that you were wondering what they were doing. During the subsequent conversation note how much useful information is exchanged. This is a form of networking (it is also a very pleasant experience that can brighten a gray day). The last time I made three such calls I unexpectedly ended up helping someone hire a good professional, I was informed of some new technical material, and I committed myself to writing a chapter in a book.

The experiments just described also suggest useful management actions. By regularizing and encouraging professional-to-professional exchanges between people in the organization and others, a reciprocal flow of information will be generated, bringing valuable information into the organization, possibly including recruitment and business opportunities. Professionals should be encouraged to keep a mailing and telephone list of professionals they have met, and to keep them active through calls, mailing of working papers, articles, and correspondence. Institutional mailing will have far less effect than person-to-person mailings. Managers of professionals might also promote the establishment and maintenance of regular information means, such as working-paper series, newsletters, reprint series, and the sponsorship of talks to other groups.

The Social-Professional Circle or Network

The professional social circle or network is built upon an aggregation of two-person bonds. A multiperson information communications system is usually referred to as a network, but the term "network" evokes an electro-mechanical model of communications that does not adequately describe the social nature of human communications. It is more useful to refer to the expression "social-professional circle," but since "network" is used so widely the terms "social-professional circle" and "social network" will be used interchangeably.

The social-professional circle is more amenable to organic/ biological or social terms of reference, which can include relevant concepts of age, attraction, norms of behavior, transactions, and the like. As was discussed in Chapter 1 ("Hiring"), social-professional circles are crucial to our lives. Our social circles determine our norms and standards, provide us with trusted and useful work-related information, and often bring us jobs or suitable employees.

Data on how information flows in social-professional networks are found in studies of the so called "invisible colleges," in the international science community, and in the literature on social networks, social change and interpersonal attraction. The literature describes a social network as based on social contacts, kinships, friendships, professional ties, and on physical propinquity (Lin, 1973).

The individual professional can be a member of many social-professional circles, for example as a member of an international professional circle linked to a group studying the phenomena in a limited field of science, or as a member of the advertising department of a corporation.

"Invisible colleges" are the social-professional circles of scientists working in a given field of basic research and found in a variety of institutions in many different locations and countries. The scientists in an invisible college maintain their social networks through correspondence, visits, small invitational meetings, and informal exchanges at larger meetings. Their exchanges are marked by a high overlap between the professional and the social. The formal meetings are marked by informality while their social meetings are filled with discussion of their work (the napkins and tablecloths at dinner might be covered with diagrams and equations). Personal bonds are formed in face-to-face meetings and strengthened by exchanges of notes and drafts of articles long before they reach formal publication. In the science community, members of so-called invisible colleges know about new findings one to two years before they are published, obtain their leads to formal sources, and receive feedback and recognition before having gone through the formal process of publication (Price, 1963; Crane, 1972; Compton, 1973).

Membership in professional social networks is obtained through sponsorship or, in the case of science, publication followed by an invitation to a meeting or a visit. To maintain membership an individual must follow the norms and standards of the network, most fundamental of which is reciprocal exchange. Those who only take from the network and do not reciprocate are dropped. An individual may be dropped from the network for not behaving according to its accepted norms: e.g., not giving due credit to the work of others, using material without attribution, taking part in the political repression of colleagues.

Extended social-professional circles are found in all professional fields, though they may not play quite as central a role as in advanced fields of science. Extended social-professional circles are particularly important to professionals who work alone or in small groups in widely scattered locales. Artists need the company and exchange of other artists. Architects who aspire to doing new and advanced work need to exchange ideas with other architects. Medical practioners, particularly specialists, need to talk to others in their specialty.

Many social-professional circles are spatially anchored in

a given city, and in professions where this occurs it is almost necessary to locate in that city or to make regular pilgrimages there to keep abreast of what is happening professionally. Examples of the latter are publishing, advertising, *haute couture* design, film making, theater, and financial analysis. In cases where a particular kind of professional activity concentrates in a region, as in electronics, social-professional circles will be made up of some of the professionals that work for the many organizations in the region.

The extended social-professional circle takes on different forms in larger organizational contexts. In such activities as engineering and industrial R & D, the extended network (beyond the organization) does not play as great a direct role in the conduct of work-in-progress as in science. Much of the information used in industrial activities comes from within the organization. What comes from outside is usually obtained and transmitted by high communicators who play the part of boundary spanners, or from sales people.

Organizational social-professional circles form within an organizational work situation. Links form between individuals for some purpose or because of some consciously recognized interest on the part of one or both of the people interacting. The links are characterized by a daily intermingling of formal and informal exchanges that include job assistance, social conversation, and personal service. The benefits obtained from daily exchanges are both intrinsic and extrinsic. Among the intrinsic benefits are information transmission and verification, friendship, and play. The extrinsic benefits include recognition and influence. In the work situation, intrinsic and extrinsic are intertwined. Joking is easily combined with recognition. Information relay and verification are easily combined with influence.

The small world of social networks. There is a great deal of interconnection between social networks. The interconnections occur because individuals within the networks have multiple memberships. All individuals, with few exceptions, are members of a large number of different kinds of social networks based on church, school, neighborhood, military service, sport, social interests, hobbies, and profession. An engineer within a given organizational social network also belongs to a church group with someone who is a scientist at a university, and is also on a committee at her child's school with someone who is an investment banker. If asked a science-related question at work, she may freely call her acquaintance for information. If the question is one of a financial nature, she can contact her fellow school committee member. Her contacts may need to reach into their professional social circles to obtain information for the requestor. The very fact of the request creates the first act in a reciprocal relationship that may strengthen with more exchanges.

Because there is so much interconnection between social networks in the United States it is usually possible to identify and locate the source of needed professional information in three to five telephone calls. In addition, starting with a fairly unstructured question, the question will become more accurate, the terminology more precise, and value judgments about the various sources of information available will be proffered and refined in the course of the calls. To illustrate, if you wanted to obtain information on what is known about the costs and benefits of alternate methods of psychotherapy, where would you start? If you went to a library to use its mechanical information retrieval system and queried it for everything on costs and benefits you would get hundreds of references. If you requested everything on psychotherapy, it would produce a similar outpouring. However, if you cross both terms to get everything that combines costs and benefits and psychotherapy you would get nothing.

Take the same question to your network of acquaintances. Where to start? You might call a psychologist friend or someone who would know a psychologist. You make your call to the psychologist, apologizing for your ignorance. Your friend might tell you "It's a dumb question" but will consider it seriously anyway and say, "Call Professor Black at State University. If anyone might have a clue about the subject, he will." You call Professor Black, telling him that your friend suggested that you get in touch with him, and admitting that it might be "a dumb question." Professor Black is sociable and asks about your friend. He tells you, "It is an odd question, but it seems to me that White, at the University of California, spoke about something on those lines."

You now call White, telling him that Black had referred you, ask your question, and apologize again for your ignorance. White is immediately responsive. He tells you your question is improperly framed. "The terms are all wrong! We don't use those economic terms in our field, and you'll never find anything under those terms. We use cures per time of treatment per person." White tells you of the work of Brown and Green, stating, "Green is an idiot! Her work is misdirected and dated. Brown is first class! Brown's done the only useful work on the subject." He goes on to say, "Brown did a lot of his work at Cambridge, but he's now at Sussex." Now, you are on target, and are able to go to the library and ask for everything by Brown of Sussex.

Analyze the process in the example. You started in almost complete ignorance. You used a personal bond in your social network to start. You followed a trail of personal bonds through personal references which meant that you would be given thoughtful responses no matter how far-fetched your question. You have had your question and terminology reframed to fit the field. Because you have come through social networks, you have been given value judgments that no retrieval system would contain.

This would be relatively fast and efficient, and in the process you might learn much more about the subject and about attitudes in the field. You might even form an acquaintanceship with someone in your chain of questions who shares other interests or who wants to know what you learn. If you reciprocate, you have created the beginnings of a two-person bond.

The question was raised some years ago, how many personal social links it would take to link up two individuals picked at random from the two hundred twenty million people in the United States. A preliminary answer was provided by Milgram (1967) in an elegant study called "The Small World Study." Packets were mailed to individual names picked at random in the Midwest. Each packet contained the name and description of an individual in the Boston area, giving the person's home and work addresses. The recipients were asked to send the packet to the target person if they knew him by first name, and, if not, to send it to someone they knew by first name who might be more likely to know him. Each of the chain of recipients were asked to return an attached postal card describing their relationship to the person to whom they sent the packet.

Of the completed chains of referral, the average number of links was five. The study was a demonstration of the effective way in which two-person bonds imbedded in social networks link up a very large population. Typically, someone in Nebraska sent the packet to a fellow engineer raised in Massachusetts who, in turn, sent it to a former high school teacher in a small Massachusetts town. The former teacher sent the packet to a haberdasher in the town where the target person lived, who then completed the chain. Other packets reached the target person at his or her place of work in Boston, most of them coming through work colleagues. Two of his or her colleagues at work and a shopkeeper in his or her living area were the principal conduits, and they could be high communicators or boundary spanners.

Managing Information–Communication Behavior at the Individual Level

Management can affect information-communication behavior by who and how they hire, the resources they make available to the individual professional, education, and motivation.

Hire high communicators. Make extra efforts to hire high communicators. Hiring the high communicator is probably the most direct way to improve the information content of an entire organization. The high communicator brings an organization (1) access to an extended body of information imbedded in links with many sources of information, (2) an active information-seeking mode, and (3) an active information-communication–transmission style that creatively connects people and information within the organization (i.e., the individual who thrusts information on you, saying, "Remember you were asking about . . ."). Hiring the high communicator is not just a matter of accessing the information in the individual's head, but of accessing the information made available to the organization through that individual's information-communication behavior.

To identify a high communicator when hiring, look for a record of continuing information-dependent output (a number of recently published and unpublished papers, patents, etc.), evidence of continuing professional networking (professional meetings frequently and recently attended, honors and awards, professional directory listings), and evidence of continuing active information-seeking behavior (number of journals read). Of course, these characteristics should be looked for in addition to what is sought in any professional—a good work record and reputation and likableness (both of which are commonly found in high-communicators).

Hire "nice" people. To maximize the information available within your organization, hire people whom others will readily go to for information and to whom they'll readily give information. The most impressive formal education without the ability to make that information readily available can result in a net loss to an organization. The measure to be applied is "net available information."

Facilitate your high communicators. If you are fortunate enough to have one or more high communicators in your organization, make it easier for them to play the part. Give them unlimited budgets for books and journals—they will get the information to more people than most libraries. Locate them where they are easily accessed by others. Encourage them to travel to see what is going on in their fields. Do not make the mistake of designating them as "information specialists" and removing them from the normal working processes and tasks. High communicators function best in context, where they are part of the regular flow of work and social exchange.

Provide liberal budgets for formal information. Information serves to enhance and save professional labor, and is cheap relative to the cost of that labor. The price of a book or an annual subscription to a technical journal may be roughly equivalent to one fully costed hour of professional labor. If a book or journal saves one hour of labor, it has already earned its way, and if it has improved the output of a professional its payout may be very large. Unlike the professional hour, the book or journal remains available after being used. In light of their potential worth and economy, it is startling to find organizations surrounding the acquisition of books, journals, and reports with an amazing amount of bureaucratic procedure that lowers or prevents the use of the formal sources of information. Typically, the purchase of information is treated as the purchase of materials and equipment, and is justified and inventoried accordingly.

Remember that information serves a "nutritive" purpose as well as a logistic one. The preferred rule is to have a larger quantity and diversity of books, journals, and reports around than is needed for any given project rather than to require justification on the basis of identified, and often painful, immediate and explicit need. If you make the book budget unlimited, probably only one or two people will make heavy demands on it. The individual who does "abuse the privilege" will likely be the high communicator who will subsequently distribute the information within the organization. It may be a good way to identify your high communicators.

Education. Education is one means of achieving improved information-communication behavior. Informing professionals how they can get and use information can make some difference in their behavior. When formal materials are combined with exercises in improved methods for obtaining information and are reinforced through practice and reminder, new behavior patterns can be established and maintained. Seminars have been successfully held in which, for example, the participants are asked to compare several modes of obtaining information such as "three to five phone calls," library search, and mechanical retrieval systems.

Motivation. Perhaps the most effective actions are those that motivate the individual to shape his or her information-communication behavior to be more effective. Eliciting the desire to read, to exchange information with other professionals within and outside the organization, and actively to improve transmission of information are tasks for the manager. Professionals can be motivated to increase and improve their information-communication behavior through positive feedback and through incentives. Among other things the manager can do are the following:

Make information-communication contributions part of the review process

Make a deliberate point of encouraging professionals to read: by managerial example, by making approving comments, and by encouraging discussion of what the professionals read (e.g., the formation of a weekly, informal "brown bag" journal club in which participants including the manager report on articles they have read)

Encourage use of the telephone to contact outside professional colleagues for information

Encourage participation in both formal and informal exchanges of information outside the immediate organizational group (e.g., seminars, classes)

Reinforce information-related activities with relevant rewards (e.g., trips to review state-of-the-art technology, subscriptions and books, time to review the literature)

Networking. Managers should encourage professionals to develop and maintain their memberships in social-professional circles that cross organizational lines. The social networks are important sources of good information for technical matters, hiring, and business-related information. Effective access to outside networks provides an organization with an extended family of information, and access to useful social-professional networks is only freely available to individuals who are "members" of them. Management should encourage and support participation in the social-professional networks to which their professionals belong for its value to the organization and its educational value to the individual professional.

Many organizations support or encourage their professionals to take part in local professional societies, and some organizations consider membership in such societies an obligation for some of their senior technical people. Membership in professional societies can lead to the kinds of personal relationships that enter a professional into a social-professional network, but this is only one form of networking. Far more effective are those things that bring the professional as a participant to smaller, less formal groups, such as seminars, small invited conferences of experts, or task forces. The preparation of articles and papers has a beneficial effect on networking just as much as it does on the individual's and organization's reputation.

At the Organizational Level

Management can affect information-communication behavior by the use of formal and informal organizational mechanisms, including rules and procedures, and by the allocation of resources.

Encourage informal workplace communications. The manager has a large effect on informal workplace communications. The manager who understands and accepts the importance of the informal, even playful, kinds of exchange that take place on the job is at ease in such an environment. With the manager at ease, the information exchange is rich. The manager who is still firmly fixed in the "production line" ethic, and who feels that "if they're just talking, they aren't working," sends out a host of signals that suppress exchange.

In addition to passive encouragement, the manager can formally help to develop an environment for productive informal information exchange by use of a number of informal mechanisms. The manager can encourage the daily coffee gathering, sponsor and take part in an informal weekly lunch with different mixes of professionals in the organization, provide architectural aids including a good lunchroom that becomes a gathering place. At one time, the Ramo-Wooldridge Corporation had coffee alcoves in their California plant to encourage just such informal exchanges. Scratch pads on cafeteria tables may encourage the exchange of information during lunch hour.

Rules, procedures, and resources. Rules, procedures, and resources channel or block desired information-communication activities. Rules regarding the buying of books and journals can make it easy or difficult to get some material when needed and, eventually, can determine whether a professional will even make the effort. The availability of resources acts in the same way and conveys a message as to what is considered to be in the organization's interests and what isn't (e.g., a rule that requires special clearance from a high level of management to use a company car tells one quickly that the management does not see company cars as just another tool.).

Uses of travel. Face-to-face communications with people in other organizations is a valuable activity that is also expensive in terms of time and money. The cost of travel makes it more difficult to be as liberal with it as with other sources of information. However, travel should be encouraged for the following reasons:

> Early-on face-to-face meetings between key professionals in your organization and others with an important role in or concern with a new project: i.e., clients, subcontractors, suppliers, public interest groups and their professionals
>
> Regular, periodic face-to-face meetings between your professionals and other parties with an important role or concern with an ongoing project
>
> Exchange of needed information on highly abstract or uncertain subjects which require very rich communications, e.g., certain kinds of professional subjects or incompletely stated problems

The first face-to-face meetings between people who will be working together on a project but are going to be separated by organizational and spatial distance provides the necessary means for each person to "calibrate" the others, to know what to expect from them. Face-to-face exchanges are vital to the establishment of trust, and make it possible subsequently to carry on reliable and useful communications over the telephone. Subsequent, periodic meetings are needed to maintain trust, to prevent misunderstanding from developing, and to defuse difficult situations. The more the work that engages two parties is of a nonroutine nature, the more the need for face-to-face exchange. In any field concerned with highly abstract material, visually dependent material, or where the questions are incompletely formed, face-to-face exchanges are essential. For example, it is difficult to conceive of an architectural project carried out completely by correspondence and telephone. It would be difficult to convey a complicated medical procedure by telephone (though this is now being tried by television hookup).

Travel should be liberally supported for the development and maintenance of linkages between professionals in an organization and professionals elsewhere. Budgets for travel to professional meetings are widespread, but travel should also be encouraged for visits and exchanges with others in the profession at universities and other institutions. The Japanese have been exemplary at understanding the value of having professionals meet other professionals to hear and to see what they are doing. Japanese recognition of what others are doing, and the Japanese custom of gift-exchange, generate the reciprocity that assures them of more information over time.

Travel by professionals from whom others in the organization will accept information should especially be encouraged. High communicators should be encouraged to travel as a way of obtaining more information.

Physical facilities. Through the design and arrangement of facilities, management can facilitate informal exchange within a group and between groups, as well as stimulating organizational changes.

Facilitate informal exchange within a group. The informal exchange of information within a group can be enhanced by locating the members fairly close together, by removing physical barriers between them, and by designing the facilities to increase "eddying" patterns (i.e., patterns that encourage encounter and interaction in the normal, daily flow of movements). Information-communication–oriented facilities design would do some or all of the following:

Locate a group in a contiguous space where possible

Place the "coffee pot" so it is easy for more than one person to share coffee and talk, and encourage group rather than individual coffee facilities

Arrange the physical layout of the group to increase the probability that all people in the group will "bump into each other"

Facilitate informal exchange between groups. Informal information exchange between different organizational groups can be aided by designing the physical facilities to enhance interactions and by arranging the way the groups are situated within the facilities. Particular attention has to be paid to increasing the opportunities for people from different groups to encounter each other casually and in the normal course of the day. Among ways to increase the probabilities for chance encounters are: (1) a central space through which different groups have to pass, on their way to other parts of the organization and on leaving the building, (2) company eating places that bring people together, (3) multigroup coffee areas which also permit small groups to meet and interact, and (4) centralized services that bring people together from various areas.

By arranging office assignments with a view to their information-communication consequences, it is possible to change the frequency of exchanges between individuals, to encourage the development of new ideas, to lay the groundwork for new coherent organizational groupings, and to break off communication patterns when that is desired.

Facility rearrangements are a constant in organizational life, particularly in large firms. The thoughtful manager can take advantage of organizational moves, when they occur, to accomplish several objectives.

One way to increase communications between individuals is to locate them in the same office or in adjacent offices. Locating them near each other can also affect the ideas that are developed in the organization. I have experimented with the use of new office assignments after a move from one facility to another. The new assignments were used to accomplish several information-communication and organizational objectives. By locating people from different disciplines in close proximity, the degree of informal and social exchange was significantly increased, and a number of innovative ideas were proposed that drew upon the varied backgrounds of the professionals newly located near each other. Placing individuals in close proximity also prepared the ground for the formation of new organizational arrangements. In one case, the deliberate grouping of individuals from different organizations resulted in a voluntary proposal by them to form a group desired by management.

Sometimes it is organizationally desirable to break off communications between individuals or groups, and the design of facilities provides an excellent means to accomplish that end. For example, in an organization of professional engineers and geologists, the partner in charge of a regional office passed on the baton of management to a younger person but wanted to keep on doing professional work. The transfer of management was not working well because the professional staff kept turning to the former manager for advice and decisions. Taking advantage of the fact that people will walk a hundred feet on the same floor, but will not go up twelve steps to the next floor, the former manager's office was moved to a different floor, and the undesired pattern of communications was broken off.

Managements should study the flow and communications patterns in their organizations to identify and understand what affects the information-communication behavior that currently exist between groups. Awareness of the effects of current facilities, and of the arrangements of groups within those facilities, can lead to conscious "tuning" of the patterns of communications. For example, studies of college dormitories showed that the most popular person in the building had the room at the head of the stairs plus or minus one room. A manager who took over as CEO of a company experiencing a great deal of legal and organizational trauma deliberately located himself in the office facing the elevators that opened on the executive offices floor. Not even his secretary buffered him from whoever came or went by the elevator. He soon was accepted by the managers and professionals of the organization and harvested valuable exchanges early in his tenure which helped him turn the company around.

Task forces and special groups. Locate task forces or special groups that have a specific task and a given deadline within the same space. A common "bull pen" is the most effective physical arrangement for such a group. The "bull pen" arrangement allows for the greatest and richest exchange between the people in the room. Though no one prefers the "bull pen" to separate offices, the evidence is that it results in rich informal exchange among professionals.

Think spaces. There is also need for facilities where one cannot be interrupted and where exchanges are minimized. Think spaces are needed for limited but intense periods of work on a final report or publication or a design presentation, particularly where deadlines are involved. Data on how professionals spend their time show that they are interrupted every twenty to thirty minutes. To get a report done, a professional or manager "hides out" from the office, either at home or in some place that only a secretary or a close family member knows about. A few organizations recognize this need for protected spaces for limited periods and set facilities aside that can be reserved by a professional when necessary. Usually such facilities are made consciously inaccessible to others when in use. They have no telephones and are places where the professional can bring and leave materials during the time of occupation. Such facilities often are equipped with plenty of surfaces to spread out on (including cork or metal walls with magnets), drafting tables, computer terminals, and shelving.

Improve information transmission. Successful professional work is not just a function of the value of the solution to a problem, the elegance of a design, or the proof of an exciting hypothesis. Full success entails that the valuable solution be accepted, the elegant design be recognized and bought, and the proof be seen and accepted. Much of the value of good professional work can be lost through ineffective transmission of its results. A major problem for many professionals in larger organizations is to get others in the organization to be interested in, and accept, their efforts and outputs.

The manager can apply the data on information-communication behavior to improve the effectiveness of the transmission of information in activities such as proposal writing, data presentations, and dealing with clients, suppliers, and important third parties such as bankers and government officials. Transmission is successful when the results are seen, understood, accepted, and leave the recipient with a continuing good relationship with the sources of the information (a guarantee of positive future exchanges). For example, R & D people who develop frequent, informal exchanges with the company's marketing people are far more likely to see their work accepted (as well as avoid market disasters through what they learn from the marketing people). All the managerial actions suggested for increasing the flow of information in an organization apply to transmission to other organizations.

Where there are continuing exchanges. When continuing exchanges over time are anticipated, as in the case of relationships between different departments of a larger organization (e.g., R & D and marketing, advertising and production) or between professional organization and client, a manager should:

Establish and increase the number of face-to-face exchanges
    between people in the different groups
Encourage telephone communications
Provide opportunities for informal exchanges

For increased acceptance. The effects of source characteristics, such as credibility and attractiveness, on the acceptance of information should be designed into important formal and information transmission efforts. The effects of credibility are recognized in practice, consciously or unconsciously, by many: by writers, when they add an authority as co-author to a submitted manuscript, thereby raising the probability of favorable reviews by their peers and subsequent publication, and by organizations, when they add a major authority to a project proposal to raise the probability that the project will be accepted.

5

Technical Obsolescence, Burnout, and Staying Alive

THE EXPRESSIONS "professional obsolescence" and "technical obsolescence" are used to describe the state of knowledge and abilities of individuals. What is an obsolete or obsolescent person? According to the dictionary, something obsolete is no longer in use or is of a style or kind no longer in use. People are not obsolete. They are the most flexible resource available to us, and it does harm to consider them no longer to be of use or out of style unless we are referring to physical form: e.g., fat is out of style. What is at issue here is a state of knowledge and/or skills that affect an individual's ability to perform well in professional work.

There is no commonly accepted definition of professional and technical obsolescence. The many available definitions include the following: (1) ineffectiveness on the job, (2) lack of new knowledge or skills, (3) a failure to keep abreast of what is going on, and (4) lack of the knowledge and skill that may be required for future jobs.

All these definitions include the idea of a reduction in effective or efficient job performance over time due to discrepancies between job needs and professional capabilities. One view is that professional or managerial obsolescence takes place when the discrepancy between job needs and performance results from innovations in the field or when, for whatever reason, the skills and knowledge of the manager or professional are insufficient for the job (Burack & Patti, 1970). According to a second definition, professional obsolescence is the failure of a once-capable professional to achieve results currently expected of him or her. Another view holds that professional obsolescence is a reduction in technical effectiveness due to a lack of knowledge of new technologies and techniques developed since the individual's education (Dubin, 1972). Another view includes all of the foregoing along with the inability to perform future work as well (Kaufman, 1974). Consideration of the future implies that a professional may be doing an adequate job today but is obsolescent unless acquiring the knowledge that may be needed for future work.

The "lack of new knowledge or skills" definition assumes that, unless acquiring or in possession of new knowledge or skills, an individual is professionally obsolescent. Of course, many examples can be thought of where new methods and techniques have not proven out, and where there is a return to old methods that work well. The widespread concern with the Japanese "miracle" has led to the rediscovery of what was taught to the Japanese by Americans who no longer use those techniques. The Japanese use of quality control, worker participation, and production methods that minimize inventory are not new but, rather, represent the use and refinement of classical American industrial techniques that date back to the 1930s and 1940s.

Linked to the lack of new knowledge or skill is the failure to keep abreast of what is going on. In this vein, one suggested measure of professional obsolescence (or incompetence) borrowed from physics is the "half-life of knowledge," defined as "the time after completion of training when, because of new developments, practicing professionals have become roughly half as competent as they were upon graduation to meet the demands of their profession" (Dubin, 1972). Dubin estimated the half-life for psychologists to be ten to eleven years on the average, with a range of five to twenty years, and quoted estimates of other half-lifes: for physicians and engineers, for example, five years.

Plausible as it sounds, the "failure to keep abreast" definition of obsolescence raises serious problems. Keeping abreast of what, and going on where? How is half-life determined, and how is it related to ineffectiveness in the work place? The "where" things are going on that determines obsolescence in the failure-to-keep-abreast version is academia. Measures of this kind of obsolescence have been based on the numbers of publications that have appeared since training and on course offerings, additions, and deletions in the catalogs of five engineering colleges at five-year intervals (Zellikoff, 1969). Course offering changes were used to develop "erosion curves" of applicable knowledge an erosion curve is determined by the year of graduation and the subsequent change in courses.

The "failure to keep abreast" definition of obsolescence assumes that what is being published and taught by academics is necessarily applicable and crucial to professional performance. The assumption is open to question. There is serious doubt that the bulk of what is published is necessarily good and, if good, applicable. The rate of publication is more a product of the "publish or perish" syndrome that drives the more than 350,000 faculty members in American colleges and universities than it is of the expansion of knowledge. According to Dubin (1972), a professional would have to spend 20% of working time to keep abreast. Dubin also quotes a leading engineering psychologist who estimated that "a compulsive, well-versed engineering psychologist would have to read thirty to forty articles, books, theses, and technical reports every day of the year to merely keep abreast of the current literature." In other fields with higher rates of publication, the time demand would be greater. No working professional can possibly keep up with this outpouring of publications, nor does it seem to be necessary.

It would be difficult to defend the argument that course offerings are an index of applicable knowledge. In many of the most advanced fields practice is ahead of scholarship, and academics argue that it is necessary for them to consult with industry to keep up with their fields. A study of the ratings of scientists and engineers in an industrial laboratory (Oberg, 1960), found that those under thirty years of age (those with the most recent education) were rated as contributing least to their laboratory.

As was shown in Chapter 4 ("Managing Information"), professionals obtain most of their information from personal sources and through informal channels, not through the literature. A study that tracked the flow of information by means of radio, TV, newspapers, magazines, books, and point-to-point communications (i.e., first class mail, mailgram, facsimile, telex, and telephone), calculated that between 1960 and 1977 the number of words supplied to Americans grew at the rate of 8.9% per year, but that the words consumed went up only at the rate of 2.9% per year. The point-to-point media (person to person communications) were most productive, and the data show that people were willing to spend much more per-word-transmitted in these media (Poole, 1983). The productivity of person-to-person communications vs. print media would have been even more pronounced if the study had included the richest of all communications media—informal, face-to-face conversations.

All the measures of obsolescence used have elements of plausibility, but none hold up to serious examination. The concept of professional obsolescence is too vague. It is difficult to define what is to be measured, the dimensions to use, and the validity and reliability of the measures. How can we determine a standard of performance against which we will measure an individual? The definitions of professional obsolescence all include some statement about performance not being what it should be. How do we determine what it should be? How do we tease out the input of the individual from all of the other factors influencing productivity? What new knowledge should the professional have not to be obsolescent? How do we know which techniques and knowledge, of all that is churned out, are relevant and effective?

Managers assume that there is something to the notion of decrements of performance with time. They intuit that they can do something about preventing or ameliorating those decrements by taking some actions. When we stand back from the narrow focus imposed by the limited notions of "professional obsolescence," however, it is possible to discern a larger question that includes plateauing, burnout, and middle age crisis. We become aware of the more pervasive problems of adult growth, development, and aging. The more useful question becomes, how can we help both the professionals who work for us and ourselves as individuals stay intellectually and professionally alive throughout our working lives? Surely the answer is not to allot 20% or 50% of our time to a desperate ingestion of everything published in the fields of our interest.

POSSIBLE CAUSES OF OBSOLESCENCE

What might cause obsolescence? Is obsolescence inherent, a matter of time and age, of some inexorable accumulation of physiological, sociological, and psychological fat that cannot be avoided? Is obsolescence induced by physiolological deterioration? Is it genetic? Is it a result of social, psychological, or motivational factors that include burnout?

Age and Performance

Research shows little uniform deterioration with time, and, though many older workers stop developing, it is not possible to attribute obsolescence solely or primarily to aging. Some people stay professionally and intellectually alive and keep developing throughout their careers. As a consequence of the many myths about age and professional performance, inaccurate assumptions are made about older workers that lead to costly and harmful managerial practices. Only limited efforts are made to maintain the professional capabilities of the older worker, on the assumption that the effort is wasted. Older professionals are overlooked for the kinds of assignments that lead to growth and professional development.

One of the most widespread assumptions about age and performance is that peak intellectual and professional performance is achieved by about age thirty-five, with steady deterioration thereafter. The assumption has drawn much of its sustenance from studies using historical evidence on the "greats" of all time. A twenty-year study was made by Lehman (1953) of creative achievement by scientists (in both abstract and applied disciplines), philosophers, and composers. Lehman asked experts to identify the greatest achievements in their fields, and then plotted the age of the responsible individual at the time of his great achievement. He concluded that achievement peaked in the late thirties to early forties.

There are reasons to doubt whether the conclusion reached by Lehman is valid today. Lehman studied the greatest creators of all time, and therefore most of his subjects lived in times of short life expectancy. Mozart and Schubert died in their thirties: what would they have accomplished if they had lived longer? Beethoven, who lived into his fifties, composed his greatest works in the last years of his life. Another question is whether the accomplishments of the very great, those bordering on genius, are relevant to the work of the great bulk of professional and creative people. In fact, when Lehman studied a larger number of lesser contributions he found that their production continued over a far longer age span.

Cross-sectional studies of the productivity of scientists and engineers in relation to their age (Pelz & Andrews, 1976) found a saddle-shaped curve with two peaks of productivity, one in the mid-forties and one in the mid-fifties! The two-peaked curve is interesting in that there appears to be a sharp drop in productivity in the late forties followed by a sharp return to productivity. Research has shown there is no physiological basis for the drop. It is apparently the result of social and emotional factors,—what is now referred to as the mid-life crisis. At this age, a professional or manager has been working for over twenty years and suddenly realizes that a fiftieth birthday is looming. It is a time of taking account of what one has done, where one is, and where one is going. It is a very sobering and restless time in the lives of many professionals and managers, a time when many drop everything to "find themselves." The drop in productivity may be good evidence that the late forties is a critical time for many professional workers. Happily, according to the data, the drop in productivity passes (or else those who are seriously affected leave).

A study of age and the "relative value" of over nine hundred technical professional employees in an industrial laboratory (Oberg, 1960) also found a two-peaked curve, with the second peak occurring in the late fifties. In a first round of studies, using the laboratory's evaluation results, Oberg found the ages associated with highest relative value were thirty-six to forty years of age, followed by fifty-six to sixty years of age. The professionals under thirty years old received the lowest ratings. The first round was questioned because it included supervisors in the total population studied, and it was suggested that the supervisors would tend to raise the average age of those judged to have highest relative value. The data was reanalyzed, excluding supervisors, and as can be seen from Table 5–1, the age of those with the highest ratings went up instead of down: those fifty-six to sixty were first, followed by a tie between those fifty-one to fifty-five and those thirty-six to forty. There was a difference between the technical professionals in R & D and the engineers, with the most valued engineers tending to be older.

It is important to realize that most studies of age vs. performance, as measured by a variety of psychological instruments,

TABLE 5–1
Most Valued Professional by Age

	Most Valued	Next in Value
All professionals	36–40	56–60
Excluding managers	56–60	51–55 & 36–40
R & D professionals	31–35	36–40 & 51–55
Engineers	56–60 & 51–55	41–45 & 36–40

Source: From Oberg (1960).

are based on cross-sectional studies. It should be remembered that cross-sectional methods measure different age groups at the same point in time while longitudinal studies measure what happens to an age group at different periods through time. In study comparing age vs. performance, using a battery of psychological instruments which included both cross-sectional and longitudinal methods (Schaie & Strother, 1968), the longitudinal studies showed far less decrement in performance with age over time than did the cross-sectional studies.

The Schaie & Strother study demonstrates little decrement in basic intellectual capabilities with age, and suggests that the causes of technical obsolescence will be found elsewhere. In recent years, the records of performance of such great figures in the world of the arts as Picasso, Chagall, Jacques Lipchitz, Georgia O'Keeffe, and Pablo Casals have helped change the general perception of performance and age. A Japanese scholar has developed curves of human physical and intellectual capabilities that identify the different ages at which specific kinds of capabilities peak. He defines an envelope of curves bounded by an upper curve of those who function well and a lower curve of those whose capabilities decline early in life. On the higher performance curve of intellectual capabilities, memory is shown as peaking early, by the twenties. Mathematics peaks early, too, as everyone familiar with the world of mathematics would agree. Great mathematicians usually appear in their early twenties. One either is or is not a great mathematician, and thirty years of experience will not transform an average mathematician into a great one. The curve shows music as peaking early, too, and there is some evidence that music and mathematics are almost inborn talents. Engineering, management, architecture, and design peak in the mid-forties. The curve also shows that a quality labelled "judgment" peaks in the sixties and stays high until the eighties. Judgment might be defined as knowing where to put one's effort, where to make a stand, what is important, and what is not. In most professional fields experience makes a difference, and an intelligent, alert, older professional can give better performance than an intelligent, alert, younger professional.

Physiology and Obsolescence

Can professional obsolescence be linked to physiological changes? For almost every physiological and psychological variable (measured in large groups of people) the highest average value is found between ages twenty and thirty, with a steady, linear decline thereafter. What is masked by average results for large groups is the amount of variability around the averages (Fries & Crapo, 1981). When it comes to age vs. performance, there is a great deal of variability, demonstrating that chronological age is not a good measure of aging. Individuals age at very different rates.

The data are also influenced by the higher incidence of illness with age. Much of the functional decrement attributable to illness is hidden by the aggregate statistics. Attention has already been called to the inaccuracies introduced by the use of cross-sectional rather than longitudinal data. Some longitudinal data have shown actual improvements in performance with age (Nesselrode et al., 1972).

Because of the variability in human attributes with age, Fries and Crapo (1981) propose the notion of "plasticity," that the future capability for a given attribute is not fixed and inevitable but may be modified. They write, "We may anticipate success, [in human attribute] in some instances and lack of success in others. Given our present knowledge we cannot be certain of all the areas where improvement is impossible." They further suggest that positive changes can be effected by eliminating the variability caused by disease, taking advantage of favorable changes that are occurring to an entire age group, and/or improving the individual with time.

There is some intriguing evidence that the external environment may have a large role in determining whether brain cells are maintained during aging (Diamond, 1978). Some data suggest that mammalian brain development can result from environmental stimulation even in advanced age. It has been found, in experiments with laboratory animals, that when litter mates were separated into three different environments—standard, enriched and improverished—those raised in the rich environment had thicker and heavier cerebral cortexes (that part of the brain responsible for the highest brain functions) and showed more brain growth compared with those raised in the impoverished environments. This may indicate that the brain of humans can be maintained and even regenerated through physical and mental stimuli (Pelletier, 1981). What seems clear is that lively, rich environments can play an important role in maintaining the physiological capabilities related to intellectual, and thus professional, capacity.

Studies of performance vs. age and of the effects of the environment on the physiological capabilities associated with higher brain functions lead to a number of salient conclusions with regard to technical obsolescence and its management:

1. Though there appear to be some physiologically caused decrements in physical performance with age, such as muscle strength and motor speed, there is no convincing evidence of a physiologically necessary decrement in intellectual performance.
2. There is very wide individual variability when it comes to age and performance, and it is almost impossible to predict physiologically based individual capability solely on the basis of chronological age.
3. Illness is a major cause of decrements in performance with age, since there is a higher incidence of illness with age.
4. There appears to be a long-term, significant interaction between the kind of environment in which an individual lives and works and some of the work-related physiological capacities of that individual.

Sociological Explanations of Professional Obsolescence

Social pressures are serious contributors to professional obsolescence. One of the ironies of professional life is that success often leads to obsolescence, and the greater the professional success of the individual the greater the difficulty encountered in trying to do the things that keep one professionally alive. For example, a surgeon becomes noted because of knowledge, skills, and publications in his or her particular subfield of surgery (e.g., a particular cardiovascular procedure). Recognition brings with it many kinds of positive returns: invitations to speak at professional meetings, more demand for one's professional services, higher fees, promotions, and a large number of callers who provide the most flattering of feedback. For a research professional, success can mean the kind of power that comes with command of a laboratory, the budget and staff that goes with it, and election to prestigious positions in professional associations.

Once success has been achieved, many people find it socially difficult to do the things that keep them alive professionally. They perceive a risk to their professional status in undertaking something new and different that might not succeed. Many feel embarrassment in being seen taking a class to learn some new skill or technique, such as computer programming, (particularly when they are in a position to hire the possessors of such skills). The perceptions of risk and possible embarrassment are reinforced by the social environment and by actual threat of sanctions. One noted Nobel laureate informally confided to a group of listeners that every time he thought of trying something in a quite different field from his own, everyone would look at him with shocked surprise. The common response was, "But you can't do that! You're Dr. So-and-so, the Nobel laureate!"

In the organizational situation, there are many built-in incentives to avoid risks that go with doing the things that maintain intellectual growth. It is in the short-term interests of an organization to keep a successful professional doing what he or she has already been successful at, rather than to provide new and challenging opportunities. In preparing proposals for grants or research contracts, an organization claims distinction on the basis of the successful past performance of its best professionals, and, in effect, promises that those professionals will do the same kinds of things if funded. There is little competitive advantage in suggesting that someone will be used in a field in which he or she hasn't had extensive experience. Where a very competent professional is promoted into a managerial position, he or she often cannot develop professionally without an actual loss of position and status. In a research laboratory, the successful professional who is now director finds it almost impossible ever to get to a laboratory bench. The demands of administration, of going to meetings within the organization, of participating in conferences in interesting countries throughout the world, or of being chosen for special government panels—as well as the gratification to the ego—leave little time for the growth that can come only through doing the work of the profession.

Burnout

One possible root of technological obsolescence in some professionals is so-called burnout. "Burnout" has been used as an omnibus term to include everything from serious emotional difficulties arising from work of a highly traumatic nature, to simple boredom, to the loss of "idealism" experienced by social workers on their intitial encounter with the realities of working life. Realistically, the term "burnout"—that is, the loss of the capacity to function due to an overloading of one's emotional circuits—is applicable to very few professional activities and situations. Jobs that lead to burnout are those that regularly place a professional under extremes of emotional stress or demand. Burnout, in this sense, is a problem of maintaining human resources, and personal or managerial intervention is required if the individuals engaged in such activities are to be able to function through time or to remain in their professions.

There is evidence that nurses who work with the most extreme cases of mentally deficient children or with the dying do suffer from burnout and must be frequently rotated or replaced if they are to keep working. Other victims of burnout might include reporters on the police beat, health professionals working in emergency rooms, and police in combat. There are, of course, high-stress situations in every profession when there is work to be done under difficult conditions and tough deadlines. However, these pressures occur temporarily and are seldom frequent enough or of long enough duration to be a major professional problem.

Midcareer Crisis

A common phenomenon that can be termed "midlife transition" affects a large percentage of the U.S. population. Many refer to the midlife transition experience as the "midlife crisis," or, from the work viewpoint, the "midcareer crisis." Midlife transition, whether or not seen as a crisis, is a period of personal examination and appraisal of oneself and one's situation heightened by a realization of aging and mortality. The onset of the midlife transition phenomenon comes from many different sources: graying of hair, appearance of wrinkles, significant birthdays such as the fortieth or fiftieth, and the onset of grandparenthood. A special case is the mother and housewife whose children have left home and who experiences the "empty nest syndrome." Midlife transition is a turbulent experience in which the individual takes stock of where he or she has been and is going. The individual often experiences serious discords internally and externally.

One study of adult development (Levinson & Darrow, 1978) found that approximately 80% of the men studied experienced some form of midlife crisis (there were no women in the study). Few go through the period smoothly and without crisis. In some cases the response to this period is extreme. Some respond to midlife crises by "dropping out": they change careers, go back to school, join the ministry, get divorced and remarry, even commit suicide. Most go through the experience making many kinds of adjustments. Evidence of the crisis and recovery are found in the two-peak curves of performance of scientists and engineers described above. On average, for the professional worker, the "crisis" and subsequent decline in performance occur somewhere between the ages of forty-five and fifty-five.

Adjustment and recovery typically occurs within five to seven years.

Midlife transition becomes a problem for the manager of professionals when it becomes midlife crisis and affects the ability of an individual to work at full capacity. Awareness of this period of transition helps sensitize the manager to the problems being faced by the professionals going through the experience and prepares the manager to handle its effects on work and the organization. Management can take steps to minimize the negative effects of this tumultuous period of personal transition on both the individual and the firm. By work-related actions such as assignments, changes of function, opportunities for new experiences, and feedback, managers can minimize the drop in performance associated with midlife transition (keeping it from becoming a midlife crisis) and can help the professional who is going through the transition. On a more positive note, the fact that midlife transition is a period of personal evaluation and stock-taking makes it an ideal time to work with the individual to achieve major advances in personal professional development. The act of personal stock-taking makes it a time when the individual may be most open to change.

Summary

The maintenance of human resources is important in the management of professionals. The condition and future capabilities of its professionals must be a matter of concern to managers unless the organization has a life expectancy of one project. It is obvious that professionals are the key resource in professional work and their skills and knowledge determine whether an organization will get work and whether the work is successful.

The Age Discrimination in Employment Act of 1967 and long-term demographic trends have already determined that management will have no choice but to come to grips with the issue of older professionals. The professional work force will include a growing percentage of older professionals, and it is legally difficult to fire them. Thus, management has a vested interest in making sure that the younger professional becomes the productive older professional and that the older professional remains highly productive.

From a human point of view we must be concerned with keeping professionals productive throughout their working lifetime. Employers cannot ethically justify profiting from the most productive years of individuals and then getting rid of them. From a personal point of view every professional and manager has a vital interest in staying alive intellectually and professionally. If management does not take the initiative in professional development, the individual professional ought to take charge of his or her own personal and professional development. And whatever managers do for others with regard to staying alive professionally is something that they should be doing for themselves.

MAINTAINING HUMAN RESOURCES

Each professional worker represents a sizable investment by an organization. The hard, measurable costs of hiring and orienting a professional for an organization have been estimated to be on the order of $20,000–$30,000, and the hard costs fall short of realistic total costs. The hard costs don't include management time, the time of colleagues who help orient the newcomer to the organization, and all the other elements that go into a newcomer's learning curve. Over time, the total investment in a professional's competence in terms of experience, management, formal, and informal education is very large.

It is impossible to assign a cost figure to the special competencies required to work well in an organization. Even for the professional, skilled in communications and interpersonal relationships, it still takes at least a year to reach a full-tilt level of performance. Company-related skills are an amalgam of knowing who to talk to get things done, why things are done a certain way, what the social and political relationships that go beyond the organization chart are, and all that goes into what is now called "the corporate culture"—the social, business, and political values held strongly in the organization and the acceptable boundaries of social and work behavior.

The full replacement costs for a competent, experienced, long-term professional employee are incalculable. Despite the large investments made in professional workers, and despite the fact that they are the primary resource in professional activities, organizations let their human resources run down, become technically obsolete, or burn out. With equipment, organizations are very conscious of the investment made. Equipment is accounted for, carefully tended, maintained, oiled, polished, cleaned, and, where possible, updated. Preventive maintenance is practiced to keep equipment from faulty performance or breakdown. Management would quickly reprimand or replace someone who abused the equipment. Human resources are not given the same level of care and attention.

Organizations expend much effort on "personnel" or "human resources" with a view to evoking a higher current output, but only limited efforts are expended on the maintenance of capacity through time. Despite the abundance of training and development programs offered by organizations, they are seldom taken as seriously as equipment maintenance programs. There are no well-trained, well-equipped, round-the-clock human maintenance crews ready to respond to incipient problems. There are few instances of serious, data-based preventive maintenance efforts when it comes to the work-related (as opposed to emotional) needs of human resources. Organizations are ready to deal, in a repair sense, with such problems as drug addiction, alcoholism, and emotional breakdown, but much less ready to do repair on work capabilities. The work-related capability problems labeled "obsolescence," "plateauing," and "burnout" are handled by getting rid of the individuals, by counseling them through critical performance evaluations (and zero or small pay increases), or by avoidance. The plateaued senior professional is an embarrassment to management, and a cause of discomfort: "He's been here fifteen years, and he used to do very good work. What can we do with him?"

Dimensions of the Human Resource Maintenance Problem

The problem of maintenance of professional human resources is large and growing sharply in size and importance. The problem has economic, legal, and personal dimensions. The marketing of professional work is first a function of quality and ability to deliver, and second, of costs. In professional activities, the capabilities of the professional workers make the difference between success and failure and determine the competitive position of the organization. The capabilities, experience, and reputations of the professional people in an organization determine whether it will even be considered for research and development, design, medical, and educational work. Costs become an issue only when the price is beyond some given threshold.

Maintaining and improving the abilities of its professionals can make a significant difference in the productivity of an organization. In large organizations, decrements in individual performance are often not noted until they are serious. An aggregation of minor decrements can keep an organization from realizing its optimum performance. Managements respond slowly to decrements in the performance of their people. Since professional work is not a matter of discrete, measurable, daily output, it often takes time to realize that performance has been going down.

The legal dimension has brought the maintenance of human resources to a new level of serious consideration. Organizations will have more older workers in their work forces, and they will stay longer than in the past. Consequently, it makes sense to ensure that professionals in the work force maintain and improve their abilities throughout their careers. The Age Discrimination in Employment Act of 1967 which extended mandatory retirement in the private sector to age 70 as of 1979 has revolutionized industrial retirement policies. Today in the United States, managements must realize that a large percentage of all workers will continue to work beyond age 65, the percentage of the work force in the over-65 bracket is already increasing rapidly. It can be tougher to justify firing someone who is over 65 than someone who is a woman or in a minority group. When it comes to professional workers all of the problems are amplified since professional workers opt to keep working more often than others. The percentage of professional workers over age 65 is going up more rapidly than the age of other workers, and it may be tougher legally to make a case for firing a professional than a blue-collar or white-collar worker.

The demographic trends in the United States are clear. In 1955, average life expectancy was 69.6 years of age. In 1980, life expectancy had gone up to 73.6 years of age (Hacker, 1983). Between 1968 and 1980, the total number of people over 65 years of age climbed from 16,559,580 to 25,544,133, a rise of 54.3%. By the year 2000, it is estimated that the over-65 group will represent about 20% of the population. The 65+ age group will number well over 45 million by 1990, and the number of people 65 or older who are eligible to work will rise to approximately 30,000,000.

Naturally, the death rate for older people is higher, and not all of them will want to continue working. However, even with regard to death rates and voluntary work rates, the numbers are changing in directions that mean more older workers, particularly professionals, will remain in the work force. Though the death rate for those over 65 is relatively high, it is dropping. Between 1970 and 1980, the death rate for those between 65 and 74 dropped from 37 to 30 per thousand, and the death rate for those between 65 and 69 was 24.6. There has been a general assumption that most workers, given the chance to retire, would happily opt out, and the statistics tend to support that idea. In 1960, 81% of men between 60 and 64 were in the labor force, and by 1979 it was only 62%. For women the equivalent numbers were 31% and 34%. Here, too, the numbers are changing.

The numbers representing those 65 and older in the labor force before 1980 do not reflect the effects of the Age Discrimination Act which began to apply in 1979, or of the cuts in Social Security benefits for early retirees, or of the tendency for people in higher occupational levels to want to continue working. A picture of the effect the opportunity to continue working has on decisions of the older worker can be obtained from the experiences of companies that suspended mandatory retirement before the act was passed (Thompson, 1979). Sears, Roebuck suspended mandatory retirement in 1978, and, to the surprise of management, 77% of the salaried and 60.6% of the hourly workers stayed on. In 1976 Polaroid suspended mandatory retirement, and by 1978 70% decided to continue working. Note that salaried employees stayed on at a higher rate than hourly workers. There is also some indication that more productive people opt to stay on. In 1979, Polaroid's corporate retirement administrator observed that retirement is a very self-selective process. Those with health or performance problems wanted to leave. Those who were productive were likely to stay, and their absentee rate was almost half the corporate average. A survey of 3,800 top executives of major companies who had retired between 1961 and 1976 found that half continued to work: 17% at paying jobs, 11% at paid volunteer jobs, and 22% at nonpaying volunteer jobs (Wikstrom, 1978).

The human dimension has several aspects. The worker who has plateaued, to whom work is not a positive experience anymore, is a burden to the organization, has stopped growing as an individual, and is often a problem for his or her family. The plateaued worker stops contributing to others in the organization, and becomes isolated from the professional exchanges flowing through the informal social-professional circles in and outside the organization. The negative effects are cumulative and compounded. The less the individual is included in professional exchanges, the less he or she contributes, the fewer the exchanges and so on. The plateaued individual often has a negative effect on the expectations of newcomers, and tends to be the cynical counterpoint to every effort to do something new in the organization. Perhaps one of the most poignant problems facing a manager of professionals is the plateaued individual. Few start out on a plateau. The majority of workers begin with high hopes and expectations. Somewhere along the line, the expectations and hopes disappear for the plateaued worker. It is a challenge for management to keep workers from plateauing, and to renew the growth of those who have plateaued.

The phenomenon labeled "burnout" is a special aspect of the human resources maintenance problem. Burnout refers to a process in which the professional's attitudes and behavior change in negative ways in response to job stress (Cherniss, 1980). Much has been written about stress and its causes, effects, and management. There is evidence that unmanaged stress can have deleterious effects on health, and certainly health affects performance. The term "burnout" has been used widely to describe a variety of phenomena including boredom, middle-age crisis, and serious emotional exhaustion that results from working in highly stressful or depressing jobs. The subject is included here because many of the managerial considerations and actions that apply to technological obsolescence pertain to the non-physchopathological aspects of burnout.

Maintenance of professional capabilities is not just a concern for organizations that hire professionals. It is also a personal question for the individual professional and manager. Each of us is faced with the problem of keeping alive professionally and intellectually, and of finding ways to maintain a personal interest in the world of ideas and work.

What the Manager Can Do About Professional Obsolescence

Definitions of professional obsolescence vary, and some make little sense, but the underlying idea of a need to maintain professional effectiveness is sound. Serious questions are raised by the available evidence about inherent decrements of performance with age or about the physiological basis for obsolescence. The results of many studies show that a substantial amount of what we call professional obsolescence may be socially induced and managable. It is reasonable to suggest that there are many things that managements can do to prevent or even reverse what is called professional obsolescence.

In all managerial functions there are elements, from hiring and firing to retirement, that can be used to achieve and maintain the capabilities of an organization's professionals. Much of what maintains professional capabilities throughout a working career is identical with what is required to achieve high performance in the short run. A management that is aware of what is needed and what is possible for maintenance of professional capabilities throughout a working career can design its functions to serve both the short run and the long run simultaneously.

First, management must take an overall viewpoint not based on the assumption that performance declines inexorably with age and that older workers are to be tolerated, not used. Management can provide (1) good hiring that includes consideration of the long run, (2) appropriate motivation, reward, and incentive structures that reinforce work behaviors leading to high performance in the long run, (3) policies, planning, and procedures that provide diversity, (4) an environment that is lively and enriching, and (5) health maintenance programs and incentives that help assure continued high performance (and lower insurance costs).

Hiring. Management can start by hiring the kinds of people that are least likely to become professionally obsolete. Some of the clues to who is least likely to become obsolete have already been given in our discussions of hiring and information-communication behavior:

1. *Performance persists.* Individuals who are high performers tend to remain high performers, and high-performing individuals tend to take care of their own professional development. The best indication that someone will not become professionally obsolete is a past record of continuing high performance over time. In addition, a record of good personal responses to life events strongly indicate an ability to adjust to changes. Individuals who are healthy emotionally tend to remain so through life, and "adjust their personalities and values to reflect changes throughout the life cycle," (Casady, 1975).

2. *Generalists outlast specialists.* The odds are in favor of the competent generalist (with at least one area of special competence) over the competent specialist when it comes to remaining professionally useful over time. Professional obsolescence comes most disastrously when a field changes radically. Specialists can always be used as consultants, and as the profession

changes so can your repertoire of consultants. The generalist will most easily adjust to a shift in a profession.

3. *High communicators are more likely to remain current in their profession than others.* The high communicator reads more and reads more widely than others, and is constantly in communication with others in a wide variety of social-professional networks. The high communicator functions by being aware, and keeping others aware, of what is going on in his or her fields of interest.

A picture of what the individual should be like in the last part of a professional career helps us put hiring and subsequent human resource maintenance activities into perspective. By characterizing the capable, productive, lively, older individual it is possible to obtain a model to work toward with others and for oneself. Think of the most lively older professional (or just older person) you can remember: what characterized that individual? In characterizing the competent older professional you probably will include most of the following in your list:

1. *A future orientation:* looking forward to what is going to happen rather than to the past
2. *Optimism:* a positive feeling about making things work rather than a firm conviction that nothing will work
3. *Curiosity:* a strong interest in many things and in new things, and a curiosity expressed both by reading and talking to many people
4. *Humor:* an ability to laugh at things including oneself
5. *Energy and activity:* a high level of energy, and probably good health
6. *Diversity:* working and interested in a wide range of things

It would be worthwhile, at the time of hiring, to look at a potential hire and try to visualize that person in midcareer and in late career. Can that individual be seen as having, or being likely to gain the characteristics associated with the productive older professional?

The characteristics most desirable in any hire are those that have the highest probability of assuring long-term development: good past performance, a positive, optimistic outlook on life, a broad-based set of professional interests, and positive information-communication habits.

Motivation, rewards, and incentives. The formal and informal personnel feedback systems should deliberately reinforce activities that maintain professional vitality. The formal systems should be designed to reward risk-taking (or at least not to penalize the taking of risks), especially among younger professionals. If failed efforts are penalized severely, the organization will lose those it should be keeping, and reinforce the propensity to avoid new approaches among those who remain. Individuals should be reinforced in their efforts to try fields or techniques new to them.

Positive reinforcement should also be given for the information-communication behavior that enhances the individual and the organization: reading, attending conferences, taking courses, and transmitting information to others. The incentive system should include incentives that reward good professional performance with development opportunities such as study trips, courses (perhaps a chance to get an advanced degree), personal subscriptions to professional journals, professional society dues, and trips to professional conferences.

The informal feedback system is even more important than the formal system. The formal system can make explicit what the organization values. A formal review system can explicitly give points for innovative behavior or for desirable information-communication behavior. However, it is management, especially the first-line manager, that is most effective in determining how the formal system works operationally. It is the first-line manager who provides the vital, daily feedback which most affects work behavior. Making the first-line manager aware of an overall organizational interest in the long-term development of its professionals is the first step, and can be accomplished by making the maintenance function a key part of the manager's formal and informal evaluation and incentive system. Typically, first-line managers tend to restrict themselves to a short-term perspective on performance except when it comes to promotions, and it takes explicit and consistent emphasis by top management to change this perspective.

Even without the prodding of higher management and the formal evaluation system for managers, the thoughtful manager can provide informal feedback that encourages the younger professional to try new things, to read, to explore new ideas. By judicious use of work assignments, the manager can diversify the experiences of all the professionals for whom he or she is responsible. Sometimes, in providing diverse work assignments for the professionals, a manager must consciously take the risk that someone else who has been doing the kind of work assigned for a long time might do it better, on the grounds that the longer term effects will be better for both professionals.

The youngest professionals should be encouraged to develop at least one or more areas of special competence, but the professionals in their thirties should be encouraged to broaden their field of professional interests. It is critical to help the professional who is in the thirties develop a desire and ability for self-direction and self-confidence in undertaking professional risks. If professionals have not developed those abilities and feelings by the time they reach their forties, it is very difficult, if not impossible, to develop them at that time.

From a maintenance viewpoint, performance evaluation is a monitoring system for professional obsolescence that should be used to trigger managerial actions. High performers should be provided support for what they are already doing to maintain their own professional capabilities: a budget for development, an unlimited publications budget, a portion of self-determined time. The persistent low performers should be moved. If they have always been low performers they should be fired and provided with outplacement counseling. The low performer who has performed well in the past is worth taking some time to examine. In some cases, the decline in performance may be due to something in the individual's personal life that has nothing to do with work. In other cases, it may be simply a case of boredom or midlife transition. If the latter is true, low performance may be overcome by moving the individual to a different group, giving that person a new and very different assignment, or shifting him or her to an entirely different kind of function (e.g., from basic to applied research, from operational activities to analysis, from design to testing).

It is the middle performer who should receive the most maintenance effort. The middle performer has the highest propensity to shift in level of performance, and the shift can be upward or downward. The focus should be on helping those evaluated as middle performers to develop a long-term outlook on their own development. Those in their thirties should be encouraged to undertake a program of courses or to obtain an advanced degree. Most attention should be paid to the individuals who have been with the organization for three or more years. They are most likely to stay, and an investment in them is most likely to be retained by the organization.

An enriching environment. As was already pointed out, on the basis of animal experiments, an enriched environment may have positive effects on the development of higher brain functions. Extrapolating to the work situation, it can reasonably be claimed that an enriched work environment is important to the maintenance and growth of professionals. Management can enrich the work environment in many ways.

The work environment is the sum total of the physical, social, and cultural elements in the work situation to which an individual is responsive. The environment includes formal elements such as the organization's policies, administrative systems and procedures, and the organization's formal organization structure. The informal elements include the organization's culture and its informal organization. An organization's culture affects the patterns of behavior of the people in the organization, and determines the way things are done. The informal organization includes the relationships between people which fall outside the formal organization chart, and which influence what gets done and the way it gets done within the organization. Management has direct control of the formal elements in the work environment, and can have a significant influence on some of the informal elements.

It is important to develop an organizational climate that will enhance the self-confidence of the professionals and their willingness and ability to take chances professionally. Policies and procedures that penalize risk, that do not include the professional in the decision-making process, and that make it difficult to get support for anything new and different will drive away the high performers, prevent the development of risk-takers among the younger professionals, and attract and retain those who are threatened by change.

Management policies should include consideration of the long-run development of professional workers, and can be expressed in the organization's administrative systems and procedures. The most important area of policy and procedure should be concerned with encouraging and institutionalizing diversity. Diversity is achieved for the individual by diverse assignments, by having more than one project to work on at a time, by being assigned more than one function to perform, by frequent contact with many kinds of professionals, by travel, by an occasional move to a different group and location, and by a mix or alternation of administration and professional work. Procedurally, management can assure that diversity is encouraged, even required, and certainly not penalized. Some examples of ways to encourage risk-taking (new and diverse experiences) have already been discussed. Many others can be developed in areas such as job rotation, intracorporate moves, and transfers that are thoughtful rather than ham-handed.

The individual manager can do much to influence the informal elements in the office culture by the feedback provided to individuals, by the assignments made, by the people an individual is assigned to work with, by physical location of individuals, and by personal example. The personal example of managers is a primary source informing an individual about the culture of an organization. The manager who is seen reading, taking courses, attending conferences, trying out new things, and taking risks is the strongest signal the individual professional can receive. The top manager who "walks the plant" and who takes a favorable interest in new ideas can increase risk-taking in the organization, and also help the individuals to do those things that lead to personal development.

Health. Health may be the critical *sine qua non* for maintaining an individual's professional ability in the later years of a career. The most important cause of decrements in performance of the older worker is a decline in health. An organization that formally undertakes to enhance the health of its workers has taken a big step toward maintaining professional capabilities for the long run (as well as minimizing its health-related insurance burden). Fortunately, there is a widespread and growing involvement of Americans with health, and encouraging health-related programs is easier today than it once was.

Management should take active steps to encourage health maintenance and enhancement activities by its professional staff. The same kinds of incentives that have been applied to educational programs can be used: partial or complete payment of health programs, intensive health programs, incentives for not smoking and controlling weight, and providing company health facilities.

6

Creativity

A HIGH PREMIUM is placed on creativity in all the professions. It is a compliment to be called a creative scientist, lawyer, advertising person, professor, manager, or market researcher. In the design professions such as architecture, engineering, industrial design, and in the plastic arts, creativity is a prime differentiator between very good and ordinary work. Even in professions that deliver services, like the health professions, it is a compliment to be called a creative surgeon or diagnostician. Only in accounting, and a few other fields, is the term "creative" one of criticism, and only when it refers to someone who finds ways to "creatively" fix the books. Many top managements complain that they need more creativity in their organizations and specify it as something desired in a candidate for hire.

> The reasonable man adapts himself to the world, the unreasonable man adapts the world to himself, therefore, all progress depends on the unreasonable man.
>
> —George Bernard Shaw

The high value placed on creativity throughout society comes from a desire for something akin to magic. Creativity is seen as a special human power that will dissolve difficult problems, generate spectacular ideas and products, break new intellectual ground, and transform lackluster organizations into lively ones. In the popular view a creative person is one who comes up with new and different ideas, designs, theories, and works of art in ways that are not amenable to explanation.

Creativity has fascinated humans from the earliest beginnings of history. It has always been seen as something mysterious, irrational, spontaneous, intuitive. In early history, creativity was openly treated like a form of magic. At times, creativity was seen as divine, partaking of the work of the Creator. At other times, it was seen as superhuman, supernatural, and satanic, and appropriately feared. Today, after almost a hundred years of research on the subject, creativity is still seen by the majority as an infrequent, irregularly distributed, and mysterious human power. For the most part creativity and the creative person are viewed as good for society. The current worldwide infatuation with high technology is a manifestation of the positive, popular view of creativity and the closely associated terms, invention and innovation. Creativity is seen as a means for saving countries from unemployment and cities from stagnation. Corporate executives often see it as a means to increase productivity and profitability.

WHAT IS CREATIVITY?

References to creativity can be found in ancient legends, but systematic research on the subject did not begin until Sir Francis Galton undertook his studies of genius and human faculties in the latter half of the nineteenth century. Since Galton, several lines of research have been pursued on aspects of exceptional human intellectual or cognitive abilities, including creativity and intelligence, without producing general agreement on what is meant by creativity, how to measure it, or how to elicit or develop it.

Creativity has been defined in relation to various frames
of reference: as a process, as a product, and as a set of human
characteristics. The dictionary views creativity as the power
or ability to create, to originate, or to produce. In dictionary
definitions, creativity carries implications of originality and
productivity. In the broad literature that discusses creativity,
the term overlaps (and is often used interchangeably with) terms
such as "inventiveness," "innovativeness," "productive thinking," and the act of "discovery." The literature includes contributions from psychology, philosophy, sociology, anthropology,
the history of science and technology, the history of thought,
economics, biography, and from the specific fields in which
creativity plays a conspicuous role, such as the plastic and performing arts, scientific and engineering fields, management,
and medicine.

Almost all the literature concerned with creativity differentiates the creative from the noncreative in terms of product.
Considerations of creativity, particularly from the perspective
of managers, must be concerned with product. A few psychologists treat creativity from the viewpoint of process and/or or
the meaning of the process to the individual engaged in it.
However, the latter approach precludes differentiating between
two exercises of creativity.

Two individuals may have a personal experience validly
identified as "creative," but one may result in a product with
no redeeming features, and the other result in something beautiful, useful, and elegant. Under the influence of psychedelic
drugs, a person may experience vivid, original, beautiful visions,
and consider the experience as "creative." However, unless
those visions result in some tangible work of art, cure, invention, design, or concept, they do not enter the world of recognized creativity, nor are they of concern to anyone beyond
the individual who experienced them. The creative experience
that does not result in a product is in the same class as the
sound of the tree falling in the forest that no one hears.

The experiential view of creativity is also misleading in
implying that all creative work results from personally dramatic
experiences, including a heightened state of feeling, and that

creativity cannot proceed without that feeling. In an interview, John Kenneth Galbraith, the economist and prolific author, commented that there was no difference in the quality of what he produced when he felt "inspired" and when he was just working at writing. Galbraith also commented on the fragility of academic colleagues who waited for inspiration to strike and who produced little or nothing.

In the literature concerned with creativity and creative thinking, the majority of definitions include the criteria of novelty and utility. The definitions insist on "newness," "novelty," "originality":

> "new combinations of ideas and things" (Edel, 1967)
> "a new association of existing elements" (Bailey, 1978)
> "newness or novelty" (Rothenberg & Hausman, 1976)
> "the forming of associative elements into new combinations" (Mednick, 1976)
> "a response that is novel or at least statistically infrequent" (MacKinnon, 1968)
> "the production of an idea, concept, creation, or discovery that is new or original to its creator" (Gregory, 1967)

There are problems with using "originality" as a criterion in the definition. If someone creates something without knowing it has already been created by someone else, can that individual be creative? The answer is, yes. There have been cases of simultaneous invention by individuals who knew nothing of each other's work. The inventions are evidence of the creativity of each of the individuals. Though one inventor may be credited with the discovery, it does not take away from the magnitude or quality of the creative effort achieved by the other.

Originality refers to something statistically infrequent. The schizophrenic who babbles incoherent sentences may be expressing something original, in the sense of its being statistically infrequent, but no one would call the babble creative. "Thus, 7,363,474 is quite an original answer to the problem 'How much is 12 + 12?' However, it is only when . . . this answer is useful that we can also call it creative" (Mednick, 1976). The chances of an original idea being useful, and thereby creative, is small.

Often managements place high hopes on creativity-enhancing programs without realizing that generating a large number of original ideas will lead to very few useful ones. A hypothetical example (from Bourne et al., 1971) may make the point. If only one out of five thousand original ideas meets the criteria for creativity, and an individual produces 20 original ideas in a typical working period, the odds are 1/250 that one of the ideas will be creative. If, by great effort, it is possible to double that individual's production of original ideas (a massive increase), the odds for generating a creative idea are still only 1/125.

Value is the second major criterion for judging creativity. Value is expressed as "utility," "satisfaction," "acceptance," "meeting requirements," "meaningfulness." Creativity is an activity with social implications, since utility implies value to someone in addition to the creator. The role of social utility in creativity is pointed out by many scholars in the field of creativity:

> "although the literal definition of the term creation does not necessarily include the attribute of value . . . the term is almost invariably used to convey value either tacitly or explicitly" (Rothenberg & Hausman, 1976)
>
> "useful or satisfying to its creator or someone else in some period of time" (Gregory, 1967)
>
> "satisfy some expressed or implied human need" (Taylor, 1961)
>
> "acceptable as tenable or useful or satisfying [to] a group in some point of time" (Stein, 1963)

References to time are included in definitions to take into account creative products not accepted or seen to have value for decades or even centuries after they appear. History is full of examples of works of art, music, inventions, and scientific discoveries not recognized or even noticed when first exposed to others. Some definitions make the point that humans do not create something out of nothing, and include in the concept of creativity the association or combination of existing things and ideas—an important notion when considering what it takes to do something creative.

Creativity, Invention, and Innovation

"Innovation," "invention," and "creativity" are often used interchangeably, particularly in everyday language. Among scholars in the field of creativity, "innovation" is used to define the process by which a new product or idea is introduced into use or practice. Innovation sometimes refers only to the first use of a new thing or idea. In this sense, discussions of innovation are concerned with the recognition, first use, or diffusion of an innovation, and take into account such things as entrepreneurship and marketing.

It is convenient to use "invention" to refer to the process that generates an idea, develops it, and brings it into practice. In this sense of the word, creativity is then the first step in the invention process. As Edison said, "Invention is 5% inspiration and 95% perspiration." Creativity is what Edison called "inspiration," the generation of an original, useful idea, the critical first step in the process. Invention is the process of selection of the idea to be worked on and its detailed development into producible, usable form. Innovation is the process by which the invention is first brought into use by an individual, company, or agency.

Differentiating creativity, invention, and innovation help us to see the differences in the required process elements more clearly. Creativity requires the ability to reach out to widely separated components, and to synthesize them. The creative effort does best by generating as many useful, new ideas as possible from which to select one or two to develop. The rest of the overall invention process consists of selecting the idea(s) to develop, requires convergent thinking and the ability to discard irrelevant ideas, and it includes analysis as opposed to synthesis. The rest of the invention process consists of detailed development of the idea(s) into producable, workable form, a continuous (often tedious) effort which includes the solution of a myriad of design problems, each of which may entail repeating the selection process many times at a micro level. The invention process also includes tests or trials of all the detailed parts as well as the whole, and many repetitions of the efforts.

THE WHO AND HOW OF CREATIVITY:
THROUGH THE PRISM OF RESEARCH

In trying to evoke and develop creativity in an organization, managers are interested in such questions as: Can creative people be identified for the purpose of hiring? Are there valid and reliable tests that can predict who will be creative? Can creativity be developed or enhanced in employees? Are there creativity techniques that can be taught to employees that will increase creativity within the organization? What kinds of management actions help or retard creativity? What kinds of environments enhance or deter creativity? What differentiates the creative organization from those that aren't creative? Researchers on creativity have generated data that provide some answers to these managerial questions.

The questions guiding creativity research have been: Who is creative? What is the creative process? What influences the creative process? Answers to the research questions have been sought by identifying creations and their creators, by studying the characteristics of both, by inquiring into the way the creators went about their tasks, and by examining the external factors that influenced creativity. Research into questions about the creative person has been primarily carried out by psychologists, but has also attracted the interest of educators and scientists from a variety of fields who have been curious about creative people in general or creative people in a particular field. Research into questions about the creativity process has also been primarily undertaken by psychologists interested in the psychology of thinking, and also by sociologists interested in social and environmental influences on the creative process, by philosophers, and by engineers, artists, and scientists interested in teaching the process to others or adopting it for personal use.

All this research has led to the development of tests that attempt to identify creative people, techniques for enhancing creativity, and a number of findings concerning managerial and organizational factors that appear to influence the presence and quality of creativity.

The Creative Individual

Is everyone creative? When the creative individual is discussed there is often a mistaken implication that creativity is a special gift, shared by few. However, all functioning humans are creative to some extent and in some activity. To get through a single week, perhaps even a single day, of our lives each person is required to draw upon and usefully associate a multitude of previously unrelated ideas, things, and ways of acting. Think of all of the ideas published in popular magazine or newspaper columns, such as "Hints From Heloise," in which everyday people demonstrate their creativity, and remember Shapero's Second Law, "No matter how you design a system, humans make it work anyway."

Everyone is creative, but there are individuals who are demonstrably more creative than others. Managers can look to studies of creative individuals to see what characteristics they display, and the way they go about their work, to learn how to identify such people and facilitate their creativeness. In addition, the data on creative individuals help illustrate how to raise the creative level of all employees through the way they are managed, the environment they work in, and the human development activities provided.

Studies of creative individuals have been predominantly studies of professionals. The professionals studied have included scientists, architects, writers, artists, managers, mathematicians, engineers, and inventors. From the studies a composite profile of the creative individual has emerged, with some variations that reflect intrinsic differences between the professions. For example, writers are found to be more psychology-oriented, while scientists and engineers are found to prefer working with things and abstractions to working with people. Creative managers are found to be more power-oriented, practically a requirement in the profession. Creative scientists are found to have higher IQs than creative people in other professions, a reflection on the entry requirements for science. On the other hand, creative scientists perform less well than artists and writers on tests for divergent thinking, one characteristic highly associated with creativity.

From the beginnings of research on creativity, highly creative individuals have been distinguished from less creative people by their intellectual and personal characteristics. Many researchers in the field agree on several of these characteristics, though there are differences of opinion in explaining their meaning. Despite the degree of agreement, a cautionary note should be sounded. The characteristics of highly creative people have been identified after they have demonstrated creativity. There has been little success in predicting that someone who has never been creative before will be creative, on the basis of the identified characteristics alone. Prediction is weakest when based on personality characteristics. "The strength of the association between creativity and the identified personality characteristics is modest" (Parloff & Datta, 1967). There may be more predictive value in intellectual characteristics, but here too the record is not impressive. It must be remembered that it takes a high order of motivation and straightforward (not necessarily creative) intellectual capabilities to create.

Intellectual characteristics. The list of intellectual characteristics identified with highly creative individuals can be clustered under the general headings of fluency, originality, flexibility, tolerance of ambiguity, playfulness, and IQ. It is difficult, of course, to make a neat separation between the intellectual characteristics identified in the literature and those characterized as personality characteristics. Some characteristics such as "nonconformity" are cited both in terms of intellect and personality since there are scholars in the field who find that high creatives may be nonconformist in their intellectual and professional activities but not socially.

Fluency entails the ability to generate a large number of different ideas rapidly (Guilford, 1967). Creativity is the ability to come up with useful ideas, and the highly creative person is someone who has a rich flow of ideas. Fluency is associated with originality.

Originality is the quality of generating "unusual, atypical (therefore more probably new) answers to questions, responses to situation, interpretations of events" (Steiner, 1965). The combination of fluency and originality almost read like a definition of creative activity: the rapid generation of a large number of original (preferably useful) ideas.

Flexibility is the ability to move from one frame of reference and one method of approach to another. It is the ability to produce a great variety of ideas and to solve problems by using conventional or unconventional methods (Guilford, 1967). Flexibility can also be interpreted to include intellectual *nonconformity*. The highly creative person does not readily accept intellectual authorities, and is much more likely than less creative people to question conventional wisdom. Both fluency and flexibility are associated with broad interests and exposure to many ideas. The highly creative person tends to read widely, and continuously expands his or her interests and circle of acquaintances, seeking new experiences and traveling.

Tolerance of ambiguity is the ability to live, perform, and be comfortable with situations in which the questions aren't clearly defined, the methods are unfamiliar, the resources are not all in hand, and the rules are not in order. It is the ability to commit oneself to solve a problem without quite knowing how to go about it. Tolerance of ambiguity is manifested by some apparently contradictory characteristics identified with creative people: (1) an interest in contradictions along with a desire to bring order, (2) a strong drive to finish a problem, but a resistance to finishing in the latter stages of solution, and (3) a tendency to defer judgment, a liking for complexity in problems, and a drive for simplicity. A closer look at the apparent contradictions suggests that they are not as opposed as they appear at first glance. The creative person wants to create form out of chaos, simplicity out of complexity, and resists closure as the time for solution approaches because of the new possibilities revealed by the process of creation. The high creative evaluates ideas on the basis of content rather than source, and follows the idea where it leads. The high creative prefers risks that lie between the sure thing (no risk) and the lottery (high risk), and is happiest where the individual plays a part in overcoming the risk.

Playfulness and humor are hallmarks of the high creative. The high creative likes to play with ideas, enjoys combining them in unlikely ways. There is a relationship between humor and creativity. Both require that you see things out of the usual pattern. In this regard the high creative and the humorist are akin. Koestler (1964), in his masterpiece on creativity, devotes his first four chapters to the subject of humor. Koestler's description of the pattern underlying humor holds true for all creativity: "[Humor involves] perceiving a situation or event in two habitually incompatible associative contexts. This causes an abrupt transfer of the train of thought from one matrix to another governed by a different logic." The creative person is at ease with fantasy, and has the ability to regress easily into it. However, the ability to fantasize is combined with an ability to switch back to a high level of rationality (Crosby, 1968). Both flexibility and playfulness result in behavior that may appear impulsive, with quick shifts of focus and direction.

IQ, as scored on tests, has little correlation with creativity. It takes a fairly high IQ to enter a profession, but beyond that creativity and IQ are unrelated.

Left-brain, right-brain functions and differences have received much attention, particularly in the popular literature. Much research and interest have focussed in the functions and roles of the lateral halves of the brain, especially with relation to creativity. Evidence suggests that each half of the brain may house different kinds of capabilities and activities. The left brain appears to be dominant in handling language, classifying objects into standard categories, and in selecting individual objects from large mixes of objects. The right brain appears to be dominant in dealing with shapes, forms, and spatial relationships, and in recognizing patterns. Indications (as yet, not fully demonstrated) are that the left brain is the seat of analytical thinking, and the right brain is the seat of synthetic, integrative thinking. Most of the thinking identified with creativity are attributed to the right hemisphere of the brain. Spatial visualization and spatial thinking, integration, intuition, and emotion are all considered to be functions of the right hemisphere. Creativity is seen as the association or combination of widely separated items, an act of synthesizing dependent on pattern recognition and intuition, and therefore a right-brain function.

It is, therefore, believed by many that high creatives are far more right-brain–oriented than others.

The left-brain, right-brain subject has to be treated with caution (Gardner, 1982). The data are insufficient as yet to come to the sweeping conclusions being made about the brain hemisphere location of various kinds of thinking. There is also very little known about how the two hemispheres interact, something that appears vital to carrying out any function attributed to either hemisphere itself.

Personality characteristics. Researchers have characterized high creatives by a host of qualities that can be roughly described as: strong work motivation, independent, nonconformist, high energy.

Strong work motivation characterizes the highly creative person. High creatives are motivated by problems and the work at hand. They show strong curiosity and tend to be positive, enthusiastic, and optimistic about the work they are doing and the problems they are undertaking. High creatives are intrigued and captured by problems, and are more likely to be motivated by the appeal of a problem than by an appeal based on the needs of the organization. It is hard to think of someone consistently generating creative solutions without a strong interest in the problems being addressed and a positive or optimistic feeling about the chances for solution. They get more immersed in the project than others, and are apt to work longer and harder without any external pressures or incentives (Steiner, 1965). They are more likely to express a positive interest in the intrinsic challenge of the job than in such extrinsic incentives as salary and status.

Independence and autonomy are attributed to high creatives by all writers on the subject. High creatives have their own standards and are less concerned with what others think or of making a good impression on others when it comes to their work. Along with an independent, internal set of standards goes a strong sense of self-acceptance that is often seen by others as self-assertiveness. High creatives are strongly self-disciplined and display self-confidence in attacking new and unfamiliar problems. In the discussion of the high creatives' tolerance of ambiguity it was pointed out that they are able to commit themselves to a problem without knowing yet how to solve it. The high creative is at the opposite pole from the person whose immediate response is, "It won't work! It can't be done."

Often, to the chagrin of managers and co-workers, high creatives tend to think more in terms of their profession than of the organization. They have been described as more "cosmopolitan" than their colleagues. "Cosmopolitan" is used as the opposite of "provincial": meaning that the high creatives are more at ease in a larger variety of contexts and organizations than others. Again, it is almost axiomatic that creating something new requires independence of thought and an ability to swim against the tide.

Nonconformity, both intellectually and personally, appears to be a central characteristic of high creatives. Part of the non-conformist characterization stems from the high creative's un-concern with making a good impression on others. They tend to belong to fewer organizations than others in their profession. High creatives often see themselves as "different."

Nonconformity raises two issues. Is bizarre behavior the hallmark of the highly creative person? How can nonconformity coexist with self-discipline? Not many people who are bizarre are judged to be creative, and not many creative people act in bizarre ways. The nonconformity identified with highly creative people does not mean nonconformity in all aspects of life. (Also, highly creative people are not creative in all aspects of their lives.) Creative people are nonconformist in their ideas and work, but not necessarily in their social lives. Creative scientists are usually not social nonconformists. Adolescents identified as high creatives in science were found to exercise self-discipline and to be reasonably circumspect in dealings with others (Parloff & Datta, 1967).

Nonconformity and self-discipline are not necessarily antagonists. Creative people are strongly goal-oriented, and to achieve their goals they must exercise much self-discipline. High creatives are known to resist closure as they continue to see new possibilities as their work unfolds, though typically they also feel a strong desire to finish the work they start.

Creativity is a social activity in the sense that its results must be appreciated by someone besides the creator. To be judged creative, an idea, invention, design, book, or work of art must meet the test of acceptance by others at some period of time. In professional fields that depend on working with others and where acceptance of the product depends on others, social nonconformity can prevent the creation from full acceptance in the marketplace. There is an historic tradition in literature, music, and the plastic arts of creative people who are social nonconformists. These are fields where the creative person works alone and is often not recognized or appreciated in his or her lifetime. In other professions, such as science, engineering, architecture, and medicine, one is almost always required to work with colleagues and clients to realize one's creation, and social nonconformity can get in the way.

Nevertheless, creative professionals have characteristics, and often behave in ways, that do not conform with the norms of behavior in most large, bureaucratic organizations. They are nonconformist, they are playful, they are independent. In a study of highly creative vs. high IQ students it was found that both parents and teachers preferred the high IQ students to the high creatives, because they were more apt to want to please parents and teachers. The high creatives, with their humor, independence, nonconformity, and playfulness tended to make parents and teachers uneasy. In organizational life, the intelligent, but conforming, professional keeps management happy, does a good job, and doesn't rock the boat. The high creatives among the employees will tend to make most managers a bit uncomfortable. They will tend to be irreverent and often will be the sources of jokes about the organization and management. They will be irreverent towards company procedures, and will be subject to the charge of not showing the proper amount of "loyalty" (Getzels & Jackson, 1962).

High energy also characterizes the high creative. Several researchers depict the high creative as having great drive, and as being "quick." Whether the perceived high levels of energy result from great motivation or physiological inheritance is not clear. One manifestation of the high creative's level of energy is a tendency to work on several projects at once.

Predicting Creativity

From the beginning, much research on creativity has focussed on developing ways of predicting who will demonstrate high creativity in the future. One approach, based on biographical and autobiographical studies of individuals with demonstrated high creativity, attempts to develop predictive profiles. Included among the profile methods is factor analysis. Other attempts have produced psychometric instruments to measure intellectual capabilities considered by the researcher as central to creativity. Most of the latter have measured divergent thinking. Despite several decades of research effort on creativity and highly creative individuals, there is as yet no profile or test that reliably predicts who will be highly creative in the future. Efforts to develop tests to predict later creativity in students have borne little result. Longitudinal studies of the predictive strength of divergent-thinking tests given to students have been disappointing (Howieson, 1981; Kogan, 1974). So far, the only good indication that an individual will be highly creative in the future has been demonstrated high creativity in the past. (See box on Edison's test.)

The Environment for Creativity

Two aspects of the environment for creativity have been examined by researchers: (1) the kinds of familial and educational environments in childhood that lead to creativity in adulthood, and (2) the kinds of immediate, organizational, and physical environments associated with high creativity. The effect of childhood environments in subsequent creativity is of special interest to educators and psychologists (and concerned parents), though of little utility for managers. One finding worth noting, however, was that high creatives, unlike those with high IQs, came from families in which parents put little stress on grades (Getzels & Jackson, 1962). It should also be noted, however, that many of the prescriptions for encouraging creative development in children are at odds with the way creative geniuses in the past were raised.

The manager of professionals is concerned with organiza-

THOMAS EDISON'S TEST FOR APPLICANTS
FOR JOBS IN HIS LABORATORY

A small controversy was created in 1921 by the publication of questions used by Thomas Edison as a test of applicants for positions in his laboratory. According to reports in the *New York Times*, the information about the test was provided by two young men who had taken the test and flunked, but who demonstrated phenomenal memories by reconstructing 146 questions which Edison refused to provide. At one testing of six hundred applicants only twenty-seven were marked eligible, and according to Edison the rest failed, "most of them miserably." Edison was also quoted to the effect that "college men are amazingly ignorant." The *Times* articles raised a flurry of responses in *Harper's Magazine*, *The Literary Digest*, and *Current Opinion*, which reported the results of research on answers to the questions showing learned disagreements about the answers to the questions and questioned the validity of the questionnaire as a means for identifying inventive people.

According to the *Times* sources and experts, some of Edison's questions and answers were the following:

What city and country produce the finest china?
Some said Limoges, France, some said Sevres, France, some said Dresden, Germany, and some said Copenhagen, Denmark.

---

tional environments associated with high creativity and how they might be generated. Most of the organizational characteristics that appear to enhance creativity relate to the characteristics attributed to highly creative individuals (Steiner, 1965). For example, since nonconformity in both thought and action characterizes high creatives, the organization that is tolerant of a large variety of deviance from the norm is more likely to enhance creativity. It is not surprising to find many "high tech" companies, architectural firms, advertising organizations, and academic faculties are marked by unconventional dress and little rigidity concerning hours of work.

What country consumed the most tea before the war?
(World War I) Russia.
Where do we get prunes from?
Prunes are grown in the Santa Clara Valley and elsewhere.
Who was Bessemer and what did he do?
An English engineer. He invented the process for making steel by taking the carbon out of molten iron by the air-blast.

The questions included many about famous historical figures, about physical and economic geography, about science, and about inventions:

Where is Korea?
From where do we import figs?
Who was Bolivar?
Who was Plutarch?
What is the speed of sound?
What causes the tides?
Who invented the cotton gin?
How is window glass made?
What is porcelain?

Many characteristics of creative organizations (Steiner, 1965) are identical with those recommended in other chapters. They include the following:

Open channels of communications are maintained.
Contacts with outside sources are encouraged.
Nonspecialists are assigned to problems.
Ideas are evaluated on their merits rather than on the status of their originator.
Management encourages experiments with new ideas rather than making "rational" prejudgments.

Decentralization is practiced.
Much autonomy is allowed professional employees.
Management is tolerant of risk-taking.
The organization is not run tightly or rigidly.
Participative decision making is encouraged.
Employees have fun.

THE PROCESS OF CREATING

Each individual develops a unique approach to the act of creation. Biographies of creative geniuses are replete with descriptions of seemingly ludicrous conditions insisted upon by great creators. "Schiller seems to have depended on the smell of decomposing apples which he habitually kept concealed in his desk! . . . Kipling reports . . . [an] inability to write creatively with a lead pencil. . . . [He] seemed to demand the blackest ink, all blue-blacks being 'an abomination' to his creative tendencies. . . . At certain precise times of the day Kant worked in bed. There he . . . had some intellectual dependence upon the tactile stimulation provided by the blankets, which were arranged round him in a highly original way invented by himself" (McKellar, 1957).

In spite of the apparent uniqueness of the creative process in each individual and the idiosyncratic patterns followed by many creative individuals, studies of the process are in fair agreement that it follows a recognizable overall pattern. The creative process has been variously described, but most descriptions include a series of steps, varying in number, that can be subsumed within the following four steps: (1) preparation, (2) incubation, (3) illumination, and (4) verification.

Preparation

The creative process begins with a problem perceived or experienced. Whenever humans have a problem, and don't know how to solve it by direct action, they resort to thinking, problem-solving, and creativity. The problems that lead to creative responses arise from many sources. They can be thrust upon one or assigned from the outside, be perceived as a threat or opportunity, be encountered, or be sought out because humans are dreaming, restless creatures who enjoy the creative process. Once a problem is perceived, the creative process begins.

Popular writings on creativity feature the dramatic insight, the lightning-like flash of recognition leading to a creative solution. However, research shows that the conscious "creative" moment comes only after intensive preparation and a period of subconscious incubation. Louis Pasteur put it succinctly: "Chance only favors the prepared mind." Helmholz, the great physiologist, described his own creative process: "It was always necessary, first of all, that I should have turned my problem over on all sides to such an extent that I had all its angles and complexities 'in my head' and could run through them freely without writing" (McKellar, 1957). In a study of highly productive inventors, Rossman (1964) found that they all started the process by "soaking themselves in the problem." Though Rossman reports that some inventors reviewed all previous efforts to solve the problem and others avoided being influenced by previous attempts, all spent time thoroughly exploring the problem to be solved.

The preparation process can include literature searches, talking to many people about aspects of the problem, experimentation, and doodling. Sometimes the preparation process can appear as unplanned, unfocused meandering through a variety of materials. McKellar (1957) considers it as almost a form of "overlearning" to the point where some of the materials become "automatic" in one's consciousness. The gathering of information is a critical part of the process in which the individual examines the materials critically, but not negatively. The creative process requires discriminating criticism that does not reject, but builds upon the materials examined.

Incubation

Incubation is a process that goes on below the level of consciousness. It cannot be commanded. Incubation appears to be a gestation period in which the process goes on subsconsciously, and it works best when the individual is inactive with regard to the problem or working on something else. A passage of time, vital to the process, varies with the problem and individual (McKellar, 1957). The philosopher Nietzsche spoke of a period of eighteen months, and the poetess Amy Lowell spoke of six months. It can be a period of frustration for the individual working against a deadline, for it cannot be pushed or rushed. It is a period when apparently nothing is happening.

One soaks oneself in the problem and then waits. The passage of time is often accomplished by sleep. It is as if sleep provides the time and the opportunity to abandon consciousness of the problem and let the unconscious work. Some great creative discoveries have surfaced in sleep. Kekulé, discoverer of the benzene ring, one of the most important and original discoveries in organic chemistry, realized his discovery as the result of a dream of the image of a snake that seized hold of its own tail. Many of Descartes' basic notions of analytical geometry formed in his dreams. Everyone has had the experience of "fighting" a problem to an impasse, and having the solution suddenly crystallize while visiting with friends or discussing other things. The need for a period of incubation may explain why professionals who work on more than one project at a time are more productive than others. Having more than one project permits a person to switch to another project when apparently at an impasse. Switching from one project to another permits the first project to incubate until it is ready, while one is still doing something productive.

The incubation process is recognized but not understood. One plausible explanation is that it is a period in which the mind tests different asociations, matches different frames of reference and different conceptual elements to see if they make sense. This explantion fits with the most accepted view of creativity as a process of association.

Probably the most widely held psychological conception is that creativity is the ability to call up and make new and useful combinations out of divergent bits of stored information (Guilford, 1964). The more creative the individual the greater the ability to synthesize remote bits of information. The likelihood of a solution being creative is a function of the number and uncommoness of associative elements an individual brings together (Mednick, 1962). The latter notion has been incorporated into a test for creative ability, The Remote Associations test (Mednick & Mednick, 1964). The test taker is asked to "make sense" out of each of thirty sets of three, not obviously related, terms by providing a fourth term related to them (e.g., the fourth term related to "cookies," "sixteen," and "heart" would be "sweet"). Another associationist view is Koestler's "bisociation of matrices," expressed by the metaphor of creativity as a "dumping together on the floor the contents of different drawers in one's mind" (Koestler, 1964).

Illumination

The Gestalt psychologists refer to illumination as the "aha!" phenomenon. It is that sudden insight, that flash of understanding, in which the solution appears. The mathematician Polya describes it as entering an unfamiliar room in the dark, and stumbling around, falling over pieces of furniture, looking for the light switch. When the switch is found and activated, everything falls into place. All historic examples of the incubation process end with that moment of illumination.

Verification

After the exhilaration of illumination comes the tedious, time-consuming stage of verification. The creative idea must pass the tests of validity, reality, utility, realizability, costs, time, and acceptance in the marketplace.

CREATIVITY FROM THE VIEWPOINT OF THE MANAGER

Can anything systematic be done to increase creativity in individuals and in an organization? Does management really want creativity and the somewhat less controlled conditions necessary to foster it?

To individuals, more creativity carries an implication of special, personally gratifying experiences. To managers, more creativity means new ideas, inventions, and solutions that will do wonderful things for the organization in the marketplace. Few, however, have thought through the consequences of having more creative people and of allowing the conditions that enhance creative behavior in their organizations.

Can Anything Be Done to Increase Creativity?

Trying to answer the converse of the question, "Can anything be done to increase creativity?" quickly illustrates how much is generally known about conditions for creativity. Pose the question "Can anything be done to kill creativity in an individual or an organization?" and the mind immediately fills with answers:

Discourage and penalize risk-taking.
Discourage and ridicule new ideas.
Reject and discourage attempts to try unusual methods.
Make sure all communications follow formal organizational lines and all employees cover themselves.
Discourage reading and communications with people outside the immediate organization.
Discourage nonconformity of any kind.
Discourage joking and humor.
Provide no recognition.
Provide no resources.

We easily intuit what it takes to minimize creative behavior, which suggests that it must be possible to improve creativity or, at least, to minimize barriers to creativity. The available information strongly indicates that it is possible to improve one's own creativity and the creativity of employees. It is possible to increase the creative activities and products of an organization. Increasing creativity in an organization is achievable, but it takes a lot more effort than preventing it from occurring. Continuity and stability are important attributes in society, and, of necessity, the dice are loaded against divergence and change.

Does Management Really Want to Live with More Creativity in the Organization?

Highly creative people are attracted by the work, by the problem being worked on, which is good from an organizational viewpoint, but they don't respond in satisfactory ways to the political or organizational constraints that are involved in every problem. Creative people are nonconformists. They are jokers. They have little reverence for authority or procedures. They are short on apparent "loyalty" to the organizations they work for. They don't respond to the kinds of incentives that stir others. They are not moved by status. High creatives don't seem to care about what others think, and they don't easily become part of a general consensus. (Could a preference for consensus management be why the Japanese have recently expressed concern about a lack of creativity in Japan?) In short, creative people can make most managers very uncomfortable. As was stated above teachers and even parents were far more comfortable with students and children with high IQs than with those who were highly creative.

A case can be always made for creativity, but managers should carefully and honestly think about whether they truly need more creativity and can live with it. If successful at hiring and retaining high creatives, and at generating the conditions needed to keep them creative, management may be creating conditions that make it difficult for its own natural style of doing things. New methods, processes and products can be purchased, copied, and stolen. According to one ironic maxim, it doesn't pay to be first—pioneers get killed. Some years ago, the head of a metal machining company producing thousands of metal fasteners picked through his catalog and fondly indicated product after product that had been invented by other companies. "You know," he said, "we don't know anything about managing creative people, but we're very, very good at designing around other people's designs. What we're really competent at is production and marketing, and we beat the hell out of the creative companies. I can't wait for their next products." Cynical? Perhaps, but it highlights the questions raised here. Many can benefit from the creativity of a few, and there are industries, companies, and fields where creativity is far less needed than in others.

On the Road to More Creativity

If desired, creativity can be consciously and systematically enhanced in an organization through hiring, motivation, organization, and management actions.

Hiring. The number of highly creative people in an organization can be increased by a hiring policy that deliberately attempts to identify, locate, and hire them. The only valid and reliable way to identify individuals with a high probability of future creative performance is through evidence of past creative performance. The more recent and continuous the past creative performance, the more likely there will be future creative performance.

It is the convention in some professional fields to come to an employment interview with evidence of past creative performance. Architects, artists, advertising professionals, writers, composers, and reporters come to an interview with portfolios of their work. Even where portfolio evidence is presented, questions remain in the mind of the interviewer. A newspaper editor may wonder whether the folio of articles submitted by a candidate for a position as reporter represents the abilities of the reporter or of his or her editor.

Where examples of a professional's work are not as easily demonstrated as in the arts and architecture, the task of determining past creative performance is harder. It is difficult to tease out evidence of the individual creative contributions of an engineer or scientist who has worked on a project that employed scores or hundreds of professionals. How can the creative performance of a teacher or accountant be ascertained? One way to tackle the problem is to put the questions directly to the individual: "What are the most creative things you have done on the job in the past three years? What are the most creative things you have ever done?" Similar questions about the individual's work can be asked of others who are familiar with it. In some fields patents, in others publications, may serve the purpose, though they should be examined for their content.

Tests, profiles of traits, and checklists are neither valid nor reliable. No available test can determine who will perform creatively in the future with any reliability. (One may be tempted to follow the example of the author who tried to hire on the basis of the apparent relationship between a good sense of humor and creativity. The rationale was, "If they don't turn out to be creative, at least they'll be a barrel of laughs.")

Motivation. Creative behavior can be maintained and enhanced through incentives that reward creative output and encourage risk-taking, and the use of new methods, processes, and materials. For those who are already highly creative, incentives can maintain and encourage their creative efforts and help retain them in the organization. For other professionals, incentives and positive feedback from management can encourage them to overcome some of the natural blocks to creativity and to take more risks and be more curious. As with any other desired behavior, feedback from management, the performance evaluation system, and the example of management can help stimulate creativity. If a manager smiles on "far out" ideas when they are ventured, lets them be tried (even when he or she is personally sure they won't work), and will even express some extravagant ideas himself, others may feel freer to think and act creatively.

Providing the necessaries. The availability of resources for initial creative efforts is a powerful indicator of management support for creative activities. The resources required to give an idea a preliminary investigation are seldom of any magnitude. Direct provision of resources, or turning a blind and benevolent eye on the inevitable "bootlegging" of an unauthorized project, both serve the purpose of support for creative experimentation. Providing resources for preliminary explorations of ideas without requiring exhaustive justification is a form of intellectual overhead and should be treated as such, formally or informally. (Remember that time is one of the most important resources required for creative activities.)

Some boost to creativity can be obtained through educational programs, though management should be wary of "patented" techniques. All creativity-enhancing techniques have some limited value in terms of stirring up new ideas for a short time. An inherent limitation in almost all of the techniques is that they purport to provide *the* way to the generation of creative ideas or to problem solving. The overall process follows a broad general pattern, but individuals must find their own personal approach.

Managing. Managers should assign tough deadlines but stay out of the operating details of a project. There is no conflict between a deadline and creativity. Creative people resist closure because they see new possibilities as the project unfolds. For all the complaints, deadlines are necessary. Without deadlines few creative projects would ever finish.

Both productivity and creativity can be enhanced by assigning more than one project to a professional. Not all the projects have to be of equal weight, or size, or value. The ability to switch to a second project and let the first project incubate in the subconscious is important to creativity. With only one project and a tough deadline, there is a tendency to try to force the project at times when it can't be forced. Having other projects provides a legitimate (forgivable) and productive way to back off from a stymied project when a pause is needed.

At the beginning of a project, managers might ask for two distinctly different solutions to a problem, two design approaches, two different experimental treatments. This is best done at the conceptual design stage before it is necessary to commit large amounts of time or resources to elaborate the solution.

New projects need fresh, unchanneled thinking. Managers might make up project groups to include people of different backgrounds, and refrain from always assigning projects to the individuals who have done that kind of work before and are apparently most suited to it.

Each professional's assignments should provide diversity for that individual. And highly productive groups of five or more years duration should be made more diverse through the addition of new people and by making certain that the individuals in the group get occasional assignments to work with other groups.

Organization. Organizational mechanisms to assure that new ideas don't get turned down for the wrong reasons (such as middle-management cautiousness) are important. One company set up a new products committee to which any employee, and not just professionals, could submit ideas. The committee, made up of senior scientists, product development people, and a patent lawyer, investigated and discussed each idea and wrote up a decision stating why the idea was accepted, rejected, or recommended for more research. By taking a positive and encouraging stance the company developed a strong flow of ideas from throughout the organization.

There should be a legitimate (nonthreatening) means for taking an idea up the management line if it is rejected by first-line management. The means may be a new product committee, of the type described above, or a procedure for periodic review of ideas people feel strongly about. After many attempts to correlate creativity with personal characteristics, GE found that a key variable was the ability not to be dissuaded from their intuitions. The former director of technical systems and materials Jerome Suran believes that high creatives are stubborn types, "because you don't get past the first level of management in a big company unless you feel strongly about your ideas" (Cullem, 1981).

A periodic review of organizational procedures and forms, with a view to identifying and removing those that cannot pass a test of necessity, is often a good idea. Too many required administrative procedures and forms sop up time and energy and impede creative activity. Procedures and forms are pervasive forces for conformity, and the more there are, the less space and time is left for nonconforming, creative thought and effort. Professional organizations should follow the role that for every procedure or form that is added, at least one should be removed.

A Little Bit of Theory About Motivation

THEORIES ABOUT WORK MOTIVATION provide frameworks that can help a manager understand the kinds of personnel actions and incentives that might be appropriate at different times.

McGREGOR'S THEORY X AND THEORY Y

McGregor pointed out the belief systems of a manager with regard to subordinates has an effect on the behavior of those subordinates. He illustrated his theory with two opposite management belief systems he labeled Theory X and Theory Y.

Theory X is typical of approaches to management current in factories at the turn of the century. Theory X represents an authoritarian viewpoint characterized by the following assumptions about humans:

1. The average human has an inherent dislike of work, and will avoid it if possible.

2. Because of an inherent dislike of work, most people have to be coerced, controlled, directed, and threatened with punishment to get them to put forth adequate effort to achieve organizational goals.
3. The average person prefers to be directed, wishes to avoid responsibility, has relatively little ambition, and wants security above all.

Theory Y is characterized by a very different set of assumptions about humans:

1. The expenditure of physical and mental effort in work is as natural as play or rest.
2. External control and the threat of punishment are not the only means for bringing about effort toward organizational objectives. Humans will exercise self-direction and self-control in the service of objectives to which they are committed.
3. Commitment to objectives is a function of the rewards associated with achievement.
4. The average human learns, under proper conditions, not only to accept but to seek responsibility.
5. The capacity to exercise a relatively high degree of imagination, ingenuity, and creativity in the solution of organizational problems is widely, not narrowly, distributed in the population.
6. Under the conditions of modern industrial life, the intellectual potentialities of the average human being are only partially used.

A Theory X management depends heavily on direction from above, detailed procedures for doing work, and does not permit much decision-making responsibility among employees. Theory X management is characterized by conformity, mistrust, and antagonism, and depends heavily on the carrot-and-stick approach to motivation.

A Theory Y management takes a far more participative approach. Theory Y management is marked by delegation of authority, increasing variety of activities and responsibilities, and by efforts to improve the free flow of communications within the organization. Theory Y puts responsibility for the work performance of employees squarely on the shoulders of management. If employees are lazy, uncreative, difficult to deal with, it is the responsbility of management.

MASLOW'S HIERARCHY OF NEEDS

Maslow's theory postulates that humans have basic needs and are motivated to act to satisfy those needs. Once people satisfy a given need, it will no longer have motivating power until it is once again unsatisfied. Further, Maslow holds that there is a basic needs hierarchy, and that each lower set of needs in the hierarchy must be satisfied before the next set will act as a motivator. When someone is unsatisfied at the physiological level, higher order levels of need are not as important. Someone suffering from hunger will not be motivated by incentives based on recognition. Maslow's hierarchy of basic human needs starting from the most basic are:

1. Physiological needs: hunger, thirst, air, shelter, sex
2. Safety needs: security, freedom from threats, a minimum level of predictability
3. Social needs: friendship, acceptance by peers, affection
4. Esteem needs: respect, recognition beyond peer acceptance, status, prestige
5. Self-actualization: self-fulfillment, realization of one's full potential, and growth

In the work situation physiological needs include a salary and basic working conditions. Safety needs include job security, fringe benefits such as insurance and medical coverage, and regular salary increases. Social needs include personal professional relationships, the compatibility of one's work group, and treatment by one's supervisor. Esteem needs concern job titles, recognition by one's supervisor and peers, promotion, adequate pay compared to others, merit pay increases, and awards. Self-actualization needs include the chance to express creativity and to try challenging new kinds of work.

Maslow's theory provides a useful way to look at practical

aspects of employee motivation, and at the kinds of incentives to be considered for different occupational levels and different individuals.

The hierarchy of needs suggests a progression of incentives effective at different stages of a professional career. To the newly graduated professional, safety needs are important. The young professional will tend to be more concerned with salary and housing. In hard economic times there will be a stronger interest in getting some assurance about job security. It is important to understand this at the time of hiring, and to provide the kinds of responses that reflect this understanding.

With time, safety needs are satisfied. Love or social needs come to the fore. The professional is integrated into the organization and establishes personal and professional ties with colleagues on the job. The approval and friendship of colleagues are needed, and the alert manager recognizes the need for compatible working groups. The quality of supervision is an important ingredient in satisfying the social needs of the professional.

As the individual develops professionally through time, the need for esteem replaces the need for social acceptance. Recognition of professional achievement becomes very important. Promotions, awards, and merit pay increases are the incentives that are most effective at this level. The opportunity to participate in professional organizations with the attendant election to positions of responsibility is an appropriate incentive, as is formal recognition by the organization. It is useful for management to establish awards for professional activities given by peers and management.

Perhaps the most difficult level for management to deal with is that of self-actualization. This is the level where the professional feels a need to learn and try new experiences. Self-actualization needs are most prominant at the height of the career of a successful professional who has established a reputation for expertise in particular areas and has been promoted to a position of responsibility level. It is difficult for both the individual and management to encourage ventures into new fields. For the individual there is risk, though the need for something different is strongly felt. Management faces the possibility of foregoing a known professional output. It is important for management to institutionalize ways to allow its most proven and valuable professionals to try something new.

THE TWO-FACTOR THEORY OF HERZBERG AND ASSOCIATES

Herzberg's theory states that there are two separate states of employee feeling: one that goes from strong dissatisfaction to no dissatisfaction, and one that goes from nonsatisfaction to strong satisfaction. The two states are not continuous and are assymetrical. Dissatisfaction is not the opposite of satisfaction. The opposite of satisfaction is nonsatisfaction, and the opposite of dissatisfaction is nondissatisfaction.

Removal of whatever factors cause dissatisfaction shifts the employee to a condition of no dissatisfaction, but it does not lead to satisfaction. Herzberg refers to the actions to remove dissatisfiers as "hygiene" and calls dissatisfiers "hygiene factors": necessary, like brushing teeth, they do not lead to satisfaction. Another set of factors contributes to satisfaction, and Herzberg designates them as "motivators." Dissatisfiers or demotivators have to be taken into account and removed before motivators can take full effect.

Demotivators include the following in descending order of importance: company policy and administration, supervision and relationships with supervisors, work conditions, salary, relationships with peers, personal life, relationships with subordinates, status, and security. Of course, the situation is not just black and white. According to Herzberg's studies, the "demotivators" account for 69% of job dissatisfaction and only 19% of job satisfaction.

Motivators or satisfiers include the following in descending order of importance: achievement, recognition, the work itself, responsibility, advancement, and growth. The absence of motivators can contribute to dissatisfaction as well. Being deprived of a chance for achievement, for recognition for responsibility, or for advancement are causes for dissatisfaction and are demotivating. Nevertheless, according to Herzberg, the "motivators" account for 81% of job satisfaction and 31% of dissatisfaction.

Ask any group of professionals (or managers) to cite the most satisfying and most dissatisfying work experiences of the last six months. The largest number of dissatisfers will be concerned with company policies and administration, ranging from the way the company assigns offices and parking places and handles expense vouchers, to its policies on promotion. Professionals are also often sensitive to items considered incompatible with their status, such as a requirement to punch a time clock, a rigid monitoring of working hours, with no allowance for individual schedules of work, or over-bureaucratic policies on obtaining technical books.

Most satisfying experiences have to do with achievements: "I brought the project in on time in spite of an inadequate budget" or "I cracked a problem that everyone thought couldn't be done." Recognition is a frequent source of satisfaction, as is pleasure in the work itself.

The theory suggests that before you can develop an effective approach to motivating the employee, you must first take care of the hygiene factors. Efforts to motivate will not work or work well if company policies and administration, supervision, work conditions, salary, and security are bad or insufficient. It would be useful to audit the demotivators in one's organization before embarking on an ambitious program of incentives.

Items that demotivate should not be considered incentives. An increase in health benefits will be gladly accepted but will not motivate. (It is unlikely that a professional would boast to a colleague at a professional meeting about the "great" health plan in his organization.) A program for motivating professional employees must use incentives that give the individual a chance for achievement, recognition, interesting work, responsibility, advancement (which is another form of recognition), and personal growth. Enhancement of the motivators in the work situation will generate satisfaction and positive motivation.

A Spectrum of Techniques for Overcoming Perceptual Barriers to Creativity

TECHNIQUES to overcome perceptual barriers to creativity are designed to force individuals to change the way they perceive a problem and its elements, to shift the elements into different frames of reference, or to stretch the abilities to associate diverse elements.

ANALOGIES

Historically, the most prevalent and most powerful creativity "technique" is the use of analogies. An analogy is a resemblance in form or function between two things that are essentially different. A current widely used analogy is that of the computer as a brain. When the computer is considered as a brain we attribute to it, and therefore design into it, brainlike functions.

Mathematics

Some recommend that mathematics be used instead of verbal analogies. Mathematics is the queen of analogies. When an equation or a mathematical model is constructed, it is intended to be a mathematical analogue of some physical, behavioral, or social phenomena. In science or engineering, the equation $y = ax + b$ represents a linear relationship between two physical, social, or behaviorial entities, y, and x. It is more convenient to manipulate the equation than the entities and thus to "create" new perceptions of what might be understood about or done with those entities.

Physical and Biological Analogies

Probably the first analogies used by humans were physical and biological analogies. Observing nature, primitive humans observed the turtle and noted that its shell provided it with protection. The thought must have occurred that analogous protection could be provided for humans: in a creative flash the shield was invented, possibly using the shell of the turtle.

CHANGING THE FRAME OF REFERENCE

By changing the frame of reference in which a problem has been stated, an individual is able to see the problem in a different light, gain new insights, and see new elements and potential associations.

Lateral Thinking

De Bono (1970) differentiates two kinds of thinking, "vertical thinking" and "lateral thinking." Vertical thinking takes a known pattern and extends and develops it. Lateral thinking tries to restructure the pattern by putting its parts together in different ways. Lateral thinking is not so much a technique as a way of thinking that goes about deliberately seeking other ways to state the problem, or to restructure the patterns. It is a way of trying to release information that might be hidden by the normal ways problems are stated.

Synectics

"Synectics" is a technique that uses analogies and metaphors in a systematic way to change the frame of reference in which the problem is perceived (Gordon (1961). The initial problem is restated and looked at variously through the use of analogies and metaphors. The kinds of analogies used include an effort personally to identify with the problem. The personal analogy approach is one in which the individual tries to project himself or herself into the midst of the problem.

Forced Associations

A number of techniques build upon the idea of the association of unlikely elements, and upon the great power of association present in all humans. The techniques vary from ways of deliberately associating selected and structured elements to ways of stimulating creativity by making deliberate random associations.

Matrices

A two-dimensional or three-dimensional matrix using problem and solution attributes as its headings is a convenient tool for examining each intersection of columns and rows, one at a time. By examining each of the intersections in the matrix, the individual is forced to consider a great number of associations that suggest problem and solution possibilities that would not otherwise be thought of. One approach to the use of matrices for creativity purposes is that of Zwicky (1969), the noted astrophysicist, who called his matrix the "morphological manifold" or the "morphological box." Zwicky's morphological matrix used such problem attributes as materials, functions, and media as headings for rows and columns, and then examined the intersections to see what they suggested.

Random Associations

The associative capabilities of the human mind are so great that, bringing two randomly selected elements together, most people can make sense of them. Creativity techniques using random associations are good ways of breaking the perceptual set of one's mind and stretching one's imaginative horizon. One of the simplest ways of using random associations is to find a word randomly, using any book or a dictionary, and to then associate that word with the problem being addressed.

OVERCOMING SOCIAL AND EMOTIONAL BLOCKS

Beginning with adolescence, the individual feels social pressure to conform with accepted norms of thought and action. Some authorities believe that all children start out with a high potential for creativity, but that much of the potential is suppressed in adolescence, a period of great conformity. Consequently, a major barrier to creativity is the pressure to conform and the individual's fear of appearing a fool in front of supervisors and collegues. A number of creativity techniques are designed to overcome such social and emotional blocks as well as to break perceptual habits.

Brainstorming

The best known of the creativity techniques used to overcome social and emotional barriers is known as brainstorming. Brainstorming is based on four operating rules (Osborne, 1963; Stein, 1975): (1) criticism is ruled out, (2) freewheeling is welcomed, (3) quantity is desirable, and (4) combination and improvement are sought. The operating rules are designed to encourage deferment of judgment—to encourage maximum stretching of the imagination by delaying analytical, judgmental braking on the mind, and to make sure that individuals are encouraged to express "crazy" ideas without fear of negative social judgment. Quantity is encouraged on the assumption that it will breed quality, by eventually simply getting beyond the conventional through sheer force of numbers.

Brainstorming is conducted in group sessions, with a leader who is charged with keeping the session moving along by questions, encouragement, and by stopping any criticisms. Participants are encouraged to build on each other's ideas, but they are stopped short if they criticize. Records of the ideas are kept by a secretary or taped.

Guidelines for Creative Problem Solving

1. Soak yourself in the problem. Read, review, examine, and analyze any material you can find on the problem. Talk to people who know about it. Look at the problem from every side. Do not accept authority uncritically; question the premises. Insist on finding a way to solve the problem, rejecting any conclusion that there is no way to solve it.

As a manager, always challenge the judgment that "it can't be done." One successful manager listens to all the reasons the section can give as to why something won't work, then counters: "I agree it can't be done, but if we had to do it or be shot, what could we do?" That always changes the atmosphere and turns the group to finding ways to attack the problem rather than judge it. Provide your people with all the information you can, erring on the side of overload. Encourage them to contact a wide variety of sources for information and to soak themselves in the problem.

2. Play with the problem. Stay loose and flexible when considering the problem. Try out different assumptions; imagine that one of the conditions affecting the problem is removed, and see where the problem leads now. Approach the problem from different directions and turn it inside out. Assume different environments. Mentally shift the positions of various parts of the problem spatially and temporally. Change the order of events or the situation.

As a manager, encourage your people to explore the problem from every conceivable viewpoint. Through discussion and questioning, suggest "wild" approaches in the early stages of a project.

3. Suspend judgment. Don't draw early conclusions, which will lock you in and hamper your creative freedom. Do not become fixated on a particular part of the problem definition, losing sight of the larger ramifications. Avoid settling on an early partial or total solution, but stay open to new information and possibilities not yet considered. As solutions occur to you, write them down in a notebook and deliberately set them on a back burner until later in the project. Get them out of your mind.

As a manager, remember that you represent deadlines and budgets, and your people will tend to believe you expect early solutions from them. Help them to suspend judgment by keeping the pressure off and encouraging them to write down and defer their solutions until later.

4. Come up with at least two solutions. When you decide to produce two solutions, you are sure to keep thinking about the problem instead of fixating on one idea. Studies have shown that second solutions tend to be more creative. In one experiment, the request for a second solution increased the number of "creative" solutions from 16 to 52 percent. A further request for a third solution pushed the subjects to the limit, but still resulted in a 25 percent increase in very good, creative solutions (Hyman and Anderson, 1965).

As a manager, call for two distinct solutions to the problem, not necessarily worked out in detail, but substantially different. In most cases, all the anxieties and rigidities of the professional go into the first solution, whereas the second is more free-flowing. A group asked for ways of delivering high-quality education for less money, for example, will come up with a first solution calling for cutting costs, increasing tuition, and putting facilities to money-making uses outside of teaching. Second solutions will then involve engaging academics who are not research-oriented but good teachers to teach double loads for more money and (in lieu of student loans) investing in students in expectation of a percentage of their first five years' earnings (which would extend a university's concern with its products in a positive way).

5. *What do you do when you're stuck?* Try a variety of ways of picturing the problem and the solution: from verbal description to graphics to abstractions. Many creative scientists, mathematicians, and writers get a new perspective on problems by making sketches and diagrams.

Try your problem on outsiders. When you discuss your problem with others, you see it differently because you have to put it into terms intelligible to them. Their answers may be less important than your own presentation, but their unexpected questions may bring new areas of your brain into play.

Take a break. Give your subconscious a chance to work. When you're really stumped, go on to something else for a while. Creative problem solving is a ripening process, remember, so you can't force it. Working on it around the clock will only exhaust you.

As a manager, make yourself available as one of the people on whom to try out problems. Ask the problem solver to "draw you a picture" to help you understand the problem. When a person becomes too intense and is making no progress, give that person some short different assignment, to give the subconscious a chance to work.

Bibliography

Chapter 1. HIRING

AZEVEDO, R. E. "Scientists, Engineers and the Job Search Process." *California Management Review* 17, no. 2 (Winter 1974).

BASSETT, G. A. *A Study of Factors Associated with Turnover of Exempt Personnel.* Crotonville, N. Y.: Behavioral Research Service, General Electric Co., 1967.

BREAUGH, J. A. "Relationship between Recruiting Sources and Employee Performance, Absenteeism and Work Attitudes." *Academy of Management Journal* 24, no. 1 (1981).

CAMPBELL, J. P., M. D. DUNNETTE, E. E. LAWLER III, and K. E. WEICK, JR. *Managerial Behavior, Performance, and Effectiveness.* New York: McGraw-Hill, 1970.

CASCIO, W. F. "Accuracy of Verifiable Biographical Information Blank Responses." *Journal of Applied Psychology* 60 (1975).

DRAHEIM, K., R. HOWELL, and A. SHAPERO. *The Development of a Potential Defense R & D Complex: A Study of Minneapolis–St. Paul.* Menlo Park, Calif.: Stanford Research Institute, 1966.

DRAKE, L. R., H. R. KAPLAN, and R. A. STONE. "Organizational Performance as a Function of Recruitment Criteria and Effectiveness." *Personnel Journal* 5, no. 52 (October 1973).

FARRIS, G. F. "A Predictive Study of Turnover." *Personnel Psychology* 24 (Summer 1971).

HALL, D. T., and I. F. C. HALL. "What's New in Career Management." *Organizational Dynamics* 5 (Summer 1976).

HAMMOND, G., and J. KERN. *Teaching Comprehensive Medical Care.* Cambridge, Mass.: Harvard University Press, 1959.

HARRELL, T. W., and M. S. HARRELL. *Predictors of Business Manager Success at 10 Years Out of MBA.* Technical Report no. 10. Stanford, Calif.: Graduate School of Business, Stanford University, May 1976.

HOWELL, R. P., M. GORFINKEL, and D. BENT. *Individual Characteristics Significant to Salary Levels of Engineers and Scientists.* Menlo Park, Calif.: Stanford Research Institute, 1966.

JARRELL, D. W. "An Evaluation of Recruitment Sources for R & D." *Research Management* (March 1974).

JINDAL, G. R., and C. H. SANDBERG. "What It Costs to Hire a Professional." *Research Management* (July 1978).

LANDY, F. J., and D. A. TRUMBO. *Psychology of Work Behavior.* Rev. ed. Homewood, Ill.: Dorsey Press, 1980.

LEVENSON, H. "Distinctions within the Concept of Internal-External Control: Development of a New Scale." *Proceedings of the 80th Annual Convention of the American Psychological Association* (1972).

LIVINGSTON, J. S. "Myth of the Well-Educated Manager." *Harvard Business Review* 49, no. 1 (January–February 1971).

MARTIN, D. D., W. J. KEARNEY, and G. D. HOLDEFER. "The Decision to Hire: A Comparison of Selection Tools." *Business Perspectives,* Southern Illinois University (Spring 1971).

MARTIN, R. A., and J. PACHERES. "Good Scholars Not Always the Best." *Business Week,* February 1962, 24.

MEYER, H., and S. CUOMO. *Who Leaves? A Study of Background Characteristics of Engineers Associated with Turnover.* Crotonville, N. Y.: Behavioral Research Service, General Electric Co. 1962.

MOSEL, J. N., and H. W. GOHEEN. "The Validity of the Employment Recommendation Questionnaire in Personnel Selection." *Personnel Psychology* 12 (1959).

PORTER, L. W., and R. M. STEERS. "Organizational Work and Personal

Factors in Employee Turnover and Absenteeism." *Psychological Bulletin* 8, no. 2 (1973).

POSNER, B. Z. "Comparing Recruiter, Students, and Faculty Perceptions of Important Applicant and Job Characteristics." *Personnel Psychology* 34, no. 2 (1981).

PRICE, J. L. *The Study of Turnover.* Ames, Iowa: Iowa State University Press, 1977.

PRICE, R. L., P. H. THOMPSON, and G. W. DALTON. "A Longitudinal Study of Technological Obsolescence." *Research Management* 18, no. 6 (November 1975).

ROTTER, J. B. "Generalized Expectancies for Internal vs. External Control of Reinforcement." *Psychological Monographs* 80 (1966).

SCHICK, G. J., and B. F. KUNNECKE. "Do High Grades, Top Schools, or an Advanced Degree Lead to Job Security and Extraordinary Salary Progression?" *Interfaces* 11, no. 6 (December 1981).

SCHNEIDER, B. *Staffing Organizations.* Palisades, Calif.: Goodyear Publishing, 1976.

SHAPERO, A. "The Decision to Hire." *Chemtech* (February 1977).

————, D. M. HUFFMAN, and A. M. CHAMMAH. *The Effective Use of Scientific and Technical Information in Industrial and Non-Profit Settings.* Austin: University of Texas at Austin, 1978.

————, R. HOWELL, and J. R. TOMBAUGH. *The Structure and Dynamics of the Defense R & D Industry: The Los Angeles and Boston Complexes.* Menlo Park, Calif.: Stanford Research Institute, 1965.

SHETTY, Y. K., and N. S. PEERY. "Are Top Executives Transferable Across Companies?" *Business Horizons* 19, no. 3. (1976).

WILLIAMS, F. J., and T. W. HARRELL. "Predicting Success in Business." *Journal of Applied Psychology* 48 (1964).

Chapter 2. MOTIVATION

ALBANESE, R., and D. D. VAN FLEET. *Organizational Behavior.* New York: Dryden Press, 1983.

ARONOFF, C. "The Rise of the Behavioral Perspective in Selected General Management Textbooks: An Empirical Investigation through Content Analysis." *Academy of Management Journal* 18, no. 4 (December 1975).

BRIM, O. G., JR. "Socialization Through the Life Cycle." In *Socializa-*

tion After Childhood, edited by O. G. Brim, Jr., and S. Wheeler. New York: John Wiley and Sons, 1966.

DEWHIRST, H. D. "The Socialization of the Young Professional: A Study of Changes in the Career Values of Engineers and Scientists During the First Five Years of Employment." Ph.D. diss., University of Texas at Austin, 1970.

GELLERMAN, S. W. *Management by Motivation*. New York: American Management Association, 1968.

HERBERT, T. T. *Dimensions of Organizational Behavior*. 2d ed. New York: Macmillan, 1981.

HERZBERG, F., B. MAUSNER, and B. SNYDERMAN. *The Motivation to Work*. 2d ed. New York: John Wiley and Sons, 1959.

JONES, M. R., ed. *Nebraska Symposium on Motivation*. Lincoln: University of Nebraska Press, 1955.

LANDY, F. J., and D. A. TRUMBO. *Psychology of Work Behavior*. Rev. ed. Homewood, Illinois: The Dorsey Press, 1980.

MCGREGOR, D. *The Human Side of Enterprise*. New York: McGraw-Hill, 1960.

MASLOW, A. H. *Motivation and Personality*. 2d ed. New York: Harper and Row, 1970.

PELZ, F. M., and D. C. ANDREWS. *Scientists in Organizations*. Rev. ed. Ann Arbor: University of Michigan Press, 1976.

ROGERS, R. E., and R. H. MCINTIRE. *Organization and Management Theory*. New York: John Wiley and Sons, 1983.

STEERS, R. M., and L. W. PORTER. *Motivation and Work Behavior*. 3d ed. New York: McGraw-Hill, 1983.

SZILYAGI, A. D., JR., and M. J. WALLACE. *Organizational Behavior and Performance*. 3d ed. Santa Monica, Calif.: Goodyear Publishing, 1983.

Chapter 3.   PERFORMANCE EVALUATION

Appraising Management Performance: Current Practices and Future Direction. New York: Conference Board, no. 723, 1977.

DRUCKER, P. *The Practice of Management*. New York: Harper and Bros., 1954.

GORDON, G., and S. MARQUIS. "Effect of Differing Administrative Authority on Scientific Innovation." Working Paper no. 4, Graduate School of Business, University of Chicago, 1963.

IVANCEVICH, J. M. "Changes in Performance in a Management by Objectives Program." *Administrative Science Quarterly* 19 (1974).

KANE, J. S. and E. E. LAWLER, III. "Performance Appraisal Effectiveness: Its Assessment and Determinants." In *Research in Organizational Behavior,* edited by B. M. Staw. Greenwich, Conn.: JAI Press, 1979.

KONDRASUK, J. N. "Studies in MBO Effectiveness." *Academy of Management Review* 6, no. 3 (1981).

KRANTZ, I. W. "Evaluating the Technical Employee: Results Approach." *Personnel* (January–February 1964).

LANDY, F. J., J. L. BARNES, J. CLEVELAND, and K. MURPHY. "Attitudes Toward Performance Appraisal." University Park, Pa.: Penn State Report Series, 1978.

LANDY, F. J., and D. A. TRUMBO. *Psychology of Work Behavior.* Rev. ed. Homewood, Ill.: Dorsey Press, 1980.

LOCKE, E. A. "Toward a Theory of Task Motivation and Incentives." *Organizational Behavior and Human Performance.* May 1968.

MEYER, H. H., E. KAY, and J. R. P. FRENCH, JR. "Split Roles in Performance Appraisal." *Harvard Business Review* (January–February 1965).

ODIORNE, G. S. *Management by Objectives.* New York: Pitman, 1965.

PELZ, D. C., and F. M. ANDREWS. *Scientists in Organizations: Productive Climates for Research and Development.* Rev. ed. Ann Arbor: University of Michigan Press, 1976.

SZILYAGYI, A. D., JR., and M. J. WALLACE, JR. *Organizational Behavior and Performance.* 2d ed. Santa Monica: Goodyear Publishing Company, 1980.

WEXLEY, K. N., and G. A. YUKL. *Organizational Behavior and Personnel Psychology.* Homewood, Ill.: Richard D. Irwin, 1977.

WIKSTROM, W. S. "Managing by and with Objectives." *Studies in Personnel Policy,* no. 212. New York: National Industrial Conference Board, 1968.

Chapter 4.   MANAGING INFORMATION

ALLEN, T. J., "Managing the Flow of Scientific and Technological Information." Ph.D. diss., Massachusetts Institute of Technology, 1966.

————. *Managing the Flow of Technology: Technology Transfer and the Dissemination of Technological Information within the R & D Organization.* Cambridge: MIT Press, 1977.

ALLEN, T. J., D. M. S. LEE, and M. L. TUSHMAN. "R & D Performance as a Function of Internal Communications, Project Management, and the Nature of the Work." *IEEE Transactions of Engineering Management* (February 1980).

BERNAL, J. D. "The Transmission of Scientific Information." *The Proceedings of the International Conference on Scientific Information, Part 1.* Washington, D.C. (1959).

BERSCHEID, E., and E. H. WALSTER. *Interpersonal Attraction.* Reading, Pa.: Addison-Wesley Publishing, 1969.

BODENSTEINER, W. D. "Information Channel Utilization Under Varying Research and Development Project Conditions." Ph.D. diss., University of Texas at Austin, 1970.

CHADWICK-JONES, J. K. *Social Exchange Theory.* London: Academic Press, 1976.

COMPTON, B. E. "Scientific Communication." In *Handbook of Communication,* edited by I. de Sola Pool and W. Schramm. Chicago: Rand McNally College Publishing, 1973.

CRANE, D. *Invisible Colleges.* Chicago: University of Chicago Press, 1972.

GOLDHAR, J. D. "An Exploratory Study of Technological Innovation." D.B.A. diss., George Washington University, 1971.

GOLDMARK, P. C. *Maverick Inventor: My Turbulent Years.* New York: E. P. Dutton, 1973.

GROSS, A. E., and J. G. LATANE. "Receiving Help, Reciprocation and Interpersonal Attraction." *Journal of Applied Social Psychology* (July-September 1974).

HODGE, D. M., and G. H. NELSON. *Biological Laboratories Communication.* Fort Detrick, Frederick, Md.: U.S. Biological Laboratories, 1965.

HOLLAND, W. E. "Intra- and Inter-organizational Communications Behavior of Scientists and Engineers with High Information Potential." Ph.D. diss., University of Texas at Austin, 1970.

JENNY, H. K., and W. J. UNDERWOOD. *Engineering Information Survey Results.* New York: RCA, 1978.

KOESTLER, A. *The Act of Creation.* New York: Macmillan, 1964.

LIN, N. *The Study of Human Communications.* Indianapolis, Ind.: Bobbs-Merrill, 1973.

McGuire, W. J. "The Nature of Attitudes and Attitude Change." In *The Handbook of Social Psychology*, Vol. 3. 2d ed., edited by G. Lindzey and E. Aronson. Reading, Mass.: Addison-Wesley, 1969.

———. "Persuasion, Resistance, and Attitude Change." In *Handbook of Communication*, Chicago: Rand McNally College Publishing, 1973.

Menzel, H. *The Flow of Information among Scientists: Report*. New York: Bureau of Applied Research, Columbia University, 1958.

———. "The Information Needs of Current Scientific Research." *Library Quarterly* 34 (January 1964).

Myers, L. A., Jr., and D. M. Huffman. "Information Systems in Research and Development: Global Gatekeepers versus Specialist Gatekeepers." Austin, Texas, *Department of Management Working Paper*, no. 81/82–4–31 (July 1982).

Milgram, S. "The Small World Problem." *Psychology Today*, January 1967.

Parker, E. B., D. A. Lingwood, and W. J. Paisley. *Communication and Research Productivity in an Interdisciplinary Behavioral Science Research Area*. Stanford: Institute for Communication Research, Stanford University, 1968.

Pelz, D. C., and F. M. Andrews. *Scientists in Organizations: Productive Climates for Research and Development*. Rev. ed. Ann Arbor: University of Michigan Press, 1976.

Price, D. J. de Solla. *Little Science, Big Science*. New York: Columbia University Press, 1963.

Shapero, A., D. M. Huffman, and A. M. Chammah. *The Effective Use of Scientific and Technical Information in Industrial and Non-Profit Settings: A Study of Managerial Interventions*. Austin: University of Texas, 1978.

Vorwerk, E. G. *Time Usage by Municipal Managers: An Exploratory Study*. Ph.D. diss., University of Texas at Austin, 1979.

Chapter 5. TECHNICAL OBSOLESCENCE, BURNOUT, AND STAYING ALIVE

Burack, E. H., and G. C. Pati. "Technology and Managerial Obsolescence." *MSU Business Topics* 18, no. 2 (Michigan State University, 1970).

Casady, M. "If You're Active and Savvy at 30, You'll Be Warm and Witty at 70." *Psychology Today*, November 1975.

CHERNISS, C. *Professional Burnout in Human Service Organizations.* New York: Praeger, 1980.

DIAMOND, M. C. "The Aging Brain: Some Enlightening and Optimistic Results." *American Scientist* 66 (January–February 1978).

DUBIN, S. S. "Obsolescence or Lifelong Education: A Choice for the Professional." *American Psychologist,* May 1972.

FRIES, J. F. and L. M. CRAPO. *Vitality and Aging.* San Francisco: W. H. Freeman, 1981.

HACKER, A., ed. *U.S.: A Statistical Portrait of the American People.* New York: The Viking Press, 1983.

KAUFMAN, H. G. *Obsolescence and Professional Career Development.* New York: AMACOM, 1974.

LEHMAN, H. C. *Age and Achievement.* Princeton, N. J.: Princeton University Press, 1953.

LEVINSON, D. J., and C. N. DARROW. *The Seasons of a Man's Life.* New York: Knopf, 1978.

NESSELRODE, J. F., K. W. SCHAIE, and P. B. BALTES. "Ontogenetic and Generational Components of Structural and Quantitative Change in Adult Behavior." *Journal of Gerontology,* no. 27 (1972).

OBERG, W. "Age and Achievement and the Technical Man." *Personnel Psychology* 13 (Summer 1960).

PELLETIER, K. R. *Longevity.* New York: Delacorte Press/Seymour Lawrence, 1981.

PELZ, D. C., and F. M. ANDREWS. *Scientists in Organizations.* 2d ed. Ann Arbor: University of Michigan Press, 1976.

POOL, I. DE SOLA. "Tracking the Flow of Information." *Science* 12 (August 1983).

SCHAIE, K. W., and C. R. STROTHER. "A Cross-Sequential Study of Age Changes in Cognitive Behavior." *Psychological Bulletin* 70, no. 6 (1968).

THOMPSON, D. B. "Aging Workers: Experienced or Exhausted." *Industry Week,* July 9, 1979.

WICKSTROM, W. S. "The Productive Years of Former Managers." Conference Board Report no. 747. New York: The Conference Board, 1978.

ZELLIKOFF, S. B. "On the Obsolescence and Retraining of Engineering Personnel." *Training and Development Journal* (May 1969).

Chapter 6. CREATIVITY

BAILEY, R. L. *Disciplined Creativity for Engineers.* Ann Arbor: Ann Arbor Science, 1978.

BARRON, F. "The Psychology of Creativity." In *The Creativity Question,* edited by A. Rothenberg and C. R. Hausman. Durham, N.C.: Duke University Press, 1976.

BOURNE, L. E., JR., B. R. EKSTRAND, and R. L. DOMINOWSKI. *The Psychology of Thinking.* Englewood Cliffs, N.J.: Prentice-Hall, 1971.

CROSBY, A. *Creativity and Performance in Industrial Organizations.* London: Tavistock, 1968.

CULLEM, T. "Stimulating Creativity." *Electronic Engineering Times,* July 20, 1981.

DE BONO, E. *Lateral Thinking.* New York: Harper & Row, 1970.

EDEL, D. H. *Introduction to Creative Design.* Englewood Cliffs, N.J.: Prentice-Hall, 1967.

GARDNER, J. *Art, Mind and Brain.* New York: Basic Books, 1982.

GETZELS, J. W., and P. W. JACKSON. *Creativity and Intelligence.* New York: John Wiley and Sons, 1962.

GORDON, W. J. J. *Synectics.* New York: Harper, 1961.

GREGORY, C. E. *The Management of Intelligence.* New York: McGraw-Hill, 1967.

GUILFORD, J. P. *The Nature of Human Intelligence.* New York: McGraw-Hill, 1967.

HOWIESON, N. "A Longitudinal Study of Creativity: 1965–1975." *Journal of Creative Behavior* 15, no. 2 (April–June 1981).

HYMAN, R., and B. ANDERSON. "Solving Problems." *International Science and Technology* (September 1965).

KOESTLER, A. *The Act of Creation.* New York: Macmillan, 1964.

KOGAN, N., and E. PANKOVE. "Long Term Predictive Validity of Divergent Thinking Tests. Some negative evidence." *Journal of Educational Psychology* 66, no. 6 (1974).

MACKINNON, D. W. "Identification and Development of Creative Personnel." *Personnel Administration* (January–February 1968).

MCKELLAR, P. *Imagination and Thinking.* New York: Basic Books, 1957.

MEDNICK, S. A. "The Associative Basis of the Creative Process." *Psychology Review,* 69, no. 3 (1962).

———. "The Associative Basis of the Creative Process." In *The Creativ-*

ity Question, edited by A. Rothenberg and C. R. Hausman. Durham: N.C.: Duke University Press, 1976.

MEDNICK, S. A., and M. T. MEDNICK. *Remote Associates Test.* Boston: Houghton Mifflin, 1964.

OSBORN, A. F. *Applied Imagination.* New York: Scribner, 1963.

PARLOFF, M. B., L. DATTA, M. KLEMAN, and J. H. HANDLON. "Personality Characteristics Which Differentiate Creative Male Adolescents and Adults." NIMH Creativity Reports, 1967.

PRENTKY, R. A. *Creativity and Psychopathology.* New York: Praeger, 1980.

ROSSMAN, J. *Industrial Creativity.* New Hyde Park, N.Y.: University Books, 1964.

ROTHENBERG, A., and C. R. HAUSMAN, eds. *The Creativity Question.* Durham, N.C.: Duke University Press, 1976.

STEIN, M. I. *Stimulating Creativity,* Vol. 2. New York: Academic Press, 1975.

———. "A Transactional Approach to Creativity." In *Scientific Creativity: Its Recognition and Development,* edited by C. W. Taylor and F. Barron. New York: John Wiley and Sons, 1963.

STEINER, G. A. "Introduction." In *The Creative Organization,* edited by G. A. Steiner. Chicago: University of Chicago Press, 1965.

TAYLOR, JACK W. *How to Create New Ideas.* Englewood Cliffs, N.J.: Prentice-Hall, 1961.

ZWICKY, F. *Discovery, Invention, Research: Through the Morphological Approach.* New York: Macmillan, 1969.

APPENDIX B

DE BONO, E. *Lateral Thinking.* New York: Harper & Row, 1970.

APPENDIX C

HYMAN, R., and B. ANDERSON. "Solving Problems." *International Science and Technology* (1965).

Index